Florida Basic Recruit Training Program:
HIGH LIABILITY
VOLUME 2

Disclaimer

Florida BRT Curriculum Volume 2
© 2012 by the Florida Department of Law Enforcement (FDLE). All rights reserved.
ISBN 13: 978-1-58152-837-4
ISBN 10: 1-58152-837-X

FDLE makes a sincere effort to ensure accuracy and quality of its published materials; however, no warranty, expressed or implied, is provided. FDLE disclaims any responsibility or liability for any direct or indirect damages resulting from the use of the information in this course or products described in it.

Mention of any product does not constitute an endorsement by FDLE of that product. All referenced persons, places, or situations are intended to be fictional, unless otherwise stated. Any resemblance to real persons, places, or situations is coincidental.

The training in this course is provided to familiarize students with issues that may involve high liability and/or high stress. FDLE urges students to ensure that their practices are correct in accordance with their agencies' policies and procedures. Employing agencies are solely responsible for guiding their employees' actions in actual situations.

Designed by Kessler Creative
Cover art by Saeedeh Posey, FDLE
Published by Copley Custom Textbooks, an imprint of XanEdu Publishing, Inc., 138 Great Road, Acton, Massachusetts 07120.

TABLE OF CONTENTS
Florida Basic Recruit Training Program: High Liability, Volume 2

Chapter 1 CMS Law Enforcement Vehicle Operations

Chapter 2 CMS First Aid for Criminal Justice Officers

Chapter 3 CMS Criminal Justice Firearms

Chapter 4 CMS Criminal Justice Defensive Tactics

Chapter 5 Dart-Firing Stun Gun

UNIT 1: USE OF THE DART-FIRING STUN GUN

Chapter 6 Criminal Justice Officer Physical Fitness Training

PREFACE

The mission of the Florida Criminal Justice Standards and Training Commission is to ensure that all citizens of Florida are served by criminal justice officers who are ethical, qualified, and well-trained. The Commission certifies officers who complete a Florida Basic Recruit Training Program and gain sworn employment through a Florida criminal justice agency, or who are diversely qualified through experience and training and who meet minimum employment standards.

As staff for the Commission, the Florida Department of Law Enforcement (FDLE) Professionalism Program is responsible for establishing and maintaining officer training programs. Criminal Justice officer training is conducted at 41 Commission-certified training schools housed in Florida criminal justice agencies, community colleges, and vocational technical schools. By statute, entrance into the basic recruit training programs for law enforcement, correctional, and correctional probation officers is limited to those who have passed a basic skills examination and assessment instrument, which is based on a job task analysis in accordance with §943.17(g), F.S. The same job analysis process is used to develop job related training and performance standards for basic recruit training. Hundreds of officers, citizens, and instructors have participated in the development of the officer job analysis and training curricula.

In 2001, the FDLE Professionalism Program established the Curriculum Maintenance System (CMS) to ensure that officer training remains job-related, valid, and up-to-date. Through CMS, basic recruit training curricula is reviewed and revised on an annual basis and further ensures that basic recruit graduates are prepared for sworn employment with state or local criminal justice agencies in Florida.

CHAPTER 1

CMS Law Enforcement Vehicle Operations

The operation of a motor vehicle in a law enforcement setting is a dynamic and challenging task. The ability to drive in emergency mode, communicate with dispatch, and remain aware of the actions of other drivers presents complexities not experienced in normal driving. This course is designed to help officers understand a vehicle's limits as well as their personal limits. An officer's awareness of the effects of physiological and psychological stressors on his or her driving is critical. It is also important that officers understand how the public views them as drivers. This course will help officers to develop the skills required to operate a motor vehicle safely.

UNIT 1 | VEHICLE INSPECTION

LESSON 1 | Exterior, Under the Hood, and Interior Vehicle Inspection

OBJECTIVES

VO901.1. Check the operational readiness of the exterior of the vehicle.

VO901.2. Check the fluid levels, hoses, wires, and belts.

VO901.4. Inspect the rear seat compartment to locate all visible damage, weapons, and contraband.

VO901.3. Inspect the restraint devices, door locks, rear view mirror, and improperly secured equipment.

VO901.5. Start the vehicle to check for operational readiness.

The Basics of Vehicle Inspection

There are guidelines for properly inspecting your assigned vehicle. Inspection includes checking the proper fluid levels, electrical wiring, belts, hoses, and tires. The vehicle interior and exterior must also be inspected.

Most agencies will have a similar form that all officers will be required to complete when they use an agency vehicle. The form helps officers remember what equipment must be inspected and allows them to report failing equipment. Each agency has its own policy or procedure for handling failing equipment. Some agencies may require officers to complete a report detailing the problem. Others may require officers to handle some problems themselves, such as changing a tire or a bulb or adding fluids, or to notify a particular shop that will repair the vehicle. The comments section on the inspection form is useful for all these purposes.

Exterior Vehicle Inspection

It is essential to inspect a vehicle before taking control of it and operating it on the road. Unlike a personal vehicle (which should also be periodically inspected), an officer will drive his or her police vehicle in extreme conditions. Therefore, before using the vehicle, the officer must locate any potential problems so they can be repaired.

For personal safety, an officer should perform inspections before and after every use of the vehicle. When an officer fails to inspect a vehicle properly, that officer faces potential safety hazards. In addition, failing to complete an inspection may violate agency policy. An officer creates potential for liability if something happens because of a vehicle problem, especially if inspection and correction could have prevented that problem.

Before using a vehicle, its body must be inspected to identify any damage. An officer should be able to conduct a quick visual examination of the vehicle's body and undercarriage and look for the following:

- scratched paint that may be the result of contact with an object or intentional damage

- dents that are more obvious signs of contact with another object, perhaps a vehicle

- missing or broken light covers that can present a hazard to other drivers and may be a traffic violation

- damaged emergency equipment such as a siren, light bar, or other emergency lights that could prevent an officer from operating the vehicle in emergency mode (An officer should be aware of malfunctioning equipment so it can be repaired before he or she attempts to use it.)

- broken or cracked glass that could injure the officer and impair vision

- broken or cracked mirrors that could impair vision

- a dirty windshield that could impair observation ability

- foreign objects, such as tree limbs and road debris trapped under the vehicle, which could cause serious problems if they strike one of the vehicle's moving parts

- foreign objects on the undercarriage other than natural objects or road debris, which means a potentially harmful device such as an explosive (In the event an explosive or other harmful device is detected, an officer should back away from the vehicle and contact the appropriate personnel as designated by the agency's policies and procedures.)

- fluid leaks visible on the ground under the vehicle *(VO901.1.)*

Tires and Rims

Inspection of the vehicle's exterior also includes its tires and rims. Tires should be checked for uneven wear that may result from improper balance or alignment, over inflation, or under inflation. These problems can make a vehicle difficult to handle. Proper tire inflation ensures tires are inflated at or above the manufacturer's recommended **PSI** (pounds per square inch). The recommended PSI can be found on the doorjamb. If wear bars are even with the tread surface, the tires will not dissipate fluids. Embedded foreign objects can deflate or blow out a tire. However, an officer should not pull out the object but allow the dealer or maintenance personnel to handle the removal. The dealer or maintenance personnel should also look at any bulges on the sidewall. Cuts in a tire can also cause a blowout and should be observed and addressed. Officers should also inspect the rims on the vehicle for dents, cracks, or damage to the bead.

Tire Failure

If the front tire fails, the vehicle may lose traction. The officer may have difficulty steering, feel vibration in the steering wheel, and feel the vehicle pulling in the direction of the affected tire. If the rear tire fails, the vehicle may also lose traction and pull in an unpredictable direction.

Under the Hood

After inspecting a vehicle's exterior, an officer should not drive it without checking under the hood. A good-looking exterior does not guarantee proper vehicle operation. An officer should examine levels of fluid that are under the vehicle's hood and identify the proper fluid levels according to the vehicle manufacturer's recommended levels before moving the vehicle.

The fluid levels to be checked include the following:

- engine oil (measured in quarts)

- transmission fluid (measured in pints)

- brake fluid

- power steering fluid

- coolant reservoir

- windshield washer fluid

Belts, hoses, and wires are essential for the safe operation of the vehicle and should be inspected each day before operating the vehicle. Belts should be checked for fraying, cuts, cracking, and gouges. Hoses should be checked for dry rot, cracking, holes, bulges, and leaks. In addition, wires should be checked for fraying, corrosion, cracked or missing insulation, and exposure. *(VO901.2.)*

Due to the communications and emergency equipment installed in a police vehicle, there is a tremendous strain on the battery. The battery should be checked for proper operation. The inspection should include terminal connections, water level (if applicable), and signs of damage to the battery's exterior.

Interior Vehicle Inspection

Before using a vehicle, an officer should also inspect its interior. This is essential to ensuring safe operation while driving. Loose items like briefcases, flashlights, and coffee cups travel at the same speed as the vehicle. If an officer must stop abruptly, unsecured items become severe hazards in the vehicle.

An officer should always check seats for tears or other damage. Before and after every shift and after every transport, officers must check under the back seat for possible weapons or contraband left in the car by suspects. Seat belts should be observed for fraying and binding and to make sure the clasp locks properly *(VO901.4.)*. Headlights, interior lights, turn signals, and hazard flashers should be tested to ensure that they operate normally. Officers should also check the rearview mirror to see if it is securely attached or if it is cracked or broken. *(VO901.3.)*

Communications equipment will be tested to make certain that radio transmissions can be made and received. Officers should ensure that manual or electric windows and door locks operate properly. The officer should observe gauges for visible damage and see if they react properly to input. The gas and battery gauges should move when the vehicle is turned on. Emergency equipment (i.e., horn, siren, and light bar) must be tested to ensure it works properly.

After the initial inspection, an officer can start the vehicle's engine, and windows and doors should be checked for proper operation. The officer should be aware of unusual sounds, smells, or other indicators that may warrant further inspection of the vehicle. While the vehicle is running, the officer should look under it (standing to the side of the vehicle, not in front of it) to check for leaks that may not be apparent when the vehicle is off. After completing this check, the officer can turn off the engine. *(VO901.5.)*

Trunk

The trunk should be opened and its contents inspected. Inside should be a spare tire, vehicle jack, tire tool, and assorted equipment for use on duty (usually issued by the agency). An officer should ensure that all the trunk's contents are properly restrained; shifting equipment may damage the vehicle or change the way it handles. Long and protruding equipment (i.e., long guns, long-handled tools, and equipment) must be stored across the width of the trunk (side-to-side, not front to back). This will eliminate protrusion into the passenger compartments or the gas tank in the event of a rear end collision.

UNIT 2 I PROACTIVE DRIVING SKILLS

LESSON 1 I Hazard Detection and Observation Skills

Officers drive agency vehicles much more than personal vehicles. Enhanced observation and driving skills are assets that greatly assist in law enforcement duties. While officers cannot predict every driver's actions or what hazards may be encountered, officers must be prepared to react. The Federal Motor Carrier Safety Administration handbook, *Countermeasures*, lists the following tips officers should follow to prevent accidents:

- Learn to recognize driving situations that can be hazardous.

- Assume other drivers will make errors.

- Adjust speed, position, direction, and attention to be able to maneuver safely if a hazard develops.

- Scan far enough ahead to be able to react safely to approaching situations.

- Scan frequently to the side and rear for passing or approaching vehicles.

- Scan thoroughly before changing speed or direction. *(VO909.2.A.1.)*

An officer must utilize all the senses to detect and verify a potential hazard or problem. If the officer determines that a safety hazard exists, he or she should pull the vehicle off the road to a safe location and notify dispatch (also known as the public safety telecommunicator). The officer should always follow agency policy and procedures for handling a vehicle problem.

OBJECTIVES

VO909.2.A.1. Identify driving tips for preventing accidents.

VO909.2.A. Identify the importance of vision in identifying potential hazards.

VO909.1.B. Describe encountered hazards.

VO909.2. Detect potential hazards through the use of the senses.

VO909.3. Describe techniques that can enhance or impede awareness.

VO909.3.B.2. Identify temporary factors that may impact observation.

VO909.3.B.1. Identify medical conditions that may impact observation.

Vision

Vision supplies approximately 90–95 percent of incoming data to a driver. It gives valuable information needed to detect and avoid hazards. Several components of vision may affect the ability to operate and control a vehicle:

- *acuity*—sharpness of vision

- *depth perception*—ability to judge distance and perceive space to determine how far away an object is

- *peripheral vision*—ability to see above, below, and to the sides (A person who is in a stationary vehicle and who has good peripheral vision can see about 180 degrees from side to side.)

- *color vision*—ability to distinguish colors

- *night vision*—ability to see clearly in darkness

Environmental and physical conditions, alertness, and aging are factors that affect vision *(VO909.2.A.)*. All officers should have optimum vision before operating their police vehicles and have any nearsightedness or farsightedness corrected. Other factors, including vehicle speed and glare from the sun or other lighting sources, may also influence an officer's observation skills. In addition, window tinting in both police and other vehicles can reduce general visibility. An officer who approaches a vehicle with heavily tinted windows faces a safety hazard.

There are various frequently encountered or predictable road hazards. Unanticipated movement of pedestrians crossing streets at unlikely points may require a driver's immediate action. Bicyclists and motorcyclists share traffic lanes with other vehicles and sometimes fall. Skateboarders and roller skaters often make unexpected, risky moves and fall as well. Striking large animals poses obvious risks to vehicles and drivers, as does suddenly stopping or swerving to avoid smaller animals, which may cause worse damage. Animals most active at dusk or night, such as opossums, raccoons, armadillos, and deer also present risks. Improperly parked vehicles that block the roadway and vehicles that suddenly pull into traffic or obstruct vision are other dangers. Additionally, roadway obstructions and surface anomalies, including debris or fluid on the roadway and damage or change to road surfaces, are a safety threat. *(VO909.1.B.)*

Hearing

Hearing lets officers locate the source of sounds that may indicate a problem with a vehicle, a suspicious incident, or a crime. Several factors can make the source of a sound difficult to find, such as whether the driver's windows are open or closed, if there are surrounding buildings, etc. It is necessary for an officer to visually scan the surroundings to locate the source and direction of the sound. An officer could drive with the driver's side window down so he or she can hear and see hazardous situations such as citizens who need help (people fighting, arguing, screaming for help), crimes in progress (glass breaking, indicating a possible burglary in progress, screaming and yelling, gunshots), or suspicious activity (unknown persons loitering or prowling, transients). Driving with the window down also helps alert the officer to other emergency vehicles (fire trucks, rescue vehicles, and police or other emergency vehicles responding to the same scene).

Smell

Officers can use their sense of smell to detect many problems. If an officer detects an unusual odor while operating a vehicle, he or she should determine whether the odor is coming from the patrol vehicle or from an outside source. He or she should look for smoke or other indicators of the odor's source. If the odor is not as readily identifiable as smoke, gasoline, or propane, the officer should drive away from the area and call for additional resources to investigate. Unusual odors may indicate unusual hazards. Officers should be clear of those hazards before continuing to investigate.

Officers should be aware that a fire can start if the vehicle is left running while parked over a grassy area for an extended period of time. This is usually caused by the extreme heat from a catalytic converter. The odor of bitter smoke is usually the first sign of a grass fire.

Touch

Touch can help an officer detect problems that can affect vehicle operation and control. For example, if an officer feels the steering wheel vibrating excessively, the vehicle may have a steering or tire problem. If the officer feels the steering wheel pulling in one direction, the vehicle may have an alignment problem. What the officer feels in his or her hands, feet, and other parts of the body provides feedback about the vehicle's handling. When an officer is driving and senses something unusual, he or she should determine whether it is a safety concern by applying the brake pedal to verify that the brakes work, checking the steering, and looking for smoke or signs of an engine fire. *(VO909.2.)*

Observation Skills

Several techniques can enhance an officer's ability to be a keen observer and be aware of his or her surroundings. Officers should drive at or below the posted speed limit so they can observe and respond appropriately to the environment. To improve awareness, officers can make adjustments to their meal times and lifestyle, such as eating smaller meals frequently throughout the shift and getting sufficient rest and sleep before a shift. *(VO909.3.)*

Some temporary factors can weaken a driver's observation skills. These include stress, emotions, fatigue, and frequent shift changes. Prescription and over-the-counter drugs and poor driving habits can also have an effect on an officer's observational levels, resulting in inattention, loss of control, and even crashes *(VO909.3.B.2.)*. Medical conditions such as high blood pressure, diabetes, heart conditions, or epilepsy may also impair observation skills. *(VO909.3.B.1.)*

Section Vocabulary
acuity
color vision
depth perception
night vision
peripheral vision

UNIT 2 | PROACTIVE DRIVING SKILLS
LESSON 2 | Road and Weather Conditions

OBJECTIVES

V0909.1. Identify corrective action to take upon encountering a road or weather hazard.

Officers are likely to encounter potential hazards due to road and weather conditions. Variable road and weather conditions affect a vehicle's operation. Though these conditions cannot be controlled, officers can prepare for them by being aware of their causes. Observation skills and techniques can help officers be aware of potential road hazards. By recognizing their effects and threats, officers can prepare to react and minimize the chances of being involved in a crash and incurring injury or liability.

Officers will probably encounter road surface abnormalities that can be hazardous if officers are not aware of them and the specific methods of handling or correcting for them. Such hazards include construction areas, other vehicles, or intersection debris as well as fluids, wet surfaces, or standing water. When an officer sees fluid on the road, he or she can take corrective action by slowing down and trying to avoid driving over or through the hazard if possible.

Damaged or altered surfaces may include potholes and sinkholes, curbs, and railroad tracks. When an officer cannot avoid striking or driving over obstacles, the officer should strike it at a slight angle (when possible) with free rolling tires. If two or more vehicle tires roll from a paved surface onto an unpaved surface, the officer should not attempt to return to the paved surface by abruptly turning the steering wheel. This can cause the vehicle to flip or cross several traffic lanes. Instead, the officer should decelerate and steer as straight as distance allows. After reducing speed, the officer can firmly grip the wheel and steer smoothly and steadily back onto the roadway.

Variable Road Surfaces

Road surfaces are very important to law enforcement drivers because they affect vehicle operation. Officers should always watch the road, look ahead, and try to anticipate what kind of traction their tires will have on the surface they are approaching. While driving, officers may encounter concrete (a nonporous supportive surface), asphalt (a porous distributive surface), clay, dirt, gravel, or brick roadways.

Weather

Weather has many effects on a vehicle's operation. Brakes often become wet when driven through deep water or heavy rain. Rain can cause a vehicle to lose traction and skid out of control. Even a small amount of rain can cause a car to float off the road. Though they are designed to disperse water, tires sometimes hydroplane. They pull to one side or the other or may not hold at all. If possible, officers should avoid driving through water if the tires will be immersed halfway or more. At that point, the water reaches the area on the tire that may cause mechanical malfunctions. Extreme wind may also affect the performance and handling of the vehicle. *(V0909.1)*

UNIT 2 | PROACTIVE DRIVING SKILLS
LESSON 3 | Proactive Measures

It is important for officers to be able to identify types of crashes and master techniques for avoiding them. Sometimes, another driver's actions or an officer's failure to recognize a hazard makes a crash unavoidable. An example is a phantom vehicle, which is a vehicle that pulls out suddenly, forcing the officer to take evasive action to avoid a collision. Officers should be especially careful at intersections, as they represent the single greatest threat to safe vehicle operation. Some frequently occurring crashes include the following:

- side swipes
- right-angle collisions at intersections
- collisions with fixed objects
- accidents caused by improper backing
- head-on collisions
- rear-end collisions *(VO909.4.A.1.)*

There are several measures that an officer can take to avoid a crash. The officer might take his or her foot off the accelerator to decrease speed, use evasive maneuvers, or apply the brakes. Steering to a safe location in the direction the officer wants to go is also a good tactic for avoiding a crash. *(VO909.4.)*

Avoiding Head-on Collisions

If a vehicle is moving toward an officer in his or her lane of travel, the officer can act to avoid a collision or reduce its effects by reading the road, that is, by examining the surroundings for obstacles. The officer can also reduce speed to increase the time to react. Driving to the right gives the other vehicle more space and puts the officer in position to drive off the road if necessary. Finally, an officer can drive off the road to avoid the collision.

If an oncoming vehicle forces an officer off the road, the officer can reduce the chances of serious injury by attempting to select what to hit (items listed from least to most dangerous):

- soft objects (bushes, small trees, fences, etc.)
- objects moving in the same direction (including another vehicle)
- a fixed object (tree, sign, or parked car) *(VO909.4.C.4.)*

If the officer cannot avoid hitting a fixed object or an oncoming vehicle, the officer should hit the object with the side of the vehicle rather than head on, glancing off the object or vehicle.

OBJECTIVES

VO909.4.A.1. Identify types of frequently occurring crashes.

VO909.4. Demonstrate crash avoidance techniques.

VO909.4.C.4. Identify possible reactions to take to avoid injury or further vehicle damage.

VO909.3.A. Describe techniques and principles to enhance awareness, including the two- and four-second rules.

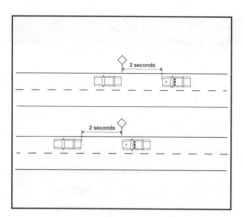

Two-second Rule   *Figure 1-1*

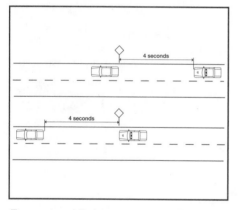

Four-second Rule   *Figure 1-2*

Two-second Rule

The two-second rule establishes a minimum safe following distance for all vehicles and provides space and time for the driver to react to potential hazards. This rule applies at the posted speed limit when weather and road conditions are good. An officer can use the two-second rule at any speed to determine if he or she is a safe distance from the car in front of the officer. To follow the principles of the two-second rule, an officer should watch the vehicle traveling in the same direction in front of the officer pass a fixed point, then count off the seconds it takes the patrol vehicle to reach the same fixed point. The officer should count the seconds saying, "one thousand and one, one thousand and two." If the patrol vehicle reaches or passes the fixed point before two seconds are counted, the officer should choose another fixed point and count again. The officer should make sure his or her vehicle passes the fixed point after counting two seconds. This means the officer is following at a safe distance.

Four-second Rule

Under poor road conditions or in inclement weather, officers should use the four-second rule. Its principles are the same as those of the two-second rule, except that four seconds are counted after the vehicle ahead passes a fixed object. Events and situations that call for the four-second rule include traveling at higher than normal rates of speed, driving during emergency responses, or traveling with other responding units. Inclement weather, fog, and smoke also require the four-second rule. Also, oncoming headlights/streetlights, hazards and debris, and construction areas all make for situations that call for application of the four-second rule. *(V0909.3.A.)*

UNIT 3 | PRINCIPLES OF DRIVING
LESSON 1 | Physical Laws and Handling Characteristics

This section teaches officers how physical forces affect their ability to control and safely maneuver a police vehicle. It is important to remember that vehicles react to driver input, road conditions, and natural forces. A police vehicle is usually a full-size vehicle with more weight and horsepower than many cars. It is a 3,500-pound body resting on four, six-inch squares (tire contact). All the factors just listed affect those four small areas and what happens to the vehicle.

Physical Laws

If an officer understands the Laws of Motion from physics, then that officer can better understand the forces acting on a stopped or moving vehicle. (*Note:* The Laws of Motion taught here are Newton's Physical Laws adapted and applied to vehicle operations.)

Every body continues in a state of rest or uniform motion in a straight line unless physical forces compel it to change that state. This means that once set in motion, a vehicle continues to move in a straight line unless an outside force compels it to do otherwise.

The acceleration of a body is directly proportional to the net force acting on that body and inversely proportional to the mass of the body. This simply means that a small car with more horsepower accelerates more rapidly than a large car with less horsepower.

Vehicular Motion

There are three types of vehicular motion. *Pitch* occurs during acceleration or braking. Motion transfers weight from front to rear or from rear to front. *Roll* occurs when turning and shifts the vehicle's weight from side to side. *Yaw* is the end-to-end motion on a horizontal plane.

Stability

Vehicular stability affects the degree of pitch, roll, and yaw that a vehicle experiences. A stable vehicle does not pitch and roll as easily as an unstable vehicle. The center of gravity on the most stable vehicle is low and centered, like a Formula One or Indy race car. The higher a vehicle's center of gravity, the lower its stability. For example, trucks and SUVs are less stable because of their high center of gravity. A vehicle with a wider tracking width, like a military Humvee, is more stable. As a vehicle's tracking width decreases, so does its stability. Trucks and SUVs are less stable because of their narrow tracking width.

Weight Transfer and Distribution

Equipment and passenger loads affect weight transfer and could change a police vehicle's stability. An officer should be sure to load all equipment in such a way as to distribute

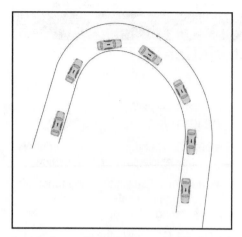

Increasing radius turn
(from left)

Figure 1-3

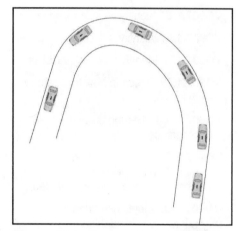

Decreasing radius turn
(from right)

Figure 1-4

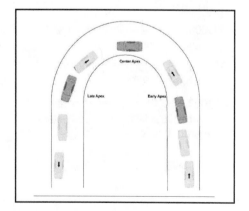

Apexing technique from right –
Early, Center, Late Apex

Figure 1-5

weight evenly. Weight transfer and distribution occurs when the vehicle's speed changes and influences the vehicle's handling ability. Weight is distributed on only four six-inch squares where the tires contact the surface. The more dramatically the brakes or accelerator are applied, the more dramatic the weight transfer and its effects.

As an officer applies the brakes, weight transfers in the direction the vehicle is traveling—forward or backward. This transfer affects the distance it takes to stop the vehicle. When a vehicle accelerates, weight transfers to the rear tires, affecting acceleration and the handling of the vehicle. Weight transfer and distribution also occurs when a vehicle changes direction. When a vehicle turns a corner, weight is transferred from one side to the other. The transfer is more noticeable in a less stable vehicle (a van, truck, or SUV) than in more stable vehicles (a standard vehicle). This transfer of weight can force the vehicle out of a driver's travel lane or off the road. In extreme situations, it can cause the vehicle to roll over. *(VO903.8.)*

When a vehicle turns a corner, weight transfers toward the tires on the outside of the turn. The front outside wheel carries the most weight, while the rear wheel on the outside of the turn carries less, followed by the front wheel on the inside of the turn, and, finally, the rear wheel on the inside of the turn. Because of this diminished steering capability, an officer should not attempt to brake and steer at the same time. The officer should always brake before turning and then steer into the turn. *(VO907.1.B., VO907.1.C.)*

Turns

A *radius* is the distance from the center of a circle to the outside of the circle. A turn or curve is a portion of a circle. An *increasing radius* is a turn that gets wider during the turn much like a circle getting larger (Figure 1-3). *(VO907.1.E.)*

A *decreasing radius* is a turn that gets tighter during the turn much like a circle getting smaller (Figure 1-4). *(VO907.1.D.)*

A *constant radius* is a turn that remains the same throughout, getting neither wider nor smaller. An example could be a 90-degree turn, such as a turn made at an intersection *(VO907.1.F.)*. Safely negotiating a tight turn requires less speed and more steering input.

Corner Negotiating Techniques

An *apex* is the center point of any curve *(VO907.1.A.)*. The apexing technique is how the vehicle is steered in relation to a curve's apex. The vehicle's position in relation to the curve defines the early, center, or late apexing techniques. The early apexing technique is when the vehicle is steered so it is closest to the inside of the curve before reaching the apex. This technique increases centrifugal force and can cause loss of control. (Figure 1-5).

The center apexing technique is when the vehicle is steered closest to the middle of the curve (Figure 1-6).

The late apexing technique is when the vehicle is steered so it passes closest to the inside of the curve after reaching the apex. This technique decreases centrifugal force, reducing the potential for loss of control. The late apexing technique, in most cases, is the best cornering or turning method. It allows the most room for driver error. *(VO907.1.A.1.)*

The two general forces that act upon a vehicle as it turns a corner are centripetal force and centrifugal force. **Centripetal force** is the force that is necessary to keep a vehicle moving in a curved path and is directed inward toward the center of rotation. **Centrifugal force** is the force enacted on a vehicle moving in a curved path that acts outwardly away from the center of rotation. *(VO907.2.A.)*

Steering has a direct relationship on vehicle dynamics, vehicle handling, and traction control. The speed of a vehicle and the forcefulness of steering influence these forces. Speed and steering also greatly affect the weight transfer of the vehicle, which in turn affects the driver's control of the vehicle. *(VO903.7.D.)*

Under steer and over steer describe certain vehicle movements resulting in a loss of traction by the front or rear tires. Officers should not confuse the word steering in these terms with the actual movement of the vehicle's steering wheel. However, recovery from these events may require steering input. **Under steer** is the tendency of a vehicle to turn less sharply than the driver intends. The cause of under steering may be a combination of excessive speed, lack of traction on the steering tires, and improper braking in a turn or curve. A combination of two or more of these errors can cause an officer to lose control. The correction for under steer is to remove the foot from the accelerator, maintain steering input but do not apply brakes, and if necessary, steer the car to a safe place and stop. *(VO903.7.A.2.)*

Over steer is the tendency of a vehicle to steer into a sharper turn than the driver intends, sometimes with a loss of traction of the rear to the outside. Over steer generally occurs at higher speeds when the rear tires lose traction and excessive braking occurs in a turn or curve. The correction for over steer is to remove the foot from the accelerator and/or brake, steer the car where desired (when the front tires have not lost traction), refrain from applying the brakes and if necessary, steer the car to a safe place and stop. *(VO903.7.A.1.)*

Wheel tracking is an occurrence that causes the rear wheels to follow a tighter path than the path the front wheels traveled in a turn *(VO903.8.B.1.)*. When trying to avoid a fixed object, an officer must steer the front of the vehicle wide of the object to prevent the rear wheels from striking it *(VO903.8.B.)*. Applying the correct inputs makes an officer a more capable driver in both normal and extreme conditions.

Section Vocabulary

apex

centrifugal force

centripetal force

constant radius

decreasing radius

increasing radius

over steer

pitch

radius

roll

under steer

wheel tracking

yaw

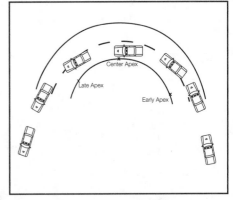

Apexing technique from left – Early, Center, Late Apex   *Figure 1-6*

UNIT 3 | PRINCIPLES OF DRIVING

LESSON 2 | Steering the Vehicle

OBJECTIVES

VO903.1. Identify how to make the necessary adjustments to the vehicle while seated.

VO903.8.C.1. Identify the caster effect.

VO903.3. Identify how to initiate the steering input for directing the vehicle.

Steering is one of the most important aspects of driving a vehicle. How an officer sits in a vehicle is also important because it enables him or her to correctly steer, accelerate, use mirrors, use proper seat position, and brake.

Steering Wheel Grip

Facing the steering wheel, the top center of the wheel is in the 12 o'clock position. The bottom center of the wheel represents 6 o'clock. On the right side of the wheel, the 3 o'clock position is centered between 12 o'clock and 6 o'clock. On the left side of the wheel, 9 o'clock is centered between 12 o'clock and 6 o'clock. Officers should place their right hand in the 3 o'clock position and their left hand in the 9 o'clock position. This position reduces injury if the air bag deploys.

The steering wheel will be held in a firm yet relaxed grip. The thumbs should rest on the rim of the steering wheel and should never be held too tightly; this will tire the officer more quickly. An officer must use proper hand position and grip each time he or she takes control of a vehicle.

Shuffle Steering

After properly adjusting the equipment, officers should place their hands in the required position and grip the steering wheel correctly. They should perform the shuffle steering technique to make a right turn and a left turn. Driving in reverse does not involve shuffle steering.

To turn right, officers should move the right hand into the 12 o'clock position at the top of the steering wheel and pull the steering wheel down in a smooth motion into a right turn:

1. Simultaneously maintain contact with the steering wheel with the left hand, and slide the left hand into the 6 o'clock position.

2. Continue as the hands meet at the 6 o'clock position to turn by gripping with the left hand and loosening the right hand while maintaining contact with the right hand. Shuffle the wheel from hand to hand, rotating the left hand up toward the 12 o'clock position.

3. Simultaneously maintain contact with the right hand, and slide the right hand into the 12 o'clock position.

4. Make sure that neither hand crosses the steering wheel's top (12 o'clock position) or bottom (6 o'clock position). The right hand stays on the right side of the wheel; the left hand stays on the left side of the wheel.

To turn left, officers should move the left hand into the 12 o'clock position at the top of the steering wheel and then pull the steering wheel down in a smooth motion into a left turn:

1. Simultaneously maintain contact with the steering wheel with the right hand, and slide the right hand into the 6 o'clock position.

2. Continue to turn as the hands meet at the 6 o'clock position by gripping with the right hand and loosening the left hand while maintaining contact with that left hand. Shuffle the wheel from hand to hand, rotating the right hand up toward the 12 o'clock position.

3. Simultaneously maintain contact with the steering wheel with the left hand, and slide the left hand to the 12 o'clock position.

4. Make sure neither hand crosses the steering wheel's top (12 o'clock position) or bottom (6 o'clock position). The left hand stays on the left side of the wheel; the right hand stays on the right side of the wheel. *(VO903.1.)*

It is imperative to use this steering technique because it helps maintain control of the steering wheel, especially when the caster effect occurs. The ***caster effect*** is the forward motion that causes a vehicle to straighten from a turn when releasing the steering wheel *(VO903.8.C.1.)*. Using the shuffle steering technique allows the caster effect to work for officers rather than against them. The caster effect does not apply when driving in reverse.

Optical Driving and Hand-Eye Coordination

Optical driving is looking in the desired direction of travel to avoid an obstacle and steering in that direction. This is also referred to as ***eye-targeting***. *(VO903.3.)*

Section Vocabulary
caster effect
eye-targeting

UNIT 3 | PRINCIPLES OF DRIVING
LESSON 3 | Threshold Braking

OBJECTIVES

VO905.2.A.2. Explain principles of threshold braking.

VO904.3.B. Describe how to avoid applying brakes to maintain rolling friction.

VO905.2.A.3. Describe an incipient skid.

VO905.2.A.1. Identify type of brake system on the vehicle.

VO905.2.A. Demonstrate how to maintain pressure on the brake pedal according to the type of vehicle braking system, using threshold braking, if necessary, to avoid wheel lockup.

VO904.3.A.1. Identify incipient spin and its effect on vehicle traction.

VO904.3. Demonstrate how to decrease the rate of acceleration to control loss of traction.

To complete the driving exercise successfully, you must learn and demonstrate the proper acceleration and threshold braking techniques. An officer must know how to use the threshold braking technique in case the patrol vehicle's ABS (anti-lock braking system) malfunctions. If it does, the vehicle's conventional braking system is still operational. With *threshold braking*, the driver presses the brake pedal by applying light pressure, and gradually increases pressure to slow or stop as quickly as possible without locking the brakes or engaging the ABS system. *(VO905.2.A.2.)*

When practicing and demonstrating threshold braking, an officer should do the following:

1. Rotate the right foot from the accelerator to the brake while leaving the heel on the floor.

2. Place the ball of the right foot on the center of the brake pedal.

3. Apply light pressure to the brake pedal.

4. Gradually increase pressure on the brake pedal to stop the vehicle in the shortest distance without the wheel locking up. (If the wheel locks, an officer may lose steering control and begin to skid.)

5. To correct wheel lock-up, slightly decrease pressure on the brake pedal to allow the tires to regain traction. The officer should immediately reapply the threshold braking technique. *(VO904.3.B.)*

An *incipient skid* happens just before the tires lose traction during braking. The tires lock, causing loss of steering control and a skid. *(VO905.2.A.3.)*

Anti-lock Braking System

Some vehicles have an enhancement to the conventional braking system called *anti-lock braking system (ABS)* *(VO905.2.A.1.)*. ABS and non-ABS work alike under normal (gradual) braking pressure. When an emergency (hard or sudden) stop is required, the two systems operate differently.

When a driver applies a steady downward pressure to the brake pedal, the computerized ABS automatically slows and stops the vehicle. If the ABS fails, an officer must use the threshold braking technique to control the stop. To stop a vehicle equipped with ABS quickly, an officer will apply the brakes hard to engage the ABS. The officer will feel the brake pedal pulsing, which is a normal condition indicating that the vehicle is in ABS mode. *(VO905.2.A.)*

Proper Acceleration

An *incipient spin* occurs just before the drive tires lose traction during acceleration. (The drive tires are the front tires on a front-wheel drive vehicle or rear tires on a rear-wheel drive vehicle.) *(VO904.3.A.1.)*

The following steps explain the proper technique for accelerating a vehicle while avoiding loss of traction and controlling weight transfer:

1. Position the foot properly; rest the right heel at the base of the accelerator.

2. Rest the ball of the right foot squarely on the accelerator pedal.

3. With the ball of the right foot, apply pressure to the accelerator, pressing it down.

4. Apply smooth consistent pressure to the accelerator until the desired acceleration rate has been reached.

5. Apply proper pressure without losing traction and passing the point of incipient spin.

6. Release the pressure on the pedal as needed to control loss of traction or decrease the acceleration rate.

It is important to remember that proper acceleration is best done in a smooth, straight line using steady pressure. If the tires begin to spin, the officer should immediately release the accelerator; this stops the tires from spinning *(VO904.3.)*. The officer can then smoothly reapply the accelerator and move the vehicle forward.

Section Vocabulary
anti-lock braking system (ABS)
incipient skid
incipient spin
threshold braking

UNIT 3 | PRINCIPLES OF DRIVING
LESSON 4 | Vehicle Slide Control

OBJECTIVES

VO904.3.B.1. Describe rolling friction and its effect on vehicle traction.

VO906.1. Identify the importance of not accelerating.

VO906.1.B. Identify the importance of not braking.

VO906.2.A. Define *counter steering*.

VO906.2. Identify the importance of counter steering to avoid a secondary slide.

Section Vocabulary

counter steering

rolling friction

skid

slide

Control of a vehicle depends on traction. Traction is the result of the friction a vehicle's tires create on the road surface. The best traction is ***rolling friction***, which is the tires constantly rotating on the road surface without losing contact *(VO904.3.B.1.)*. Loss of traction is, therefore, the result of loss of rolling friction, which causes loss of control of the vehicle as the tires skid or slide on the road surface. Loss of traction equals loss of control.

A ***skid*** results when the wheels lock and do not turn while the vehicle is moving. Both rolling friction and traction are lost. If a driver follows a vehicle too closely, does not pay attention, and then slams on the brakes to avoid a collision, the result is a common skid in which both rolling friction and traction are lost. Weight transfer and centrifugal force can also influence a skid. If a driver enters a turn too quickly and brakes improperly to slow down, he or she will lose control and begin to skid.

A ***slide*** also results from loss of both rolling friction and traction. In a slide, the wheels still rotate, but they do not control the vehicle's movement. A power slide happens when a driver over-accelerates, and the tires spin; the wheels are not locked, but the driver has lost traction. That is why the vehicle is not accelerating forward. A slide can cause loss of control. Accelerating too much on a turn or a slick surface causes a power slide. *(VO906.1.)*

Generally, officers will not have to drive on icy roadways in Florida. However, rainstorms cause similar hazards. Of particular concern on Florida roadways is oil and tar. When moistened by rainfall, they increase the possibility of skidding. When a vehicle rides on top of water on the roadway, it is hydroplaning and may slide or skid.

Recovering from a Slide

If the vehicle skids or slides, follow these basic steps to recover and to avoid a secondary skid or slide:

1. Remove the foot from the gas pedal to stop accelerating.

2. Do not apply the brakes. This may lock the wheels and make the skid or slide worse *(VO906.1.B.)*. The only way to recover is to regain traction.

3. Use ***counter steering*** when traction is regained. Turn the vehicle's front tires in the direction you want to go. *(VO906.2.A.)*

If you follow these steps correctly, you will also avoid a secondary slide *(VO906.2.)*.

UNIT 3 | PRINCIPLES OF DRIVING
LESSON 5 | Vehicle Cornering

Cornering requires entering an intersection safely and properly at normal driving speeds and making a 90-degree turn to the right or left. Threshold braking is an important element of negotiating a turn. Officers should also recognize the apex of the turn and properly adjust the vehicle's location to fully use the available space. Steering input with inappropriate speed keeps a vehicle from going in a straight line.

Officers must demonstrate effective cornering by making right and left turns following these steps:

- Drive straight forward when approaching the turn.

- Reach and maintain a speed of 35 mph.

- Be sure to operate turn signals before the turn.

- Brake to slow to a safe speed before entering the turn. Complete braking while driving straight forward.

- Align the vehicle in the appropriate traffic lane outside the turn or corner. *(VO907.1.)*

- Determine the apex or path of travel through the turn.

- To ensure steady weight transfer, maintain a constant speed while entering the turn. *(VO907.2.)*

- Provide steering input; shuffle steer through the curve. *(VO903.7.)*

- Look through the turn to observe and react to obstacles, hazards, and road conditions.

- Begin accelerating while exiting the curve.

OBJECTIVES

VO907.1. Position the vehicle for entry into a turn or corner.

VO907.2. Maintain control of the vehicle through the turn.

VO903.7. Demonstrate how to control the amount of steering input.

UNIT 3 | PRINCIPLES OF DRIVING
LESSON 6 | Vehicle Backing

OBJECTIVES

VO908.1. Identify how to achieve the pivot position by turning the upper body to the right, placing the right arm on the top portion of the passenger seat, and looking through the rear window to navigate.

VO908.2. Identify how to steer in reverse with your left hand while slowly accelerating and maintaining control of the steering wheel.

Many crashes occur when drivers are backing up. The ability to back a vehicle safely out of a particular location or situation is an officer safety skill. If an officer fails to back the vehicle properly, he or she might hit a person or an object. The majority of law enforcement vehicle crashes are a result of backing into a fixed object.

All dynamics apply to the vehicle in any direction of travel. In reverse, the vehicle should be driven slowly to compensate for an increase in weight transfer and a decrease in the driver's field of vision. The rear brakes, which handle a great amount of weight transfer while driving in reverse, are not as efficient as the front brakes. Therefore, the ability to stop when backing is significantly lowered.

Driving in reverse requires less steering input to produce a larger change in direction. Officers will find this especially evident when they drive the Reverse Serpentine course.

Large or quick steering movements may cause uncontrolled oscillation. Officers will find this evident when they drive the Emergency Backing course.

Officers must demonstrate effective backing of a law enforcement vehicle. When backing, officers should perform the following steps:

- Press the brake with the right foot while shifting the transmission into reverse.
- Turn the upper body to the right, placing the right arm on the top of the upper portion of the passenger seat.
- Look through the rear window; scan the area the vehicle should back into.
- Place the left hand in the 12 o'clock position and, with upper body turned, release the brake and slowly accelerate. *(VO908.1.)*
- Back the vehicle while steering, using the left hand and a smooth motion.
- When driving in reverse, use the mirrors only as an option, not as sole sources of visual perception.
- Except in an emergency, always back slowly. *(VO908.2.)*

UNIT 4 | LIGHTS AND SIRENS

LESSON 1 | Preparation for Emergency Mode

The decision to operate a law enforcement vehicle in emergency mode is one an officer must never take lightly. Driving in emergency mode can place the officer and the public at risk. Responding in emergency mode or pursuing a vehicle are among the most dangerous driving situations because the officer may experience psychological and physiological effects.

An officer must follow specific Florida laws that relate to the operation of emergency vehicles. Individual agency policies can add further restrictions to state law as to when and how officers will operate vehicles in emergency mode. Officers must revert to specific agency policy relating to emergency mode operation. Court opinions and legislation change laws continuously. Officers should consult their supervisors and their agency legal advisors about issues specific to their respective agencies to stay up-to-date.

According to F.S. §316.003(1), an authorized emergency vehicle refers to

> Vehicles of the fire department (fire patrol), police vehicles, and such ambulances and emergency vehicles of municipal departments, public service corporations operated by private corporations, the Department of Environmental Protection, the Department of Health, and the Department of Transportation as are designated or authorized by their respective department or the chief of police of an incorporated city or any sheriff of any of the various counties.

According to F.S. §316.271(6),

> Every authorized emergency vehicle shall be equipped with a siren, whistle, or bell capable of emitting sound audible under normal conditions from a distance of not less than 500 feet and of a type approved by the department, but such siren, whistle, or bell shall not be used except when the vehicle is operated in response to an emergency call or in the immediate pursuit of an actual or suspected violator of the law, in which event the driver of the vehicle shall sound the siren, whistle, or bell when reasonably necessary to warn pedestrians and other drivers of the approach thereof.

According to F.S. §316.126(3),

> Any authorized emergency vehicle, when en route to meet an existing emergency, shall warn all other vehicular traffic along the emergency route by an audible signal, siren, exhaust whistle, or other adequate device or by a visible signal by the use of displayed blue or red lights. While en route to such emergency, the emergency vehicle shall otherwise proceed in a manner consistent with the laws regulating vehicular traffic upon the highways of this state.

OBJECTIVES

VO910.1.A.3. Identify Florida Statutes that govern vehicles operating in emergency mode.

VO910.1.A. Identify guidelines for operating in emergency mode.

According to F.S. §316.126(1),

> Upon the immediate approach of an authorized emergency vehicle, while en route to meet an existing emergency, the driver of every other vehicle shall, when such emergency vehicle is giving audible signals by siren, exhaust whistle, or other adequate device, or visible signals by the use of displayed blue or red lights, yield the right-of-way to the emergency vehicle and shall immediately proceed to a position parallel to, and as close as reasonable to the closest edge of the curb of the roadway, clear of any intersection and shall stop and remain in position until the authorized emergency vehicle has passed, unless otherwise directed by any law enforcement officer.

According to F.S. §316.072(5)(a) 1.,

> The driver of an authorized emergency vehicle, when responding to an emergency call, when in the pursuit of an actual or suspected violator of the law, or when responding to a fire alarm, but not upon returning from a fire … may exercise the privileges set forth in this section, but subject to the conditions herein stated.

According to F.S. §316.072 (5)(b), a driver operating in emergency mode may do the following:

> park or stand, irrespective of the provisions of this chapter

> proceed past a red or stop signal, or stop sign but only after slowing down as may be necessary for safe operation

> exceed the maximum speed limits so long as the driver does not endanger life or property

> disregard regulations governing direction or movement or turning in specified directions so long as the driver does not endanger life or property *(VO910.1.A.3.)*

These provisions do not relieve the law enforcement driver of a vehicle specified in F.S. §316.072(5)(a)1 and 4(c) from the duty to drive with due regard for safety of all persons, nor do they protect the driver from the consequences of his or her reckless disregard for the safety of others. *(VO910.1.A.)*

UNIT 4 I LIGHTS AND SIRENS
LESSON 2 I **Night and Subdued Light Driving**

Although only one-third of all driving is done at night, more than half of all fatal crashes occur during hours of darkness. This happens because drivers believe that they can drive as fast at night as they can during the day. This perception and false confidence combine with reduced visibility to create a more hazardous driving environment.

Several factors may influence driving performance at night. They include the following:

- **overdriving of vehicle headlights:** The most common night driving error is to overdrive the distance the vehicle's headlights project. According to F.S. §316.237, vehicle headlights reveal a person 450 feet away with the high beams and a distance of 150 feet with the low beams. When increasing speed, an officer may not be able to stop his or her vehicle within the visible area the vehicle's headlights create. This factor is most important when driving in emergency mode. High speed increases stopping distance and decreases reaction time.

- **reaction distance:** Reaction time remains the same whether driving during the day or night. However, lack of light increases the time required to initially observe a hazard.

- **field of vision:** At night, peripheral vision decreases. Less light narrows the field of vision.

- **loss of visual cues:** At night, it is easy to lose many visual cues that are available during the day, which lowers the ability to judge distance and the speed of oncoming traffic.

- **glare:** Glare from oncoming vehicles or other outside sources can temporarily blind a driver. When driving at night, human eyes adjust to the lack of light and use night vision. When the light suddenly changes, eyes need time to readjust.

- **emergency lights:** When driving in emergency mode, emergency lights can increase the amount of glare encountered. The high intensity of the emergency lights easily reflects off objects. *(VO910.6.A.)*

There are techniques officers can use to improve their vision while driving at night and react properly to oncoming vehicular traffic. These techniques include the following:

- reducing speed and not looking directly at the headlights of oncoming vehicles
- looking off to the shoulder of the roadway to protect night vision while using the white line at the edge of the road for guidance
- dimming the headlights for oncoming traffic to reduce glare and protect the night vision of other drivers
- using low beams while driving in fog or smoke during the day or at night, which limits the amount of glare reflected back at the driver
- controlling interior lights by lowering instrument panel lights to reduce glare *(VO910.6.B.)*

OBJECTIVES

VO910.6.A. Identify types of sensory influences the driver may experience at night.

VO910.6.B. Identify techniques that may improve vision at night.

UNIT 4 | LIGHTS AND SIRENS

LESSON 3 | Operating in Emergency Mode

OBJECTIVES

VO910.5.A. Identify possible psychological effects on the driver in emergency mode.

VO910.5.B. Identify possible physiological effects on the driver in emergency mode.

VO910.4. Identify safe emergency driving techniques.

After deciding to drive in emergency mode, an officer must be continuously concerned about certain safety factors while responding.

Effects of Driving in Emergency Mode

Responding to an emergency call causes stress, which can lead to many psychological and physiological reactions. The psychological stress of an emergency call may cause you to exceed your ability or your vehicle's ability in trying to "catch the bad guy at any cost" or "get there before anyone else" *(VO910.5.A.)*. Physiological effects are the measurable changes to normal body functions. These include tunnel vision, selective hearing, increased heart rate, time distortion, and loss of spatial awareness or fine motor skills *(VO910.5.B.)*. It is important for officers to be aware of these effects and keep them under control when responding in emergency mode.

Several techniques help officers respond safely in emergency mode. Officers must use all available emergency equipment properly. They are responsible for ensuring a safe response. Any decision to use lights should be based on factors associated with the response, not on extraneous factors such as concerns about waking citizens during the night hours, inconvenience to traffic, etc. Officers should also realize that a siren is not a protective shield. Many motorists drive with their radios and air conditioners on and their windows up. They may not hear a siren.

There are many concerns that accompany operating a vehicle in emergency mode. Officers should remember to always control their vehicles by using proper steering, braking, and accelerating techniques. It is possible to respond rapidly and safely when using good judgment and good driving techniques.

Officers must approach intersections correctly, yielding or stopping when the situation warrants to ensure that they adhere to due regard for the safety of others when requesting right of way. It is recommended that an officer make eye contact with other drivers at an intersection before driving through that intersection.

It is necessary to maintain proper following distances from citizens' vehicles and other emergency vehicles. If an officer follows a vehicle too closely, the driver may not see the officer's lights in the rearview mirrors.

An officer should always offset his or her vehicle to the left of the available roadway but within his or her lane. That makes the vehicle more visible to the vehicles the officer is following as well as those approaching from the opposite direction. The driver in front of the officer should see his or her car in both the rear and side mirrors. *(VO910.4.)*

Always keep in contact with the dispatcher and other responding units when driving in emergency mode.

UNIT 4 | LIGHTS AND SIRENS
LESSON 4 | Pursuit Considerations

The goal of pursuit is to apprehend a fleeing violator. The violator's driving or the route the violator takes cannot be controlled. Therefore, driving functions as a reaction to the violator's actions both during the driving and after he or she stops. An officer must never let a violator's driving dictate the officer's driving.

The officer's decision to initiate a pursuit is contingent upon the officer's knowledge of agency policy and Florida Statutes as well as current conditions and circumstances. An officer must weigh the risks to him- or herself and the public against the benefits of apprehending a violator after a pursuit. *(VO910.1.)*

Pursuit is an active attempt by an officer, driving an authorized emergency vehicle (with emergency equipment activated), to apprehend occupants of a moving vehicle if the offender increases vehicle speed, takes other evasive actions, or refuses to stop in an apparent attempt to avoid apprehension *(VO910.1.B.).* An officer must be aware of his or her duties to the public as they relate to emergency and pursuit driving. The decision must be considered in relation to engaging the fleeing vehicle as well as in terms of the consequences that might come of beginning a pursuit and terminating it, if the violator then continues to operate the vehicle recklessly.

Some court cases address officers' duty to care for the public while operating police vehicles. In *DeShaney v. Winnebago County Department of Social Services*, 489 U.S.189 (1989), the U.S. Supreme Court stated that an officer or agency has no duty to guarantee a person's safety unless a special relationship exists between the police and that person. This type of relationship exists, for example, between police and a person in custody. After police restrict the person's freedom of movement, they assume responsibility for that person's safety and must keep the person reasonably free from harm.

In pursuit situations, this means that an officer who begins a pursuit generally has no duty to continue it. The officer who terminates a pursuit is unlikely to be liable if the violator continues to drive recklessly. However, according to the Florida case *City of Pinellas Park v. Brown*, 604 So.2d 1222 (Fla. 1990), law enforcement has a duty to protect the public when choosing to continue a pursuit.

In the *Pinellas Park* case, officers and deputies from three different jurisdictions engaged approximately 15 police cars in a pursuit on the main roadway. All officers and deputies violated department policies by continuing the pursuit. Another officer driving an unmarked police vehicle entered the roadway from a side street in an attempt to join the pursuit. At the same time, a civilian vehicle occupied by two sisters waited to cross the roadway. Without warning the women, the officer entered from the side street and turned right onto the main road in an effort to get ahead of the pursuit. When the light

---

OBJECTIVES

VO910.1. Identify how to make a decision to operate in emergency mode.

VO910.1.B. Define *pursuit*.

VO910.1.A.2. Explain case law regarding operating a vehicle in emergency mode.

VO910.2. Notify communications and supervisor when a pursuit is initiated.

VO910.3. Activate the emergency equipment.

VO910.7. Identify when to coordinate with other responding units and with dispatch via radio.

VO910.9. Identify the conclusions to a pursuit.

LE278.9.A. Choose the appropriate report form for the pursuit report.

turned green, the sisters pulled into the path of the pursued vehicle. Both sisters and the fleeing driver were killed.

The Florida Supreme Court held that the police action in this case created a risk to the public that was foreseeable and preventable. The court did not prohibit police pursuits; it simply stated that any police decision to start or continue a pursuit is subject to court review under the doctrine of negligence, not just as a use of force under the Fourth Amendment. If police have a duty of care to a citizen, and police action or inaction causes injury or death to that person, then the court must determine whether police acted reasonably. The court also noted that in modern times, "losing" a vehicle during pursuit does not mean the police will never find the car nor bring its occupants to justice. It is not always a matter of "catching them now or never." Police may identify a violator for apprehension later. Following agency policy is the best way to avoid liability in a pursuit scenario.

In *Brower v. Inyo County*, 489 U.S. 593 (1989), the U.S. Supreme Court addressed the issue of deadly force in a police pursuit. In that case, the court held that certain pursuit tactics might result in a claim of a constitutional violation as a seizure by deadly force. In *Brower*, the police set up a roadblock by parking an 18-wheeler around a curve in the roadway and placing a police car with its headlights positioned to blind Brower as he drove around the curve. The combination of these caused Brower to strike the stationary truck, resulting in his death.

In reaching its opinion, the court relied heavily on its earlier decision regarding deadly force in *Tennessee v. Garner*, 471 U.S. 1 (1985). The court was concerned with the use of deadly force to apprehend an individual for commission of a "nondangerous crime" and drew a distinction between the act of pursuing and the act of blocking or seizing a person. Brower clearly was seized; the police actively tried to block him, so responsibilities associated with seizure applied to their actions.

In *Brower*, as in *Garner*, the court took the position that deadly force should not be used to apprehend citizens for minor offenses such as traffic violations. This distinction also highlights the relationship between the violator and officers' actions. When merely pursuing, officers have no special relationship with the violator and assume no responsibility for the violator's injury or death. However, if the officers take affirmative steps to halt or force the fleeing individual to stop—whether by roadblock or physical contact between vehicles—the officers are responsible for the results. Their actions become a seizure under the Fourth Amendment.

The issue of using a police vehicle as deadly force is best addressed in specific policy. When police intentionally use a vehicle as a weapon, it becomes a deadly weapon. An agency's use of force policy governs the vehicle's use just as it governs any other weapon of opportunity. Questions often arise regarding use of tactics such as Pursuit Immobilization Technique (PIT), ramming, and other forcible vehicle tactics. *Graham v. Connor*, 490 U.S. 386 (1989) is the U.S. Supreme Court's key case regarding use of force. In this case, the court made an observation about law enforcement's decisions during emergency and pursuit driving. Chief Justice Rehnquist wrote: "… [P]olice officers are often forced to make split-second judgments—in circumstances that are tense, uncertain, and rapidly evolving—about the amount of force that is necessary in a particular situation." Rehnquist went on to say the courts will not second guess those judgments as long as they are objectively reasonable in light of the totality of circumstances.

Another issue is the standard for judging an officer responsible for injury or death caused by pursuit or emergency response. In *County of Sacramento v. Lewis*, 523 U.S. 883 (1998), the Supreme Court adopted the standard referred to in earlier cases involving force. The officers may be liable if their actions were sufficient to "shock the conscience" of the court. This standard must be decided on a case-by-case basis. The court distinguished between mere carelessness or negligence, deliberate indifference, and the intent to cause harm. To "shock the conscience" under the conditions of a high-speed pursuit, the officer must have intended to cause harm to the violator without justification for the use of deadly force.

Although the *Lewis* decision involved a minor offense that resulted in the death of a passenger on a motorcycle, the Court again recognized the dynamic nature of some law enforcement activities. Writing for the majority, Justice Souter wrote, "A police officer in deciding to give chase must balance on one hand the need to stop a suspect and show that flight from the law is no way to freedom, and, on the other, the high-speed threat to everyone within stopping range, be they suspects, their passengers, other drivers, or bystanders." This "balancing test" is what officers must consider when deciding to engage in, continue, or terminate a pursuit.

In 2007, the Supreme Court decided another pursuit/use of force case in *Scott v. Harris*, 550 U.S. 372, 127 S.Ct. 1769 (2007). Deputy Scott pursued Victor Harris for a traffic offense at high speeds for several minutes before attempting to terminate the chase using PIT, though at much higher speed than was recommended by PIT training. Writing for the majority, Justice Scalia said, "Whether or not Scott's actions constituted application of 'deadly force,' all that matters is whether Scott's actions were reasonable." He went on to deride Harris' argument that the public endangered by the chase could have been protected if Scott and the other officers had just stopped chasing Harris. "Whereas Scott's action—ramming respondent off the road—was certain to eliminate the risk that respondent posed to the public, ceasing pursuit was not…Second, we are loath to lay down a rule requiring the police to allow fleeing suspects to get away whenever they drive so recklessly that they put other people's lives in danger. It is obvious the perverse incentives such a rule would create; every fleeing motorist would know that escape is within his grasp, if only he accelerates to 90 miles per hour, crosses the double-yellow line a few times, and runs a few red lights. The Constitution assuredly does not impose this invitation to impunity-earned-by-recklessness. Instead, we lay down a more sensible rule; a police officer's attempt to terminate a dangerous high-speed car chase that threatens the lives of innocent bystanders does not violate the Fourth Amendment, even when it places the fleeing motorist at risk of serious injury or death." *(VO910.1.A.2.)*

Because Florida officers are bound by the *Pinellas Park v. Brown* decision which imposed a negligence standard for injuries caused during chases, the *Scott* decision does not give the green light for an "anything goes" approach to pursuits. However, under the Fourth Amendment's use of force analysis, injury to the fleeing driver will generally not be considered to be the result of unreasonable force.

Once engaged in a pursuit, an officer must notify dispatch that he or she is initiating or terminating a pursuit *(VO910.2.)*. The officer must activate and properly use all available emergency equipment during the pursuit *(VO910.3.)*. He or she must keep in contact with the dispatcher and other assisting units during the entire pursuit. They must be notified of any changes or additional help needed *(VO910.7.)*. The officer in pursuit must also control his or her vehicle as well as speed by pacing the violator's vehicle, using the four-second rule to establish a safe distance between his or her vehicle and the violator's vehicle. The officer must practice good driving techniques. An officer should keep in mind that the chance of brake fading or loss of traction increases as the pursuit continues and immediately terminate a pursuit when risk to the public or the officer (or other officers) outweighs the benefit of apprehending the violator. Officers should also remember that it is necessary to alter driving methods to accommodate nighttime conditions.

A pursuit has five possible conclusions:

1. The violator stops voluntarily, and the pursuit ends.

2. The violator is stopped involuntarily, resulting in the violator's apprehension or death.

3. The officer ends the pursuit without apprehending the violator, permitting the violator to escape, at least temporarily.

4. The violator crashes.

5. The officer crashes.

Pursuit Termination Techniques

Some Florida law enforcement agencies use tactics and technologies to conclude vehicular pursuits more safely and more rapidly. Those agencies have training and policies that teach and govern the application of forcible-stop techniques.

Roadblocks

A *roadblock* is the use of vehicles, barricades, cones, or other objects to block traffic flow completely. Its purpose is to demonstrate overwhelming police superiority and position so that the violator will stop and surrender. According to *Brower v. County of Inyo*, a roadblock must be positioned so the violator has sufficient time to stop. Using a roadblock poses a hazard to the officer, other motorists, pedestrians, and the suspect. Therefore, it is necessary to use care and caution when choosing a location for a roadblock and while setting it up.

Appropriate locations for roadblocks include areas that provide a clear view of the roadblock from both sides and highways, streets, or roads. Inappropriate locations for roadblocks include locations over the crest of a hill and locations in, on, or around a curve. Officers should never select a location where the violator has no warning that the crash may occur, unless the use of deadly force is necessary. Officers should never use non-police equipment to block the roadway, and they should never remain seated in vehicles used to obstruct the roadway. This places officers in extreme danger. Communication between officers establishing the roadblock and officers in pursuit is vital. All officers involved in the pursuit should be informed of the road block technique to be used.

Tire-deflation Devices

Many brands of tire-deflation devices are available for law enforcement agencies. The employing agency's policy and training will provide guidelines for using tire-deflation devices. All tire-deflation devices share common characteristics:

• hollow spikes that puncture a vehicle's tire and allow air to be released, causing the tire to deflate

• track or mat base

• some form of officer deployment

Pursuit Immobilization Technique (PIT)

Some law enforcement agencies around the country currently use the *Pursuit Immobilization Technique (PIT)*. The purpose of this technique is to stop a violator's vehicle by using the police vehicle to apply force to either the rear right or left side of the violator's vehicle to end the pursuit. Only properly trained officers following agency policy may use this technique. *(VO910.9.)*

Pursuit Reporting

When an officer is involved in a pursuit, he or she should promptly report the details of the pursuit to the agency. Policy on reporting differs between agencies, but prompt reporting is always required. After conducting a pursuit according to agency policy and procedures, the officer will probably be required to complete a written report of the pursuit's circumstances and results. If the suspect is arrested, the officer should detail the pursuit on the arrest report. If issuing a citation, the officer should note the pursuit information in the citation's narrative or if the vehicle is towed, the pursuit information should be recorded on the impound tow sheet. *(LE278.9.A.)*

Section Vocabulary

pursuit

Pursuit Immobilization Technique (PIT)

roadblock

CHAPTER 2

CMS First Aid For Criminal Justice Officers

As the first person on the scene of an emergency, you have a special role. You can make a difference in a life-threatening situation. By appropriately applying your knowledge, skills, and abilities, you can stabilize patients and possibly prevent the deterioration of their conditions until EMS arrives. Your ability to assist with emergency medical situations and your ability to remember legal guidelines are important skills, as are your sound judgment and good common sense.

When called to respond to an emergency, be aware of your attitude, appearance, and behavior at all times. As a criminal justice officer, convey the message that you are competent and trustworthy. A professional and confident manner will reassure and comfort the patient, family, and bystanders in times of panic or chaos.

UNIT 1 | PREPARING TO RESPOND TO EMERGENCIES
LESSON 1 | Introduction to First Aid

OBJECTIVES

FR004.1. Identify the role of the Emergency Medical Services System (EMS) in preparing to respond to a medical emergency.

FR004.1.A. Identify how the roles and responsibilities of the criminal justice first aid provider differ from other professionals within the EMS system.

FR004.2. Uphold responsibilities for medical treatment in accordance with Criminal Justice Standards and Training Commission (CJSTC) standards when responding to a medical emergency.

The criminal justice officer ensures the safety of victims and bystanders, gains access to patients, provides basic first aid, and alerts the EMS system. The *EMS system* is a network of trained professionals linked to provide advanced, out-of-hospital care for victims of sudden traumatic injury or illness. *(FR004.1.)*

Laws, regulations, policies, and procedures govern Florida's EMS system. The Division of Emergency Medical Services and Community Health Resources provide leadership to local jurisdictions and municipalities. Florida law mandates that all patients have equal access to the EMS system. Although each state regulates its EMS system, the National Highway Traffic Safety Administration and the United States Department of Transportation (*USDOT*) sets the standard.

The roles and responsibilities of criminal justice officers differ from those of other professional out-of-hospital caregivers. At the scene of a medical emergency, the criminal justice officer can be the first person providing basic first aid. Advanced, specialized training prepares paramedics, emergency medical technicians (*EMTs*), and other responders to provide more comprehensive care than criminal justice officers can provide. The EMS system has at its disposal teams of highly skilled individuals trained to respond to emergencies on a daily basis.

Criminal Justice First Aid Provider Levels of Training

- airway care
- patient assessment
- cardiopulmonary resuscitation (*CPR*)
- bleeding control
- stabilization of injuries to the spine and extremities or limbs
- care for medical and trauma emergencies
- use of limited amount of equipment
- assistance to other EMS providers
- cannot administer medications

EMS Levels of Training
First Responder

- airway care with use of adjunctive equipment
- patient assessment
- CPR

- bleeding control

- stabilization of injuries to the spine and extremities

- care for medical and trauma emergencies

- use of limited amount of equipment

- assistance to other EMS providers

- other skills or procedures as local or state regulations permit

EMT—Basic
- performs all techniques of a first aid provider and a first responder

- performs complex immobilization procedures

- restrains patients

- staffs and drives ambulance

EMT—Paramedic
- performs all functions of previous two levels

- administers medications

- performs advanced techniques, including cardiac monitoring *(FR004.1.A.)*

Criminal Justice First Aid Provider Responsibilities

As criminal justice officers, you will encounter people of different races, ages, genders, cultures, and socioeconomic backgrounds. Your primary concern as a first aid provider is the patient. However, you do have other responsibilities to fulfill while maintaining the appropriate standard of care.

- Protect your safety, the safety of the patient, and the safety of bystanders. Wear personal protective equipment. You cannot help the patient if you are injured. Injury forces other rescuers to rescue you. After ensuring safety at the scene, you must make the patient's needs your primary concern.

- Gain access to the patient. In some emergencies, you may need to move one patient to reach a more critically injured patient.

- Determine life-threatening emergencies. As soon as possible, perform an initial assessment to identify and correct Airway, Breathing, and Circulation (***ABCs***) problems.

- Maintain composure. Some emergencies are life-threatening or emotionally charged situations. Maintaining your composure is important. It enables you to assess the scene and establish priorities. Maintaining a calm demeanor at all times is imperative. Communicate clearly with the patient and responding EMS personnel so that nothing is misunderstood. Working efficiently and avoiding undue haste can prevent mistakes or misunderstandings.

- Keep your appearance neat, clean, and professional. Your appearance can instill confidence in the patient. It can portray you as knowledgeable and trustworthy. Cleanliness reduces contamination of wounds.

- Maintain a caring attitude. Often when arriving on a scene, you meet emotional patients, family members, and bystanders. Identify yourself, give reassurance, and begin to stabilize the patient. Let everyone know more assistance is on the way.

Section Vocabulary

ABCs

CPR

EMS system

EMT

USDOT

• Alert EMS. When a patient requires transport to advanced medical facilities, you must remain with that patient until other EMS personnel relieve you. When they arrive, relay all pertinent information.

• Provide care based on your assessment. As you await EMS, provide the patient with care based on needs you identified during your assessment.

• Assist EMS personnel. When asked, assist EMS personnel by following their instructions.

• Keep your skills current. The medical community and researchers often discover better ways officers can perform their jobs as criminal justice first aid providers. Take advantage of opportunities to continue your education and maintain your skills.

• Participate in the record keeping and data collection your agency requires. You may be required to provide documentation if the patient refuses care.

• Act as liaison with other public safety personnel. Personnel include local, state, and federal law enforcement, fire department personnel, and other EMS providers.

As criminal justice officers providing basic first aid, you play a vital role in delivering emergency care to patients who experience sudden illness or injury. What makes your role so vital is that you are responsible for the patient in the first few minutes after the trauma. The EMS system depends on your actions during those minutes. What you do sets the foundation for the remainder of the rescue. Correcting a breathing problem or stopping bleeding actually can save a life. In this role, you also assist other patients who are not in critical condition by preventing further injuries, performing proper assessments, gathering medical histories, and preparing for EMS personnel to arrive and assist. *(FR004.2.)*

UNIT 1 | PREPARING TO RESPOND TO EMERGENCIES
LESSON 2 | Legal and Ethical Issues

Ethical Responsibilities

Legal and ethical issues significantly affect your roles and responsibilities. These issues may be as easy as asking for and receiving a patient's consent or as problematic as a patient's refusal of treatment. The public has come to expect—and the law requires you to be—competent criminal justice officers whose behavior is always above reproach. You will encounter a variety of individuals throughout the course of your law enforcement career. You must protect them, their families, and their confidentiality while providing appropriate care. Placing the public's well-being first during an emergency reduces your likelihood of acting unethically.

Make the patient's physical and emotional needs a priority. Respect their needs without regard to nationality, race, gender, or age. Practice your skills, continue your education, and uphold professional standards. Show respect for the competence of others in the medical field. Review your performance; seek ways to improve your actions and communication skills. Maintain patient confidentiality, unless the law requires you reveal it. Work in accord with other medical professionals to reach a positive outcome to the emergency. *(FR005.1.)*

Duty to Act

According to *Black's Law Dictionary,* **duty to act** is

> "a duty to take some action to prevent harm to another and for the failure of which one may be liable depending on the relationship of the parties and the circumstances." (Garner, 1999)

Advisory Legal Opinion
(Attorney General's Opinion 89-62)

Number: AGO 89-62
Date: September 15, 1989
Subject: Officer's duty to provide aid to ill or injured

Mr. Michael A. Berg
Chairman
Florida Criminal Justice Standards and Training Commission
Post Office Box 1489
Tallahassee, Florida 32302

Dear Mr. Berg:

You have asked for my opinion on the following questions:

OBJECTIVES

FR005.1. Identify legal and ethical issues for a criminal justice first aid provider when responding lawfully to a medical emergency.

FR005.2.A. Identify how the duty to act applies to the criminal justice first aid provider.

FR005.2.B. Identify how the standard or scope of care applies to the criminal justice first aid provider.

FR005.2. Identify how the Good Samaritan Act affects the criminal justice first aid provider.

FR005.3. Identify the implications of abandonment, negligence, and battery for the criminal justice first aid provider.

FR005.4. Identify the legal and ethical considerations of patient consent for a criminal justice first aid provider.

FR005.5. Identify the role of a Do Not Resuscitate (DNR) Order (DNRO) for a criminal justice first aid provider in patient refusal of care.

FR005.6. Identify the role of organ donor notification for a criminal justice first aid provider when responding to a medical emergency.

FR005.7. Identify the legal and ethical considerations of the Health Insurance Portability and Accountability Act of 1996 (HIPAA) for the criminal justice first aid provider.

FR005.8. Identify actions a criminal justice first aid provider should take to assist in preservation of a crime scene.

1. Does a law enforcement officer have a legal duty to provide aid to ill, injured, and distressed persons, who are not in police custody, during an emergency?

   a. If yes, are the provisions of §768.13, F.S., as amended by Ch. 89-71, Laws of Florida, the Good Samaritan Act, applicable to officers acting within the scope of their employment?

   b. If no, is §768.13, F.S., supra, applicable?

2. Is a police officer protected from liability by the "Good Samaritan Act" if rendering emergency aid to persons not in police custody while off-duty?

3. Is a correctional officer protected from liability by the Good Samaritan Act if rendering emergency aid to persons not in custody while off-duty?

4. What standard of care is required of law enforcement and correctional officers rendering emergency aid within the scope of their employment? While off-duty?

5. What are the limits of liability for an officer, a supervisor, an employing agency, and the officer's first responder instructor if the emergency aid rendered is less than the established standard of care?

Summary:

1. & 2. A law enforcement officer, including a police officer, has a legal duty to provide aid to ill, injured, and distressed persons who are not in police custody during an emergency whether the law enforcement officer is on-duty or acting in a law enforcement capacity off-duty. Thus, the Good Samaritan Act does not apply to such officers.

3. A correctional officer is not a peace officer and, therefore, does not have a legal duty to provide aid to ill, injured, and distressed persons. As a volunteer, a correctional officer would be covered under the Good Samaritan Act to the extent provided therein from liability for civil damages as a result of such care or treatment.

4. The standard of care required of law enforcement and correctional officers rendering emergency aid whether on-duty or off-duty is the same: to render such competence and skill as he or she possesses.

5. A law enforcement officer rendering emergency aid to ill, injured, or distressed persons on-duty or acting in a law enforcement capacity while off-duty is acting within the scope of his or her employment. The liability of the officer and his or her employing agency would, therefore, be subject to the terms and limitations of §768.28, F.S.

A correctional officer providing emergency aid acts as a volunteer and would be protected by the Good Samaritan Act. The provisions of §768.28, F.S. (1988 Supp.), would not apply because the correctional officer is acting outside the scope of his or her employment.

I am not aware of, nor have you brought to my attention, a situation in which the supervisor or the first responder instructor of a law enforcement or correctional officer would be liable for the actions of an officer providing emergency assistance to an injured, ill, or distressed person.

You have asked that this office reconsider the conclusion expressed in AGO 78-140 that a municipal police officer has a common law duty to render aid to ill, injured, or distressed persons during an emergency. Your request is based on a change in the judicially created test to determine a governmental employer's liability under §768.28, F.S. (1988 Supp.), for the actions of its employee/agents. The holdings in these cases are based on the distinction between operational and planning level activities. While AGO 78-140 was rendered prior to the change in this area of the law expressed by The Florida Supreme Court in *Commercial Carrier Corporation v. Indian River County,* 371 So.2d 1010 (Fla.1979), the common law duty of a law enforcement officer as identified in AGO 78-140 continues to be viable, and, as discussed herein, appears to have been extended.

Your letter states that the relevant training required for basic certification as a law enforcement officer or correctional officer is the 40 hour First Responder Training Course developed by the U.S. Department of Transportation.

As to Questions 1 and 2:

Your first and second questions are interrelated and will be answered together.

Florida's "Good Samaritan Act" 1 provides in part that:

> Any person, including those licensed to practice medicine, who gratuitously and in good faith renders emergency care or treatment at the scene of an emergency outside of a hospital, doctor's office, or other place having proper medical equipment, without objection of the injured victim or victims thereof, shall not be held liable for any civil damages as a result of such care or treatment or as a result of any act or failure to act in providing or arranging further medical treatment where the person acts as an ordinary reasonably prudent man would have acted under the same or similar circumstances.

Generally, in the absence of a contractual, special professional, or trustee relationship or a statutory requirement, a person is not under a legal duty to assist or care for the injured when the injury is not due to the fault of the person sought to be charged.

The term "law enforcement officer" is defined in several statutory sections. The most comprehensive definition is found in §943.10(1), F.S., which states that: "Law enforcement officer" means any person who is elected, appointed, or employed full time by any municipality or the state or any political subdivision thereof; who is vested with authority to bear arms and make arrests; and whose primary responsibility is the prevention and detection of crime or the enforcement of the penal, criminal, traffic, or highway laws of the state. This definition includes all certified supervisory and command personnel whose duties include, in whole or in part, the supervision, training, guidance, and management responsibilities of full-time law enforcement officers, part-time law enforcement officers, or auxiliary law enforcement officers but does not include support personnel employed by the employing agency.

Thus, it does not appear that the Legislature has distinguished between municipal police officers and law enforcement officers in general and the statutory duties and responsibilities, as well as the training, of all law enforcement officers are comparable.

In AGO 78-140 this office considered a Florida appellate court holding that a sheriff's officer is charged with the common law duty to render aid in emergencies to the ill, the injured, or the distressed, and concluded that in view of this holding municipal police officers are under a legal duty to provide such aid.

In *Webster v. State*, the district court held that the right of officers of the sheriff's department to enter and to investigate in an emergency situation, without an accompanying intent to seize or arrest, "is inherent in the very nature of their duties as peace officers and derives from the common law." Thus, no search warrant was required to legalize an entry by police for the purpose of rendering aid to an injured or distressed person, "their duty certainly being to effect a rescue or to render aid to someone whom they had reasonable belief was in dire peril." The Webster court declared that it is part of the nature and duty of a police officer, derived from the common law duties of a peace officer, to render aid in emergency situations. Subsequent Florida court decisions have upheld warrant-less searches and seizures based on this common law duty of police officers.

A "peace officer" is generally defined to "include[s] sheriffs and their deputies, constables, marshals, members of the police force of cities, and other officers whose duty is to enforce and preserve the public peace." (e.s.)

Thus, the common law duty to render aid to an ill, injured, or distressed person would appear to apply to all law enforcement officers whose duty it is to enforce and preserve the public peace, not just police or sheriff's officers.

However, the authority of a law enforcement officer is subject to territorial limitations. As a general rule, the authority of a law enforcement officer is coextensive with the boundaries of his employing agency and, when acting outside his or her jurisdiction, a law enforcement officer possesses no more authority to act than a private citizen.

Thus, as the power of a law enforcement officer to act as a peace officer is coextensive with his or her territorial jurisdiction, the common law duty of such officer to render aid in emergency situations would also be subject to such limitations and a law enforcement officer would act as a private citizen otherwise.

At the discretion of their superior officers, all certified law enforcement officers have the right to carry, on or about their persons, concealed firearms, during off-duty hours and may perform the same law enforcement functions that they normally perform during duty hours, utilizing their weapons in a manner, which is reasonably expected of on-duty officers in similar situations.

The officers specified in §790.052(1), F.S., may act as peace officers while off-duty and perform law enforcement functions. Therefore, these officers, although off-duty, would continue to be subject to the common law duty to render aid that applies to an on-duty officer to the extent they are performing law enforcement functions.

Because a law enforcement officer is under a common law duty to render aid while on-duty and when acting in a law enforcement capacity while off-duty, the provisions of §768.13, F.S. (1988 Supp.), Florida's Good Samaritan Act, would not be applicable.

As to Question 3:

A correctional officer is defined as:

> [A]ny person who is appointed or employed full time by the state or any political subdivision thereof, or by any private entity which has contracted with the state or county, and whose primary responsibility is the supervision, protection, care, custody, and control, or investigation, of inmates within a correctional institution; however, the term "correctional officer" does not include any secretarial, clerical, or professionally trained personnel.

Because the duties and responsibilities of a correctional officer are directed to the supervision, protection, and control of inmates within the correctional system of this state rather than the general public, I cannot conclude that such officers are under the common law duty to aid the injured, ill, or distressed in an emergency, as are law enforcement officers.

Thus, as a correctional officer is not under a common law duty to render aid in emergencies to ill, injured, or distressed persons, he or she acts as a volunteer outside the scope of employment when rendering such aid off-duty. Pursuant to the Good Samaritan Act, if a correctional officer provides emergency care and aid in good faith and in a reasonably prudent manner, he or she would be immune from liability provided that such care is rendered at the scene of an emergency outside of a place with proper emergency equipment and without the objection of the victim.

As to Question 4:

I am aware of, and you have called to my attention, no Florida case law which prescribes a standard of care to be used by law enforcement or correctional officers rendering emergency aid. However, the following general comments may be of assistance to you.

The Good Samaritan Act prescribes as the standard of care for purposes of that statute the responsibility to "act[s] as an ordinary reasonably prudent man would have acted under the same or similar circumstances."

General authority suggests that the duty of one who voluntarily undertakes to care for and assist an ill or injured person is the same as that of one who is legally obligated to render such care or assistance.

One who is under a duty to care for an ill or injured person is bound to use reasonable or ordinary care and to have a proper regard for the safety of such person, and is liable for further injury resulting from lack of proper care. The generally accepted rule is that one who provides relief or assistance to an ill, injured, or helpless person is under a legal obligation to use reasonable care and prudence in what he does. In such case the measure of the duty assumed is to exercise ordinary or common humanity, or to exercise with reasonable care such competence and skill as he possesses, or to exercise such care in the treatment of the injured person as the circumstances will allow.

As discussed above, law enforcement officers are under a legal duty to render emergency aid to the injured, ill, or distressed whether such officers are on-duty or acting in a law enforcement capacity while off-duty. Thus, a law enforcement officer who renders emergency assistance to an injured, ill, or distressed person must exercise with reasonable care such competence and skill as he possesses, i.e., such skill as a person with 40 hours of "first responder training" would possess.

A correctional officer rendering aid in an emergency situation would be held to the same duty of care, i.e., commensurate with the competence and skill he or she possesses, but such officer acts as a volunteer outside the scope of his or her employment when rendering such aid.

As to Question 5:

Section 768.28(1), F.S. (1988 Supp.), provides in part that an action at law may be brought against the state and its agencies or subdivisions to recover damages in tort for injuries caused by the negligent acts of an employee acting within the scope of his or her employment, if a private person would be liable under the same circumstances. Since the actions of a law enforcement officer in rendering aid in emergencies would be within the scope of his or her employment, the agency employing the officer may be liable for the actions of its employee. A law enforcement officer, however, would not be subject to personal liability in tort for any injuries or damages suffered as a result of any act or omission of action done within the scope of his employment or function unless he acted in bad faith, or with malicious purpose, or in a manner exhibiting wanton and willful disregard of human rights, safety, or property. Any liability of an employing agency of a law enforcement officer would be limited to the monetary limits set forth in §768.28(5), F.S. (1988 Supp.), which are currently provided to be $100,000 for any claim or judgment by any one person or $200,000 for all claims or judgments paid by the state or its agencies or subdivisions arising out of the same incident or occurrence.

A correctional officer, who is under no legal duty to render emergency aid, acts as a volunteer outside the scope of his or her employment when rendering such aid. Therefore, a correctional officer may be held personally liable for injuries resulting from his actions or omission of action unless he is held immune under the terms of the Good Samaritan Act. A correctional officer who in good faith and in a reasonably prudent manner provides care and aid at the scene of an emergency, without any duty to do so, would be immune from liability provided that he or she renders such care outside of a place with proper emergency equipment and without the objection of the injured person.

However, the employing agency would not be liable pursuant to §768.28, F.S. (1988 Supp.), for the torts or negligence of a correctional officer under such circumstances as the officer is not acting within the scope of his or her employment.

I am not aware of, nor have you related, any situation in which the supervisor of either a law enforcement officer or correctional officer or the first responder instructor of such officer would be held personally liable for the actions of an officer in providing emergency aid.

Sincerely,

Robert A. Butterworth
Attorney General

(gh)

Duty to act refers to your contractual or legal obligation to provide care. While on duty as a correctional officer or correctional probation officer, you have an obligation to provide care to a patient in your custody who needs and consents to care. As a law enforcement officer, you have a duty to act 24/7 within your jurisdictional boundaries. Refer to your agency policy and procedure as jurisdictional boundaries can extend due to a mutual aid agreement. **Breach of duty** occurs when you either fail to act or act inappropriately. *(FR005.2.A.)*

Standard or Scope of Care

Black's Law Dictionary defines standard or scope of care as the following:

> "In the law of negligence, the degree of care that a reasonable person should exercise; under the law of negligence, the conduct demanded of a person in a given situation. Typically, this involves a person's giving attention both to possible dangers, mistakes, and pitfalls and to ways of ensuring that these risks do not materialize." (Garner, 1999)

Standard or scope of care is care that you are expected to provide to the same patient under the same conditions as would any criminal justice first aid provider who received the same level of training. For example, providing CPR is within your scope of care as a criminal justice officer while performing open-heart surgery is not. *(FR005.2.B.)*

Good Samaritan Act

Enacted in 1959 in California, the first Good Samaritan Act provides protection from civil suits to physicians who render emergency care. Most states, including Florida, now have the Good Samaritan Act that also protects first aid providers.

The ***Good Samaritan Act***, based on § 768.13, F.S., Good Samaritan Act, protects a civilian first aid provider from liability for medical care performed in good faith or medical care similar to that expected of another first aid provider with equal training. Medical care includes using an automated external defibrillator (***AED***) as provided for in § 768.1325, F.S. The Good Samaritan Act does not stop someone from filing a lawsuit; however, it does provide a defense if you performed according to the standard of care for a first aid provider. Always render care to the best of your ability. Do not go beyond the scope and level of your training. Maintain the patient's best interests.

According to the Advisory Legal Opinion (89–62), the Good Samaritan Act does not apply to law enforcement officers within their jurisdiction. However, the Good Samaritan Act does apply to correctional officers unless they deal with persons reduced to their custody. The Advisory Legal Opinion does not address correctional probation officers. *(FR005.2.)*

Abandonment

Abandonment is:

> "The relinquishing of a right or interest with the intention of never again claiming it." (Garner, 1999)

You abandon the patient when you stop providing care without ensuring that the patient continues or begins to receive the same or better care. You must continue providing emergency first aid until another medical professional with the same or higher-level training replaces you, or you are unable to continue.

Negligence

> "The failure to exercise the standard of care that a reasonably prudent person would have exercised in a similar situation; any conduct that falls below the legal standard established to protect others against unreasonable risk of harm, except for conduct that is intentionally, wantonly, or willfully disregardful of other's rights." (Garner, 1999)

Negligence occurs if all these conditions are present:

- Duty to act—You were supposed to be there.
- Breach of standard of care—What you did was wrong.
- Causation—What you did caused the injury.
- Damages—The patient suffered an injury; the injury is additional to the original injury.

If patient care deviates from accepted standards and causes further injury, negligence can become a legal liability. Your best defense against negligence is to conduct yourself with a professional attitude and demeanor, provide consistently high standards of care within the scope of your training, and document the care you provide.

Battery

"The use of force against another resulting in harmful or offensive contact; an intentional and offensive touching of another without lawful justification—also termed tortuous battery" (Garner, 1999)

Battery is unlawful physical contact. When you provide emergency care without the patient's consent, you can face a battery charge if you touch a patient's body or clothes. *(FR005.3.)*

Consent

"Agreement, approval, or permission as to some act of purpose, especially given voluntarily by a competent person" (Garner, 1999)

Gain the patient's consent, or permission, before providing emergency first aid. For consent to be valid, the patient must be competent and the consent informed. As a criminal justice first aid provider, you are responsible for fully explaining the care you plan to render, and its possible related risks.

To refuse medical care, a patient must be competent. A competent adult is one who can make an informed decision about medical care. The patient must understand your question and the implications of decisions made about medical care. Consider an adult incompetent if he or she is under the influence of alcohol or drugs and meets the criteria for a Marchman Act (refer to the chapter on Human Issues). An incompetent adult can be in an altered mental state and meet the criteria of a Baker Act (refer to the chapter on Human Issues). Consider an adult incompetent if he or she is seriously ill, has an injury that affects judgment, or is mentally ill or mentally challenged.

You must have a responsive, competent adult's consent before rendering first aid. To obtain consent from an adult, begin by identifying yourself. State your level of training. Carefully explain to the patient what first aid you need to render. Explain your plan for rendering aid in terms the patient understands. Be sure to state possible risks involved. The patient needs a clear idea of all factors that may affect a reasonable person's decision to either accept or refuse.

There are three types of consent:

- *expressed consent*—"Consent that is clearly and unmistakably stated" (Garner, 1999). Expressed consent is affirmative consent, such as verbal or physical assertion of the affirmative. For example, in *State v. Swank*, 399 So.2d.510 (Fla. App. 1981) persons expressly invited officers into a hotel room where they found contraband.

- *implied consent*—"Consent inferred from one's conduct rather than from one's direct expression" (Garner, 1999). Implied consent "may be found by circumstantial evidence suggesting implicit consent." See *Ming v. Interamerican Car Rental, Inc.*, 913 So.2d.650, 656 (Fla. 5th/DCA 2005) for details. You make assumptions of implied consent. You may assume that the unresponsive patient is at risk of death, disability, or deterioration of condition and would agree to care if able to consent. Implied consent may also apply to conscious patients who do not stop you from providing treatment, refuse care, and then become unresponsive and are not competent to refuse care.

- *informed consent*—"A person's agreement to allow something to happen made with full knowledge of the risks involved and the alternatives" (Garner, 1999).

When a patient chooses a treatment or a procedure, he or she makes this choice after a physician or other healthcare provider discloses whatever information a reasonably prudent provider in the medical community would provide to a patient about the risks involved in the proposed treatment.

In Florida, children under age 18 are minors. You must have a parent or legal guardian's permission before providing care. However, if the parent or legal guardian is not available in life-threatening or disabling emergencies, provide emergency care based on the principle of implied consent. An emancipated minor is one who is married, an active member of the military, or financially independent or lives away from home with court permission. You do not need a parent or legal guardian's permission to treat an emancipated minor. The minor's consent is sufficient.

A mentally ill person who has been found to need care under the Baker Act is not considered competent to give expressed consent. Therefore, you must have a legal guardian's permission to treat a mentally ill person. If the legal guardian is not available and the emergency is life threatening, act on the principle of implied consent, and provide care.

Competent adults have the right to refuse treatment for themselves and their children. Follow the law. Inform them of the treatment and the possible risks involved in refusing it. A competent adult may refuse verbally or physically by pulling away, pushing you away, or shaking his or her head in a negative manner. Competent adults also have the right to withdraw from treatment after it begins. This is true for patients who consent and then change their minds. It also applies to a patient who is unconscious when treatment begins, regains consciousness and mental competence, and asks you to stop. Refusal of first aid must follow the rules of expressed consent. Make every effort to persuade the patient to consent to treatment. Be sure the patient is able to make a competent, rational decision.

A person involved in a traumatic incident such as an auto accident may be emotionally, intellectually, and/or physically impaired. If the person continues to refuse treatment, keep him or her under observation. If the patient loses consciousness, and you believe a life-threatening situation exists, immediately begin first aid.

For situations involving minors in life-threatening emergencies needing medical care against parental consent, refer to your agency policy and procedure and Florida Statute §39.401 for guidance. Notify the Department of Children and Family Services by calling 1-800-96-ABUSE. *(FR005.4.)*

Do Not Resuscitate/Advanced Directive

A terminally ill patient may have a directive in place, written in advance, and signed by both the patient and a physician. Commonly known as a Do Not Resuscitate (***DNR***) Order (***DNRO***) or an advanced directive, it is legally binding in Florida according to Florida Statute §401.45. See Figure 2-1 below for an example. The DNR documents the terminally or chronically ill patient's wish to refuse resuscitation. An ***advanced directive*** documents the patient's request to withhold specific medical care.

Criminal justice first aid providers do not have authorization to honor a DNR Order or an advanced directive. You cannot withhold resuscitation or first aid. You must immediately begin first aid. Licensed medical professionals, EMTs, or paramedics, however, can honor a DNR Order or advanced directive. *(FR005.5.)*

FLORIDA
DO NOT RESUSCITATE ORDER
(Please use ink)

Patient's Full Legal Name ____________________
(Print or Type Name) (Date)

PATIENT'S STATEMENT

Based upon informed consent, I, the undersigned, hereby direct that CPR be withheld or withdrawn.
(If not signed by patient, check applicable box):

- ☐ Surrogate
- ☐ Court appointed guardian
- ☐ Proxy (both as defined in Chapter 765 F.S.)
- ☐ Durable power of attorney (pursuant to Chapter 709, F.S.)

(Applicable Signature) (Print or Type Name)

PHYSICIAN'S STATEMENT

I, the undersigned , a physician licensed pursuant to Chapter 458 or 459, F.S., am the physician of the patient named above. I hereby direct the withholding or withdrawing of cardiopulmonary resuscitation (artificial ventilation, cardiac compression, endotracheal intubation and defibrillation) from the patient in the event of the patient's cardiac or respiratory arrest.

(Signature of Physician (Date) Telephone Number (Emergency)

(Print or Type Name) (Physician's Medical License Number)

Pursuant to s. 401.45, F.S., a copy or original of this DNRO may be honored by hospital emergency services, nursing homes, assisted living facilities, home health agencies, hospices, adult family -care and emergency medical services.

DH Form 1896, Revised February 2000

DH Form 1896, Revised February 2000
PHYSICIAN'S STATEMENT

I, the undersigned, a physician licensed pursuant to Chapter 458 or 459, F.S., am the physician of the patient named above. I hereby direct the withholding or withdrawing of cardiopulmonary resuscitation (artificial ventilation, cardiac compression, endotracheal intubation and defibrillation) from the patient in the event of the patient's cardiac or respiratory arrest.

(Signature of Physician) (Date) Telephone Number (Emergency)

(Print or Type Name) (Physician's Medical License Number)

Pursuant to s. 401.45, F.S., a copy or original of this DNRO may be honored by hospital emergency services, nursing homes, assisted living facilities, home health agencies, hospices, adult family -care, and emergency medical services.
DH Form 1896, Revised February 2000

FLORIDA
DO NOT RESUSCITATE ORDER
(Please use ink)

EMS

(Print or Type Patient's Full Legal Name) (Date)

PATIENT'S STATEMENT

Based upon informed consent, I, the undersigned, hereby direct that CPR be withheld or withdrawn. (If not signed by patient, check applicable box):

- ☐ Surrogate
- ☐ Proxy (both as defined in Chapter 765, F.S.)
- ☐ Court appointed guardian
- ☐ Durable power of attorney (pursuant to Chapter 709, F.S.)

(Applicable Signature) (Print or Type Name)

FLORIDA DO NOT RESUSCITATE ORDER
This form is usually yellow

Figure 2-1

REVISIONS TO CHAPTER 64E-2, FLORIDA ADMINISTRATIVE CODE

64E-2.031 Do Not Resuscitate Order (DNRO) Form and Patient Identification Device.

(1) An emergency medical technician or paramedic shall withhold or withdraw cardiopulmonary resuscitation:

  (a) upon the presentation of an original or a completed copy of DH Form 1896, Florida Do Not Resuscitate Order Form, May 2002, which is incorporated by reference and available from the department at no cost, or, any previous edition of DH Form 1896; or

  (b) upon the presentation or observation, on the patient, of a Do Not Resuscitate Order patient identification device.

(2) The Do Not Resuscitate Order:

  (a) form shall be printed on yellow paper and have the words "DO NOT RESUSCITATE ORDER" printed in black and displayed across the top of the form. DH Form 1896 may be duplicated, provided that the content of the form is unaltered, the reproduction is of good quality, and it is duplicated on yellow paper. The shade of yellow does not have to be an exact duplicate;

  (b) patient identification device is a miniature version of DH Form 1896 and is incorporated by reference as part of the DNRO form. Use of the patient identification device is voluntary and is intended to provide a convenient and portable DNRO which travels with the patient. The device is perforated so that it can be separated from the DNRO form. It can also be hole-punched, attached to a chain in some fashion and visibly displayed on the patient. In order to protect this device from hazardous conditions, it shall be laminated after completing it. Failure to laminate the device shall not be grounds for not honoring a patient's DNRO order, if the device is otherwise properly completed.

(3) The DNRO form and patient identification device must be signed by the patient's physician. In addition, the patient, or, if the patient is incapable of providing informed consent, the patient's health care surrogate or proxy as defined in Section 765.101, F.S., or court appointed guardian or person acting pursuant to a durable power of attorney established pursuant to Section 709.08, F.S., must sign the form and the patient identification device in order for them to be valid.

(4) An emergency medical technician or paramedic shall verify the identity of the patient who is the subject of the DNRO form or patient identification device. Verification shall be obtained from the patient's driver license, other photo identification, or from a witness in the presence of the patient.

(5) During each transport, the EMS provider shall ensure that a copy of the DNRO form or the patient identification device accompanies the live patient. The EMS provider shall provide comforting, pain-relieving and any other medically indicated care, short of respiratory or cardiac resuscitation.

(6) A DNRO may be revoked at any time by the patient, if signed by the patient, or the patient's health care surrogate, or proxy or court appointed guardian or person acting pursuant to a durable power of attorney established pursuant to Section 709.08, F.S. Pursuant to Section 765.104, F.S., the revocation may be in writing, by physical destruction, by failure to present it, or by orally expressing a contrary intent.

Specific Authority 381.0011, 401.45(3) FS. Law Implemented 381.0205, 401.45, 765.401 FS History-New 11-30-93. Amended 3-19-95, 1-26-97. Formerly 10D-66.325. Amended 2-20-00, 11-3-02.

Medic Alert

You may have a patient who wears an identification bracelet or necklace or carries a card in his or her wallet that alerts you to a specific medical condition such as an allergy, epilepsy, or diabetes. On the jewelry or card, you may find a telephone number to call for detailed information about the patient. This bracelet, necklace, or card is known as a *medic alert*.

Organ Donor

You may also have a patient who, according to Florida Statute §765.521, has written legal documentation, a signed donor card, or an organ donor designation on his or her driver's license that indicates the patient is an organ donor. Treat potential organ donors as you would treat any other patient. Remember, they are patients first and organ donors last. *(FR005.6.)*

Health Insurance Portability and Accountability Act of 1996 (HIPAA)

NOTICE OF PRIVACY PRACTICES

This notice describes how medical information about you may be used and disclosed and how you can get access to this information.

PLEASE READ CAREFULLY

**FLORIDA DEPARTMENT OF HEALTH,
OFFICE OF THE INSPECTOR GENERAL**

Department of Health Duties

The Department of Health is required by law to maintain the privacy of your protected health information. This Notice of Privacy Practices tells you how your protected health information may be used and how the department keeps your information private and confidential. This notice explains the legal duties and practices relating to your protected health information. As part of the department's legal duties this Notice of Privacy Practices must be given to you. The department is required to follow the terms of the Notice of Privacy Practices currently in effect.

The Department of Health may change the terms of its notice. The change, if made, will be effective for all protected health information that it maintains. New or revised notices of privacy practices will be posted on the Department of Health website at www.myflorida.com and will be available by email and at all Department of Health buildings.

Uses and Disclosures of Your Protected Health Information

Protected health information includes demographic and medical information that concerns the past, present, or future physical or mental health of an individual. Demographic information could include your name, address, telephone number, social security number and any other means of identifying you as a specific person. Protected health information contains specific information that identifies a person or can be used to identify a person. Protected health information is health information created or received by a health care provider, health plan, employer, or health care clearinghouse. The Department of Health can act as each of the above business types. This medical information is used by the Department of Health in many ways while performing normal business activities. Your protected health information may be used or disclosed by the Department of Health for purposes of treatment, payment, and health care operations. Health care professionals use medical information in the clinics or hospital to take care of you. Your protected health information may be shared, with or without your consent, with another health care provider for purposes of your treatment. The Department of Health may use or disclose your health information for case management and services. The Department of Health clinic or hospital may send the medical information to insurance companies, Medicaid, or community agencies to pay for the services provided to you. Your information may be used by certain department personnel to improve the department's health care operations. The department also may send you appointment reminders, information about treatment options or other health-related benefits and services. Some protected health information can be disclosed without your written authorization as allowed by law. Those circumstances include:

- Reporting abuse of children, adults, or disabled persons
- Investigations related to a missing child
- Internal investigations and audits by the department's divisions, bureaus, and offices
- Investigations and audits by the State Inspector General and Auditor Generaland the legislature's Office of Program Policy Analysis and Government Accountability
- Public health purposes including vital statistics, disease reporting, public health surveillance, investigations, interventions and regulation of health professionals
- District medical examiner investigations
- Research approved by the department
- Court orders, warrants, or subpoenas
- Law enforcement purposes, administrative investigations, and judicial and administrative proceedings

Other uses and disclosures of your protected health information by the department will require your written authorization. This authorization will have an expiration date that can be revoked by you in writing. These uses and disclosures may be for marketing and for research purposes. Certain uses and disclosure of psychotherapist notes will also require your written authorization.

Individual Rights

You have the right to request the Department of Health to restrict the use and disclosure of your protected health information to carry out treatment, payment, or health care operations. You may also limit disclosures to individuals involved with your care. The department is not required to agree to any restriction.

You have the right to be assured that your information will be kept confidential. The Department of Health may mail or call you with health care appointment reminders. We will make contact with you in the manner and at the address or phone number you select. You may be asked to put your request in writing. If you are responsible to pay for services, you may provide an address other than your residence where you can receive mail and where we may contact you.

You have the right to inspect and receive a copy of your protected health information. Your inspection of information will be supervised at an appointed time and place. You may be denied access as specified by law. If access is denied, you have the right to request a review by a licensed health care professional who was not involved in the decision to deny access. This licensed health care professional will be designated by the department.

You have the right to correct your protected health information. Your request to correct your protected health information must be in writing and provide a reason to support your requested correction. The Department of Health may deny your request, in whole or part, if it finds the protected health information:

- Was not created by the department,
- Is not protected health information,
- Is by law not available for your inspection, or
- Is accurate and complete.

If your correction is accepted, the department will make the correction and tell you and others who need to know about the correction. If your request is denied, you may send a letter detailing the reason you disagree with the decision. The department will respond to your letter in writing. You also may file a complaint, as described below in the section titled Complaints.

You have the right to receive a summary of certain disclosures the Department of Health may have made of your protected health information. This summary does not include:

- Disclosures made to you.
- Disclosures to individuals involved with your care.
- Disclosures authorized by you.
- Disclosures made to carry out treatment, payment, and health care operations.
- Disclosures for public health.
- Disclosures for health professional regulatory purposes.
- Disclosures to report abuse of children, adults, or disabled.
- Disclosures prior to April 14, 2003.

This summary does include disclosures made for:

- Purposes of research, other than those you authorized in writing.
- Responses to court orders, subpoenas, or warrants.

You may request a summary for not more than a 6-year period from the date of your request. If you received this Notice of Privacy Practices electronically, you have the right to a paper copy upon request.

For Further Information

Requests for further information about the matters covered by this notice may be directed to the person who gave you the notice, to the director or administrator of the Department of Health facility where you received the notice, or to the Department of Health, Inspector General at 4052 Bald Cypress Way, BIN A03/ Tallahassee, FL 32399-1704/ telephone 850-245-4141.

Complaints

If you believe your privacy rights have been violated, you may file a complaint with the: Department of Health's Inspector General at 4052 Bald Cypress Way, BIN A03/ Tallahassee, FL 32399-1704/ telephone 850-245-4141 and with the Secretary of the U.S. Department of Health and Human Services at 200 Independence Avenue, S.W./ Washington, D.C. 20201/ telephone 202-619-0257 or toll free 877-696-6775. The complaint must be in writing, describe the acts or omissions that you believe violate your privacy rights, and be filed within 180 days of when you knew or should have known that the act or omission occurred. The Department of Health will not retaliate against you for filing a complaint.

Effective Date

This Notice of Privacy Practices is effective beginning April 14, 2003, and shall be in effect until a new Notice of Privacy Practices is approved and posted.

References

"Health Insurance Portability and Accountability Act of 1996." Public Law 104-191. Available at http://www.gpoaccess.gov/cfr/index.html.

"Standards for the Privacy of Individually Identifiable Health Information; Final Rule." 45 CFR Part 160. Federal Register 65, no. 250 (December 28, 2000).

"Standards for the Privacy of Individually Identifiable Health Information; Final Rule." 45 CFR Parts 160 through 164. Federal Register, Vol. 67, No. 157 (August 14, 2002).

Florida Department of Health
Office of the Inspector General
4052 Bald Cypress Way, BIN A-03
Tallahassee FL 32399-1704
DH 150-741, 4/03; Stock Number: 5730-741-0150-0

A patient's privacy, medical history, condition, and emergency care are, by law, confidential information. The patient or a legal guardian must sign a written release before the dissemination of any medical information, except when relaying information to EMS.

The Health Insurance Portability and Accountability Act of 1996 (***HIPAA***) protects the rights of patients and the release of patient information. Do not release patient health information without a signature unless another health care provider needs patient information in order to continue medical care or you receive a request to provide patient information as part of a criminal investigation. The law requires you to report special situations such as child abuse, elder abuse, spouse abuse, etc. As long as you make the report in good faith, related laws often grant immunity from liability for libel, slander, or defamation of character. A legal subpoena requires you to provide patient information in court. *(FR005.7.)*

Section Vocabulary

abandonment

advanced directive

AED

breach of duty

DNR/DNRO

duty to act

expressed consent

Good Samaritan Act

HIPAA

implied consent

informed consent

medic alert

negligence

Every Scene is a Potential Crime Scene

You may respond to a call that could be both a crime scene and a medical emergency. Examples may include any scene involving a suicide, homicide, a drug overdose, a domestic dispute, abuse, a hit-and-run, robbery, or any scene involving battery, gunfire, or a weapon. As always, your first concern is your personal safety. If you believe the perpetrator remains in the area, ensure scene safety before caring for the patient. When the scene is safe, the patient becomes your priority.

Remember that any item on the scene may be evidence. Observe and document anything unusual at the scene. Touch only what you need to touch. Move only items you need to move to render emergency care. To avoid contaminating evidence, do not use the telephone found on the scene unless doing so is necessary. Move the patient only if he or she is in imminent danger and advanced emergency care is not nearby. Try to preserve the patient's clothing; it may be evidence. If you suspect rape, do not allow the person to bathe or wash. Explain the need to collect evidence.

It is important that you understand legal and ethical issues surrounding your responsibility as a criminal justice first aid provider. Remember to provide care to the best of your ability and within the scope of your training. *(FR005.8.)*

UNIT 1 | PREPARING TO RESPOND TO EMERGENCIES
LESSON 3 | Professionalism and Communication

Communication

When responding to a crisis or medical emergency, effective communication skills help you obtain needed information and give reassurance to patients, their families, and bystanders. By responding in a calm and compassionate way and using a courteous and caring tone of voice, you can convey a sense of confidence and assurance in a frightening situation.

Do not base the standard of care given to a patient on his or her culture, gender, age, or socioeconomic status; treat the patient as an individual. Do not alter your standard of care by stereotyping the patient. Remember, all patients deserve equal care.

Confident Manner—According to Merriam-Webster's Collegiate Dictionary (Mish, 2002), confident means "characterized by assurance….full of conviction." Manner is a "characteristic or customary mode of acting, custom…a mode or procedure or way of acting."

Possessing these skills enhances your ability to communicate in a confident manner. Identify yourself and let the patient know you came to help. Position yourself in a non-threatening manner. Establish eye contact. Ask questions in a calm, steady voice. Tell the patient what you will do before you do it. Do not make false statements or give false assurances. Address patients by their surnames, if possible.

Nonverbal communication such as offering a tissue or a warm blanket or placing your hand on the patient's shoulder comforts patients and families. Simple acts of kindness can humanize a frightening situation and provide reassurance that someone cares. Communication involves not only talking but also listening. To show a patient that you are listening, rephrase or restate his or her words and repeat them back to the patient. This is more helpful than saying, "I know what you mean."

When dealing with a hysterical patient, family member, or bystander, redirect the conversation to divert his or her attention. Recognize the person's concerns or focus his or her attention on the immediate situation or a meaningful task. Remember, your main goal is to treat the medical emergency the patient experiences; family members and bystanders are secondary concerns.

Being able to see yourself in another person's situation and share his or her feelings or concerns helps you understand what the patient experiences. Empathy is one of the most helpful tools you can use to deal with a crisis.

Caring Attitude—Good listening skills display a caring attitude and are part of good communication. Let the patient tell what happened. Listen carefully to what he or she says. Acknowledge the patient's feelings. Do not say, "I know how you feel."

OBJECTIVES

FR006.3. Reassure patients, family members, and bystanders while working in a confident and efficient manner.

FR006.4. Communicate professionally with patients with special considerations when responding to a medical emergency.

FR006.5. Approach and communicate appropriately with a family confronted with death and dying when responding to a medical emergency.

Effective communication skills include not only how you talk and act but also how you present yourself. Be well groomed, clean, and neat. Present a professional appearance at all times. Your professional attitude, conduct, and neat appearance convey much-needed reassurance to the patient, family, and bystanders. *(FR006.3.)*

Patients with Special Considerations

You may need to help or render first aid care to patients who have special needs or require special considerations. These patients include the visually impaired, the hearing impaired, the elderly, the chronically ill, the developmentally disabled, those who speak a language foreign to you, and those who behave disruptively. To provide effective emergency first aid to these patients, be aware of their particular disabilities and special needs.

Visual Impairments and Blindness—When initially surveying the scene, be alert to signs indicating that the patient is visually impaired. Clues include eyeglasses, a collapsible, white cane with a red tip, or a seeing-eye dog. If you are unsure, do not hesitate to ask the patient if he or she is visually impaired. Although people learn to compensate for visual impairment by using other senses, an accident or emergency can cause disorientation. Continually speak to the patient, providing information about the surroundings. Clearly describe what you will do before you render care.

A patient with a guide dog may be more concerned about the dog than his or her own situation. If possible, keep the patient and the dog together. Let the patient direct the dog or tell you how to handle the dog. Remember that most guide dogs are protective. Taking charge of or handling the guide dog without the patient's direction can confuse the dog.

Hearing Impairments and Deafness—Communicating with a person who has a hearing impairment can be a challenge. A person who has been deaf for some time will probably indicate the condition to you by pointing to an ear and shaking his or her head. If you do not know how to sign (using your hands and fingers to communicate), communicate in writing or with gestures.

One technique is to look directly at the patient, touch a place on your body, and make a face that indicates pain. Continue looking directly at the patient, and repeat the procedure on his or her body. Most hearing impaired patients will understand what you are doing. (However, do not touch a conscious patient who is hearing impaired unless that patient acknowledges your intent.) You can perform a complete patient assessment in this manner. Continue to use gestures to inform the patient. Physical touching, such as holding the patient's hand, gives comfort and reassurance.

If an accident or illness causes the patient temporary deafness, deal with the patient's panic or anxiety. Point at your ear and shake your head to indicate deafness, or write the question, "Can you hear?" on paper. This can reassure the patient that you recognize and understand the problem. Continue to write to keep the patient informed. Let the patient know that help is on the way. If the patient's "hearing" child is present, consider asking the child to interpret. Keep in mind, however, that children may not have the maturity to deal with a crisis. When you render care to a patient who is hearing impaired, identify yourself. Show your identification. Use touch to communicate. Face the patient when you speak so he or she sees your lips and expressions. Speak slowly and distinctly. Do not shout. Use simple, clear language. Watch the patient's face for indications of understanding. Use paper and pencil to communicate, if necessary. When interviewing a hearing impaired patient, an interpreter may be required.

Elderly Patients—Many senior citizens do not fit the traditional image of the elderly person. However, many older patients do have specific age-related needs. Sensitivity to their particular situations or conditions can relieve fears and secure their cooperation for treatment. Be alert to the individual patient's ability to hear, see, and understand his or her medical condition. In your initial assessment, look for such items as hearing aids, glasses, walkers, and wheelchairs.

Old age sometimes brings confusion, loss of short- or long-term memory, inability to follow directions, or hostile behavior. A gentle voice and calm attitude can be effective communication tools, even if the patient does not understand your words. Address older patients by their title and last name unless they invite you to use their first names. Elderly patients may fear change or loss of independence, resist transport to a medical facility, or feel embarrassed by their physical appearance or condition. Elderly patients may experience loss of bowel or bladder control, be unable to accurately hear or answer questions about their health histories, and be more seriously ill or injured than they appear. They may react more sensitively to hot and cold temperatures, sustain fractures because their bones are brittle, suffer from multiple medical conditions, or take multiple medications.

Chronically Ill Patients—Medical advances in treating patients with serious, chronic conditions make it possible for individuals to live in the community rather than be confined in a hospital or long-term care facility. An officer may encounter a vast number of complex medical devices: pacemakers, surgically inserted breathing tubes, ventilators, catheters, and so on. Do not be overwhelmed or distracted by the complex equipment. Patients do not expect you to understand how their machines work. Do not hesitate to question the patient or caregiver as you provide first aid.

Patients Who Speak a Language Foreign to the Criminal Justice Officer—In rendering first aid, you may encounter a patient with whom you cannot communicate because of language differences. Contact your public safety telecommunicator regarding access to an interpreter. If no interpreter is available, you can apply some techniques used to communicate with hearing impaired patients. Shouting at patients in your language does not increase their ability to understand you. Hand gestures can be the best way to communicate with the patient if no interpreter is available.

Developmentally Disabled—Communicating with developmentally disabled patients can be a challenge. Try to designate a single person to communicate with the patient. Speak in short sentences and use simple words. Repeat or rephrase your statements until the patient understands. Remember that you can easily confuse or inspire fear in the patient. Take the time needed to reassure a developmentally disabled patient.

Infants and Children—When communicating with younger patients, staying calm is important. Children are sensitive and can respond negatively to what they observe and feel. Often, their maturity regresses during a crisis. You, an unfamiliar person, may increase their anxiety and fear in an already frightening situation. Avoid removing a child from parents; separation anxiety can become a major concern. Involve parents or caregivers in the exam and treatment of their child.

While communicating with younger children, get down to their eye level. Move slowly. Include the children in your conversation, keeping them informed about what you are doing. This can help alleviate their fears. Adolescents and older children are sensitive to peer pressure and public embarrassment. Be aware of their modesty. Be aware of asking medical or legal questions and jurisdictional limitations regarding questioning children who are victims of crime. *(FR006.4.)*

Death and Dying

Dealing with death and dying is part of emergency medical care. When you or the patient realizes that death is imminent, consider the patient's emotional needs as well as injury or illness. Show the patient the greatest possible respect. Value and respect the patient's dignity by talking to the patient as if he or she were fully alert. Assure the patient that you are doing everything possible and that he or she will receive advanced medical care as quickly as possible. Do not give false assurances.

Communicate with the family. Answer their questions and explain what is happening. If possible, let the family speak to the dying patient. That may positively affect all involved and allow closure. Avoid making negative statements about the patient's condition. If the patient asks if he or she is dying, do not confirm it. Instead, say, "We are doing everything we can."

If the patient insists that death is imminent, he or she may want messages delivered to survivors or to make a dying declaration if he or she has been a victim of a crime. If necessary, take notes, as this information can be useful in court. Assure the patient that you will do what you can to honor the requests.

Accept all emotions as real and necessary. Allow family members to grieve as you maintain control of the situation. Culture influences the display of emotion, which can range from hysteria to a total lack of emotion. Hysteria, lack of emotion, or other symptoms of grief may require additional medical attention. Do what you can to comfort the family without interrupting your emergency care of the patient. *(FR006.5.)*

UNIT 1 | PREPARING TO RESPOND TO EMERGENCIES
LESSON 4 | Health Issues

Stress

An inevitable, unavoidable part of life, stress can result from providing emergency medical care. Recognizing stress is important. So is taking steps to reduce or prevent it. Learn to identify the warning signs of stress:

- inability to concentrate
- difficulty sleeping, nightmares
- anxiety
- inability to make decisions
- guilt
- changes in appetite
- changes in sexual desire
- isolation
- changes in work or recreation habits *(FR007.1.A.)*

While high stress levels may require medical intervention, individuals can make personal lifestyle choices that help them cope with, reduce, or alleviate stress.

Lifestyle Choices

Nutrition—A healthy, well-balanced diet helps prevent and reduce stress. Maintaining regular meal schedules and having healthy food available improves eating habits. Certain foods, such as sugar, caffeine, and alcohol, elevate the body's response to stress. Alcohol, tobacco products, and other kinds of self-medication actually increase stress levels.

Exercise—Exercise is a great stress reliever. Its many benefits include a release for pent-up emotions. Criminal justice officers should incorporate regular exercise programs in their daily schedules.

Relaxation—Relaxation takes many forms: meditation, religion, sports, hobbies, or other activities. Your schedule should also allow for adequate sleep and rest.

On-Scene Stress Relief

If, during an emergency, you experience irritability, inability to concentrate, or indecisiveness, stress may be the source. The following techniques may help when you know you are experiencing too much stress:

- **breathing**—Take several long, deep breaths; focus on counting each breath.
- **thought patterns**—Consciously change your thought patterns. Remind yourself that you are essential; you are in control. Think, "This too shall pass." *(FR007.1.)*

OBJECTIVES

FR007.1.A. Identify signs and symptoms of stress a criminal justice officer may display.

FR007.1. Identify possible steps the criminal justice officer may take to help reduce/alleviate stress.

FR007.1.B. Identify possible long-term emotional reactions that a criminal justice officer may experience when facing death and dying.

FR007.3. Identify ways a criminal justice officer is exposed to bloodborne pathogens and infectious diseases.

FR007.2. Identify the importance of body substance isolation (BSI) when applying first aid.

FR007.4. Identify the importance of utilizing personal protective equipment (PPE) when applying first aid.

FR007.5. Demonstrate how to put on, properly remove, and discard disposable gloves.

FR007.6. Identify personal behaviors that may help reduce the risk of contracting a bloodborne disease when applying first aid.

FR011.2. Identify how to maintain equipment and supplies for the next emergency medical response.

FR007.7. Identify how to prevent contracting hepatitis A.

FR007.8. Identify how to prevent contracting hepatitis B.

FR007.9. Identify how to prevent contracting hepatitis C.

FR007.10. Identify how to prevent contracting Human Immunodeficiency Virus.

FR007.11. Identify personal behaviors that may help reduce the risk of contracting tuberculosis when applying first aid.

FR007.12. Identify general symptoms of most food-related illnesses.

FR007.13. Identify the most common sexually transmitted diseases (STDs).

Death and Dying Stress Situations

One of the most intense types of stress occurs when a first aid provider is involved with a dying patient or the death of a patient. This type of stress can affect everyone involved. One well-recognized model describes people's reactions to death and dying as a five-stage process: denial, anger, bargaining, depression, and acceptance. While not everyone moves through all these grief stages at the same rate or in the same way, recognizing the reality and necessity of these emotions is important.

- **denial**—feeling that the death is not happening or did not happen; refusing to accept reality

- **anger**—acting out, perhaps in ways that endangers others

- **bargaining**—trying to make a deal to postpone the inevitable

- **depression**—feeling and acting unusually silent, distant, and withdrawn

- **acceptance**—unhappy, but resigned to reality

These stages are often also present in a serious trauma or crisis. Your responsibility as an officer is to recognize these emotional reactions and to give initial comfort and care to those involved, including yourself. Recognize that you may experience these stages and that you should not minimize or deny your emotional reaction. A debriefing session usually takes place shortly after a critical incident in which serious injury or death occurred. The session gives you a chance to vent feelings. Many agencies formally debrief individuals involved in crises or emergencies. In addition, public agencies provide access to mental health professionals for those affected by trauma. You are encouraged to take advantage of these services. *(FR007.1.B.)*

Officer Safety

Criminal justice officers encounter injured people who can also be sick or carriers of disease. Knowing how diseases are transmitted and how you can protect yourself from unnecessary exposure alleviates your fears so you can do your job confidently. Certain job-related tasks that involve physical contact, such as CPR, first aid care, property searches and confiscation, frisks and custodial searches, any response to resistance, crime scene investigation, or prisoner transport, are more likely to expose you to body substances that contain bloodborne pathogens than others. Regard body fluids that you encounter while you perform your duties as contaminated with bloodborne pathogens that can infect you. Bloodborne or airborne pathogens are pathogenic microorganisms in human body fluids. They can infect and cause disease in persons exposed to blood or body fluids containing the pathogens. *(FR007.3.)*

Body Substance Isolation (BSI)

The Center for Disease Control & Prevention *(CDC)* defines **universal precautions** as a set of procedures designed to prevent transmission of human immunodeficiency virus (HIV), hepatitis B virus, and other bloodborne pathogens to first aid or health care providers. The new CDC standard instructs providers to assume that all blood and body fluids are infectious.

When in doubt, treat any body fluid as if it is contaminated. Adhere to the colloquialism: "If it is wet, sticky, and not yours, do not touch it."

Called Body Substance Isolation *(BSI)*, the new standard requires using a form of infection control with all patients. Isolating body substances from yourself and other patients is critical in preventing disease and infection transmission. BSI includes two basic behaviors: use of medical personal protection equipment and personal behaviors that reduce risk. *(FR007.2.)*

Personal Protective Equipment (PPE)

Always use appropriate *PPE* in any emergency. It serves as a barrier against infection. Medical PPE includes eye protection, gloves, protective clothing (i.e., gown or coveralls, sleeves, shoe covers), masks or shields, and biohazard bags. The following sections cover guidelines for properly using personal protective equipment. *(FR007.4.)*

Gloves

Gloves minimize skin contact with blood or other body fluids. Always use gloves if you expect to have physical contact with a patient or prisoner; if you have skin contact with persons who are bleeding or have open sores, rashes, blisters, burns, or other broken skin conditions; and if you have open cuts, sores, burns, rashes, or other broken skin conditions on your hands. Universal precautions apply in any situation where you can clean and decontaminate spilled blood or other body fluids, handle body fluids or blood-contaminated equipment (such as handcuffs), or handle containers (such as red or yellow bags) labeled biohazardous or biomedical waste. See Figure 2-2 on the next page *(FR007.5.)* for instructions on using and removing disposable gloves.

Hand Washing

If your hands are visibly dirty or soiled with blood or other body fluids, wash them with plain or antimicrobial soap and water. If your hands are not visibly soiled, use an alcohol-based hand rub to decontaminate them. If you have had no contact with blood or other body fluids, consider using sanitizing hand wipes or towelettes as alternatives to washing with plain soap and water. When washing your hands with soap and water, first wet them with water. Then apply soap and rub your hands together vigorously for at least 15 seconds. Lather all hand surfaces. Rinse your hands with water, and thoroughly dry them with a disposable towel. Use the towel to turn off the faucet. When using an alcohol-based hand rub, apply it to one palm and rub your hands together. Rub all hand surfaces until they dry.

Protective Eyewear

Use protective eyewear whenever you expect that blood or body fluid will splash, spray, fly, or splatter into your eyes. A risk situation that requires protective eyewear also requires a facemask. Some face shield designs simultaneously protect your eyes, nose, and mouth.

Protective Clothing

Protective clothing serves as a barrier to prevent clothing and skin contact with blood and body fluids. It is usually single-use and disposable. Use it when you anticipate significant blood or body fluid contamination of clothing. Your uniform, leather or cloth gloves, and everyday footwear are not PPE.

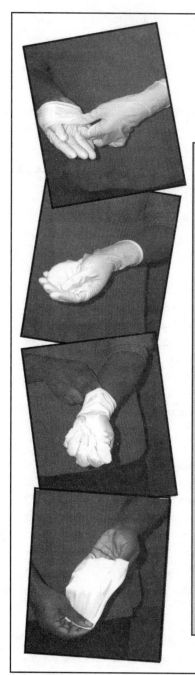

Using and Removing Disposable Gloves

Using Disposable Gloves

Before putting on protective gloves, remove any jewelry that may puncture the material of the gloves.

If the material of the gloves is fragile, it may be important to trim your fingernails to avoid puncturing the gloves while you are putting them on, using them or taking them off.

If you are going to be dealing with known hazardous materials, try to obtain and use gloves that will resist damage or permeation by a wide range of materials and consider using two pairs of gloves with different qualities.

Removing Disposable Gloves

Removing gloves without contaminating your hands takes a technique that can easily be learned with a little practice.

1. Be sure you do not touch your skin with the outside of either glove.

2. Remove the first glove either by grasping it just below the cuff on the palm side and rolling the glove off the fingers. Place it in the palm of the gloved hand.

3. Remove the second glove by inserting your ungloved fingers inside the cuff on the palm side without touching the outside of the glove and pushing or rolling the glove off the fingers.

4. Dispose of gloves properly.

5. Wash hands with soap and water.

© 2000 Florida Department of Law Enforcement

First aid–Using and removing disposable gloves

Figure 2-2

Masks

There are two different types of masks: filter masks and CPR masks. A filter mask can provide protection against airborne diseases. CPR masks are barrier devices with one-way valves used when performing ventilations. They may be disposable or multi-use. Resuscitation devices with one-way valves, designed to prevent the patient's saliva or vomitus from entering the caregiver's mouth, are available from your agency. Although there is no documentation of cases of HIV transmission through saliva, transmission of other infectious diseases can occur when performing CPR. The presence of blood or open sores in the rescuer or victim's mouth increases the transmission risk. The CPR course trains you to use these devices.

Discard disposable resuscitation devices after use. Clean and properly disinfect multi-use devices before returning them to their storage containers. Remember to wear gloves when handling resuscitation devices contaminated with blood or body fluids. Carefully place a contaminated disposable resuscitation device in a plastic bag, and discard it according to agency policy. Avoid contaminating the outside of the bag. Place a biohazard sticker on the bag unless you use a red biohazard bag. Follow agency policy for decontamination and replacement procedures.

Handling Biohazardous Wastes

You have learned that you could contract a bloodborne infection from contact with blood or body fluids on equipment and surfaces. To minimize this danger you must properly handle and discard materials contaminated with blood or body fluids. The procedures you use to handle biomedical or biohazardous wastes must comply with federal Occupational Safety and Health Administration (OSHA) requirements for identifying and segregating blood or waste material saturated with body fluids. Additional requirements include using color-coded bags or containers for storing biomedical waste, such as red or yellow bags or containers with the international biohazard symbol. Rigid plastic sharps containers secure used syringes and needles to prevent injuries. Follow local protocol or department policy for disposal of wastes classified as biomedical or biohazard.

Personal Behaviors to Help Reduce Risk

Personal behaviors can reduce your risk of occupational exposure to bloodborne pathogens. Cover cuts, scrapes, burns, sores, or broken skin on exposed portions of your face, neck, arms, and hands with suitable dressing and bandages. This helps protect these injured areas from blood or body fluid splashes. Routinely wash your hands during your work shift. Always wash your hands after removing gloves or other PPE, before eating, drinking, smoking, or applying cosmetics, after using the restroom, after contact with blood or body fluids, and at the end of your shift.

Properly remove clothing contaminated with blood or body fluids as soon as possible. Thoroughly wash contaminated skin with soap and water. In situations in which clothing and skin contamination occur, shower with soap and warm water. Contact your personal physician for additional recommendations to protect your health if you are HIV positive or receiving medical treatment that may affect your immune system. Avoid risky behaviors in your personal life that might expose you to bloodborne pathogens.

If exposure occurs, pay attention to obvious personal hygiene, such as thoroughly washing affected areas with soap and water. Change your clothing as soon as possible. Report your exposure according to local protocol and department policy.

Methicillin-Resistant Staphylococcus Aureus (MRSA)

Methicillin-Resistant Staphylococcus Aureus (MRSA) is a type of bacteria that is highly contagious and resistant to certain antibiotics. Staph infections, including MRSA, occur most frequently among persons in hospitals, healthcare facilities, and detention facilities. People are more likely to get an infection if they have skin-to-skin contact with the hands, wound drainage, or nasal secretions of a person who is infected with MRSA. People who participate in contact sports, have openings in their skin such as cuts or abrasions, or have poor hygiene are more likely to get an infection.

Signs and symptoms of a skin infection can be a wound site that is red, swollen, or painful, or an area that is warm to the touch or is draining pus. The site may look like a spider bite, pimple, or boil, and the person may have a fever.

Follow these precautions to avoid contracting MRSA:

- Shower with soap and water as soon as possible after direct contact with an open sore and use a clean, dry towel.
- Do not share equipment, towels, soap, or any personal care items.
- Do not share drinking containers.
- Do not share ointments, creams, or antibiotics.
- Keep your hands away from your nose, mouth, and eyes.
- Keep all skin wounds completely covered with a bandage.
- Wash towels, equipment, uniforms, and any other laundry in hot water and detergent daily. *(FR007.6.)*

Maintain Equipment and Supplies

Examine the condition of supplies and equipment you used during your response. Sometimes, this means only replacing gloves or replenishing first-aid supplies. Use disposable items whenever possible. If you work with reusable items, clean, disinfect, or sterilize them before next use. During this process, be sure to wear protective gloves and eyewear, if appropriate.

The cleaning process involves thoroughly washing away blood, fluids, and other contaminants. Follow these general rules:

- Disinfect items exposed to the patient's intact skin.
- Sanitize items exposed to body fluids or mucous membranes.
- Follow the manufacturer's recommendations and local protocol to clean, disinfect, and sanitize.
- Follow local protocol for contaminated equipment and uniforms.
- Clean other equipment, such as restraints, with soap and water.
- After cleaning, disinfect using a hospital-grade disinfectant or chlorine bleach and water. The acceptable standard for dilution is one part chlorine bleach to 10 parts water. Mix them just before use.

Take proper care of your equipment. As with any other tool you use on the job, be familiar with using and maintaining your medical and safety equipment. *(FR011.2.)*

Infectious Diseases and Illnesses
Bloodborne Diseases

There are multiple strains of hepatitis; the most common ones are hepatitis A, B, and C that can all cause liver disease. HIV is a virus that attacks the immune system. All these diseases are life altering.

Hepatitis A—The *hepatitis A virus* causes hepatitis A. Hepatitis A is technically not a bloodborne disease; it is found in food and waste, and is passed on when a person swallows infected matter. It is, however, highly infectious, but is preventable with BSI and appropriate PPE. Its incubation period ranges from two weeks to two months. Person-to-person contact primarily transmits hepatitis A, generally through fecal contamination and oral ingestion. Poor personal hygiene, poor sanitation, and intimate contact facilitate transmission. Common source epidemics from contaminated food and water also occur. Sharing utensils, cigarettes, or kissing does not transmit the hepatitis A virus. Signs and symptoms of hepatitis A may include fever, weakness, anorexia, nausea, abdominal discomfort, dark urine, and jaundice. *(FR007.7.)*

Hepatitis B—Outside of occupational settings, sexual contact or sharing contaminated needles (through intravenous drug abuse) primarily transmits the *hepatitis B virus*. The hepatitis B virus causes hepatitis B. Infected blood received through transfusions may infect persons with the hepatitis B virus. However, the risk of infection from a transfusion is extremely low because all donated blood is tested. The hepatitis B virus can remain infectious in dried body fluids for an undetermined time. Symptoms range from minor flu-like symptoms to severe liver damage and even death. Other symptoms include weakness, various muscle and joint pains, dark urine, diarrhea, weight loss, and an enlarged and tender liver. Not everyone infected necessarily experiences all these symptoms.

The CDC estimates that each year in the United States more than 200,000 people of all ages contract hepatitis B. Close to 5,000 die of the illnesses it causes. The disease has disabling long-term effects. Individuals with chronic hepatitis B often cannot continue to work. Some hepatitis B virus carriers are infectious for life. They can transmit the disease while not experiencing obvious symptoms. Since 1982, a vaccine has been available to prevent the disease. At the time of initial assignment, officers should receive information about the vaccine and the opportunity to receive the three separate doses. Over 90 percent effective against hepatitis B for seven or more years after vaccination, the vaccines stimulate active immunity. They are also 70 to 88 percent effective when given within one week after hepatitis B virus exposure. *(FR007.8.)*

Hepatitis C—According to CDC reports, hepatitis C is the most common chronic bloodborne infection in the United States and is caused by the *hepatitis C virus*. The incubation period varies from person to person. Direct contact with human blood primarily transmits hepatitis C. This occurs from sharing needles or drug paraphernalia, needle sticks, contaminated sharps, or an infected mother delivering her baby. Sexual contact with an infected person can also (rarely) spread the virus. Of all persons infected with the hepatitis C virus in America, approximately one-third pass through jails and prisons each year.

Hepatitis C's signs and symptoms are similar to those of hepatitis B. They range from minor flu-like symptoms to severe liver damage and even death. Other symptoms include weakness, various muscle and joint pains, dark urine, diarrhea, weight loss, and an enlarged and tender liver. Not everyone infected necessarily experiences all these symptoms. Of 100 persons infected with the hepatitis C virus, about 85 persons develop long-term infection. Seventy persons develop chronic liver disease. Fifteen persons develop cirrhosis, the scarring of liver tissue (this may take 20 to 30 years to occur). Five will eventually die of cirrhosis or liver cancer.

Because of lab testing, chances of contracting the hepatitis C virus from a blood transfusion are very low. Casual contact, coughing, sneezing, food, water, and sharing eating utensils or drinking glasses does not spread the hepatitis C virus. Preventing hepatitis C depends on avoiding direct contact with infected blood. Avoid behaviors that spread the disease, especially direct contact with blood or blood products. There is no vaccine for hepatitis C. *(FR007.9.)*

Human Immunodeficiency Virus *(HIV)*—Another bloodborne virus that attacks the immune system is HIV, which causes Acquired Immune Deficiency Syndrome *(AIDS)*. Transmission occurs primarily during sexual contact with an infected individual, when intravenous drug abusers share contaminated needles, from an infected mother to her unborn child, and from contact with blood, certain body fluids, and tissue from an infected individual.

Criminal justice officers may have a greater risk of exposure to HIV than many other public employees do. An officer encounters people who participate in high-risk behaviors, including persons who engage in unprotected sexual activity and individuals who share contaminated needles. These individuals' sexual partners also have an increased risk of infection. Individuals with histories of unsafe sexual activity or sexually transmitted diseases also face increased risk of HIV infection. Blood transfusions given from the late 1970s to early 1985 infected some individuals. Careful blood donor screening and blood testing before use have greatly reduced that risk factor. Casual contact, sneezes, coughs, or insect stings do not transmit HIV.

An individual infected with HIV may show no symptoms initially or have mild flu-like symptoms. Infected individuals may live many years without obvious symptoms of infection. An individual infected with HIV becomes a lifelong carrier who can transmit the infection to others. A chronic condition, HIV attacks the immune system and the body's natural defense mechanisms against disease. No vaccine prevents HIV. However, using BSI and appropriate PPE can prevent this highly infectious disease from spreading. Take all reasonable precautions to avoid exposure to HIV and all communicable diseases. *(FR007.10.)*

HIV and TB Infections—A growing concern is the increase in persons with HIV who develop TB. A person with both HIV and TB infections is far more likely to develop TB disease. HIV weakens the body's immune system, allowing TB bacilli to multiply rapidly and spread.

Airborne Diseases

Any infection spread from person to person through the air is an ***airborne infection***. Breathing in microscopic organisms called pathogens causes airborne infections. An infected person who coughs or sneezes into the air, particularly in a relatively confined space, transmits airborne diseases. The lungs provide accumulation sites for airborne infectious microorganisms (bacterium and viruses) that cause communicable diseases, such as the common cold, chicken pox, both forms of measles, mumps, meningitis, influenza, and tuberculosis (*TB*). Many airborne pathogen diseases require prolonged exposure for an infection to occur. For those working in an enclosed correctional environment, a greater opportunity exists for exposure than for other criminal justice personnel.

Tuberculosis

Of particular concern to officers is TB. Nearly one-third of the world's population has TB. Over 3,000,000 deaths occur yearly from this disease. The 1980s saw a resurgence of TB outbreaks in the United States and the birth of a new drug-resistant, more deadly strain.

Tuberculosis Infection versus Tuberculosis Disease—TB organism infection differs from having TB disease. Infected persons carry the TB germ or bacteria in their bodies, but their bodies' defense system protects them from the disease. Over 10 million Americans carry TB germs, but less than 10 percent of them actually develop the disease. An infected person is not contagious until he or she develops the disease. A person can be infected for years and seem perfectly healthy. However, when illness weakens the immune system, TB infection can become TB disease.

Although coughing or sneezing spreads TB germs through the air, becoming infected is not easy. Brief exposure to a TB source rarely results in infection, nor does handling bed sheets, books, furniture, or eating utensils. TB usually transmits through family members, close friends, and people who work or live together, sharing close, confined spaces over extended periods of time.

If you suspect you or someone you know has signs and symptoms of TB disease, seeing a doctor immediately is important. Without treatment, victims can spread the infection and disease to others.

People at Higher Risk—Anyone can contract TB, but some people have a higher risk of developing active TB disease such as people with HIV infections or AIDS and people in close contact with those who are infectious. People who work in or reside at long-term care facilities, such as prisons, nursing homes, and some hospitals, people who are malnourished, alcoholics, IV drug users, elderly, infants, or transplant recipients, and people with serious medical conditions are at a higher risk of developing active TB disease.

Symptoms of TB—A person with TB infection has no symptoms. A person with TB disease may have any, all, or none of the following symptoms: coughing up blood or a cough that does not go away, fever, constant fatigue, weight loss, loss of appetite, and night sweats.

Testing for TB Disease and Infection—The TB skin test determines if a person has TB infection. A chest X-ray and mucus test determines if a person has TB disease. Should your TB test result be positive, seek professional medical advice.

Preventing Tuberculosis and Other Airborne Diseases—At adequate flow rates, fresh-air ventilation disperses TB droplet nuclei, decreasing the potential for disease transmission. For example, when you transport persons suspected of TB infection or any other airborne disease, open your vehicle's windows. Maintaining good health and practicing good health habits helps strengthen your immune system. Any person in a high-risk category should have regular TB skin tests. If your work places you in contact with persons who have active TB disease, closely follow workplace policy, procedures, and OSHA guidelines for infection control. Remember to use BSI and appropriate PPE (gloves, masks, goggles). *(FR007.11.)*

Food Related Illnesses

Thousands of types of bacteria exist naturally in our environment and even our food supply. Some are beneficial, such as bacteria used to make cheese and yogurt. However, some bacteria or pathogens cause mild to serious illness if ingested with food. Hepatitis A is one serious illness transmitted by food.

Many people do not recognize food related illness, as its symptoms often mimic the flu. In addition, symptoms may not occur for two or more days after eating contaminated food. These symptoms can be severe but often last only one or two days. They range from fever, chills, headache, and backache to abdominal cramps, nausea, vomiting, diarrhea, and general weakness. *(FR007.12.)*

Section Vocabulary

AIDS

airborne disease

BSI

CDC

hepatitis A virus

hepatitis B virus

hepatitis C virus

HIV

MRSA

PPE

STD

TB

universal precautions

Other Infectious Diseases

Sexually transmitted diseases (***STDs***), or sexually transmitted infections, are among the most common infectious diseases in the United States today. Of at least 20 identifiable sexually transmitted diseases and infections, seven are most common: Chlamydia, genital herpes, genital warts, gonorrhea, HIV infection and AIDS, syphilis, and hepatitis B. All are preventable. *(FR007.13.)*

UNIT 1 | PREPARING TO RESPOND TO EMERGENCIES
LESSON 5 | Human Body

Skeletal System

The *skeletal system* is the supporting framework for the body, giving it shape and protecting vital organs. It attains mobility from the attached muscles and manufactures red blood cells. The skeletal system has six main components. The skull houses and protects the brain. It also gives shape and function to the face. The hinged jawbone attached to the skull permits the jaw to move. The spinal column protects the spinal cord and is the primary support for the entire body. It consists of separate bones called vertebrae that stack one on top of each other and are held together by muscles. The shoulder girdle consists of the collarbone and shoulder blades. The chest consists of the breastbone (sternum) and ribs. It protects the heart, lungs, liver, and spleen. The pelvis protects the reproductive organs and supports the organs in the lower abdominal cavity.

The lower extremities consist of the upper leg, lower leg, ankle, and foot. The upper leg consists of the longest, strongest bone in the human body, the thighbone (*femur*). The lower leg consists of two bones attached to the ankle. The lowest portions of the lower extremities are the feet and toe bones. The upper extremities consist of the upper arm, forearm, wrist, hand, and finger bones that comprise the arm. The upper arm consists of one bone. The lower arm, like the lower leg, contains two bones. *(FR008.1.A.)*

Muscular System

The *muscular system* gives the body shape, protects internal organs, and provides body movement. The body contains three different types of muscles. Muscles used for deliberate acts, such as chewing, bending, lifting, and running, are *voluntary muscles*. These are muscles attached to the skeleton and under the control of the nervous system and brain. The individual can contract and relax these muscles. *Involuntary muscles*, or smooth muscles, carry out many automatic body functions. They are in the walls of the tube-like organs, such as ducts, blood vessels, and the intestinal wall. The individual does not normally control these muscles. Found only in the heart, the *cardiac muscles* work constantly to expand and contract the heart. *(FR008.1.B.)*

Nervous System

The *nervous system* controls voluntary and involuntary body activity. It also supports higher mental functions, such as thought and emotion. It lets the individual be aware of and react to the environment and keeps the rest of the body's systems working together. It has two main systems. The *central nervous system* is located in the brain and in the spinal cord. Its components are the body's mainframe computer. This is where all communication and control originate. The *peripheral nervous system* includes nerves that connect to the spinal cord and branch out to every other part of the body.

OBJECTIVES

FR008.1.A. Identify function of skeletal system and six main parts.

FR008.1.B. Identify function of muscular system and types of muscle.

FR008.1.C. Identify function of nervous system and two main parts.

FR008.1.D. Identify function of respiratory system and basic parts.

FR008.1.E. Identify function of circulatory system and four major arteries.

FR008.1.F. Identify function of digestive system and main organs.

FR008.1.G. Identify function of endocrine system.

FR008.1.H. Identify function of genitourinary system.

FR008.1.I. Identify function of the skin.

These nerves serve as a two-way communication system. Some carry information from the brain and spinal cord to the body. Others carry information from the body back to the brain. *(FR008.1.C.)*

Respiratory System

The ***respiratory system*** delivers oxygen to and removes carbon dioxide from the blood. The body can go without oxygen only for a few minutes. The nose, mouth, throat, voice box, and windpipe make up the airway that brings oxygen to the lungs. The passage that connects the upper airway with the lower airway is the windpipe (trachea). At the upper end of this passageway is a small leaf-shaped flap (epiglottis) that keeps food and other foreign objects from entering the windpipe. A large muscle (diaphragm) below the lungs at the bottom of the chest cavity assists in moving air in and out of the lungs.

The respiratory systems of infants and children differ from an adults'. Their airways are smaller and more easily obstructed. Their tongues take up proportionally more space in their mouths. Their windpipes are narrower, softer, and more flexible. Very young infants breathe primarily through their noses. *(FR008.1.D.)*

Circulatory System

The ***circulatory system*** pumps blood throughout the body. The circulatory system functions to deliver oxygen and nutrients to and remove waste from the body's tissues. Basic parts of the circulatory system are the heart, veins, capillaries, arteries, and blood. Positioned behind the sternum, slightly to the left in the chest cavity, the heart is a hollow, muscular organ about the size of your fist. It functions like a two-sided pump. Blood is under constant pressure and circulation by the heart's pumping action.

The heart consists of two sides, each having an upper and lower chamber. The right side pumps blood to the lungs, which pick up oxygen, and returns the oxygenated blood to the left side of the heart. The left side delivers the oxygenated blood throughout the body and returns the blood to the right side of the heart.

Blood vessels are a system of tubes through which blood flows. Vessels called arteries carry blood away from the heart to the rest of the body. The following major arteries determine blood flow and set the patient's pulse rate:

- carotid—major artery in the neck, felt on either side of the neck
- femoral—major artery in the thigh, felt in the groin area
- radial—major artery in the lower arm, felt at the thumb side of the wrist
- brachial—major artery in the upper arm, felt on the inside of the upper arm

Vessels called veins carry blood back to the heart. Throughout the body, small vessels called capillaries connect arteries to veins.

Blood is composed of several elements. Plasma is a clear, straw-colored fluid. Red blood cells carry oxygen from the lungs to the body and bring carbon dioxide back to the lungs. White blood cells fight infection and destroy bacteria and other disease organisms. Platelets initiate the blood-clotting process. *(FR008.1.E.)*

Digestive System

The ***digestive system*** has two main functions: ingesting and digesting food and nutrients. Mainly in the abdomen, this system's organs include the stomach, pancreas, liver, gallbladder, and small and large intestines. *(FR008.1.F.)*

Endocrine System

The endocrine system regulates body systems by secreting hormones directly into the bloodstream from glands. These glands include the thyroid, adrenals, ovaries, testes, and the pituitary. Located at various places throughout the body, they affect physical strength, reproduction, hair growth, voice pitch, mental ability, and behavior. The endocrine system also maintains water balance and blood pressure in the body. *(FR008.1.G.)*

Genitourinary System

The genitourinary system is responsible for reproduction and waste removal. Urinary organs include kidneys, ureters, the urethra (tubes through which urine flows), and the bladder. Male reproductive organs include the testes and the penis. The female reproductive system consists of ovaries, fallopian tubes, the uterus, the vagina, and external genitals. *(FR008.1.H.)*

Skin

The *skin* serves as the protective covering for the inside of the body. It provides a barrier against bacteria and other harmful substances and organisms. Covering the entire body, skin helps regulate body temperature. Acting as a communication organ, the skin also receives and relays information about heat, cold, touch, pressure, and pain. It transmits this information to the brain and spinal cord through nerve endings. *(FR008.1.I.)*

Section Vocabulary

cardiac muscles

central nervous system

circulatory system

digestive system

femur

involuntary muscles

muscular system

nervous system

peripheral nervous system

respiratory system

skeletal system

skin

voluntary muscles

LESSON 1 | Scene Size-Up

OBJECTIVES

FR009.1. Visually assess a scene upon arrival to determine if the scene is safe to enter prior to providing first aid.

FR009.2. Identify the difference between a trauma and a medical patient prior to providing first aid.

FR009.4. Determine the need for additional or specialized help or assistance when providing first aid.

Scene Safety

Scene size-up begins as soon as you become aware of a situation whether you have been notified by radio or you come upon it in the course of duty. Although it takes only moments to perform, scene size-up is crucial to all involved. Before you enter the scene, take an overall view of what you are about to expose yourself to. The size-up has four components: scene safety, mechanism of injury or nature of illness, the number of victims, and the need for additional rescuers and special equipment.

Scene safety always begins with your safety. If the scene is not safe and you have no means to make it safe, do not enter! If you do, you can become an additional victim. Be aware of everything. Take note of what you see, hear, smell, and feel. Quickly put all your observations together to help determine what you and others need to do to make the scene safe. Only after determining if the scene is safe to enter can you deal with the patient's safety.

Possible dangers vary greatly depending on the scene type. Some situations commonly encountered on duty include vehicle crashes that involve specific dangers, such as unstable vehicles, entrapment, spills, fire, and scenes of violence that may involve ongoing violence, weapons, and unruly crowds or groups of inmates who dislike officers. Other situations encountered can include environmental dangers such as hurricanes, tornados, sinkholes, and floods. Downed power lines present a problem during these conditions. The presence of hazardous materials may include unseen dangers, such as chemical spills. Multiple casualties may require various personnel to respond and can be a source of mass confusion. Keep in mind that, although some scenes may be similar, none is the same. Each presents its own dangers. *(FR009.1.)*

Mechanism of Injury or Nature of Illness

While assessing scene safety, try to determine the mechanism of injury to the patient or the nature of the illness. Simply put, try to figure out what happened. Understanding what happened helps you judge the extent of injury or illness. Are you dealing with a trauma patient or a medical patient? A trauma patient is an injured person; a medical patient is a person who is ill. Knowing which type of patient you have helps you determine the type of assistance or equipment needed. A patient who belongs to both categories requires treatment for each. *(FR009.2.)*

Number of Victims

The next size-up component is determining the number of victims. If there is more than one, find out how many and their locations. In certain situations, such as rollover car crashes, patients ejected from a vehicle are difficult to find. In those situations, you may need to question other victims, witnesses, or bystanders.

Need for Additional Rescuers or Special Equipment

Assess the need and relay a request for additional resources, special equipment, or special rescue teams, such as trauma teams, fire department, K-9, search and rescue, utilities, and so on. Resources available depend on your local protocol and department policy. *(FR009.4.)*

In a clear and concise manner, verbally transmit all information gathered during your size-up. Doing so makes the communications center or responding units aware of the circumstances. Relay your information about overall scene safety, type and extent of injuries, number of patients, and the need for special units to assist. The quicker you relay information, the faster additional resources can respond. Relaying scene size-up information accurately and quickly better prepares responding units for what they might encounter when they arrive on scene.

UNIT 2 | RESPONDING TO EMERGENCIES

LESSON 2 | Patient Assessment

OBJECTIVES

FR010.1. Conduct an initial assessment when making a general observation of a patient.

FR010.2. Assess mental status when making a general observation of a patient.

FR010.5. Determine the patient's level of responsiveness.

FR010.3. Assess if a patient is breathing adequately at a normal breathing rate.

FR010.4. Assess a patient's circulation to include taking a pulse.

FR010.6. Perform a physical assessment of a patient to include assessing for external bleeding.

FR010.7. Assess a patient's pupils when conducting an initial assessment.

FR010.8. Manually stabilize a patient's head and neck when conducting an initial assessment.

FR010.9. Obtain SAMPLE history from a patient when conducting an initial assessment.

FR010.10. Conduct an ongoing assessment of a patient while awaiting additional EMS resources.

FR011.1. Update EMS during a medical emergency.

Initial Assessment

Every patient you encounter needs assessment. Some will be conscious, alert, and able to help with your assessment. Others will be unconscious or unable to provide information. Remember from CPR training that assessment begins with airway, breathing, and circulation, the ABCs. Consider the position of the patient with regard to spinal injury and airway compromise, to include positional asphyxia. As you approach, begin your assessment by generally observing the patient. Note details including the patient's gender, approximate age, and positioning. Listen for sounds the patient may make. Identify yourself and let the patient know you came to help. Gently touch and speak to the patient. *(FR010.1.)*

Consider the patient's response in determining the level of consciousness *(LOC)*. Establishing a patient's LOC includes attempting to determine if the illness or injury has changed the patient's mental status. A head or spinal injury can change a person's normal mental state and cause confusion. Speak clearly, state your name, and explain that you came to help.

Assessing an adult's mental status is often easier than determining a child's mental status. Conscious adults can tell you what is wrong. Children will often not talk to you because they are frightened. Visual assessment of an infant or child is your most valuable tool. If an infant or child appears drowsy or is in obvious respiratory distress, consider this condition serious. Ask the infant or child's caregiver why they called you, what the complaint is, and how the infant or child's behavior has changed. Infants should respond appropriately to sound, movement, and stimuli. *(FR010.2.)*

Alert, Verbal, Pain, and Unresponsiveness (AVPU)

After you rule out life-threatening injuries, obtain a general overview of the patient, including his or her mental alertness or responsiveness. Identify responsiveness on four levels:

Alert—Determine if the patient is alert. Ask simple questions such as, "What is your name? What day is it? Where are you?" Consider a patient who responds correctly and spontaneously as alert and oriented.

Verbal—A patient who responds verbally to your questions but appears disoriented, or only responds to loud noises, is responding to verbal stimuli.

Pain—A patient who does not respond to verbal stimuli but responds to pain stimuli is at the pain responsiveness level. You can assess pain responsiveness with a pinprick, by pinching the ear lobe, or giving a sternal rub.

Unresponsive—A patient who responds to none of the stimuli listed above is unresponsive or unconscious. *(FR010.5.)*

ABCs—Airway, Breathing, and Circulation

Airway and Breathing

Place the side of your face near the patient's mouth and nose to detect breathing. Watch the patient's chest. Look for the rise and fall of the chest. Are the patient's efforts to breathe increasing or decreasing? Is the patient wheezing or snoring? At the same time, listen and feel for breathing from the mouth and nose. If the patient is breathing, is he or she breathing adequately? Good skin color and effortless breathing characterize adequate breathing. Inadequate breathing causes poor skin color, particularly in the mouth and nose areas, and patients may experience labored breathing.

To calculate a patient's breathing rate, watch the patient's chest rise, count the number of breaths taken over 30 seconds, and multiply by two. This gives an average breathing rate.

Normal breathing rates:

- adult: 12–20 breaths per minute
- child: 15–30 breaths per minute
- infant: 25–50 breaths per minute

Note the quality of breathing, which includes the rhythm and depth of breath, described in the following terms:

- rhythm—the interval between breaths

    regular—equal time between breaths

    irregular—time varies between breaths

- depth or manner of breathing

    normal—breathing is average and hardly noticeable

    shallow—short gasps; very little airflow

    deep—hyperventilation; large airflow

- labored or painful breathing

Relay vital information to responding medical personnel. Report the rate first and then the qualities, for example, "slow, irregular, and shallow." *(FR010.3.)*

Circulation

Assess patient circulation by pulse rate, skin color, and skin temperature. To take a patient's pulse, place your fingers (not your thumb) on a pulse point. Count the number of beats for 15 seconds. Multiply this number by four to arrive at the patient's average pulse rate.

- On a conscious adult or child, check the radial pulse.
- On an unconscious adult or child, check the carotid pulse.
- On an infant, check the brachial pulse.

Classify pulse quality by its rate, rhythm, and force.

- rate

    adult: 60–100

    child: 100–120

    infant: 120–160

If the patient's pulse rate is outside these ranges, consider the situation a life-threatening emergency. Look for and treat uncontrolled bleeding before continuing with the assessment.

- rhythm, the interval between beats

    regular—equal time between beats

    irregular—time varies between beats
- force, strength of the pulse

    bounding—strong pulse

    weak—pulse you can barely feel; "thready"

Relay vital information to responding medical personnel. Report the rate first and then the qualities, for example, "slow, irregular, and weak." *(FR010.4.)*

Skin Color and Condition

Assess a patient's skin temperature by placing the back of your hand against the patient's skin to determine relative skin temperature. If the skin feels cool, the patient could be suffering from heat exhaustion, shock, or exposure to a cold environment. If the skin feels hot, the patient could have a fever or heat stroke. Change in body temperature can indicate poor circulation. A hot spot on the skin can indicate an infected area.

The skin quality indicates possible circulation problems:

- pale—possible shock or heart attack, fright, impaired blood flow
- red (flush)—alcohol presence, heat stroke, fever, sunburn, high blood pressure, infection, or physical exertion
- blue (*cyanosis*)—appears first in the mouth and fingertip areas, reduced oxygen level, possibly due to shock, heart attack, or poisoning. Look for changes in circulation in the color of lips, palms, and nail beds. Look inside the eyelid of a dark-skinned patient.
- yellow (jaundice)—liver problems
- moist—heart attack or possible shock
- dry—heat stroke or diabetic emergency

Treat for life-threatening injuries before continuing if the following conditions exist: decreased LOC, abnormal breathing, and/or abnormal circulation (shock). Signs of conditions that rapidly lead to shock include uncontrolled bleeding, tender and/or distended abdomen (internal bleeding), unstable pelvis, femur fractures, and/or anaphylaxis. Check vital signs every five minutes to include pulse, respirations, skin condition, and eyes. If the patient's condition worsens, repeat every step of the initial assessment.

Physical (or Secondary) Assessment

Initial assessment helps to identify life-threatening situations. After completing the initial assessment, perform a physical assessment. This is a thorough head-to-toe evaluation performed to find other signs of injury or illness by looking, listening, and feeling. It may involve removing clothing in a respectful manner to expose hidden injuries.

Make an overall observation of the patient. Observe various body parts, as well as any discomfort the patient shows. Also, note any medical alert items the patient wears. For example, the patient may wear a medic alert necklace, anklet, or bracelet indicating special medical considerations, such as diabetes or allergies.

If some clothing appears wet with blood, the patient may be bleeding externally. Carefully remove the clothing to find the bleeding. If the patient is bleeding externally, try to control it now.

Listen to what the patient says and any sounds made. Listen carefully to the patient's breathing.

Carefully work from head-to-toe, inspecting and palpating (touching) each body part before moving to the next. Compare an injured body area to a similar, uninjured area. Look for deformities, open injuries, tenderness, and swelling (**DOTS**):

Deformities

Open injuries

Tenderness

Swelling *(FR010.6.)*

Start at the head. Observe anything out of the ordinary, such as swelling, fluid loss from the ears or nose, discoloration around the eyes (raccoon eyes), mouth injuries that may obstruct the airway, and discoloration behind the ears (battle signs).

Look at the patient's pupils, the dark-colored areas of the eye. Do they appear round, equally sized, constricted (pinpointed), or dilated (enlarged)? Do they move or remain fixed? If you have a low candlepower penlight, flash it at each pupil and watch the reaction. Both pupils should react equally. This test can help you detect a head injury or the presence of alcohol, drugs, or other substances. *(FR010.7.)*

Gently palpate the scalp and skull. Feel for depressions, open wounds, and swelling. From the head, move to the neck.

Gently palpate the cervical or neck area. Feel for deformities. Look at the throat for signs of trauma or deformities, particularly those related to airway obstructions. While doing this, ask the conscious patient to wiggle his or her fingers and toes. Ask if the patient's extremities feel numb or tingly. Does the patient have neck pain?

Assess for source of injury. If the patient has fallen or been involved in a motor vehicle crash, consider stabilizing the patient's head and neck to prevent movement and further damage. When assessing a patient wearing a full coverage helmet (motorcycle, football, sports, etc.,) do not remove the helmet unless it obstructs the airway.

Spinal Injuries

If the patient has suffered a significant trauma, complains of neck or back pain, cannot move fingers or toes, or feels numbness or tingling, stabilize the head and neck to prevent movement and further damage. Injury to the head, neck, shoulders, back, and abdomen may cause injury to the spinal cord. A spinal injury can permanently interrupt the relay of messages from the brain to the body, eliminating a person's ability to move, feel, or even breathe. Difficult to identify, spinal injuries present some of these symptoms:

- constant or intermittent pain or tenderness in the spinal column
- weakness in the legs with or without movement
- respiratory distress (Constantly monitor the patient's airway and breathing.)
- injury to the head, neck, shoulders, back, and abdomen
- tingling, numbness, loss of sensation in upper or lower extremities
- obvious deformity of the spine (rarely seen)
- loss of bladder or bowel control
- persistent erection in males

If you suspect the patient has a spinal injury, your main objective is to protect the spine from further injury. To do so, follow these steps:

1. Size up the scene and perform an initial assessment.
2. Stabilize the patient's head and neck.
3. Conduct physical assessment.
4. Keep the patient in position until EMS completely immobilizes the patient.

Spinal Immobilization

If scene size-up and initial assessment suggest spinal injury, manually stabilize the patient's head and neck (cervical spine) in the position you found them.

1. Kneel at the patient's head.
2. Place your palms on either side of the patient's head below the ears.
3. Hold the patient's head in the position you found it.
4. If the patient is not breathing, use the jaw thrust to open the airway to initiate rescue breathing.
5. You must keep the patient in position until EMS completely immobilizes the patient.

Jaw Thrust with Spinal Immobilization

Perform a jaw thrust maneuver when you suspect the patient has a spinal injury and you need to establish an airway.

1. Kneel at the patient's head. Place one hand on each side of the patient's head with your thumbs resting on the cheekbones.

2. Grasp the angles of the patient's lower jaw on both sides and press down with your thumbs as you lift the jaw. If the lips close, push the lower lip open with your thumb.

3. Use a lifting motion to move the jaw forward with both hands. This pulls the tongue away from the back of the throat.

4. You must keep the patient in position until EMS completely immobilizes the patient.

After you commit to stabilizing the head and neck, you must stay with the patient until EMS relieves you. The object is to keep the breathing patient's head in the same position you found it and to prevent movement until advanced medical personnel arrives. *(FR010.8.)*

If you are not committed to stabilizing the patient's head, continue the physical assessment. Gently squeeze the shoulders inward. Palpate the chest for areas of pain or tenderness. Does the chest rise and fall equally? Are there noises coming from the chest wall? Squeeze lightly on the ribcage. Look to see if both sides of the chest rise and fall equally during breathing, feel for fractured ribs, and look for bruising. Continue to the abdomen, following the same palpating procedures. Tenderness here may indicate internal injury. Swelling may indicate abdominal injury or pregnancy. Palpate the pelvis; gently squeeze inward and down, checking for tenderness or deformities. Is the pelvis stable or unstable?

Examine the extremities. Gently palpate the entire length of each arm and leg, checking for deformities and tenderness. Check the pulse, motor, and sensory capacity (PMS) in each extremity. Check for capillary refill by squeezing the patient's finger or toe nail bed for two seconds. After releasing, measure the time it takes to return to the original color, which should be from white to pink. If it takes less than two seconds, blood flow should be sufficient.

Does the patient feel his or her toes and fingers? Can the patient move his or her toes and fingers? Place your hands along the soles of the patient's feet, and ask him or her to press them against your hands. You should feel equal pressure from both feet. Ask the patient to hold your fingers and squeeze them simultaneously. Both hands should have equal strength.

If you have a compelling medical reason and the necessary assistance, roll the patient to check his or her back. Again, follow the same palpating procedures. Feel along the spine for possible fractured ribs and deformities. Look for any bruising or swelling that could indicate internal bleeding.

SAMPLE

While conducting your physical assessment, talk to the patient. Try to learn the patient's history. If the patient is unconscious, begin by questioning family members. Any information you acquire is important because it helps in providing care to the patient.

The **SAMPLE** method may help you acquire information useful in determining causes of injury or illness. The acronym SAMPLE stands for:

Signs and symptoms—What can you see? (sign/objective) What does the patient feel? (symptom/subjective)

Allergies—Does the patient have allergies?

Medications—Is the patient currently taking medication; when was the last dose?

Past history—What other medical problems may contribute to the patient's current condition?

Last oral intake—When did the patient last eat or drink?

Events—What events led to this incident?

All this information can help you determine the extent of injuries or illness. Include the information in your report when handing the patient off to appropriate medical personnel. *(FR010.9.)*

Ongoing Assessment

If the patient is stable and maintains his or her ABCs, continue an ongoing assessment until medical personnel relieve you. In your ongoing assessment, reassess the patient's responsiveness level, airway and breathing, and pulse rate and quality. You may need to repeat parts of the physical assessment to detect changes in the patient's condition. Continue to reassure and calm a conscious patient. The patient's state of mind is important to treatment. If the patient is stable, reassess every 10 to 15 minutes. If unstable, reassess about every five minutes.

As the first person on the scene of a medical emergency, you must relay scene and patient information to medical responders when they arrive. In some situations, you will provide information by radio to EMS personnel en route. Doing so prepares them to treat the patient as soon as they arrive. *(FR010.10.)*

Updating EMS

Effective verbal communication is the key skill needed to relay patient assessment information as accurately as possible. As the first officer on the scene, you may have the earliest information about the patient's condition. In particular, the patient's baseline pulse and respiration rate are of extreme importance to medical personnel. This information helps them determine if the patient's condition is improving, stable, or deteriorating. Here are some typical questions EMS may ask:

- "How many patients are there?"
- "Where are they?"
- "Who are the high priority patients?"
- "What treatment did you render?"

EMS personnel complete a pre-hospital care form, or run report, and may include your patient information.

Specialized personnel such as fire fighters and EMS may become involved in a rescue, based on local protocol and department policy. EMS providers may ask you to assess the extent of a person's injuries, render emergency care or protection to a patient, or perform emergency moves. EMS may ask you to maintain the patient's cervical stabilization and an open airway and help lift patients onto stretchers. As a criminal justice first aid provider, do what you can safely do, use the equipment available to you, and stay within the limits of your training and qualifications. *(FR011.1.)*

Section Vocabulary

AVPU

cyanosis

DOTS

LOC

SAMPLE

UNIT 2 | RESPONDING TO EMERGENCIES
LESSON 3 | Moving Patients

Proper Lifting Techniques

In an emergency, you may have to move patients to safety or reposition them in response to their changing medical conditions. You may also be required to assist EMS in moving patients or removing an entrapped patient. Follow their direction and assist when needed. *(FR040.1.)*

Perform an ***emergency move*** when a patient is in immediate danger or the patient's location prevents providing care to that patient or another patient. Perform a non-emergency move, such as a walking assist, when the situation is not urgent. Always use BSI and appropriate PPE when moving a patient. *(FR039.1.)*

When moving patients, employing basic body mechanic principles and observing the rules of proper lifting and moving is essential. Maintain correct alignment of your spine, shoulders, hips, and feet. Use proper breathing techniques. Be aware of your physical limitations. Lift with your legs, hips, and buttocks, not your back. Contract your abdominal muscles while lifting. Keep the patient's weight as close to your body as possible. Limit the distance you need to move the patient if possible. *(FR039.3.)*

Recovery Position

Position a patient based on his or her medical condition. Place an unresponsive, breathing patient with no suspected neck or back injuries in the recovery position: roll the patient, preferably onto his or her left side, with knees slightly bent.

OBJECTIVES

FR040.1. Identify your role in assisting EMS with an entrapped patient.

FR039.1. Identify under what circumstances a criminal justice first aid provider moves a patient.

FR039.3. Lift a patient properly.

FR039.4. Place a patient in a recovery position.

FR039.5. Perform a walking assist with a patient that you may have to move.

FR039.6. Perform an emergency drag of a patient you may have to move.

FR039.7. Perform an extremity lift or carry of a patient you may have to move.

FR039.8. Perform a log roll of a patient you may have to move.

The ***recovery position*** helps maintain an open airway if the patient becomes nauseated or vomits and may prevent positional asphyxia.

Positional asphyxia is a term used to describe the placement of a body in a position that interferes with the ability to breathe. Application of physical restraints can contribute to positional asphyxia when a subject is placed face down, with his or her chest on a hard surface, arms restrained behind his or her back, and left in this position for a significant period of time. This could result in an in-custody death. *(FR039.4.)*

Walking Assist

The most common non-emergency move for a responsive, ambulatory (capable of walking) patient is the walking assist. Patients with leg injuries or visual impairments benefit from a walking assist.

1. Stand next to the patient on the same side as the injury.

2. Place the patient's arm across your shoulder.

3. Place your arm around the patient's waist. Grab his or her belt, if necessary.

4. Assist the patient to a safe or comfortable location and discourage the patient from placing body weight on the injury. *(FR039.5.)*

Emergency Drags

A critical issue when moving a patient is the danger of making an existing spine injury worse. Use an emergency drag if the patient is on the floor or ground. Make every effort to maintain the patient's head, neck, and shoulder alignment.

Clothes Drag

1. If the patient is unconscious, secure his or her hands to protect them during the move.

2. Stand at the patient's head.

3. Bend your knees.

4. Pull the patient's shirt under his or her head to form a support.

5. Using the shirt as a handle, pull the patient toward you.

Blanket Drag

1. Place a blanket directly against the patient's side.

2. Gather the blanket into accordion-style, lengthwise pleats.

3. Kneel on the patient's side opposite the blanket.

4. Reach across the patient and grasp his or her hip and shoulder.

5. Roll the patient toward you onto his or her side.

6. Tuck the pleated side of the blanket under the patient.

7. Roll the patient onto the blanket, preferably onto his or her back.

8. Wrap the blanket around the patient.

9. Grab the part of the blanket under the patient's head and drag it toward you.

Shoulder Drag/Carry

1. Stand at the patient's head.

2. Bend your knees.

3. Slide your hands under the patient's arms.

4. Firmly grasp the patient's wrists, and fold them across the patient's chest.

5. Stand up. As you do, lift the patient up and toward you.

6. Drag the patient toward you. The patient's feet will drag on the ground. *(FR039.6.)*

Extremity Lift or Carry

Extremity lifts or carries are often easier and require less time than drags. Considered non-emergency moves, these lifts require at least two officers' efforts. Use these techniques to move unresponsive patients from the floor or ground. However, do not perform an extremity lift if you suspect or know a patient has an injury to the spine or an extremity injury.

Two-Person Extremity Lift

1. Officer one, kneel on one knee at the patient's head.

2. Place your hands, palms up, under the patient's shoulders.

3. Lift the patient to a sitting position.

4. Support an unconscious patient's back with your kneeling leg.

5. Slide your hands under the patient's arms.

6. Firmly grasp the patient's wrists, and fold them across the patient's chest.

7. Officer two, stand between the patient's knees with your back to the patient. If necessary, separate the patient's feet.

8. Bend your knees and grasp under the patient's knees.

9. Officer one, standing at the patient's head, delivers all commands. Simultaneously both officers stand while lifting the patient.

Two-Person Seat Carry

Use a two-person seat carry to move a standing, conscious patient who is non-ambulatory. Remember to use proper body mechanics. However, do not perform an extremity lift if you suspect or know a patient has an injury to the spine or an extremity injury. Officers one and two stand behind the patient.

1. Face each other, with the patient centered between you.

2. Place hands, palm down, on the shoulder of the officer facing you.

3. Extend your arms, and create back support for the patient.

4. Grasp the wrists of the officer facing you.

5. Extend your arms, and create a seat for the patient.

6. Bend your knees.

7. Instruct the patient to raise his or her arms.

8. Scoop the patient up from behind his or her knees.

9. Tell the patient to place his or her arms on your shoulders.

10. Lift from your legs using proper body mechanics.

11. Move the patient, keeping step with the other officer. *(FR039.7.)*

Logroll

Use this technique only when moving the patient is necessary or when assisting medical personnel. The purpose of a logroll is to roll the patient onto his or her back, front, or side.

1. Perform a logroll on the floor or ground with at least three officers on their knees.

2. Officer one, constantly maintain head, neck, and spinal stabilization.

3. Officer two, take your position at the patient's shoulder and hip. Stay far enough away from the side of patient's body so there is room to roll the patient toward you.

4. Officer three, take your position on the same side of the patient as officer two. Stand at the patient's thigh and lower leg. Stay far enough away from the side of patient's body so there is room to roll the patient toward you.

5. Officer two, reach across the patient. Place your hand on the patient's shoulder. Place your other hand on the patient's hip.

6. Officer three, reach across the patient. Place your hand closer to the second officer's hand on the patient's hip. Place your other hand on the outside of the patient's knee area.

7. Officer one, issue all commands to roll the patient toward officers two and three. Simultaneously maintain the patient's head, neck, and cervical spine alignment.

8. Assess the patient for injuries.

9. If applicable, reverse the process to return the patient to his or her original position. *(FR039.8.)*

LESSON 4 | Multiple Casualty Incident

Unfortunately, you will respond to some incidents that involve more than one victim. Such incidents are Multiple Casualty Incidents *(MCI)*. You may be the first to arrive at the scene of an MCI, and you must know how to respond and set priorities when providing emergency medical care.

Follow local protocol and department policy when defining an MCI. Most involve only a few victims. Most agencies have a plan in place to manage an MCI. Generally, your role as the first officer on the scene involves establishing command of the scene, communicating with EMS, and beginning triage.

Establish Command of the Scene

Try to bring order to the scene to enable you to conduct a scene size-up. Ideally, you accomplish these tasks simultaneously. Establishing command of the scene allows you to perform a thorough size-up.

Communicate with EMS

Relay all information to your communications center and responding EMS personnel. Inform them of additional resources or equipment you may need. *(FR012.1.)*

Begin Triage

Your next step is to begin triage. *Triage* is the term given to sorting and classifying patients. Triage determines in which order patients receive medical attention. Although methods of performing triage differ, its basic principles remain the same. Check local protocol and department policy to determine if they recommend a specific method.

Simple Triage And Rapid Treatment (START)

This is the initial triage system based upon Florida Incident Field Operations Guide (FOG). The START method of triage assesses a large number of victims rapidly and personnel with limited medical training can use it effectively.

1. Use BSI and appropriate PPE.

2. Locate and remove all of the walking wounded into one location away from the incident if possible, but do not forget these victims. Someone should triage them as soon as possible. Say "Everyone who can hear my voice and can walk, come to this area." Now move quickly through the remaining patients.

3. If available, triage and tag the remaining injured patients with triage ribbons (color-coded plastic strips) by tying them to an upper extremity in a visible location (wrist if possible).

OBJECTIVES

FR012.1. Identify the role of the first officer on the scene of a multiple casualty incident or disaster area.

FR012.2. Identify the steps of triage used during a multiple casualty incident.

FR012.3. Identify your role when assisting in a multiple agency response.

4. Classify patients according to the START protocols.

> **RED**—immediate
>
> **YELLOW**—delayed
>
> **GREEN**—ambulatory (minor)
>
> **BLACK**—deceased (expectant/non-salvageable)

5. Remember the pneumonic RPM. (Respiration, Perfusion, Mental Status).

   • Assess respirations:

   > (a.) If respiratory rate is 30/min or less, go to perfusion assessment.
   >
   > (b.) If respiratory rate is over 30/min, tag RED.
   >
   > (c.) If victim is not breathing open the airway, remove obstructions if seen, and assess for (a) or (b) above.
   >
   > (d.) If victim is still not breathing, tag BLACK.

   • Assess perfusion:

   > (a.) Perform by palpating a radial pulse or assessing capillary refill (CR) time.
   >
   > (b.) If radial pulse is present or CR is two seconds or less, go to mental status assessment.
   >
   > (c.) If no radial pulse is present or the CR time is greater than two seconds, tag RED.
   >
   > (d.) In addition, control any major external bleeding.

   • Assess mental status:

   > (a.) Assess the victim's ability to follow simple commands and their orientation to time, place, and person.
   >
   > (b.) If the victim follows commands, tag GREEN.
   >
   > (c.) If the victim does not follow commands, is unconscious, or disoriented, tag RED.
   >
   > (d.) *Note:* Depending on injuries (burns, fractures, bleeding) it may be necessary to tag YELLOW.

6. Make independent decisions for each victim. Do not base triage decisions on the perception of too many reds, not enough greens, etc.

7. If you encounter borderline decisions, always triage to the most urgent priority (GREEN/YELLOW patient, ribbon YELLOW).

8. Direct the movement of patients to proper treatment areas, if necessary.

9. Provide appropriate medical treatment (ABCs) to patients prior to movement as incident conditions dictate.

10. The first assessment that produces a RED tag stops further assessment of that patient. During triage, only manage the correction of life-threatening problems, such as airway obstruction or severe hemorrhage.

11. The triage priority determined in the treatment phase should be the priority used for transport.

12. If you identify a victim in the initial triage phase as a RED and transport is available, do not delay transport. *(FR012.2.)*

In a multiple agency response, your role depends on your arrival time, department policy, and local protocol. Florida implements the Incident Command System *(ICS)* for multiple agency response. If you are the first person on the scene, assume command until you can transfer control to the correct authority or agency. During the transfer, you can provide a briefing or report on what occurred since your arrival.

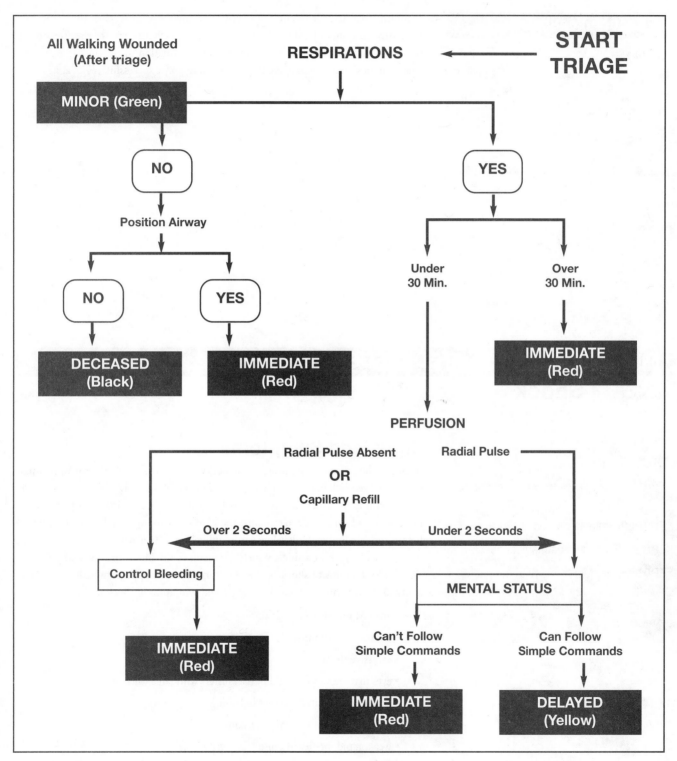

First aid triage

Figure 2-3

83

Section Vocabulary

ICS

MCI

START

triage

A multiple casualty incident can overwhelm anyone who reaches the scene first. Understanding the role of the first officer on the scene can reduce the stress of the situation. Taking control of the scene, getting information to responding personnel, and beginning triage helps make the combined response successful. *(FR012.3.)*

UNIT 3 | TRAUMA RELATED ISSUES

LESSON 1 | Shock

OBJECTIVES

FR014.2. Identify signs and symptoms of shock.

FR014.3. Identify causes of shock.

FR014.4. Identify treatment for shock.

FR014.1. Perform general treatment for shock for a patient in a medical emergency.

Signs and Symptoms

Shock is the failure of the heart and blood vessels (circulatory system) to maintain enough oxygen-rich blood flowing to the vital organs of the body. Shock occurs to some degree with every illness or injury. Shock can be life threatening. The principles of prevention and control are to recognize the signs and symptoms and to begin treatment before shock completely develops. It is unlikely that you will see all the signs and symptoms of shock in a single patient. Sometimes the illness or injury disguises the signs and symptoms of shock or the symptoms may not appear immediately. In fact, many times, they appear hours later. Signs and symptoms of shock may include:

- anxiety, restlessness, and fainting
- nausea and vomiting
- excessive thirst
- eyes that are vacant and dull (lackluster) with large (dilated) pupils
- shallow, rapid, and irregular breathing
- pale, cool, or moist (clammy) skin
- weak, rapid, or absent pulse *(FR014.2.)*

Types of Shock

Hypovolemic (low volume) shock—A decreased amount of blood or fluids in the body causes hypovolemic shock. This decrease results from injuries that produce internal and external bleeding, fluid loss due to burns, and dehydration due to severe vomiting and diarrhea.

Neurogenic shock—An abnormal enlargement of the blood vessels causes neurogenic shock, which is often caused by brain or spinal cord injury.

Psychogenic shock—Psychogenic shock is a "shock-like condition" produced by excessive fear, joy, anger, or grief. Post-Traumatic Stress Syndrome (PTSS) is a psychological adjustment reaction to extreme, stressful experiences such as war, multiple casualty incidents, etc. Care for PTSS is limited to emotional support and transportation of the patient to a medical facility.

Anaphylactic shock—Anaphylactic (allergic) shock occurs when an individual is exposed to a substance to which his or her body is sensitive. *(FR014.3.)*

To treat shock,

1. Maintain an open airway.
   - Remember your CPR training: use the head tilt-chin lift method to open the patient's airway. If you suspect spinal or neck injuries, use the jaw thrust method.
2. Prevent further blood loss by controlling bleeding.
3. Elevate the lower extremities.
   - Position the patient on his or her back, and elevate the lower extremities eight to 12 inches.
   - If you suspect the patient has serious head, neck, spinal, or pelvic injuries, do not elevate the lower extremities.
4. Keep the patient warm.
   - Maintain normal body heat by covering the patient with a blanket.
5. Perform ongoing assessment of the patient for life-threatening injuries. Maintain ABCs. *(FR014.4.) (FR014.1.)*

Section Vocabulary
shock

UNIT 3 | TRAUMA RELATED ISSUES
LESSON 2 | Bleeding and Soft Tissue Injuries

OBJECTIVES

FR013.2. Identify treatment for closed soft tissue injuries.

FR013.3. Identify treatment for open soft tissue injuries.

FR013.4. Stop the bleeding of a patient with an open wound.

FR013.5. Dress and bandage an open wound for a patient who is bleeding.

Closed Soft Tissue Injuries

Types of closed soft tissue injuries are

- *contusion* (bruising)—a closed injury that is discolored and painful at the injury site. *Bruising* is the obvious discoloration (black and blue) of the soft tissue at the injury site.
- *hematoma* (swelling)—a closed injury that appears as a discolored lump. *Swelling* is the soft tissue raised when blood or other body fluids pool beneath the skin at the injury site.

Treatment for closed soft tissue injuries—Lacking the obvious signs of open soft tissue injuries, closed soft tissue injuries can be just as life threatening.

1. Use BSI and appropriate PPE.

2. Treat large contusions by applying a cold compress to the injury site and elevating if the injury is in an extremity.

   - A contusion is an indication of internal bleeding. Internal bleeding can cause the patient to go into shock. Large contusions—those the size of the patient's fist—may indicate a 10 percent blood loss because of blood pooled at the injury site.

   - Small contusions normally require no treatment, but applying cold compresses to the injury site helps reduce pain and swelling.

3. If you cannot assess the seriousness of a closed wound, treat the patient as if he or she has internal bleeding, and monitor for shock.

4. Perform ongoing assessment of the patient for life-threatening injuries. Maintain ABCs, and treat for shock. *(FR013.2.)*

Open Soft Tissue Injuries

Types of open soft tissue injuries:

- *abrasion*—open wound caused by scraping, shearing away, or rubbing the outermost skin layer
- *amputation*—gross removal of appendage
- *avulsion*—injury characterized by a flap of torn or cut skin that may not be completely loose from the body
- *evisceration*—open wound where the organs protrude
- *laceration*—open wound in soft tissue that varies in depth and width
- *puncture wound*—result of driving a sharp or blunt, pointed object into soft tissue

The most important first aid responsibilities to a patient with an open soft tissue injury are to control bleeding and prevent further contamination of the area. To treat an open soft tissue injury,

1. Use BSI and appropriate PPE.

2. When treating avulsions,

    a. Remove any large debris from the wound.

    b. Align the torn flap to its normal position to maintain proper circulation.

    c. Secure the wound in place with a dry, clean dressing and bandage.

3. Apply direct pressure to a soft tissue injury that continues to bleed.

4. Perform ongoing assessment for life-threatening injuries. Maintain ABCs, and treat for shock. Remember, ABCs take priority over wounds. *(FR013.3.)*

Control Bleeding

There are three types of bleeding:

- In *arterial bleeding*, bright red blood spurts from a wound, indicating a severed or damaged artery.

- In *venous bleeding*, dark red blood flows steadily from a wound, indicating a severed or damaged vein.

- In *capillary bleeding*, dark red blood oozes slowly from a wound, indicating damaged capillaries.

To treat the patient by controlling bleeding,

1. Use BSI and appropriate PPE.

2. Cover the wound with a clean dressing.

3. Apply direct pressure to control bleeding.

    - If the first layer of dressing does not control the bleeding, do not remove it, and apply additional layers as needed.

4. Elevate an injured extremity to help control bleeding.

    - While applying direct pressure to a bleeding site in an upper extremity, elevate the extremity above heart level.

    - If the bleeding site is on a lower extremity, ensure that the patient is lying down, and elevate the extremity.

5. If direct pressure and elevation are not effective, compress the artery that supplies blood to the extremity at a pressure point.

    - If the bleeding is in the head, neck, face, arm, or foot, apply appropriate pressure with your fingers.

    - If the leg is bleeding, apply pressure to the artery with the heel of your hand.

6. Perform ongoing assessment for life-threatening injuries. Maintain ABCs, and treat for shock.

Two pressure points are commonly used to control bleeding: the brachial artery, located on the inner arms, just above the elbows, and the femoral artery, located on the inner portion of each leg, just below the groin. *(FR013.4.)*

Section Vocabulary

abrasion

amputation

arterial bleeding

avulsion

bruising

capillary bleeding

contusion

evisceration

hematoma

laceration

puncture wound

swelling

tourniquet

venous bleeding

Applying Dressings and Bandages

Applying dressings and bandages to wounds can stabilize the wound site, control bleeding, and limit further contamination and damage. To apply a dressing and bandage,

1. Use BSI and appropriate PPE.

2. Expose the entire injury site to ensure that there are no other hidden injuries.

3. Apply dressings first.

   • Dressings are coverings applied directly to wounds. If possible, do not touch the side of the dressing that will make contact with the wound.

4. Apply bandages.

   • Bandages are coverings that hold dressings in place. Bandages do not touch the wound. They can create pressure to help control bleeding, support an injured extremity or body part, and prevent the wound from further contamination and damage.

5. Perform ongoing assessment for life-threatening injuries. Maintain ABCs, and treat for shock. *(FR013.5.)*

Tourniquet

A ***tourniquet*** is a device that restricts blood flow to an extremity such as an arm or leg. A tourniquet is used only as a last resort when the amount of blood lost endangers the victim's life and all other methods of controlling the bleeding have failed. The vast majority of external bleeding can be controlled using direct pressure and pressure points. Bleeding from clean-edged amputations usually requires no more than pressure dressing to control bleeding. The injured blood vessels seal themselves shut as a result of spasms produced by the muscle walls of the vessels. The most common type of injury requiring a tourniquet is a rough-edged amputation. These amputations are a result of a tearing or crushing type of injury and prevent blood vessels from shutting as in a clean-edged injury.

Using a tourniquet requires wrapping a cravat (nonstretchy material such as triangular bandages found in first aid kits, terry cloth, or linen handkerchiefs) around the extremities with the use of a rigid object (stick, pen, screwdriver) and tightening the tourniquet until the bleeding stops. The band should be at least two inches wide and six to eight layers thick when applied. Place padding around the limb where the tourniquet will be applied to help protect the site and provide additional pressure. Set the tourniquet band material around the tourniquet site and tie band with a half knot. Position the rigid object on top of the half knot and tie a full knot over the rigid object. Twist the rigid object either clockwise or counter-clockwise until the tourniquet is tight and bleeding has stopped. Secure the rigid object to prevent the tourniquet from loosening. Mark the victim on the forehead by writing a "T" to alert medical personnel that a tourniquet has been applied, and note the time and date. Once the tourniquet is in place, do not remove or loosen! A tourniquet should only be removed or loosened by medical staff. Remember: The tourniquet is used only as a last resort where the loss of blood is life threatening.

UNIT 3 | TRAUMA RELATED ISSUES
LESSON 3 | Puncture Wounds

Impaled Object

Puncture wounds are usually the result of an object, blunt or sharp, penetrating the skin's soft tissue. A penetrating or puncture wound's severity depends on the wound's location, the penetrating object's size, and the forces that created the injury.

An impaled object is an object that punctures the soft tissue and stays in place. An object impaled in the head, neck, or thorax needs immediate care followed by prompt EMS transport. To treat a patient for an impaled object,

1. Use BSI and appropriate PPE.

2. Do not remove the object from the wound unless it obstructs the patient's airway. *(FR016.2.)*

3. Expose the entire injury site. Cut away clothing around the impaled object to
    a. Determine if the patient has other wounds.
    b. Expose enough skin to apply the stabilizing dressing.

4. Apply proper dressing to prevent further contamination of the injury.

5. Secure the object. Surround it with stabilizing dressing or any material that prevents the object from moving.
    - You might use, for example, two pillows, rolls of gauze, or a paper cup. *(FR016.3.)*

6. Control bleeding.
    - Only apply enough pressure to the wound site to stop bleeding. Be careful not to put pressure on the embedded object.

7. Perform ongoing assessment for life-threatening injuries. Maintain ABCs, and treat for shock. *(FR016.1.)*

Human or Animal Bites

A bite can be a serious body injury. The wound can become infected and cause severe discomfort. In rare instances, limbs are lost. To treat a patient for a human or animal bite,

1. Use BSI and appropriate PPE.

2. Wash the wound site with warm soapy water.
    - Human or animal bites are more likely to become infected than other wounds. With human bites, be aware of the possibility of bloodborne pathogens. If you receive a human bite, follow agency policy and procedures for reporting. *(FR017.2.)*

3. Look for imbedded teeth. If you find one, treat it as an impaled object.

4. Dry the wound, dress the injury, and bandage.

OBJECTIVES

FR016.2. Identify when to remove an impaled object.

FR016.3. Identify how to apply stabilizing dressing around an impaled object.

FR016.1. Identify treatment for an impaled object.

FR017.2. Identify need to clean wound if appropriate.

FR017.1. Identify treatment to control bleeding of a human or animal bite.

FR017.5. Identify the type of bite and possible need to call specialized unit.

FR018.2. Identify complications resulting from a gunshot wound.

FR018.3. Identify need to expose the entire injury site.

FR018.1. Identify treatment for a gunshot wound.

5. Apply only enough pressure to control bleeding.

6. Perform ongoing assessment for life-threatening injuries. Maintain ABCs, and treat for shock. *(FR017.1.)*

If you are treating an animal bite, make every attempt to find the animal. It may carry rabies or other infections. Follow local protocol and department policy when contacting specialized units, such as animal control. You must notify the proper agency of all dog bites. *(FR017.5.)*

Gunshot Wounds

Gunshot wounds can cause serious injury by fragmenting, penetrating, vibrating, and otherwise damaging internal organs. Complications from gunpowder, clothing, and bacteria drawn into the wound can cause infection. The damage from the wound may extend farther and deeper than just the exposed area. A small entry wound that causes little bleeding might mask severe internal injuries. Exit wounds are sometimes larger than entry wounds. Depending on the location, a gunshot wound may cause spinal cord injury. For any gunshot wound not in an extremity, consider spinal immobilization. See Figure 2-4. *(FR018.2.)*

To treat a gunshot wound,

1. Use BSI and appropriate PPE.

2. Expose the entire injury site so you can look for the entry wound and possible exit wound. *(FR018.3.)*

3. Dress the wound.

4. Apply enough pressure to stop bleeding.

5. Bandage the dressing.

6. Perform ongoing assessment for life-threatening injuries. Maintain ABCs, and treat for shock. *(FR018.1.)*

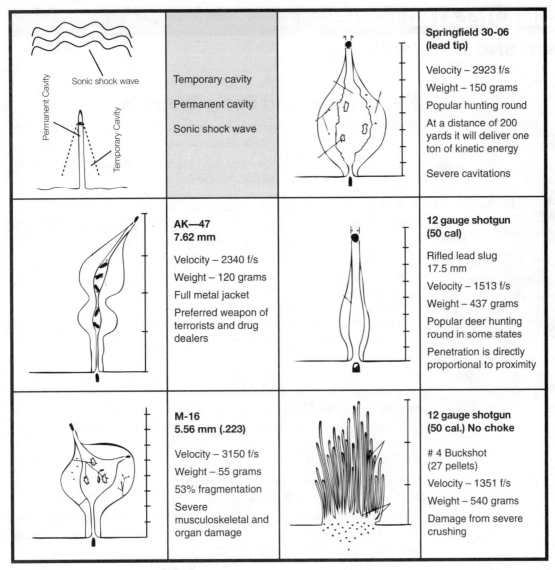

Bullet wounds

Figure 2-4

UNIT 3 | TRAUMA RELATED ISSUES

LESSON 4 | Head and Neck Injuries

OBJECTIVES

FR019.1. Identify treatment to control bleeding of head, face, and scalp wounds.

FR020.1. Identify treatment to control bleeding of a patient with a nosebleed.

FR021.2. Identify types of eye injuries.

FR021.1. Identify treatment for various types of eye injuries.

FR022.2. Identify important structures of the neck.

FR022.1. Identify treatment for a large open neck wound.

Head, Face, and Scalp Wounds

Head and neck injuries are among the most serious emergencies. They can impair the upper airway, causing breathing difficulties. Impacts to the head and neck can also cause hidden fractures. If a head or neck injury is obvious or suspected, or if a trauma patient is unresponsive, immediately stabilize the head and neck.

Scalp wounds may bleed profusely but are usually easy to control with direct pressure. Remember to protect yourself from blood by using BSI and appropriate PPE. The wound's location and severity determines if you apply direct pressure or loosely dress the wound. Never apply direct pressure to a head wound if the patient has an obvious or depressed skull fracture. You might drive fragments of bone into brain tissue, causing further damage.

For lacerations to the head, face, or scalp, use dressing to apply direct pressure to the site. Be careful not to obstruct the airway and to allow for normal breathing. If fluid drains from the ears or the head wound, loosely cover the opening with a dressing. Trauma to the mouth can cause a lot of bleeding. Your main concern is establishing and maintaining an open airway. If teeth were knocked from the patient's mouth, wrap them in moist dressing and transport them with the patient. Perform ongoing assessment for life-threatening injuries. Maintain ABCs, and treat for shock. *(FR019.1.)*

Nosebleeds

Nosebleeds are common occurrences resulting from various situations. Usually, they tend to be more annoying than serious. However, with enough blood loss a nosebleed can cause shock. A nosebleed can also be a serious threat to an unresponsive patient's airway. Because nosebleeds can bleed profusely, remember to protect yourself by using BSI and appropriate PPE.

In most cases, treat a nosebleed by keeping the patient still and calm. Instruct the patient to sit down and lean forward but not so far that the head is below the heart. If other injuries make sitting impossible and the patient is lying down, elevate the head and shoulders. Instruct the patient not to blow his or her nose for several hours. Doing so can dislodge naturally clotted blood.

To control bleeding, apply pressure to the bridge of the nose (if it is not broken) and apply an ice pack. However, do not apply pressure if you suspect trauma to the nose. Do not pack anything into the nose. Perform ongoing assessment for life-threatening injuries. Maintain ABCs, and treat for shock. *(FR020.1.)*

Eye Trauma

Types of eye injuries can be eyelid injuries, chemical burns, objects impaled in the eye, and an extruded eyeball *(FR021.2.)*. When treating a patient for an eye injury, identify the injury's cause, when it occurred, whether it affects both eyes, and when the patient first noticed symptoms. Encourage the patient not to rub the eye. This can cause more damage to the eyeball. Carefully and separately, examine each eye. Because injuries around the eye area can bleed profusely, protect yourself by using BSI and appropriate PPE.

Treatment of eye injuries varies according to the nature of the injury. If an object entered the eye, such as dirt or sand, remove it by flushing the eye with water.

These injuries may need further medical attention:

- **Eyelid injuries are trauma to the eyelid itself.** Treatment can be as simple as gently applying patches to both eyes. This limits eye movement, which can cause further injury. Control bleeding with light pressure as long as the injury does not affect the eyeball itself.

- **Chemical burn injuries to the eye require immediate attention.** Flush the affected eye immediately with water to dilute the chemical and deter further damage to the eyeball. The water does not need to be sterile, but it must be clean. The chemical can continue to burn tissue in the eye, even after dilution. Position the patient's head so that the unaffected eye is above the affected eye. Flush the injured eye from its inner portion to its outer portion for 20 minutes. This helps prevent transferring the chemical to the uninjured eye (cross contamination). Hold the eyelid open while flushing. Be aware of where the runoff goes.

- **Do not remove an impaled object or apply pressure to the eyeball or the object.** Cover the unaffected eye to limit eye movement. As with other impaled objects, if the patient must move, stabilize the object.

- **Trauma to the eye socket can cause the eyeball to come out of (extrude from) its socket.** Do not try to restore the eyeball to the socket. Cover it with a moist dressing, and apply a bandage over both eyes.

- **Perform ongoing assessment for life-threatening injuries.** Maintain ABCs, and treat for shock. *(FR021.1.)*

Neck Injuries

The neck contains major blood vessels and the windpipe (trachea). Neck wounds can bleed profusely. Air entering a blood vessel in the neck can cause stroke, heart attack, or pulmonary embolism *(FR022.2.)*. For deep lacerations, apply an ***occlusive*** (airtight) dressing. When assessing for a neck wound, look for obvious deformity of the neck, open wounds, swelling, and spinal injury.

To treat an open neck wound,

1. Use BSI and appropriate PPE.

2. Cover the wound with dressing and a bandage.

   - Do not wrap the bandage around the neck.

3. Apply only enough pressure to control bleeding while maintaining an open airway and cervical stabilization.

4. Perform ongoing assessment for life-threatening injuries. Maintain ABCs, and treat for shock. *(FR022.1.)*

UNIT 3 | TRAUMA RELATED ISSUES
LESSON 5 | Chest, Abdominal, and Genital Injuries.

OBJECTIVES

FR015.1. Identify factors that affect the severity of a chest wound.

FR015.2. Identify treatment for a closed chest injury.

FR015.3. Identify treatment for an open chest injury.

FR024.1. Identify treatment for an evisceration.

FR025.1. Identify treatment for a genital wound.

Chest Injuries

A puncture wound in the chest area can affect the patient's breathing. A patient with this life-threatening injury needs immediate emergency care, followed by prompt EMS transport to a hospital. *(FR015.1.)*

Closed Chest Injury

A *closed chest injury* results from blunt trauma to the chest area. It damages internal organs and/or causes internal bleeding. A *flail chest* is a type of closed chest injury. It occurs when two or more adjacent ribs are fractured in two or more places and become free floating.

To treat a closed chest injury,

1. Use BSI and appropriate PPE.

2. If the patient has difficulty breathing, allow the patient to position him- or herself in a sitting or semi-sitting position. Be aware that the patient may have neck and spinal injuries.

3. Perform ongoing assessment for life-threatening injuries. Maintain ABCs, and treat for shock. *(FR015.2.)*

Open Chest Injury

An *open chest injury* occurs when penetration opens the chest area.

A *sucking chest injury* is a type of open chest injury in which air and blood escape into the area surrounding the lungs, creating a change in the pressure in the chest cavity. This can create breathing difficulties because it will not allow the lungs to expand and contract properly. You may hear a sucking noise or the injury may bubble as air moves through the open injury.

To treat an open chest injury,

1. Use BSI and appropriate PPE.

2. Apply an occlusive (airtight) dressing to the injury.

3. If the patient has difficulty breathing, allow the patient to position him- or herself in a sitting or semi-sitting position. Be aware that the patient may have neck and spinal injuries. If the patient is already seated, do not elevate his or her feet.

4. Perform ongoing assessment for life-threatening injuries. Maintain ABCs, and treat for shock. *(FR015.3.)*

Evisceration

An ***abdominal evisceration*** is an open wound where the organs protrude from the abdominal cavity. The wound's appearance may alarm you and command your attention. Do not get tunnel vision! Patients with an evisceration may be unable to breathe on their own. Maintaining an open airway is your first priority. Care of the exposed organs is always secondary to ensuring that the patient can breathe. Large abdominal eviscerations may produce large amounts of blood and body fluids. Additional PPE, such as a gown (raincoat) and eye protection, should be worn if available. If the patient can breathe adequately and has no other life-threatening injuries, provide emergency care.

To treat an abdominal evisceration,

1. Use BSI and appropriate PPE.

2. Do not touch or reinsert the exposed organ(s). The patient is already at risk for infection.

   • Touching the organ(s) increases the potential for infection.

   • Repositioning the organ can stop blood flow.

3. Cover the wound with a moist dressing, and place an occlusive (airtight) dressing over the moist dressing. This prevents further contamination and moisture loss. A dry dressing pulls fluid from the organ that you need to keep moist. Drying out the organ can cause a loss of function.

4. Perform an ongoing assessment for life-threatening injuries. Maintain ABCs, and treat for shock. *(FR024.1.)*

Genital Wounds

Treating a genital injury is similar to treating other soft tissue injuries. Genital wounds may bleed profusely. If bleeding is present, use direct pressure to stop active bleeding and a cold pack to control bleeding and pain. Prevent further contamination by covering the injury site with the appropriate dressing.

Section Vocabulary

abdominal evisceration

closed chest injury

flail chest

open chest injury

sucking chest injury

To treat a female patient,

1. Use BSI and appropriate PPE.

2. Use a trauma dressing or sanitary pad to apply direct pressure and a cold pack to the area.

   • Never insert or pack anything into the vagina.

3. If there is an impaled object, leave it in place.

4. Do not discard blood-soaked materials and clothing, which may be used to determine the amount of blood lost or may be used as evidence.

5. Do not clean or allow the patient to clean the area.

6. Perform ongoing assessment for life-threatening injuries. Maintain ABCs, and treat for shock.

To treat a male patient,

1. Use BSI and appropriate PPE.

2. Use a trauma dressing to apply direct pressure and a cold pack to the area.

3. If there is an impaled object, leave it in place.

4. If a body part of the patient has been amputated, apply direct pressure to the wound. Try to find the amputated part. Wrap it in a dressing, place it in a plastic bag and keep it cool, but do not place it directly on ice.

5. For scrotal injuries, apply a cold pack.

6. Perform ongoing assessment for life-threatening injuries. Maintain ABCs, and treat for shock. *(FR025.1.)*

UNIT 3 | TRAUMA RELATED ISSUES
LESSON 6 | Extremity Injuries

Classifications of Fractured Bones

The medical term for a broken bone is *fracture*.

- *open fracture*—The skin at the injury site is broken, and the bone may protrude through the skin. If lacerations appear near the fractured bone, treat the break as an open fracture because you do not know if the bone penetrated the skin.

- *closed fracture*—The skin at the injury site remains intact. *(FR026.4.)*

Mechanism of Injury

Force breaks a bone. There are several types of force:

- Direct force causes injury at the point of impact. Force may be delivered from a blow to the head with a baseball bat or as a driver's chest hits the steering wheel.

- Indirect force causes injury past the point of impact. The break may occur when a falling person extends the arms to break the fall and breaks his or her elbows.

- Twisting force causes injury when one part of a limb remains stationary, while the other twists. The result can be a spiral fracture, a bone break often caused by a sports injury or physical abuse. *(FR026.5.)*

Assess Pulse, Motor, and Sensory Function *(PMS)*

Pulse—Assess for circulation before and after splinting by checking for distal circulation below the injury site.

- In upper extremities, check the radial pulse, or leave the fingers exposed and check for capillary refill.

- In lower extremities, check the pedal pulse on the top of the foot (finding a pedal pulse is very difficult), or leave the toes exposed and check for capillary refill.

Motor—Assess for motor function (movement) of upper extremities. Ask the patient to move his or her fingers or squeeze your hand. To assess the motor function of lower extremities, perform the following steps:

1. Use BSI and appropriate PPE.

2. Ask the patient to move his or her feet.

3. Place your hand on the bottom of the foot, and ask the patient to push against your hand.

4. Place your hand on the top of the foot, and ask the patient to pull against your hand. As the patient pushes and pulls, you can feel and evaluate the strength of the extremity.

OBJECTIVES

FR026.4. Identify classifications of broken bone injuries.

FR026.5. Identify the mechanisms of injury for a broken bone.

FR026.7. Assess for pulse, motor, and sensation for a broken bone injury.

FR026.6. Assess for open wound, painful swelling, deformity, and bleeding for a broken bone injury.

FR026.3. Identify treatment for a broken bone.

FR026.9. Identify treatment for a dislocation, sprain, and strain.

FR026.1. Splint broken bones in a lower extremity.

FR026.2. Splint broken bones in an upper extremity.

FR027.4. Identify procedures for treatment of an amputated part.

FR027.1. Identify treatment of a patient with an amputation.

Sensory—Assess for sensation before movement. Ask the patient if he or she has feeling where you touch. *(FR026.7.)*

Assess Before and After Splinting

1. Use BSI and appropriate PPE.

2. Assess the injury.

3. Check for pulse, motor, and sensory function.

4. Ask the patient if he or she feels pain in the injured area.

5. Look for swelling.

6. Compare the injured extremity to the uninjured extremity.

7. Look for deformities. *(FR026.6.)*

Treatment—To prevent movement of an injured extremity,

1. Use BSI and appropriate PPE.

2. If the bone is exposed and you feel a pulse in the injured extremity,

   • Cover the exposed bone with dressing.

   • Splint as you would any fractured bone.

If you suspect

   • a fractured rib, watch for both sides of the chest to rise and fall equally as the patient breathes. Unequal rise and fall may indicate a flail chest or collapsed lung.

   • a fractured skull, assess by gently palpating the head to find deformity. Be careful not to push bone fragments into the brain.

   • a fractured neck, back, or pelvis, assess for pain, movement, and sensation in the feet. Unless there is a life-threatening emergency, perform spinal immobilization, and wait for EMS to move the patient.

   • an ankle injury and the patient is wearing boots, leave the boot in place, and splint around it. The boot provides support; removing it can cause more ankle damage.

   • a femur (thighbone) fracture, it may be life threatening due to blood loss, and the patient is probably in extreme pain. The injured leg is usually shorter than the uninjured leg and may have rotated. The thigh may be very swollen. Treating a mid-shaft femur fracture involves applying tension to the leg by grasping the calf muscle just below the knee and leaning back until the patient feels less pain. Discontinue tension if you meet resistance or the patient complains of more pain. Maintain tension until EMS arrives or the patient's medical condition dictates other priorities.

Treating life-threatening injuries takes precedence over treating fractured bones: life over limb.

3. Perform ongoing assessment for life-threatening injuries. Maintain ABCs, and treat for shock. *(FR026.3.)*

Dislocations, Sprains, and Strains

A *dislocation* occurs when the end of a bone comes out of its socket at the joint. Treatment for dislocations, sprains, strains, and fractured bones is the same. Do not try to put the dislocated bone back into place because major blood vessels and nerves can lie near the joint. Further injury may occur if you do this improperly. Treat sprains and strains like fractured bones. *(FR026.9.)*

Splint, Sling, and Swath

1. Use BSI and appropriate PPE.

2. If possible, remove jewelry from the patient's injured extremity before splinting or have the patient or a family member remove the jewelry. Document what happens to the jewelry.

3. To splint properly, immobilize the joints above and below the injury.

    • Various materials are appropriate for splinting, such as commercial splints, magazines, and boards.

4. If you feel a distal pulse, splint the extremity as you find it.

    • If you find no distal pulse or circulation in the extremity, reposition the extremity before splinting. To reposition, gently pull the extremity and return it to its natural position.

5. To support an injured upper extremity, splint first, then sling and swath.

    • A sling should support the entire arm and elevate the hand to decrease swelling.

    • A swath supports the arm, taking pressure off the collarbone. It prevents the arm from moving away from the body.

6. Perform ongoing assessment for life-threatening injuries. Maintain ABCs and treat for shock. *(FR026.1.) (FR026.2.)*

Amputation

There are two types of amputations: complete and incomplete. Amputations are visually disturbing injuries accompanied by a large amount of bleeding.

To treat an amputation,

1. Use BSI and appropriate PPE. If there is arterial bleeding or spurting blood, you may need eye protection.

2. With a gloved hand and a dressing, apply pressure directly to the wound.

3. If bleeding continues, apply more dressing and elevate the extremity.

4. If direct pressure and elevation do not stop the bleeding, apply pressure to the appropriate pressure point:
    • brachial artery for upper extremities
    • femoral artery for lower extremities

5. When bleeding is under control, apply a bandage to secure the dressing.

6. Do not delay the patient's treatment or transport to look for the amputated part. However, when you do find the amputated part,

    a. Wrap it in dressing.

    b. In the case of multiple amputations, wrap each part separately.

    c. Place it in a plastic bag.

    d. Keep it cool, but do not place it directly on ice. *(FR027.4.)*

Section Vocabulary

closed fracture

dislocation

fracture

open fracture

PMS

7. Perform ongoing assessment for life-threatening injuries. Maintain ABCs, and treat for shock. *(FR027.1.)*

UNIT 3 | TRAUMA RELATED ISSUES
LESSON 7 | Burns

OBJECTIVES

FR023.2. Identify the seriousness of a burn as it relates to depth, location, and extent of the burn.

FR023.1.C. Identify special considerations for elderly and small patients who have burns.

FR023.1.E. Identify treatment for a patient with thermal burns.

FR023.1.F. Identify treatment for a patient with chemical burns.

FR023.1.G. Identify treatment for a patient with electrical burns.

FR023.1.D. Identify treatment for a patient with inhalation burns.

Classified by Depth

Burn injuries are classified by depth. Superficial burns are the least serious, partial thickness burns involve more skin layers and are more serious, and full thickness burns are the most serious.

- *Superficial* (first-degree) *burns* damage the first layer of skin, which becomes red and feels very painful.
- *Partial thickness* (second-degree) *burns* damage the first two skin layers, which blister and feel very painful. Do not puncture blisters, as the open wound is vulnerable to infection; try to keep the blisters intact.
- *Full thickness* (third-degree) *burns* damage all skin layers and affect muscles and nerves. Skin looks waxy, white, or charred. Because of nerve damage at the site of a full thickness burn, the patient may feel no pain. If a patient with a full thickness burn does feel pain, the pain originates from the area around the full thickness burn, which may be a partial thickness burn.

Types of Burns

- *Thermal burns* occur when an external heat source comes into contact with the skin. Sources include the sun, fire, steam, hot plates, irons, etc.

- *Chemical burns* occur when a chemical comes into contact with the skin.

- *Electrical burns* occur when manmade or natural (lightning) electricity comes into contact with the skin and body, causing the skin and perhaps internal organs to burn.

- *Inhalation burns* occur when the patient has a burn to any part of the airway.

Burn Location

In addition to the depth and type of burn, the location of the burn is also a concern. Burns on the face, hands, feet, and genitals should be considered a critical burn. A victim suffering any of these types of burns needs close monitoring and rapid transport. Burns to the hands or feet may cause swelling that cuts off circulation to the fingers or toes. Extended loss of circulation may result in the loss of the affected body part. Closely monitor the area to determine if blood is flowing.

Another area with high blood flow is the genital area. Also closely monitor the chest. A burn on the chest may limit chest expansion, resulting in breathing difficulty. If the patient's face is burned, they may also have suffered an inhalation burn; swelling may obstruct the airway. Signs are singed facial hair, burning around the mouth and nose, soot on the face, breathing difficulty, and coughing. *(FR023.2.)*

The major long-term concern about burns is preventing infection. Any skin opening increases the chance of infection. The possibility of infection increases with the size of the burn area. Intact skin helps us maintain normal body temperature. If large areas of skin are burned, the body loses its ability to shiver and cannot maintain its normal temperature. This condition can put a patient into shock.

Children and the elderly are of special concern. A small burn on a child may cover a significant amount of skin in proportion to total body area. The effects of aging make the elderly more susceptible to serious injury and they often have medical conditions that complicate the process of healing a burn. *(FR023.1.C.)*

To treat a burn patient,

1. Use BSI and appropriate PPE. Be aware of scene safety and the danger of wearing a polyester uniform in a fire situation.

2. Determine the burn type so you can choose the proper technique to stop the burning.

   - For thermal burns, separate the patient from the heat source, apply water, or if the patient is on fire, advise him or her to stop, drop, and roll. *(FR023.1.E.)*

   - For chemical burns, brush off any dry residue, and then irrigate the burn with water for at least 20 minutes. (Be careful! Some chemicals, such as dry lime, react to water.) *(FR023.1.F.)*

   - For electrical burns, personal safety is the major concern. Make sure the scene is safe before trying to treat the patient. Ask the power company to disconnect the line if it is still live, or locate a breaker box and throw the main breaker, as appropriate. Ask someone to stay at the breaker box to make sure the power remains off while you provide treatment. If lightning struck the patient, it is safe to touch the patient and move him or her to a safe location before providing emergency medical care. Be aware that electrocution sometimes causes spinal injury or cardiac arrest. Check for entrance and exit wounds to determine if exposure affected major organs. Electricity travels the path of least resistance. *(FR023.1.G.)*

Section Vocabulary

chemical burn

electrical burn

full thickness burn

inhalation burn

partial thickness burn

superficial burn

thermal burn

3. Remove any clothing necessary to expose the burn. Do not pull off clothing that is stuck to the wound.

- If the patient has a chemical burn, remove all clothing, contact lenses, and jewelry to make sure that no chemicals are trapped under them.

- If the patient has an inhalation burn, allow him or her to assume a comfortable position. Keeping the patient's airway open is always a priority. *(FR023.1.D.)*

4. For superficial burns, place clean, cool water on the area to reduce the pain, and then cover with a dry sterile dressing.

- For partial thickness burns, be careful not to break any blisters, place clean, cool water on the area to reduce the pain (only if the blisters are intact), and then cover with a dry sterile dressing.

- For full thickness burns, cut any clothing away from the burn area; if there is any clothing stuck in the burn, leave it there. Cover with a dry sterile dressing.

- Do not apply creams or salves (Aloe Vera, Vaseline, butter, etc.,) to the wound.

- Do not bandage burned fingers together.

- Do not apply ice directly to the burn.

5. Perform ongoing assessment for life-threatening injuries. Maintain ABCs, and treat for shock.

UNIT 4 | MEDICAL ISSUES
LESSON 1 | Assisting in Childbirth

The Anatomy of Childbirth

A normal and natural life process, childbirth occurs every day. Most often, it takes place without complication in a hospital or home setting. In some cases, however, the delivery process begins and progresses so quickly, the mother has no time to reach the hospital. By performing patient assessment and taking a few simple steps, you can assist in childbirth. The following anatomical structures are present in childbirth:

- *uterus*—organ that holds the developing fetus
- *cervix*—neck of the uterus; contains a mucus plug
- *placenta*—disk-shaped inner lining of the uterus; provides nourishment and oxygen to the developing fetus
- *birth canal*—passage the fetus is pushed through during delivery
- *umbilical cord*—cord connecting the fetus and the mother; transports nourishment to the fetus
- *amniotic sac*—bag of fluid surrounding the fetus *(FR028.1.)*

Stages of Labor

The final phase of pregnancy, *labor* begins the birthing process. In this very intimate procedure, patient privacy is important. Explain what you will do before you do it. Labor consists of contractions of the uterine wall that force the fetus and later the placenta into the outside world. Normal labor occurs in three stages:

1. *Dilation* (preparation)—The first stage begins with the first contraction and continues until the fetus enters the birth canal. During this stage, the amniotic sac may rupture. As a result, fluid gushes from the vagina. When this occurs the patient may say something like, "My water broke."

2. *Expulsion* (delivery of the baby)—In the second stage, the fetus moves through the birth canal and is born. As the fetus moves down the birth canal, the mother experiences considerable pressure and pain. She may have an uncontrollable urge to push down. Soon the fetus's head crowns, or becomes visible, as it emerges from the vagina. The shoulders and the rest of the body follow.

3. *Placental* (delivery of the placenta)—In the third stage, the placenta separates from the uterine wall and moves through the birth canal for delivery. This stage usually occurs within 30 minutes of the baby's delivery. *(FR028.2.A.)*

Assessing for Labor

When called to assist a woman in labor, size up the scene and perform an initial assessment. Ask calming, reassuring questions, such as:

OBJECTIVES

FR028.1. Identify the anatomical structures of a patient who requires assistance in childbirth.

FR028.2.A. Identify the stages of labor of a patient who requires assistance in childbirth.

FR028.3. Identify the steps in the pre-delivery preparation of the mother.

FR028.4. Identify the steps to assist in the delivery of a newborn.

FR028.4.B. Identify the steps in caring for a newborn immediately following the delivery.

FR028.4.C. Identify the steps in delivery of the placenta immediately following childbirth.

FR028.5. Identify post-delivery care of the mother who requires assistance in childbirth.

FR028.6. Identify treatment for a patient who suffers from complications of pregnancy.

FR028.7. Identify treatment for a patient who suffers from complications of childbirth.

- When is your due date?

- Is this a multiple pregnancy?

- Has your water broken? What color was it?

- How many children have you had?

- Do you expect complications in this delivery?

Preparing for Delivery

Never delay or restrain delivery in any way. To prepare for delivery, perform the following steps:

1. Position the patient on her back with her knees bent and legs spread apart.

2. If a blanket and towels are available,

    a. Cover the patient with a blanket.

    b. Place clean towels under the patient's buttocks to elevate the hips slightly.

3. Look to see if the fetus is crowning. If so, delivery is imminent.

Large amounts of body fluids are present during childbirth. Use BSI and all available PPE, such as protective gloves, face shield, raincoat, and so on. *(FR028.3.)*

Assisting with Delivery

Do not attempt to pull the baby at any time during delivery.

1. As crowning occurs, place a gloved hand on the top of the fetus's head. Apply light pressure to prevent an explosive delivery. This helps prevent tearing of the vagina and injury to the baby.

2. As the baby emerges, support its head.

3. If the amniotic sac did not break as the baby's head started to deliver,

    a. Tear it open with your fingers.

    b. Push it away from the baby's nose and mouth.

4. Check to see if the umbilical cord loops around the baby's neck. If it does,

    a. Encourage the mother not to push.

    b. Try to slip the cord over the baby's head.

    - Never pull on the umbilical cord.

5. Continue to support the baby's head.

6. Be ready to catch the baby in a clean towel, grasping the baby's feet as they are delivered.

    - Remember, the baby will be wet and slippery.

    - Never pick up the baby by the feet to slap the buttocks.

7. Keep the baby on the same level as the mother.

8. Be sure to record the time of the delivery. *(FR028.4.)*

Care of the Newborn

After the newborn delivers,

1. Hold the baby in a face-down position or on its side.
2. Immediately clear the baby's nose and mouth using your fingers or the edge of the blanket.
    - The baby should start to cry immediately upon delivery.

If the baby is not breathing,

1. Rub the baby's back with a dry towel.
2. Flick the soles of the baby's feet to stimulate breathing.
    - If the baby does not begin to breathe on its own within the first minute after birth, begin rescue breathing.
    - If the baby has no pulse, begin infant CPR.

After breathing begins,

1. Keep the baby warm.
    - Wrap the baby in dry towels or blankets.
    - Cover the top of the baby's head.
    - Newborns have difficulty maintaining their body temperature, so keeping the baby warm is very important.
2. Hand the baby to the mother.
3. Encourage the mother to begin nursing the newborn.
    - Nursing stimulates contraction of the uterus to deliver the placenta and helps slow bleeding.

In a normal delivery, you do not need to cut the umbilical cord. However, you must clamp or tie it. Keep the newborn warm and wait until EMS personnel arrive. *(FR028.4.B.)*

Delivery of the Placenta

Never pull on the umbilical cord to deliver the placenta. The placenta usually delivers within 10 to 30 minutes after the baby's delivery.

After the placenta delivers,

1. Place it in a clean towel or container.
2. Place the placenta at the same level as the baby to help prevent the baby's blood from flowing back into the placenta.
    - Bleeding usually decreases after the placenta delivers. *(FR028.4.C.)*
3. Place a sanitary pad or towel over the vagina.
    - Do not insert anything in the vagina.
4. Encourage the mother to massage her uterus to help stop the bleeding.
5. Continue your ongoing assessment of both the mother and newborn.

6. Keep both warm.

7. Every few minutes reassess the mother and newborn for blood loss. *(FR028.5.)*

Complications of Pregnancy

Although the vast majority of pregnancies and deliveries are normal, you must be aware of possible complications:

- poisoning of the blood (toxemia)
- vaginal bleeding
- pain in the lower stomach and/or under the diaphragm
- passage of tissue from the vagina
- tender, bloated, or rigid stomach
- missed menstrual periods
- signs of shock

Treatment for all these complications is the same:

1. Arrange immediate transport to a medical facility.

2. Monitor and treat for shock.

3. Control bleeding.

4. Save all dressings and expelled tissue. *(FR028.6.)*

Complications During Childbirth

prolapsed umbilical cord—In some deliveries the umbilical cord comes out of the vagina before the baby's birth. The fetus's head compresses the cord against the birth canal. This cuts off the fetus's supply of oxygenated blood. If you notice a prolapsed cord, arrange for rapid transport and instruct the expectant mother to assume a knee-chest position.

umbilical cord around the neck—If the umbilical cord wraps around the baby's neck and you cannot remove the cord,

1. Encourage the mother to continue breathing and stop pushing.

2. If necessary, place clamps or ties approximately three inches apart on the cord and carefully cut between them.

3. Remove the cord from the neck.

4. Follow the steps of a normal delivery.

breech birth—A breech birth occurs when the fetus's feet or buttocks present down the birth canal first. If this occurs,

1. Arrange for prompt transport to a medical center.

2. Position and prepare the mother for delivery.

3. Support the fetus's legs and body as they deliver; the head will follow.

  • Never try to pull the baby from the vagina by the legs or trunk.

If the head does not deliver within three minutes,

1. Keep the baby's airway open by forming a V with the fingers of your gloved hand.

2. Turn your palm toward the baby's face.

3. Form an airway by pushing the baby's face away from the birth canal until the head delivers.

limb presentation—A normal delivery is not possible if the fetus's leg or arm appears first. A physician needs to deliver this baby. Rapid transport to a medical facility is crucial.

excessive bleeding after delivery—A mother loses about one or two cups of blood during normal childbirth. If the mother bleeds severely,

1. Place trauma dressings or sanitary pads and/or cold packs at the vaginal opening while elevating her legs and hips.

2. Treat for shock.

3. Arrange for rapid transport to a medical facility.

If the area between the mother's vagina and anus is torn and bleeding, treat it as you would an open wound.

1. Apply direct pressure using trauma dressings, sanitary pads, or gauze dressings.

2. Do not throw away blood-soaked pads; transport them with the mother.

stillborn delivery—A baby who dies long before delivery generally has an unpleasant odor and exhibits no signs of life. Give special consideration to the stillborn baby and its mother:

1. Do not resuscitate.

2. Turn your attention to the mother, and provide physical and psychological support.

3. Carefully wrap the stillborn infant in a blanket.

multiple births—Deliver multiple babies in the same manner as single babies. The mother will have a separate set of contractions for each baby. Each baby may also have a separate placenta, although this is not always the case. The second baby is usually born within 45 minutes. Do not worry: prepare to repeat the procedures you just completed for the first birth. Call for additional personnel to assist with the first baby born while you deliver the second. *(FR028.7.)*

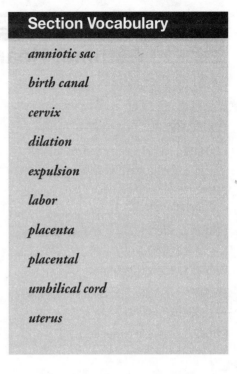

Section Vocabulary

amniotic sac

birth canal

cervix

dilation

expulsion

labor

placenta

placental

umbilical cord

uterus

UNIT 4 | MEDICAL ISSUES

LESSON 2 | Asthma, Heart Attack, and Stroke

OBJECTIVES

FR041.2. Identify signs and symptoms of a severe asthma attack.

FR041.1. Identify treatment for a severe asthma attack.

FR043.2. Identify signs and symptoms of a stroke.

FR043.1. Identify treatment for a stroke.

FR042.2. Identify signs and symptoms of a heart attack.

FR042.1. Identify treatment for a heart attack.

Asthma

Asthma results from the narrowing of airway passages, which causes breathing difficulties. Signs and symptoms of asthma are breathing difficulty while exhaling, a wheezing or whistling sound, and tense, frightened, or nervous behavior. *(FR041.2.)*

To treat a severe asthma attack,

1. Use BSI and appropriate PPE.

2. Position the patient for comfort.

3. Ask the patient if there is an accessible inhaler and encourage him or her to use it.

4. Perform an ongoing assessment for life-threatening injuries. Maintain ABCs, and treat for shock. *(FR041.1.)*

Stroke

A *stroke* is damage to part of the brain due to rupture or blockage of a blood vessel. Time is of the essence for transportation and professional treatment. Signs and symptoms of a stroke include

- numbness/paralysis of extremities, typically on one side

- confusion or dizziness

- difficulty speaking or slurred speech

- difficulty with vision

- headache

- seizures

- diminished consciousness/unconsciousness

- difficulty breathing

- facial drooping *(FR043.2.)*

To treat a stroke,

1. Use BSI and appropriate PPE.

2. Notify EMS of possible stroke patient and arrange immediate transport to a medical facility.

3. Position the patient for comfort.

4. Perform an ongoing assessment for life-threatening injuries. Maintain ABCs, and treat for shock. *(FR043.1.)*

Heart Attack

A ***heart attack*** is caused by oxygen deprivation to part of the heart, typically from a blocked blood vessel. This may lead to cardiac arrest; be prepared to administer CPR. Time is of the essence for transportation and professional treatment. Possible signs and symptoms are

- chest pain (may radiate to other parts of the body such as the arm or jaw)
- difficulty breathing
- cool, pale, moist skin/profuse sweating
- nausea/vomiting
- dizziness
- irregular pulse *(FR042.2.)*

To treat a heart attack,

1. Use BSI and appropriate PPE.
2. Notify EMS of possible heart attack patient and arrange immediate transport to a medical facility.
3. Position the patient for comfort.
4. Perform an ongoing assessment for life-threatening injuries. Maintain ABCs, and treat for shock. *(FR042.1.)*

Section Vocabulary
asthma
heart attack
stroke

UNIT 4 | MEDICAL ISSUES
LESSON 3 | Diabetes and Seizures

OBJECTIVES

FR029.3. Identify signs and symptoms of a diabetic emergency.

FR029.1. Identify treatment for a patient with a diabetic emergency.

FR030.2. Identify causes of seizures.

FR030.3. Identify how to prevent further injury to a patient experiencing a seizure.

FR030.1. Identify treatment for a patient experiencing seizures.

Diabetes

Diabetes is a disease in which the body does not produce or properly use insulin. *Insulin* is a hormone needed to convert sugar, starches, and other food into energy needed for daily life. When blood sugar is too low or too high, the body reacts and a diabetic emergency occurs. There are two types of diabetes: Type I—insulin dependant, juvenile diabetes and Type II—diabetes that can be controlled by diet or medication.

Signs and symptoms of a diabetic emergency can include

- intoxicated appearance (may mimic drunken behavior), including staggering or slurred speech
- altered mental state, including dizziness, drowsiness, and confusion
- sweet, fruity, or acetone-smelling breath that you might mistake for the odor of alcohol
- irregular breathing
- rapid or weak pulse
- flushed, dry or moist, warm skin
- seizures

Persons in a diabetic emergency often exhibit signs and symptoms that resemble drunkenness or drug overdose. Do not make assumptions; investigate further before making an arrest. *(FR029.3.)*

Treatment for Diabetic Emergencies

When assessing a conscious patient, ask if he or she has a medical condition. If the patient does say he or she has diabetes, inquire further. Ask if the person has eaten or taken medication or insulin. Also, look for medical alert tags or other obvious signs, such as syringes, insulin, insulin pumps, or blood sugar/glucose monitors. Do not give the patient anything by mouth unless he or she is fully conscious.

1. Use BSI and appropriate PPE.
2. Give or encourage the patient to consume some honey or sugar dissolved in a glass of water, or a drink rich in sugar, such as fruit juice or a non-diet soda.
3. If necessary, help the patient perform a blood sugar check.
4. Keep the patient from overheating or becoming chilled.
5. Perform ongoing assessment for life-threatening injuries. Maintain ABCs, and treat for shock. *(FR029.1.)*

Seizures

Seizure symptoms range from a blank stare into space or random shaking to twitching extremities or whole body muscle contractions. The condition causes mild to severe convulsions of the body or a body part. Seizures are rarely life threatening unless they continue indefinitely or two or more consecutive seizures occur without a period of responsiveness in between.

While having a seizure, the patient may stop breathing temporarily, bite his or her tongue, become incontinent (lose bowel or bladder control), make noises, spit and have a foamy appearance around the mouth, and be unresponsive. There are various causes of seizures, including the following:

- head injury
- trauma
- stroke
- high fever (predominately in children)
- shock
- poisoning, including alcohol and drug-related poisoning
- complications from pregnancy
- diseases such as epilepsy and diabetes
- unknown causes *(FR030.2.)*

Treatment for Seizures

Do not force anything between the patient's teeth or into the mouth.

Do not restrain the patient.

1. Use BSI and appropriate PPE.
2. Clear the area around the patient to prevent further injury. *(FR030.3.)*
3. Monitor the patient to ensure the airway is open.
4. After the seizure,
   a. Begin rescue breathing, if necessary.
   b. Turn the patient on his or her side if the airway is not obstructed.
5. Perform an ongoing assessment for life-threatening injuries. Maintain ABCs, and treat for shock. *(FR030.1.)*

Persons experiencing a minor seizure often exhibit signs and symptoms that resemble drunkenness or drug overdose and in some cases may show signs of aggression. Do not make assumptions; investigate further before making an arrest.

Section Vocabulary
diabetes
insulin

UNIT 4 I MEDICAL ISSUES

LESSON 4 I **Heat and Cold Related Injuries**

OBJECTIVES

FR031.1. Identify various ways the body adjusts to heat and cold.

FR031.2. Identify treatment for cold-related injuries.

FR031.3. Identify treatment for heat-related injuries.

Heat and cold emergencies may result in bodily injury and ultimately cause death. To adjust to outside temperatures, the human body undergoes chemical and physical changes. Many conditions contribute to heat or cold emergencies. Elderly persons, infants, diabetics, and persons with various pre-existing health conditions may be more susceptible to these types of injuries.

The body maintains heat by constricting blood vessels near its surface. Hair stands erect (goose bumps), helping to keep warm air near the skin. The body produces heat by shivering.

The body stays cool by perspiring (perspiration) and breathing (respiration). The body transfers heat without contact (radiation); the body also transfers heat with contact (conduction). *(FR031.1.)*

Cold-Related Emergencies

Exposure to cold causes two types of emergencies: *hypothermia*—an excessive cooling of the body's core temperature and *frostbite*—a localized injury from overexposure to cold.

Causes of hypothermia can include overexposure to cold, weather conditions, such as wind-chill, improper clothing, submersion in cool water for an extended time, and an inability to heat physical surroundings adequately.

Signs and symptoms of hypothermia, ranging from mild to severe, include

- shivering
- numbness
- changes in pulse rate and breathing
- alert but with possible drowsiness
- decreased muscle function
- sluggish pupils
- altered mental status
- bluish skin
- cardiac arrest

Never consider a hypothermic patient deceased until the patient is warmed in an appropriate medical facility. Continue to care for the patient until EMS relieves you.

To treat for hypothermia,

1. Use BSI and appropriate PPE.

2. Perform initial assessment.

3. Handle the patient gently.

4. Remove the patient from the cold environment, if possible.

5. Remove wet clothing and dry the patient.

6. Warm the body gradually by wrapping the patient in dry blankets or dry clothing.

7. Encourage a fully conscious patient to drink hot, non-alcoholic, non-caffeinated liquids.

8. Perform ongoing assessment for life-threatening injuries. Maintain ABCs, and treat for shock.

Frostbite, or local cold injury, is the freezing or near freezing of a body part. Fluid in the cells freezes and swells, destroying or damaging them. Frostbite usually occurs in exposed body areas or areas with lower blood supply, such as ears, nose, fingertips, and toes. Frostbite can cause loss of the affected areas. Signs and symptoms of frostbite include skin that remains soft and turns very pale when touched, an affected area that tingles as it re-warms, and the affected person losing feeling or sensation.

As frostbite progresses, the skin appears waxy and firm and becomes mottled and blotchy. The affected area swells, blisters, and turns white. Thawed skin may appear flushed or mottled with areas of blanching (lightening).

To treat for frostbite,

1. Use BSI and appropriate PPE.

2. Handle affected parts gently.

3. Remove wet clothing and cover the patient with a blanket.

4. If in a remote area or if transport is delayed, warm the frostbite area in tepid, not hot, water. Do not warm the area if there is the possibility of refreezing.

5. Cover the affected area with a dry dressing or padding.

6. Perform an ongoing assessment for life-threatening injuries. Maintain ABCs, and treat for shock. (FR031.2.)

Heat-Related Emergencies

Heat-related emergencies can occur from loss of fluids and salts through heavy sweating. ***Hyperthermia*** occurs when the body cannot recover from this fluid loss. Hyperthermia has three stages: heat cramps, heat exhaustion, and heatstroke. Heatstroke can be life threatening. Signs and symptoms of heat-related emergencies can include

- cramps in legs, arms, or abdominal muscles

- weakness, exhaustion

- dizziness, fainting

- strong, rapid pulse that weakens as damage progresses

- headache

Section Vocabulary

frostbite

hyperthermia

hypothermia

- appetite loss, vomiting
- altered mental state or unresponsiveness
- seizures
- moist, cool skin during the heat cramps or heat exhaustion stage
- hot, dry skin during the heatstroke stage—a sign of a life-threatening emergency that requires prompt EMS transport

To treat heat cramps or heat exhaustion,

1. Use BSI and appropriate PPE.

2. Remove the patient from the hot environment, and attempt to cool slowly.

3. Loosen or remove clothing.

4. Fan the body or apply a light mist of water.

5. Encourage an alert patient who is not nauseated to drink half a glass of cool water every 15 minutes.

6. Perform ongoing assessment for life-threatening injuries. Maintain ABCs, and treat for shock.

To treat heatstroke,

1. Use BSI and appropriate PPE.

2. Remove the patient from the hot environment.

3. Cool the patient immediately.

4. Apply cold packs to the patient's neck, armpits, and groin, frequently replacing warm packs with cold packs.

5. Keep skin wet with towels or wet clothing.

6. If possible, place patient on his or her back with legs elevated.

7. Perform ongoing assessment of the patient for life-threatening injuries. Monitor ABCs, and treat for shock. *(FR031.3.)*

It is important to remember that heat- and cold-related injuries range from mild to extreme and can cause death. Assessing and caring for the patient may stop the injury's progress as you await medical help.

UNIT 4 | MEDICAL ISSUES
LESSON 5 | Abdominal Pain, Poisoning, and Drug Overdose

Abdominal Pain

Separated from the chest cavity by the diaphragm, the abdominal cavity contains several body systems. The abdomen is a large part of the body, and abdominal pain is a common complaint. The patient may feel abdominal pain directly over the affected organ, or the pain may radiate to a different body part.

As the first officer on the scene, do not spend time trying to determine the pain's cause. Instead, recognize that the patient has an abdominal problem, complete a thorough patient assessment, and wait for EMS. Abdominal pain that is significant enough for the patient to call for help may be an emergency. Patients with abdominal pain may seem extremely ill. Signs and symptoms of abdominal pain include

- localized or radiating abdominal pain
- anxiety, reluctance to move
- loss of appetite
- nausea and vomiting
- fever
- abdominal distention
- patient may assume the fetal position
- signs of shock *(FR032.2.)*

General treatment for severe abdominal pain:

1. Use BSI and appropriate PPE.
2. Allow the patient to assume a comfortable position.
3. Conduct an initial assessment.
4. Treat for shock, if necessary.
5. Never give the patient anything by mouth, including medication.
6. Perform an ongoing assessment for life-threatening injuries. Maintain ABCs, and treat for shock. *(FR032.1.)*

Poisoning

Poisons are substances that may cause an allergic reaction, injury, or death if introduced into the body. Poisons can be solids, liquids, or gases that enter the body through ingestion, inhalation, injection, or absorption. *(FR033.2.)*

OBJECTIVES

FR032.2. Identify signs and symptoms of abdominal pain or distress.

FR032.1. Identify treatment for a patient with acute abdominal pain or distress.

FR033.2. Identify modes of poisoning.

FR033.3. Identify signs and symptoms of poisoning.

FR033.4. Identify the need for specialized assistance in caring for a patient with poisoning.

FR033.1. Identify treatment for poisoning.

FR034.2. Identify signs and symptoms of insect bites or stings.

FR034.1. Identify treatment for insect bites or stings.

FR035.2. Identify signs and symptoms of snakebites.

FR035.1. Identify treatment for snakebites.

FR036.2. Identify signs and symptoms of marine life stings.

FR036.1. Identify treatment for marine life stings.

FR037.2. Identify signs and symptoms of an allergic reaction.

FR037.1. Identify treatment for an allergic reaction.

FR038.2. Identify signs and symptoms of a drug overdose.

FR038.1. Identify treatment for a drug overdose.

Poisoning by ingestion occurs when poison enters the body through the mouth. Sources of poisoning by ingestion can be over-the-counter drugs, alcoholic beverages, contaminated food, illicit drugs, cleaning supplies, gasoline, or antifreeze. Signs and symptoms of poisoning by ingestion can include

- burns around the mouth
- odd breath odor
- nausea, vomiting
- stomach pains
- diarrhea
- altered mental status
- breathing difficulty
- seizures

To treat poisoning by ingestion,

1. Use BSI and appropriate PPE.
2. Make every attempt to identify the ingested substance by questioning the patient's family and bystanders.
3. Contact poison control to determine the course of treatment.
4. Provide appropriate treatment as recommended by poison control.
5. Notify responding personnel of type of poison.
6. Look for a container or a Material Safety Data Sheet (MSDS), and read instructions for treating poisoning.
7. Perform an ongoing assessment for life-threatening injuries. Maintain ABCs, and treat for shock.

Poisoning by inhalation occurs when poison enters the body through the mouth or nose. Possible inhaled poisons include by-products of fire, cyanide, chlorine, and other gases including carbon monoxide (CO), which is a byproduct of combustion. Some poisonous gases are colorless, odorless, and tasteless. Signs and symptoms of poisoning by inhalation can include

- breathing difficulty
- chest pain
- cough and/or burning sensation in the throat
- cyanosis
- dizziness
- confusion
- seizures
- unresponsiveness
- reddening around the mouth (late sign)

To treat poisoning by inhalation,

1. Ensure scene safety by making sure the area is adequately ventilated. If you suspect hazardous conditions, follow agency policy and procedure prior to entering.

2. Use BSI and appropriate PPE.

3. Remove the patient from the source of poison.

4. Follow local protocol or department policy for contacting poison control or the HAZMAT (hazardous materials) unit to determine course of treatment.

5. Notify responding personnel of the type of poison.

6. Perform an ongoing assessment for life-threatening injuries. Maintain ABCs, and treat for shock.

Poisoning by injection occurs when poison is inserted into the body through a small opening in the skin. Sources of poisoning by injection may include bites, stings, and toxic injections. Signs and symptoms of poisoning by injection may include

- bite or sting mark
- stinger, tentacle, or venom sac that remains in the skin
- redness at and around the entry site
- swelling at and around the entry site
- pain or tenderness at and around the entry site
- dizziness
- itching
- convulsions or seizures
- nausea, vomiting
- breathing difficulty
- sweating

To treat poisoning by injection,

1. Use BSI and appropriate PPE.

2. Separate the patient from the source of poison.

3. Notify responding personnel of type of poison.

4. Perform an ongoing assessment for life-threatening injuries. Maintain ABCs, and treat for shock.

Poisoning by absorption occurs when poison enters the body through contact with the surface of the skin. Sources of poisoning by absorption can be poisonous plants such as poison ivy, poison sumac, poison oak, poisonwood, etc., corrosives, insecticides and herbicides, and cleaning products. Signs and symptoms of poisoning by absorption may include

- liquid or powder on the skin
- burns
- itching and/or irritation

- redness, rash, and blistering
- shock
- dizziness
- nausea, vomiting
- convulsions or seizures *(FR003.3.)*

To treat poisoning by absorption,

1. Use BSI and appropriate PPE.
2. Separate the patient from the source of poison.
3. Notify responding personnel of type of poison.
4. Remove clothing, jewelry, and contact lenses from the affected area or ask a family member to do so.
5. Follow local protocol or department policy for contacting poison control or the HAZMAT unit to determine course of treatment. *(FR033.4.)*
6. If the poison is a dry powder, brush it off.
7. Flush the area with a large amount of clean water for at least 20 minutes.
   - Caution: Water may activate some dry chemicals and cause a burning reaction.
8. If the eye area is affected, follow procedures for eye trauma.
9. Perform an ongoing assessment for life-threatening injuries. Maintain ABCs, and treat for shock. *(FR033.1.)*

Poisoning from Insect Stings

Africanized Honey Bees are very aggressive in nature and are sometimes referred to as Killer Bees. These bees have been known to chase victims to distances of 1/4 mile. These bees can travel approximately 200 miles per year and are now in Florida.

Vibrations of machines and disturbances of their nest agitate Africanized Honey Bees. When common honeybee hives are agitated, approximately half the colony will exit the hive and attack victims. With Africanized Honey Bees, the entire colony will attack their victims. Although their venom is not any more toxic than the common honeybee, it is the number of stings that cause the victim to experience a possible life-threatening emergency.

When the first Africanized Honey Bee attacks someone, it breaks the stinger off, which leaves a scent for the rest of the colony to attack. Because these bees attack this scent, the rescuer should not seek shelter in swimming pools, streams, or areas of water as these bees will attack the victim when he or she resurfaces.

There is no way for the officer to differentiate between the common honeybee and the Africanized Honey Bee. If you suspect that a hive is of the Africanized Honey Bee type, do not enter the area, and contact an approved pest control handler.

Many people have severe allergies to substances in the venom of bees, wasps, hornets, and yellow jackets. When stung, highly allergic people need immediate medical care for ***anaphylaxis***, a severe allergic reaction in which air passages swell and restrict breathing. Signs and symptoms of an insect bite or sting, as observed in patient assessment, are similar to those of injected poison. *(FR034.2.)*

General treatment for an insect sting or bite:

1. Use BSI and appropriate PPE.

2. Lower the affected part below the heart.

3. Examine the site to see if the stinger is in the skin. If so,

    a. Remove it to prevent further poisoning and infection.

    b. Scrape the stinger away from the skin with the edge of a plastic card held at an angle.

    Do not use tweezers to remove the stinger. You may push it further into the skin and inject more poison.

4. Observe the patient for signs of an allergic reaction.

    a. If the patient has an allergic reaction, ensure that he or she has an open airway and adequate breathing.

    b. If the patient has a history of an allergic reaction and carries an insect kit, assist the patient in preparing treatment.

5. Perform an ongoing assessment for life-threatening injuries. Maintain ABCs, and treat for shock. *(FR034.1.)*

Poisoning from Snakebites

Snake venom contains some of the most complex poisons known. These poisons can affect the central nervous system, heart, kidneys, and blood. Snake venom is a digestive enzyme. It "digests" (eats) the tissue into which it is injected. Signs and symptoms of poisoning from snakebites include

- one or two puncture wounds that may or may not bleed
- a semicircular bite site that may or may not bleed
- severe pain and burning sensation at the wound site
- swelling and discoloration at the wound site beginning within 30 minutes and perhaps lasting several hours
- fainting from the emotional distress of the bite
- shock
- nausea, vomiting
- blurred vision
- drowsiness, slurred speech
- increased sweating and salivation
- weakness, paralysis
- seizures, unresponsiveness *(FR035.2.)*

Treatment for a snakebite:

1. Presume that the snakebite was from a poisonous snake until proven otherwise.

2. Use BSI and appropriate PPE.

3. Immobilize the affected part.

4. Keep the affected area lower than the heart.

5. Minimize the patient's movement: Keep the patient quiet and lying down.

6. Remove, or ask family members to remove, rings, bracelets, and other constricting items from the bitten extremity.

7. If possible, safely bring the snake with you or give it to EMS personnel.

8. Perform an ongoing assessment for life-threatening injuries. Maintain ABCs, and treat for shock. *(FR035.1.)*

When treating snakebites:

- Do not apply ice to the bite site.

- Do not cut the wound.

- Do not apply a tourniquet.

- Do not apply alcohol to the wound.

- Do not use your mouth to suck venom from the wound.

Poisoning from Marine Life Stings

Stings from some marine life are very painful. They can also make a person ill. Signs of poisoning from marine life stings are swelling and redness on the skin's surface. *(FR036.2.)*

Treatment for a marine life sting:

If the patient is stung by a jellyfish, sea anemone, hydra, coral, or Portuguese man-of-war,

1. Use BSI and appropriate PPE.

2. Immediately rinse with seawater and continue rinsing for approximately 30 minutes or until the pain is gone.

3. Remove dried tentacles.

4. Remove stingers as you would remove a bee stinger: Scrape the stinger away from the skin with the edge of a plastic card.

5. If possible, pour vinegar on the affected area.
   - Vinegar often works best to offset the toxin and reduce pain.
   - Do not use meat tenderizer. Most tenderizers no longer include the active ingredient once used to reduce pain.
   - Do not rub the wound.

6. Perform an ongoing assessment for life-threatening injuries. Maintain ABCs, and treat for shock.

If the patient is stung by a stingray, sea urchin, or spiny fish,

1. Use BSI and appropriate PPE.

2. Flush the area with seawater.

3. Immobilize and soak the affected area in water as hot as the patient can stand. Continue soaking about 30 minutes or until the pain goes away.

   • Toxins from stingrays, sea urchins, or spiny fish are heat sensitive. Often a single application of hot water dramatically relieves local pain.

4. Treat a spine embedded in the skin as an impaled object: Stabilize it in place and arrange for transport to a medical facility.

5. Perform an ongoing assessment for life-threatening injuries. Maintain ABCs, and treat for shock. *(FR036.1.)*

Anaphylactic Shock

Anaphylactic shock, or anaphylaxis, results from insect bites or stings, medications, pollen, foods, chemicals, or any substance that triggers an allergic reaction. Anaphylactic shock is a life-threatening emergency! Reaction can occur within seconds after a sting, ingestion, or exposure. The more quickly signs and symptoms appear, the greater the risk of fatality. Signs and symptoms of anaphylactic shock may include

- warm, tingling feeling in the mouth, face, chest, feet, and hands
- itching skin and hives
- swollen eyes, hands, and feet
- cyanosis
- paleness
- swollen mouth, tongue, or throat that obstructs the airway
- painful, squeezing sensation in the chest
- cough
- whistling sound prior to loss of voice
- rapid or labored breathing
- noisy breathing, wheezing
- increased heart rate
- dizziness
- restlessness
- itchy, watery eyes
- headache
- runny nose
- sense of impending doom
- decreasing mental status *(FR037.2.)*

Treatment for anaphylactic shock:

1. Use BSI and appropriate PPE.

2. Assess the patient's airway and breathing.

3. Arrange for immediate transport.

4. Perform an ongoing assessment for life-threatening injuries. Maintain ABCs, and treat for shock.

Patients who know they have allergies usually try to avoid substances that cause reactions. Avoidance is sometimes impossible, so these patients carry an anaphylaxis kit. Available only by a prescription, the kit contains a single dose of the drug epinephrine. When injected into the body, epinephrine counteracts the allergic reaction. You may assist, but the patient must inject the medication. *(FR037.1.)*

Drug Overdose

A drug overdose is an emergency that involves poisoning by legal or illegal drugs. Most drug overdoses involve drug abuse by long-time users. However, a drug overdose can also result from an accident, miscalculation, confusion, use of more than one drug, or a suicide attempt. An overdose occurs when someone uses an excessive amount of a substance. It causes adverse reactions ranging from excited delirium to coma and death.

The most reliable indications of a drug overdose come from the scene and patient history. Similar to those of many medical conditions, signs and symptoms of an overdose vary widely and may include

- unresponsiveness
- breathing difficulty
- abnormal pulse
- fever
- vomiting
- convulsions or seizures
- sweating
- tremors
- abnormal pupil reactions
- blurred vision
- slurred speech
- muscle spasms
- signs of illicit drug use (track marks, burns on fingers/lips)
- combativeness
- extraordinary strength
- endurance without fatigue
- sudden tranquility after frenzied activity
- paranoia
- memory loss
- hallucinations
- altered mental status/abnormal behavior

Excited delirium is neither a medical nor a psychiatric condition. It is a term used to describe the mental and physical effects of extreme drug abuse that can lead to death. Increased attention has been paid to the sudden and seemingly inexplicable deaths of some subjects being held in police custody. In most cases, the force required to subdue the suspect was not sufficient to cause death. Medical authorities have typically had extreme difficulty in identifying the cause of death. Signs and symptoms of excited delirium may include

- unbelievable strength
- imperviousness to pain
- ability to offer resistance against multiple officers for an extended period of time
- hyperthermia (temperatures can spike to between 105–113°F)
- sweating
- shedding clothes or nudity
- bizarre and violent behavior
- aggression
- hyperactivity
- extreme paranoia
- incoherent shouting or nonsensical speech
- hallucinations
- attraction to glass (smashing glass is common)
- confusion or disorientation
- grunting or animal-like sounds while struggling with officers
- foaming at the mouth
- drooling
- dilated pupils *(FR038.2.)*

Gaining physical control of the subject may be dangerous and difficult. If possible, request assistance before approaching the subject. The method for dealing with suspected excited delirium is to provide medical treatment to the individual according to substance abuse procedures and be aware of positional asphyxia.

Treatment for a drug overdose:

1. Use BSI and appropriate PPE.
2. Establish and maintain an open airway and breathing.
3. Monitor the patient's mental status.
4. In the presence of hyperthermia, cool the patient appropriately.
5. Prevent or decrease the patient's agitation.
6. Place the patient in a position to prevent asphyxiation.

Section Vocabulary
anaphylaxis
CO
excited delirium

7. Notify responding personnel of drug used (if known).

8. Perform an ongoing assessment for life-threatening injuries. Maintain ABCs, and treat for shock. *(FR038.1.)*

CHAPTER 3

CMS Criminal Justice Firearms

Officers face many dangers as part of their jobs. Yet, danger can come from the most unexpected place, such as an officer's own firearm. Failure to cautiously and consistently follow rules of firearm handling can result in injury or death. Every officer must acquire proper training on the specific model of firearm he or she will carry and use before touching, handling, or loading any firearm.

UNIT 1 | FIREARMS SAFETY

LESSON 1 | Firearms Safety Procedures

OBJECTIVES

FA603.2.A.1. Identify shooting hand.

FA603.2.A.2. Identify support hand.

FA611.1. Identify the common cause of most firearm accidents.

FA611.1.A. Identify the general rules of safety that should be applied to all firearms.

FA611.1.A.2. Identify what safety rules to follow on the range.

FA611.4. Identify the requirements in the Florida Statutes for storing a firearm.

When studying firearms, the terms *shooting hand* and *support hand* are used to describe the hand used to shoot the firearm and the hand that aids the other in shooting, respectively. The support hand is the hand that assists the shooting hand. *(FA603.2.A.1., FA603.2.A.2.)*

Safety is the most important element of firearms training. Negligence is the most common cause of firearms accidents. No matter how proficient you become at marksmanship, you and those around you are not safe if you negligently handle or discharge a weapon. The highest standards of firearms safety are required at all times. As students and later as officers, you will follow all firearms safety rules. Facilitators and instructors will enforce those rules any time firearms are present, issued, or handled. *(FA611.1.)*

Always refer to the manufacturer's manual for safety recommendations.

General Rules of Firearms Safety

1. Always treat every firearm as if it were loaded, whether you think it is or not.

2. Each time you pick up, put down, or hand a firearm to another, open the firearm's action and physically and visually inspect it to make sure that it is not loaded. This is called a safety check.

Safety Note: Never rely on memory to decide if a firearm is unloaded. Open the action and physically and visually check every firearm you handle during this course. If you touch it, first open the action and check it.

3. Always point the muzzle in a safe direction. If a weapon pointed in a safe direction fires, it causes no personal injury and minor, if any, property damage. The environment dictates what direction is safe. In a building, for instance, people may be above or below you.

Safety Note: A safe direction is generally muzzle pointed down at a 45 degree angle away from your body with your finger outside the trigger guard.

4. Never point a firearm at anyone or anything that you do not intend to shoot.

5. Keep your trigger finger off the trigger and against the frame when drawing the firearm from or returning it to your holster.

6. Never leave a loaded firearm unattended.

7. Clean the firearm each time it is fired, and fully inspect the firearm once a week. Safety check the firearm each time you use it.

Safety Note: Before cleaning or handling a firearm, make sure that it is unloaded and is pointed in a safe direction. Never clean a loaded firearm. *(FA611.1.A.)*

Rules for Firearms Safety on the Range

Follow these safety rules while on the firing range:

1. Immediately obey all directions and commands from the range instructor.

2. Care for and respect all firearms.

    a. Never abuse firearms.

    b. Perform a safety check each time you are issued or return a firearm. Open the cylinder or action to make sure the firearm is unloaded and perform a physical/visual check.

    c. If loose screws and/or loose sights are discovered, report this to the range instructor.

3. Before training, the range instructor will inspect all firearms for proper function.

4. Always keep the firearm secure and in its holster unless otherwise instructed.

    a. Keep all safety/retention devices securely engaged on holstered firearms at all times.

    b. Never unholster a firearm behind the firing line.

    c. When carrying unholstered firearms to and from the range, keep the action of the firearms open.

    Carry revolvers by the tops of their frames with your fingers through the cylinder opening and the muzzle pointed in a safe direction.

    Carry pistols with their magazines removed, action open, and muzzle pointed in a safe direction (safety on, if applicable).

    Carry shotguns and rifles with their muzzles pointing in a safe direction, actions open and with the safety on.

5. Keep your trigger finger off the trigger and against the frame when drawing the firearm from or returning it to your holster.

6. Never anticipate any command.

    a. Load only on the range instructor's command.

    b. Retrieve dropped ammunition, speed loaders, magazines or equipment only when the range instructor declares it safe to do so.

    Safety Note: Perform unloading procedures even if the firearm is unloaded when the range instructor issues the unload command.

7. When you are on the firing line, you may leave only at the range instructor's command.

8. Always point unholstered firearms in a safe direction.

9. Stop firing immediately at the cease fire command.

10. Never handle firearms on the firing line while someone is down the range.

11. Dry fire on the firing line only under a range instructor's supervision.

12. Only fire approved ammunition.

13. Always wear ear and eye protection on or near the firing line.

14. Never talk on the firing line unless your instructor speaks to you or in an emergency.

15. No tobacco products are allowed on the firing line.

16. Never eat on the firing line.

17. Be courteous to fellow shooters.

18. When not training, watch other shooters and listen to the range instructor.

19. If you drop a firearm, do not pick it up; notify the range instructor immediately.

20. If a weapon fails to fire, keep it pointed in a safe direction and immediately attempt to clear the malfunction. If the attempt to clear the malfunction fails, notify the range instructor by raising your support hand.

21. Immediately report all injuries to an academy staff member. Learn the location of the first aid kit on the range. *(FA611.1.A.2.)*

Storing Firearms Safely

As officers and perhaps first-time gun owners, you are responsible for making sure your weapon is secure while you are off duty. Section 790.174, F.S. addresses requirements for storing firearms safely.

1. A person who stores or leaves, on a premise under his or her control, a loaded firearm, as defined in §790.001, and who knows or reasonably should know that a minor is likely to gain access to the firearm without the lawful permission of the minor's parent or the person having charge of the minor, or without the supervision required by law, shall keep the firearm in a securely locked box or container or in a location which a reasonable person would believe to be secure or shall secure it with a trigger lock, except when the person is carrying the firearm on his or her body or within such close proximity thereto that he or she can retrieve and use it as easily and quickly as if he or she carried it on his or her body.

2. It is a misdemeanor of the second degree, punishable as provided in §775.082 or §775.083, if a person violates subsection (1) by failing to store or leave a firearm in the required manner and as a result thereof a minor gains access to the firearm, without the lawful permission of the minor's parent or the person having charge of the minor, and possesses or exhibits it, without the supervision required by law:

   a. In a public place; or

   b. In a rude, careless, angry, or threatening manner in violation of §790.10.

This subsection does not apply if the minor obtains the firearm as a result of an unlawful entry by any person.

As used in this act, the term "minor" means any person under the age of 16. *(FA611.4.)*

UNIT 2 | FIREARMS FAMILIARIZATION

Firearms Familiarization

These next sections cover the nomenclature of the four weapons used in this training: revolver, semiautomatic pistol, shotgun, and semiautomatic rifle/carbine. The section also covers how each of these weapons works, and how their parts interrelate. You will learn to fieldstrip the weapons correctly and reassemble them to their original operational status.

All firearms have many of the same types of parts to achieve the same function. It is important to learn the nomenclature of the four weapons and how their parts function together to make the weapons work. This knowledge allows safe weapons operation on the range and in the field. It also helps you to better communicate with the armorer and to testify in court in a clear and credible manner.

UNIT 2 | FIREARMS FAMILIARIZATION

LESSON 1 | Revolver

Nomenclature of the Revolver

Revolvers may operate differently based upon who manufactured them. Refer to the Double Action Revolver Nomenclature Diagram (see next page). Make sure you are familiar with the nomenclature, each part's location, and function for the revolver that you use.

Following is the nomenclature associated with a revolver, a description of the parts of a revolver, and their functions:

- backstrap—portion of the grip that is placed in the palm of the shooting hand
- barrel—provides a path for the fired bullet
- center pin—on a Smith & Wesson revolver, it is the spring-loaded part that holds the cylinder closed
- crane—attaches the cylinder to the frame so the cylinder can swing in and out of the frame opening; Colt uses the term crane; Smith & Wesson uses the term yoke (internal part)
- cylinder—houses the extractor rod and contains the chambers that hold the cartridges

OBJECTIVES

FA609.3.B. Identify revolver parts with correct nomenclature.

FA609.3.C. Describe the function of revolver parts.

FA611.2.A. Identify the steps to follow to safely handle a revolver.

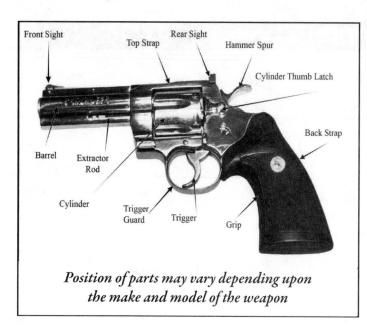

Front Sight

Top Strap

Rear Sight

Hammer Spur

Cylinder Thumb Latch

Back Strap

Barrel

Extractor Rod

Cylinder

Trigger Guard

Trigger

Grip

Position of parts may vary depending upon the make and model of the weapon

Double action revolver

Figure 3-1

- cylinder release latch—disengages the cylinder from the frame
- cylinder stop—locks the cylinder
- extractor—star-shaped device attached to the extractor rod that fits inside the cylinder that the rounds rest on (internal part)
- extractor rod—when depressed, it causes the extractor to push the cartridge from the cylinder
- frame—internal structure that holds the parts of the revolver and provides a way of gripping the firearm
- front sight—located on the end of the barrel near the muzzle; it is designed for the swift location of the target and for bringing the firearm into alignment for accuracy.
- grip—made of wood, plastic, or rubber; designed to allow the shooter to grip the firearm easily for control
- hammer—when the trigger is pulled, this part falls forward to activate the primer
- hammer nose—pin or firing pin—part of the hammer or frame that protrudes through the frame and strikes the primer (internal part)
- hammer spur—part of the hammer used for cocking the weapon to single-action mode
- hand—part of a revolver that turns the cylinder as the gun is cocked, thus aligning a cartridge with the hammer or firing pin (internal part)
- rear sight—located on the rear of the frame; it can be adjustable or fixed
- top strap—part of the frame that houses the rear sight, positioned over cylinder
- trigger—activates the revolver's operation in both single and double action
- trigger guard—part of the frame that protects the trigger *(FA609.3.B., FA609.3.C.)*

How the Revolver Works

When the trigger is squeezed, the cylinder unlocks and rotates, placing a live cartridge in line with the firing pin. When the hammer falls, the hammer nose or firing pin strikes the primer and ignites the powder charge. The burning powder creates a gas, and pressure builds from the gas. This pressure sends the projectile (bullet) down and out of the barrel. The trigger releases forward, resetting the mechanism.

The direction of the cylinder rotation depends upon the manufacturer. A Smith & Wesson revolver rotates counterclockwise and the cylinder release latch pushes forward to release the cylinder. Ruger's revolver rotates counterclockwise; the cylinder release latch is depressed into the frame. A Colt revolver rotates clockwise. The cylinder release latch is pulled rearward to release the cylinder.

Cycle of Operation

- loading—placing live rounds into the open cylinder and closing the cylinder into the frame
- locking—locking the cylinder into the frame

- unlocking/feeding/locking—releasing the locked cylinder by squeezing the trigger so the cylinder can rotate and place a live round in front of the barrel in line with the firing pin; the cylinder then locks, allowing the firing pin to strike the live round that has been locked in place. The cylinder repeats this process with each pull of the trigger until all cartridges have been fired.

- firing—ignition of the primer and firing the cartridge

- extraction/ejecting—pushing or pulling the cylinder release latch; this rotates the cylinder out of the frame. Pushing the extractor rod ejects all cartridges.

Handing the Revolver to Another Person

As officers, you will handle many firearms. In the course of your duties, you will hand over your firearm or a confiscated firearm. Safely handling the firearm is essential to protect yourself and ensure the safety of others.

To hand a revolver to another person, follow these steps:

1. With the barrel pointed in a safe direction, open the cylinder.

2. Visually and physically inspect the cylinder to make sure it is not loaded. If it is loaded, unload the revolver and ensure that all rounds have been removed.

3. With two or three fingers through the top strap, hand the revolver to the other person, grip first. *(FA611.2.A.)*

The person receiving the firearm should physically and visually check to make sure that the firearm is unloaded.

UNIT 2 | FIREARMS FAMILIARIZATION
LESSON 2 | Semiautomatic Pistol

OBJECTIVES

FA619.3.B. Identify semiautomatic pistol parts with correct nomenclature.

FA619.3.C. Describe the function of semiautomatic pistol parts.

FA611.2.B. Identify the steps to safely handle a semiautomatic pistol.

Nomenclature of the Semiautomatic Pistol

Semiautomatic pistols may operate differently based upon who manufactured them. Refer to the Semiautomatic Double Action Pistol Nomenclature Diagram. Make sure you are familiar with the part names, locations, and functions of the pistol you use.

Following is the nomenclature associated with the semiautomatic pistol, a description of the parts of a semiautomatic pistol, and their functions:

- accessory rail—provides space for lighting and sighting devices
- back strap—portion of the grip that is placed in the palm of the shooting hand
- frame/receiver—holds the internal parts, as well as the slide assembly, and provides a way to grip the pistol
- front sight—located on the slide's front; used to bring the firearm into alignment for accuracy
- front strap—position of the grip that allows the fingers of the shooting hand to rest
- grip panel—made of polymer designed to allow the shooter to easily grip and control the weapon

- magazine catch—releases the magazine from the frame (magazine well)
- magazine floor plate—base of the magazine
- muzzle barrel—provides a path for the fired bullet and is chambered to hold the cartridge
- rear sight—located on the rear of the slide that aligns with the front sight to bring the firearm into alignment for accuracy
- slide—houses the firing pin, safety, drop safety, sights, and extractor
- slide cover plate—allows access of the firing pin assembly
- slide lock—device that allows quick and simple field stripping of the pistol
- slide stop lever—device that locks the slide in the open position
- thumb rest—place for the thumb to rest while gripping the pistol
- trigger—activates the pistol's operation
- trigger guard—part of the frame that protects the trigger
- trigger safety—allows the trigger to move when pressed *(FA619.3.B.), (FA619.3.C.)*

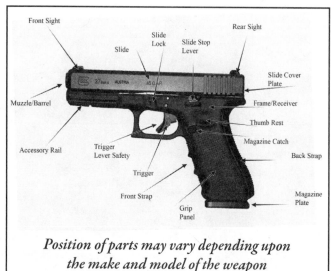

Position of parts may vary depending upon the make and model of the weapon

Semiautomatic pistol

Figure 3-2a

The magazine holds the ammunition. It contains a spring and follower that pushes each round up to be stripped off by the forward movement of the slide. The follower also activates the slide stop. The floor/butt plate holds the magazine spring and follower in the magazine. You can remove it to clean inside the magazine. When reassembling the magazine, make sure to replace the spring and follower correctly.

The magazine consists of five main parts:

1. follower
2. spring
3. magazine insert
4. floor plate
5. magazine tube

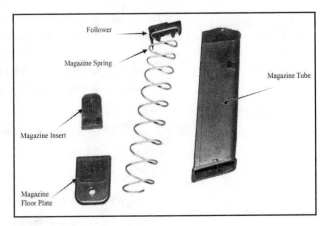

Semiautomatic pistol – magazine

Figure 3-2b

Some additional parts of the semiautomatic pistol include the recoil guide, recoil spring, and slide. The recoil guide directs the recoil spring. It absorbs the recoil and returns the slide to the following position. The recoil spring pushes the slide forward.

Types of Pistols

Pistols are categorized by their type of trigger mechanism. A ***single-action*** mechanism performs the single action of releasing the hammer or striker. Once the first round is fired the automatic movement of the slide resets the mechanism for each subsequent shot.

When a pistol is ***double action only***, every round fires double action with the hammer at rest against the rear of the slide. Every time the trigger is pulled to the rear, it manually cocks and releases the hammer to fire the pistol. As the slide cycles and goes forward, the hammer safety follows, coming to rest against the slide's rear. The hammer never stays cocked. The weapon's trigger pull is the same each time.

In a ***double/single*** pistol, the first round fires double action. (The trigger being pulled to the rear manually cocks the hammer and releases it.) The second and subsequent rounds fire single action as the hammer remains cocked each time the slide cycles. After firing is complete, the hammer remains cocked. Before holstering the weapon, it must be de-cocked using the de-cocking lever.

How the Semiautomatic Pistol Works

A semiautomatic pistol functions by using the energy from the recoil of a single round of ammunition to extract and eject a fired cartridge from the pistol's chamber and load an unfired round from a magazine into the chamber for the next shot.

As you draw the trigger fully to the rear in double action mode, the hammer moves back and then releases to strike the firing pin. Upon firing, the slide moves back, extracting and ejecting the spent cartridge case and pushing the hammer to the fully cocked position. As the slide moves to the rear, the recoil spring compresses. When all the energy has been used, the spring decompresses, pushing the slide forward. Then the slide returns forward, feeding the next cartridge from the magazine to the barrel chamber. The hammer remains cocked and the trigger is in the rear position, so subsequent shots fire in single-action mode. This sequence repeats until the last round fires. Then the magazine follower exerts upward pressure on the slide stop, causing it to engage and hold the slide in the open position. (This example describes a double action/single action pistol.)

Cycle of Operation (open action)

- loading—seating a loaded magazine into the magazine well

- feeding/chambering—moving the round from the magazine to the chamber by releasing the slide, picking up the round from the magazine and seating the round into the chamber

- locking—the breech end of the barrel locks into the slide

- firing—ignition of the primer and firing the cartridge

- unlocking—unseating the breech end of the barrel from the slide

- extraction—"pulling" the spent cartridge from the chamber

- ejecting—"pushing" the spent cartridge out of the ejection port

- cocking—returning the firing mechanism to the fire position

Performing a Function Check

A function check ensures that the weapon functions properly. It is usually performed after fieldstripping or cleaning and reassembling the pistol. To perform a function check, follow these steps:

Glock:

1. Press the trigger and hold it to the rear.

2. Cycle the slide with the support hand and slowly release the pressure of the trigger until the trigger resets; you should hear a click and feel the reset on the trigger.

Other types of semiautomatic pistols:

1. Visually and physically check the firearm to make sure it is unloaded.

2. Operate the slide several times to ensure that it operates freely.

3. If the firearm has a magazine disconnect, follow the manufacturer's instructions to perform a function check.

4. Put the manual de-cocking/safety lever in the off position.

5. Pull the trigger. The weapon should function properly.

6. If the weapon has an external hammer, then manually cock the hammer and pull the trigger. The weapon should function properly. If the weapon has a de-cocking lever, operate the slide and depress the lever. The pistol's hammer should de-cock.

7. Lock the slide to the rear.

8. Insert an empty magazine into the magazine well until the magazine engages.

9. Depress the magazine release. The magazine should fall free.

10. Depress the slide release or pull the slide to the rear and then release. The slide should function properly.

Handing the Semiautomatic Pistol to Another Person

To hand a semiautomatic pistol to another person, do the following:

1. Locate the manual safety on the semiautomatic pistol (if applicable). Put the safety in the on position.

2. Press the magazine release button and remove the magazine from the magazine well.

3. Secure the magazine.

4. Point the weapon in a safe direction, and pull the slide to the rear to extract and eject the live round from the chamber.

5. Lock the slide to the rear using the slide stop on the weapon's frame.

6. Visually and physically inspect the chamber and magazine well to make sure they are empty.

7. With the slide locked to the rear and the magazine well empty, hand the semiautomatic pistol to the other person, grip first. *(FA611.2.B.)*

The person receiving the firearm should physically and visually check to make sure the firearm is unloaded.

Section Vocabulary
double action only
double/single
single-action

UNIT 2 | FIREARMS FAMILIARIZATION
LESSON 3 | Shotgun

A shotgun is a smooth bore gun designed for firing at short distances. This weapon's general specifications are as follows:

- gauge—12 gauge (ga) most common; chamber 2 3/4 or 3 inches
- magazine tube capacity—see manufacturer's specifications
- length—overall 38 inches with an 18-inch barrel (standard)
- weight—see manufacturer's specifications
- sights—rifle or bead
- choke—full, modified, improved cylinder
- stock—see manufacturer's specifications
- barrel—18-, 20-, and 22-inch barrels most commonly used
- safety—see manufacturer's specifications

Nomenclature of the Shotgun

Make sure you are familiar with the part locations and functions for the shotgun you are using. Part names and locations, and some part designs, vary from model to model. Refer to the Shotgun Pump Action Nomenclature Diagram.

Following is the nomenclature associated with a shotgun, a description of the parts of a shotgun, and their functions:

- action/slide release—mechanical device that, when activated, releases the slide
- barrel—long cylinder-shaped tube through which the projectile travels from the chamber
- bolt—cylindrical steel part containing the firing pin and extractor, which closes the breech end of the barrel for firing
- bolt carrier—flat steel part that fits onto the action bars and on which the bolt sits
- ejection port—opening on the side or bottom of the receiver; spent casings are ejected from it and live rounds are loaded into this port
- ejector—piece of spring steel mounted on the inside left of the receiver; when the action pulls a shell to the rear, it compresses and then releases the ejector as the bolt goes past it.

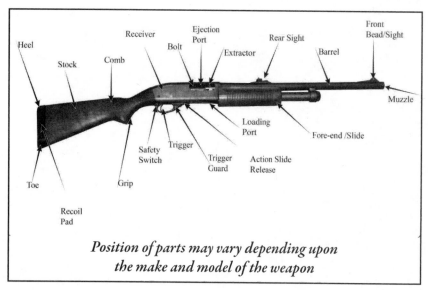

Position of parts may vary depending upon the make and model of the weapon

Shotgun pump action nomenclature

Figure 3-3

A small extension stops the shell from going further and assists in ejecting the shell from the receiver.

- extractor—metal hook-shaped part mounted on the bolt; the hook engages the rim of the cartridge so that when the action is brought to the rear, the extractor removes the shell from the chamber.

- fore-end or slide—wooden or polymer grip near the magazine

- front/bead sight or post—bead or raised post on the front of the barrel used to bring the firearm into alignment for accuracy

- loading port—bottom opening on the receiver that live rounds are fed into or removed from the magazine tube

- magazine cap—located on the magazine tube's end and keeps the barrel in place

- magazine tube—located under the barrel and holds rounds

- muzzle—barrel's front end

- rear sight—secondary aligning device located on the receiver or barrel that aligns with the front sight bead or post to bring the shotgun into alignment for accuracy

- receiver—holds the trigger group and bolt assembly

- safety—mechanical device that prevents a shooter from pulling the trigger and discharging the shotgun

- shell carrier—slightly rounded steel part that blocks the loading port; catches rounds released from the magazine and raises them into alignment with the chamber

- shell latches (stops)—two pieces of steel mounted on each side of the inside of the receiver at the magazine's rear; they help hold the cartridges in the magazine and release them one at a time when the action operates. They are also used to manually unload the shotgun.

- stock—part of the weapon attached to the receiver; a shooter places the stock on his or her shoulder when firing. Nomenclature of the stock includes the following:

  - butt—rear area of the stock that the shooter mounts against the shoulder for firing; normally covered with a metal or plastic butt plate or a recoil pad

  - comb—stock's top edge where the shooter's cheek rests

  - grip—"small of the stock," just behind the receiver; the shooter uses the grip and his or her shooting hand for control when firing or carrying it

  - heel—top corner of the butt

  - recoil pad—a butt plate, usually rubber, that reduces the effect of the shotgun's recoil or "kick"

  - toe—the bottom part of the butt

- trigger—when pulled, this releases the sear (a part that holds the hammer in the cocked position) and activates the firing pin

- trigger guard—part of the frame that protects the trigger *(FA636.3.B., FA636.3.C.)*

How the Shotgun Works
Cycle of Operation (Pump Action Shotgun)

- loading—placing live rounds in the magazine tube or open ejection port

- chambering—removing a round from the magazine tube and placing it in the barrel's chamber by cycling the weapon, or after placing a round in the open ejection port, pushing the slide forward

- locking—closing the action to a locked position by moving the fore-end forward until it stops
- firing—discharging the weapon by depressing the trigger
- unlocking—weapon unlocks when fired
- extracting/ejecting—extractor's removal of the empty casing from the chamber and pushing the empty casing out of the weapon through the ejection port by manually cycling the slide/fore-end grip to the rear

Performing a Function Check (Pump Action Shotgun)

1. With the safety in the on position and the shotgun pointed in a safe direction, cycle the action and leave it closed.

2. Depress the trigger; nothing should happen.

3. Release the trigger and move the safety to the off position. This means the trigger, sear, and hammer will work as they should.

4. Holding the trigger back, cycle the action of the shotgun. You should hear the bolt lock into position and nothing else.

5. Release the trigger. You should hear the disconnector move into place. This tells you that the disconnector is working.

6. Pull the trigger to the rear. You should hear the hammer fall and strike the firing pin.

7. Place the safety in the on position.

8. Open the action.

Handing the Shotgun to Another Person

To hand a shotgun to another person, follow these steps:

1. Place the safety in the on, or engaged, position.

2. Unload the shotgun.

3. Verify that no ammunition is in the magazine chamber and tube with a physical and visual check.

4. Make sure the fore-end is to the rear and the ejection port is open.

5. Hand the shotgun to the person in the port arms stance.

To assume the port arms stance:

a. Hold the stock with your shooting hand and the fore-end with your support hand.

b. Point the barrel in a safe direction.

c. Put the safety in the on position, the fore-end to the rear, and the ejection port open, facing the person receiving the weapon. *(FA611.2.C.)*

The person receiving the firearm should physically and visually check the firearm to make sure it is unloaded.

UNIT 2 I FIREARMS FAMILIARIZATION
LESSON 4 I Semiautomatic Rifle/Carbine

Nomenclature of the Semiautomatic Rifle/Carbine (AR-15 style, gas operated system)

Part names, locations and some part designs may vary depending on the specific make and model. Make sure you are familiar with the part names, locations, and functions for the weapon that you use. Refer to the Semiautomatic Rifle Nomenclature Diagram.

Following is the nomenclature associated with the semiautomatic rifle/carbine, a description of the parts of a semiautomatic rifle/carbine, and their functions:

- barrel—provides a path for the fired bullet; its chamber holds the cartridge

- bolt—contains the firing pin, spring, and extractor (internal part)

- buffer/buffer spring—enables the bolt to return after firing (internal part)

- butt—the end of the stock

- chamber—supports the case at rest and during firing (internal part)

- charging handle—enables withdrawal of the bolt to chamber a round

- ejection port—opening that permits the shell to exit the weapon (internal part)

- ejector—expels the shell from the ejection port (internal part of the bolt)

- extractor—grips and pulls the shell from the chamber

- forestock/hand guard—used to support the rifle with the support hand; acts as a heat shield from the barrel

- forward assist—a button assuring that the bolt is locked

- lower receiver group—contains the magazine release, magazine well, trigger housing, and trigger components

- magazine—contains ammunition ready to be chambered

- magazine release—permits removal of the magazine from the firearm

- magazine well—housing for the magazine (internal)

- muzzle flash suppressor—attachment on the barrel's forward end that reduces the flash as burning powder escapes when the bullet exits the barrel

- safety—blocks the hammer from striking the firing pin; prevents firing (located on the left side of the weapon)

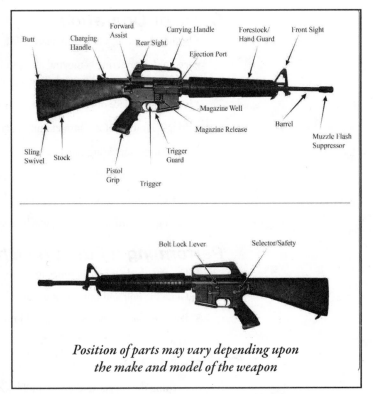

Position of parts may vary depending upon the make and model of the weapon

Semiautomatic rifle

Figure 3-4

- sights (front and rear)—used to align the firearm to the bullet's point of impact

- sling swivels—metal loops affixed to the rifle/carbine to which a carrying strap attaches

- stock—part that enables shoulder support during firing

- take down pins—enables separation of the upper receiver from the lower receiver and allows for fieldstripping and cleaning

- trigger—enables the firearm to fire when pulled

- trigger group—section consisting of the trigger, trigger springs, safety, and all firing mechanism parts

- trigger guard—part of the frame that protects the trigger

- upper receiver group—houses the bolt assembly group *(FA627.3.B., FA627.3.C.)*

How the Semiautomatic Rifle/Carbine Works

A semiautomatic gas operated AR-15 style rifle functions by using the pressurized gas from a fired cartridge tapped from the barrel as the bullet moves past a gas port located under the rifle's front sight base. The gas rushes into the port and down a gas tube which extends into the AR-15's upper receiver. This forces the bolt assembly group rearward resulting in the extraction and ejection of a fired casing from the rifle's chamber. This action also re-cocks the hammer. The bolt assembly group is then forced forward by the buffer spring causing a live round to be picked up from the magazine and seated into the chamber for the next shot.

Cycle of Operation

- loading—seating a loaded magazine into the magazine well

- feeding/chambering—moving the round from the magazine to the chamber by releasing the bolt, picking up the round from the magazine and seating the round into the chamber

- locking—the face of the bolt locks with the breech end of the barrel

- firing—ignition of the primer and firing the cartridge

- unlocking—unseating the bolt from the breech end of the barrel

- extracting—pulling the spent cartridge case from the chamber

- ejecting—pushing the spent cartridge case out of the ejection port

- cocking—returning the firing mechanism to the fire position

Performing a Function Check

1. Operate the bolt several times to make sure it moves freely.

2. Close the bolt and put the safety on.

3. Pull the trigger. The weapon should not work.

4. Move the safety to the fire position.

5. Pull the trigger to the rear, and hold it there. The hammer should fall as you pull the trigger.

6. Keeping the trigger to the rear, pull back the bolt. Allow the bolt to move slowly forward. You should hear a click as the hammer resets.

7. Release and pull the trigger again. The weapon should function properly.

8. Lock the bolt carrier assembly to the rear.

9. Insert an empty magazine into the magazine well until the magazine engages.

10. Depress the magazine release. The magazine should fall free.

Handing the Semiautomatic Rifle/Carbine to Another Person

To hand a rifle/carbine to another person, follow these steps:

1. Ensure the safety is in the on, or engaged, position.

2. Remove the magazine.

3. Lock the bolt assembly group to the rear; physically and visually inspect the chamber to ensure it is unloaded.

4. Hand the semiautomatic rifle/carbine to the person with the muzzle pointed in a safe direction. *(FA611.2.D.)*

The person receiving the firearm should physically and visually inspect the firearm to make sure it is not loaded.

UNIT 3 | AMMUNITION

LESSON 1 | Identification and Maintenance

OBJECTIVES

FA607.3.A. Identify ammunition parts and nomenclature.

FA607.1.A.1. Identify ammunition by appearance and caliber.

FA607.1.A.2. Identify shotgun ammunition by appearance and gauge.

FA607.3.B. Identify any abnormalities or defects on ammunition.

FA607.2.B. Identify proper storage procedures for ammunition.

FA607.2.B.1. Differentiate between duty life and shelf life.

FA607.2. Properly store and handle ammunition.

Cartridge Parts and Types

Please refer to the cartridge diagrams that follow. They illustrate the basic parts of ammunition for a revolver, a pistol, a shotgun, and a rifle/carbine. The definitions for these parts can also be found in the Firearms Glossary.

- *case/casings*—the metal or plastic container that holds all parts of a round of ammunition: primer, powder charge, and bullet

- *rim*—the edge on the base of a cartridge case that stops the progress of the case into the chamber

- *crimp (shotgun only)*—the part of the case mouth that bends inward to grip the bullet; with shotgun shells, the term applies to the closure at the case mouth.

- *headstamp*—markings found on the head of ammunition that indicate caliber or gauge and identify manufacturer

- *shot (shotgun)*—spherical pellets of various sizes, usually made of lead

- *primer*—small, metal cup containing the detonating mixture used to ignite the propellant or powder charge

- *powder*—propellant used in most firearms; produces a large volume of gas when ignited

- *wad(s) (shotgun)*—the only part not found in any other centerfire cartridge; this is used to seal/confine gases; can be made of plastic or compressed cardboard

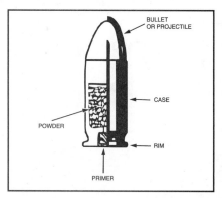

Pistol cartridge   *Figure 3-5*

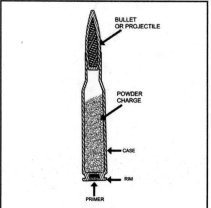

Rifle cartridge   *Figure 3-6*

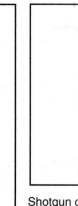
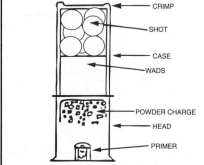

Shotgun cartridge   *Figure 3-7*

- ***bullet***—portion of the cartridge that becomes a projectile when in flight

- ***round***—complete ammunition cartridge that contains all parts of ammunition; a military term meaning one single cartridge *(FA607.3.A.)*

Ammunition can be identified by examining the caliber or gauge found on the cartridge's headstamp. ***Caliber*** is a measurement used to identify different cartridge (projectile) sizes. It is determined by measuring the diameter of the bore of the firearm. This helps identify the correct ammunition for a specific weapon. ***Gauge*** is a measurement of shotgun bores derived from the number of bore-sized balls of lead per pound. For example, 12 balls that fit the bore of a 12-gauge shotgun weigh one pound.

Law enforcement most often uses these caliber and gauge types:

- revolver—.38 Special, the 357 Magnum

Note: You can safely use .38 caliber ammunition in a .357 revolver. However, you cannot use .357 ammunition in a .38 caliber revolver. A .357 cartridge casing is longer than a .38 cartridge and so does not fit into the chamber of a .38 revolver.

- semiautomatic pistol—.40 caliber, .45 caliber, 9 mm, and 10 mm
- shotgun—12 gauge
- rifle/carbine—223 Remington, 9 mm, and 10 mm

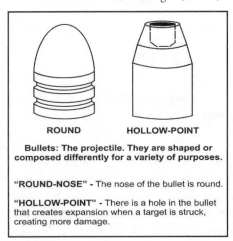

Bullet (projectile) design   *Figure 3-8*

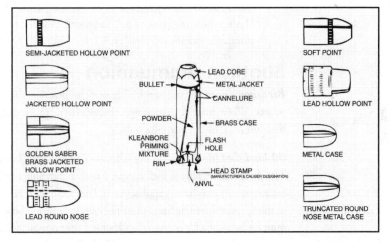

Handgun bullet styles   *Figure 3-9*

Refer to the Bullet (Projectile) Design diagrams. Learn the definitions and ballistic characteristics of each ammunition type so that you can identify them:

- blank round—a round designed for training or noise; the casing's cardboard material becomes a projectile when fired; the projectile cannot penetrate drywall or hollow core doors. However, it can penetrate soft body tissue. When fired at close range, it can cause serious injury or death. Do not discharge in the direction of others. Use extreme caution.

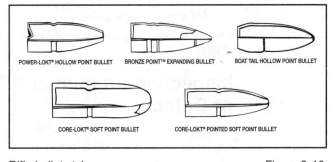

Rifle bullet styles   *Figure 3-10*

- lead round nose—cartridge design that features a solid lead bullet with a round nose; this bullet has a medium velocity. By design, it easily penetrates interior walls or hollow core doors and then ricochets.

- jacketed soft point—one-half to three-quarters of this lead bullet is jacketed with copper; the exposed lead on the flat nose allows for expansion upon impact. Usually of high velocity, this bullet is designed for antipersonnel. The round easily penetrates interior walls and solid doors.

- hollowpoint—lead or copper-jacketed lead with a hollow cavity in the bullet's nose; as the bullet expands upon impact, it expends its kinetic energy. Since a hollowpoint expands quickly, it does not penetrate as deeply as a round-nose bullet. This design reduces ricochet. Usually of high velocity, it delivers maximum shock upon striking a surface of soft tissue.

- full metal jacket—a round-nose lead bullet completely covered with a copper jacket; sometimes called ball ammunition, it is normally of medium to high velocity. Used extensively by the military, it has low expansion and high penetration capabilities. The chance for ricochet is high.

- frangible—normally made of brass or copper dust held together with a resin material that disintegrates upon impact with steel or concrete; it can penetrate hollow core doors, drywall, or thin wood material

- armor piercing—made of solid carbon or tungsten steel coated with bright green Teflon; it has a considerably sharper point than most manufactured rounds. The round can pierce protective body armor or steel. In Florida, its use or possession is illegal for anyone but law enforcement.

- tracer—full metal-jacketed bullet with incendiary material in the casing of its base; when fired, the round can be visually tracked by the burning material. The bullet tip is normally painted red or orange. Having the same velocity as a full metal-jacketed bullet, it is most often used by the military in fully automatic weapons. *(FA607.1.A.1.)*

Shotgun Ammunition

Birdshot is normally used for bird hunting or practice; this shell has a load of small diameter lead or steel shot pellets. When fired at close range, these pellets can be dangerous and cause injury. Law enforcement uses birdshot for training purposes only.

00 buckshot (double-aught buckshot)—The standard 2 3/4-inch shell contains nine .33 caliber lead pellets. The three-inch magnum shell contains twelve .32 caliber pellets. The spread pattern from a 20-inch barrel is approximately one-inch spread per yard. For example, at 20 yards, the spread pattern equals 20 inches. Because of the spread pattern, officers must use extreme caution when shooting 00 buckshot in populated areas. They must be aware of what is around and behind the targeted area. Accurate maximum distance for law enforcement purposes is approximately 40 yards. The pellets penetrate solid wood doors, drywall, and wood walls at close range. The pellets can ricochet when they hit hard surfaces.

A **rifled slug** is a single, hollow lead bullet that weighs from 7/8 to 1 1/8 ounce. It is .72 caliber with an effective range of approximately 100 yards. The round penetrates most materials but not solid steel. *(FA607.1.A.2.)*

Inspecting Ammunition for Possible Abnormalities or Defects

It is important to know how to inspect ammunition for functionality and dependability. Your ammunition may be the correct type, caliber, and gauge, but it must still be checked for damage or defects. This section covers the most common types of ammunition defects and how to inspect ammunition for those abnormalities or defects.

When inspecting ammunition, these abnormalities and defects may be encountered:

- scrape—indentation in the case that may weaken the case wall; a scrape makes a layer of the case wall metal look as if it has been scratched or torn away
- dent—dimple or depression in the case; the case looks like someone struck it with a hard object, crushing part of it inward
- corrosion—layering of the case with oxidation or foreign material, such as mold, fungi layers, congealed oil, and lubricants
- puncture—actual tear, avulsion, or rip that looks like an opening in the case body *(FA607.3.B.)*

Inspecting ammunition before loading is important. As you do so, identify and separate less than perfect rounds from service ammunition. Before heading out on duty, check your ammunition to make sure it operates properly.

1. Make sure that the casing is free of defects. Look and feel for scrapes, dents, corrosion, and punctures.

2. Determine that the projectile is firmly seated in the casing. Feel both ends of the ammunition to make sure the projectile is not loose.

3. Ensure that the primer is seated properly and free of indentations. Look at and feel the cartridge to see if the primer is flush with the rim.

4. Establish that the rim is free of defects. Look and feel for scrapes, dents, corrosion, and punctures.

Ammunition Storage

Properly storing and handling your ammunition also helps prevent defects. When storing ammunition, following the manufacturer's recommendations is crucial. Respect the manufacturer's original design: Do not alter the ammunition.

Environmental conditions affect the ammunition's shelf and duty life expectancy and may cause malfunctions when you use the cartridges. Keep your ammunition in a cool place where moisture is minimal. Do not use cartridges that have been water soaked as seeping water may affect the primers. Also, avoid keeping ammunition in locations where there is atmospheric heat, such as inside a closed vehicle, or where there is radiant heat (for example, inside a box in a sunny location). Follow your agency's standard operating procedure for storing ammunition. *(FA607.2.B.)*

Duty life is the recommended time (normally expressed in months) for which you can expect ammunition to be reliable when used on duty. Ammunition used on duty is exposed to environmental elements, such as heat and humidity, which cause it to deteriorate more quickly. Its duty life is shorter than its shelf life. It is recommended that ammunition be replaced annually.

Shelf life is the recommended time (normally expressed in years) for which you can expect ammunition to be reliable from manufacture time to issue time. Duty life is factored into shelf life, which also depends on care and protection of the ammunition. Therefore, it is important to write on the box the date you received and stored ammunition. That helps determine how long it stays on the shelf. *(FA607.2.B.1.)*

Section Vocabulary

birdshot

bullet

caliber

case

crimp

*double-aught buckshot
(00 buckshot)*

duty life

gauge

headstamp

powder

primer

rifled slug

rim

round

shelf life

shot

wad(s)

Handling Ammunition Safely

Proper maintenance of ammunition involves any care that helps provide the most safety when using and inspecting ammunition. Improperly maintained ammunition may cause a weapon to fail to fire or function. In a self-defense situation, serious injury or death may result.

Use only factory-loaded ammunition from a reputable manufacturer. Do not drop or throw ammunition—it may discharge. Do not place ammunition in the radio holder of your patrol vehicle. Contact with an electrical impulse can cause ammunition to discharge.

Avoid using solvents and lubricants when handling ammunition. To prevent solvents on your hands from seeping into the primers, wash your hands before handling ammunition. Solvents and lubricants may cause a failure to fire malfunction.

Do not use reloads for duty ammunition. Reloads are cartridges that have been prepared using previously fired brass cases. They are not as reliable as new ammunition. Also, using reloaded ammunition may void the warranties of many firearms. *(FA607.2.)*

UNIT 4 | FUNDAMENTALS OF MARKSMANSHIP
LESSON 1 | Handgun

Accurate shooting results from knowing and correctly applying these fundamentals of marksmanship: grip, sight alignment, sight picture, trigger control and follow-through, and proper stances and shooting positions. Breath control and concentration are also essentials for accuracy. The fundamentals of marksmanship are the same for both a revolver and semiautomatic pistol.

Grip

One Hand—Follow these steps to grip the handgun properly with one hand:

1. Place the handgun in your shooting hand so that its barrel points in the direction desired. Place the webbing of the shooting hand around the handgun's backstrap.

2. Center the weapon between your thumb and forefinger. It should fit directly into the V of the web of your hand between your thumb and forefinger. Your forearm, hand, and weapon should form a straight line.

3. Apply a firm, uniform grip to the firearm. Use the same firmness you would in a handshake. Gripping too tightly can cause the hand and arm to shake; muscle spasms may begin after a short time. Gripping too loosely does not give you the necessary control of the weapon or its recoil.

4. Rest the thumb of your shooting hand along the frame. Keep the trigger finger (index finger of the shooting hand) outside the trigger guard until on target and ready to fire.

Two Hands—The two-handed grip lets you steady your shooting hand with your support hand. It thereby provides maximum support while firing.

Follow these steps to grip the handgun properly with two hands:

1. Follow the steps for the one-handed grip.

2. With your thumb and index finger in proper grip positions along the frame, wrap the fingers of your support hand tightly around the fingers of your shooting hand.

3. Place your support hand's thumb on or just below the thumb of your shooting hand, holding the weapon firmly. Do not overlap your thumbs or place the thumb of your support hand over the back or in the web of your shooting hand. *(FA605.2.)*

Sight Alignment and Sight Picture

Sight alignment is the relationship of the front sight and rear sight with the shooter's eye(s). It occurs when the top of the front sight is level with the rear sight's top edge and centered in the rear sight aperture or notch. Keep your eye(s) centered behind the rear and front sights. This is the most important aspect of aiming.

OBJECTIVES

FA605.2. Acquire a proper grip with a handgun.

FA605.4. Obtain sight alignment with a handgun.

FA605.5. Obtain sight picture with a handgun.

FA605.6. Pull/squeeze the trigger until the handgun discharges (trigger control).

FA605.7. Release pressure on the trigger until the trigger reengages (trigger reset).

FA605.8. Follow through after the cartridge is fired.

FA608.5. Assume an appropriate shooting position with the handgun from behind cover.

FA605.1.A. Identify shooting stances to use when shooting a handgun.

FA605.10. Shoot a handgun while using a flashlight.

FA605.10.A. Identify techniques for shooting a handgun while using a flashlight.

For proper sight alignment,

1. Look along the top of the weapon's sight plane.

2. Center the top of the front sight on a line along the top of the rear sight.

3. Center the top of the front sight horizontally and vertically in the rear aperture or notch. (Figure 3-11)

Sight Alignment
and Sight Picture

Figure 3-11

This is the most natural method of sight alignment. Your eye instinctively accomplishes this task with little training. This method also causes the least inconsistency from shot to shot. *(FA605.4.)*

Sight picture is the relationship between the eye, front sight, rear sight, and target. Follow these steps:

1. Look through the notch of the rear sight.

2. Align the top of the front sight with the top of the rear sight with equal space on each side.

3. Place the sights on the target.

4. Focus on the front sight. (The target will be blurry.)

5. Use your dominant eye to align sights.

Though it is recommended to keep both eyes open during firing, this practice may take time to get used to. Keeping both eyes open during firing has been known to improve the focus of your dominant eye and sight picture, as well as improve your accuracy, while providing increased peripheral vision.

The act of firing without disturbing sight alignment and the muzzle is a fundamental of marksmanship. Failure to control the trigger will result in improper sight alignment and motion in the muzzle when the hammer falls. *(FA605.5.)*

Note: Controlling the trigger is a mental process; pulling the trigger is a physical process.

Breath Control

Breath control is important in the aiming process. If you breathe while trying to aim, the rise and fall of your chest moves the handgun vertically.

To hold your breath properly, inhale, exhale normally, and stop at the moment when you pause between breaths. The extended pause between breaths (**respiratory pause**) is the best time to fire the shot(s).

Trigger Control and Follow-through

Trigger control results when the trigger finger pulls the trigger straight back with increasing yet constant and steady pressure until the firearm discharges. Trigger control, the most difficult handgun fundamental to master, often determines a shot's success.

To control the trigger properly,

1. The preferred method is to contact the trigger with your index finger. Be careful not to touch the firearm elsewhere with your trigger finger. After you place your trigger finger on the trigger, keep it there until you fire.

2. When controlling the trigger, make sure to move your trigger finger straight back. This will release the hammer and discharge the handgun. *(FA605.6.)*

3. Control the trigger reset after the weapon discharges. Release pressure on the trigger until the trigger reengages. Dry drills help you improve your ability to reset the trigger without disturbing sight alignment or your muzzle. *(FA605.7.)*

Improper trigger control causes more misses than any other action in the firing process. Slightly off-center pressure of the trigger can cause the firearm to move and disturb your sight alignment and muzzle. No one can hold a firearm completely motionless. Jerking the trigger disturbs your aim before the bullet leaves the barrel. Flinching—a human reflex caused by anticipating the firearm's recoil—also disturbs your aim, but a steady, controlled squeeze of the trigger will yield the best result.

Control the trigger during the shot while keeping the sight alignment and sight picture correct. When the sight picture settles, the pressure remains steady until the handgun fires. Focus on perfect aim as you apply trigger control. A firm handgrip is essential for good trigger control. Apply pressure on the trigger with the trigger finger only and without disturbing sight picture or sight alignment. Use the same grip for each shot. By placing your trigger finger in the same position on the trigger each time, you can move the trigger straight to the rear with the same results each time.

Follow-through involves maintaining sight alignment before, during, and after firing a round. You must maintain proper grip, stance, and finger placement on the trigger. You must also acquire sight picture, re-establishing it each time you fire a weapon. Do not try to force a handgun down at the time of discharge (anticipating recoil), but rather keep your body and weapon in a controlled position during discharge. *(FA605.8.)*

Concentration

Concentration on the fundamentals is key to accurate and consistent shooting. For improved proficiency you should apply all the fundamentals simultaneously.

Shooting Stances for a Handgun

Stance is the posture a shooter assumes while firing a shot. Proper stance is important when using firearms tactically or defensively. It gives the shooter more stability. From a steady and efficient shooting stance or stable shooting position, a shooter has the ability to move and engage targets properly.

A handgun can be fired from a number of stances: Isosceles, Weaver, Modified Weaver, hip, and tactical ready, as well as two-handed high point, barricade (standing and kneeling), and prone.

The Isosceles stance most closely represents the instinctive response to a threat. This stance minimizes the exposed areas of the body not covered by armor.

Standing Position

To shoot a handgun from the standing position,

1. Stand with your feet approximately shoulder-width apart.

2. Keep your weight on the balls your feet.

3. Bend your knees slightly so you can move in any direction.

4. Move the foot on your weapon (shooting) side back slightly.

5. Square your head and shoulders to the target. Keep your back straight and head erect (unless you are using the Modified Weaver stance.)

6. Draw your weapon, raising it to eye level. Do not bend your head down to the weapon's level.

7. After you fire the weapon, continue to cover your target and scan for additional threats.

Kneeling Position

To fire a handgun from the kneeling position

1. Begin in the standing position.

2. Draw your weapon and step forward with your opposite foot.

3. Drop your shooting side knee to the ground, keeping the muzzle of your weapon pointed downrange. Keep your finger off the trigger.

4. As you drop your knee, bring your arms up, raising your weapon to eye level. Keep your head erect and your back straight.

From the waist up, the kneeling and standing positions do not differ. From the waist down, the kneeling position differs only in that your shooting side knee is on the ground and your support knee is up.

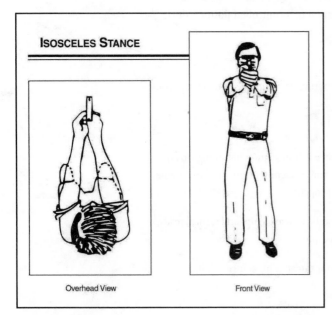

Isosceles stance

Figure 3-12

Isosceles Stance

To shoot a handgun from the Isosceles shooting stance,

1. Stand with your feet approximately shoulder-width apart. Keep your weight on the balls of your feet.

2. Bend your knees slightly to allow for movement.

3. Stand with your head and shoulders square to the target, body weight forward.

4. Lock your arms straight out in front, and bring the handgun to eye level. (Figure 3-12)

Weaver Stance

To fire the handgun from the Weaver stance,

1. Stand at a 45-degree angle to the target, with your feet shoulder-width apart. Your weapon-side foot is to the rear.

2. Bend your knees slightly so your weight is on the balls of your feet. Keep your shoulders at a 45-degree angle to the target.

3. The weapon arm should be almost fully extended while your support arm is bent at the elbow. The elbows should be fairly close together not allowing them to flare out.

4. Push forward with your shooting hand and pull back with your support hand to create isometric tension.

5. Bring your weapon to eye level and keep your head erect.

Modified Weaver Stance

The Modified Weaver Stance is similar to the Weaver Stance except the weapon arm is locked out straight. Other elements such as foot position may be modified because of a person's physical characteristics.

Hip Shooting Stance

When you are within arm's reach (three to four feet away) of a subject, use the hip shooting stance. If you extend your arms to prepare to shoot your firearm, the subject would be close enough to grab your firearm or knock your hand and firearm to the side.

To fire the handgun from a hip shooting stance, you have two options:

Option 1—Shoot your handgun from the one-handed hip stance:

1. Assume the interview stance:

    a. Stand with head, hips and feet aligned.

    b. Stand with your feet approximately shoulder-width apart with knees slightly bent.

    c. Angle your body to the subject with the weapon side away.

    d. Keep your hands above your waist.

2. Draw your firearm.

3. Place the elbow of your weapon arm against the side of your body above the holster.

4. Point your forearm, hand, and firearm against the side of your body above the holster.

5. Put your support hand in a defensive position in front of your body. Keep it close to your chest to guard against attack, should you not draw your firearm quickly enough.

Option 2 (less preferable than Option 1)—Shoot your handgun from the two-handed hip stance:

1. Assume the interview stance.

2. Draw the weapon and keep your weapon-side elbow at a 90-degree angle (in an L shape). Keep your elbow against the body, slightly above the holster.

    a. Keep your forearm and wrist and the barrel of your handgun parallel to the ground and pointed at the subject.

    b. Grip the handgun a little more tightly than normal. This helps you keep your wrist straight and makes it more difficult for a subject to take your weapon.

3. Bring your support and shooting hands together in a normal two-handed grip.

    a. Hold your weapon at waist level and both elbows tightly against your body above your gun belt.

    b. Keep your forearm, hand, and weapon horizontal to the ground.

4. With both eyes open and looking at the subject, eye and hand coordination normally adjusts the weapon to the proper aim.

Tactical Ready Stance

At times, you must cover a subject who is ready to take aggressive and perhaps deadly action. In the tactical ready stance, you can see a subject's hands. To take the tactical ready stance, you should assume the standing position described earlier, then lock your arms below your line of sight. In this stance, you will be able to observe the subject's hands/waistline.

Two-Handed, High Point Position

In the two-handed, high point position, you are in the standing or kneeling firing position with your sights on the target.

Barricade Position

A **barricade position** is a position behind cover.

To fire the handgun from the standing barricade position,

1. Start away from the barricade's outside edge.

2. Upon target stimulus or command, draw your firearm and move to cover.

3. Outstretch and lock your arms.

4. Assume a stable standing position.

5. Lean to your weapon side.

   a. Expose the necessary portion of your shoulder and head.

   b. Keep your firearm's muzzle away from and behind the barricade.

   c. Do not let your firearm or hands rest on or touch the barricade. Keep them behind the lateral line of the barricade.

To fire the handgun from the kneeling barricade position,

1. Start away from the barricade's outside edge.

2. Upon target stimulus or command, draw your firearm and move to cover.

3. Point your firearm downrange, and keep your finger off the trigger.

4. Assume a stable kneeling position behind cover.

5. Lean to your weapon side.

   a. Expose the necessary portion of your shoulder and head.

   b. Keep your firearm's muzzle away from and behind the barricade.

   c. Do not let your firearm or hands rest on or touch the barricade. Keep them behind the lateral line of the barricade. *(FA608.5.)*

Prone Position

To fire a handgun from the prone position,

1. Kneel on both knees.

2. Draw the firearm and point it toward the target.

3. Lie on your stomach, face down, using your support hand for stability.

4. Assume a two-handed grip.

To return to a standing position from a prone position,

1. Keeping the firearm pointed in a safe position, use your support hand to rise to a kneeling position.

2. Return the firearm to the holster.

3. Safely stand. *(FA605.1.A)*

General Flashlight Principles

The flashlight's main function is illumination. This includes illumination for movement, navigation, and searching, as well as for identification and engagement of a threat. The flashlight may also be used to control suspects and subjects if the light is bright enough. Its design and ergonomics are critical to its proper and safe use. Firearm and hand sizes are two important factors in choosing an appropriate flashlight.

Generally, using a flashlight lets you make a smooth transition from search to firing mode. The relationship between the flashlight and the bore of the firearm may offer some recoil control so you can place shots efficiently. In reduced light, you can execute all the fundamentals you practiced. Always positively identify a threat before using deadly force.

Varying amounts of light in the confrontation area can work for or against you. When you move quickly from a lighted area to a reduced-light area, your visual acuity may be adversely affected for a period of time. When you move from a dark area to a lighted area, your silhouette may present you as a target.

Whenever possible, consider the options of illumination for movement, navigation, searching, and to identify and control suspects.

Types of Flashlight Grips

"Watchman" grip—The flashlight is held in the support hand with the illuminating end projecting from the index finger side of the hand. The thumb controls the on/off switch with a side-mounted switch near the front of the flashlight; the little or ring finger controls it with a side-mounted switch near the back of the flashlight.

"Law enforcement" or "tactical" grip—The flashlight is held in the support hand with the illuminating end projecting from the little finger on the side of the hand. The thumb controls a rear-mounted switch; the index finger controls a side-mounted switch near the back of the flashlight; the little or ring finger controls a side-mounted switch near the back of the flashlight.

"Syringe" grip—This grip is used with a small (4–6 inch) flashlight with a rear switch and a ring around the grip to give the index and middle fingers a hold. The flashlight is held in the support hand between

Section Vocabulary

barricade position

follow-through

point shooting

respiratory pause

sight alignment

sight picture

stance

trigger control

the index and middle fingers. The switch is pulled back against the base of the hand or the knuckles of the shooting hand, depending on the technique used.

Flashlight: Firearm Techniques

Firing a handgun at night hinders sight alignment (if the weapon has no night sights), the ability to obtain a sight picture, and the ability to identify threats or targets.

You must be able to identify a target or threat before engaging it with your handgun. Ideally, you should fire in reduced light (at night) only at close proximity because of the risk involved in identifying targets and threats. Focus on your weapon's front sight if you can see it. If you cannot, you must use the point shooting technique. ***Point shooting*** is the technique used when you cannot use the sights on your weapon or you have no time to align the sight properly. The handgun becomes an extension of your arm and hand. You use this "extension" to point to the target or threat and fire. Most flashlight-assisted shooting requires point-shooting skills because point shooting can be very effective when the target is in silhouette. Also, flashlight-assisted conditions may alter how you see or use your sights. Again, you should use this method only if you are close to the target or threat. At more than seven yards, seek cover, and evaluate your options. *(FA605.10.)*

The following are techniques for shooting a handgun while using a flashlight.

Ayoob Technique—This technique is thumb-to-thumb; it uses the "watchman" grip. It provides some support for firearm control and good illumination in relationship to the weapon.

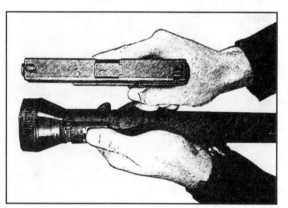

Ayoob technique   *Figure 3-13*

To use this handgun/flashlight method, you should hold the handgun in your shooting hand and the flashlight in your support hand. Then, you should hold your hands out in front of you with your arms extended and hands pressed together at your thumbs. (Figure 3-13)

The light and handgun are side by side, so the light beam and handgun are parallel and point to the same place. You can quickly assume this position and easily identify a target. This method also helps illuminate the handgun sight.

Harries Technique—To perform the Harries technique, you should hold the flashlight in your support hand and the handgun in your shooting hand. Then, put the backs of your hands together. With your hands braced together, you have more control over the handgun. (Figure 3-14)

It is important to remember that using a flashlight at any time will give away your position. Also, the Harries technique is not a natural position to take, and requires practice. The key to the Harries method is properly using the law enforcement or tactical grip. This method illuminates the sights fairly well. *(FA605.10.A.)*

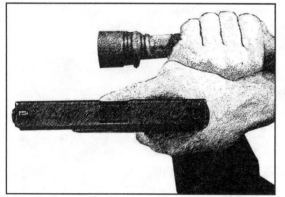

Harries technique   *Figure 3-14*

UNIT 4 | FUNDAMENTALS OF MARKSMANSHIP

LESSON 2 | Shotgun

An officer can improve their proficiency with a shotgun by applying the fundamentals of marksmanship which include grip, stance, sight alignment, sight picture, trigger control, follow-through, breath control, and concentration.

Shooting Stances for the Shotgun

This section teaches you to fire a shotgun from the standing, kneeling, low ready, and barricade positions.

Standing Position

To shoot a shotgun from the standing position, you should follow these steps:

1. Stand with your feet approximately shoulder-width apart and keep your weight on the balls of your feet.

2. Place your weapon-side foot slightly behind your support foot or stand with your head and shoulders square to the target, body weight forward. Keep your weight slightly forward on the balls of your feet. Bend your knees slightly to allow for movement.

3. With your shooting hand, grip the stock with your trigger finger alongside the receiver, and grip the fore-end with your support hand.

4. Shoulder the shotgun by placing the top of the stock between the shoulder and the collar bone so that your cheek naturally touches the comb of the stock.

5. To maintain proper sight alignment, press your cheek firmly against the comb of the stock.

Kneeling Position

To assume the kneeling position, keeping the firearm pointed in a safe direction, you should perform the following steps:

1. Kneel on your strong knee.

2. Extend your support leg toward the target with your foot flat on the ground.

3. Keep your ankle straight and the toe of your shoe in contact with the ground, curled forward by your body weight.

4. Hold the shotgun as you do in the standing position.

Low Ready Position

The low ready position is a position of readiness that allows the officer to immediately begin firing the shotgun or to take appropriate action and is used in the standing or kneeling positions.

OBJECTIVES
FA632.1.A. Identify shooting stances to use when shooting a shotgun.
FA608.5.B. Assume an appropriate shooting stance with the shotgun from behind cover.
FA632.6. Obtain sight alignment using a shotgun.
FA632.7. Obtain sight picture with a shotgun.
FA632.8. Pull/squeeze the trigger until the shotgun discharges (trigger control).
FA632.9. Release pressure on the trigger until the trigger reengages (trigger reset).
FA632.10. Follow through after the shell is fired.

To assume a low ready position, hold the shotgun's butt in the curve of your shoulder and point the barrel toward the ground at an angle of approximately 45 degrees. This helps you use your peripheral vision and quickly react to a threat. Keep the muzzle of the gun pointed up and in a safe direction. *(FA632.1.A)*

You will prepare to get into the low ready standing or kneeling positions from the port arms stance with your weapon across your chest—muzzle pointed in a safe direction, a stance normally used when you move from one safe position to another.

Barricade Position

To assume the barricade position, you would follow these steps:

1. Stand in the open, next to the barricade, with your shotgun in a ready position.

2. Upon target stimulus/command, step behind the barricade and assume a standing or kneeling position.

3. Remove the safety and fire the prescribed number of rounds.

Do not let your weapon touch the barricade's surface. The barricade is cover, not a resting place.

Stand or kneel a safe distance away from the barricade and use the roll-out technique to gain maximum protection from behind cover. Positioning your weapon-side leg to the rear makes you a smaller, harder-to-hit target for the aggressor. *(FA632.1.A, FA608.5.B.)*

Shouldering the Shotgun

To shoulder the shotgun, you must grip the shotgun and place the recoil pad firmly into your shoulder pocket. Properly placing the recoil pad reduces the effect of recoil, helps steady the shotgun, and prevents the shotgun recoil pad from slipping.

To properly shoulder the shotgun, do the following:

1. Hold the stock just behind the trigger guard with your shooting hand by placing your thumb on top of the stock and wrapping your middle, ring, and pinky fingers on the bottom of the stock just behind the trigger guard.

2. Place your trigger finger on the receiver just above the trigger guard.

3. With your support hand, grasp the fore-end from underneath with your thumb on one side and remaining fingers on the other side.

4. Raise the shotgun and place the recoil pad into your shooting shoulder pocket. Your support elbow will be bent and your shooting-side elbow will be raised to create a pocket. To seat the shotgun in your shoulder, pull back with your shooting hand.

Cheek Weld

The cheek weld provides firm contact between your cheek and the comb of the stock. To form a cheek weld, raise the stock to your cheek; do not lower your cheek to the stock. Tightly hold the flesh against the cheekbone so it acts as a buffer. The firm contact between the head, hand, and shotgun enables your head and weapon to recoil as one unit. This aids in rapid recovery between rounds. The cheek weld lets you maintain the same distance behind the receiver, further assisting in correct sight alignment.

Sight Alignment and Sight Picture

Sight alignment is the relationship of the front sight and rear sight with the shooter's eye. It occurs when the top of the front sight is level with the rear sight's top edge and centered in the rear sight. Keep your eye centered behind the rear and front sights.

Modern shotguns use two types of sighting systems: rifle sights and bead sights. Rifle-sighted shotguns have a front and rear sight. To use these sights properly, you must align the front sight with the rear sight. Bead-sighted shotguns have no rear sight. You must focus on the bead, and the barrel should not be visible. *(FA632.6.)*

Sight picture is the relationship between the eye, front sight, rear sight, and target. Follow these steps:

1. Align the top of the front sight with the top of the rear sight with equal space on each side.

2. Place the sights on the target.

3. Focus on the front sight. (The target will be slightly blurry.)

4. Use your dominant eye to align sights. This may be altered if you are cross-eye dominant.

5. For bead sights, align your eye with the top of the receiver. Locate and focus on the bead, placing it on the center mass of the target. *(FA632.7.)*

Breath Control

Breath control is important in the aiming process. If you breathe while trying to aim, the rise and fall of your chest moves the handgun vertically.

To hold your breath properly, inhale, exhale normally, and stop at the moment when you pause between breaths. The extended pause between breaths (respiratory pause) is the optimum time to fire the shot(s).

Trigger Control and Follow-through

Trigger control was previously defined on page 148. The trigger of a shotgun is called a single-action trigger because the hammer is cocked each time the weapon is cycled. The trigger moves only a short distance before the sear trips and the hammer releases. The pressure needed to trip the sear is between four and eight pounds. Control the trigger until the shotgun discharges. *(FA632.8.)*

As the weapon cycles, you must allow the trigger to return to its forward position (reset). Failure to do so prevents the weapon from firing until you release and control the trigger again. *(FA632.9.)*

Proper follow-through involves maintaining sight alignment before, during, and after firing a round. You must maintain proper grip, stance, and finger placement on the trigger. You must also acquire a sight picture each time you fire the shotgun. *(FA632.10.)*

After firing a pump shotgun, you must bring the slide to the rear to extract the spent casing and return it to the forward position to chamber a new round.

Concentration

Concentration on the fundamentals is key to accurate and consistent shooting. For improved proficiency you should apply all the fundamentals simultaneously.

UNIT 4 | FUNDAMENTALS OF MARKSMANSHIP
LESSON 3 | Semiautomatic Rifle/Carbine

OBJECTIVES

FA623.2. Acquire the proper grip with the semiautomatic rifle/carbine.

FA623.1.A. Identify shooting stances to use when shooting a semiautomatic rifle/carbine.

FA608.5.C. Assume an appropriate shooting stance with the semiautomatic rifle/carbine from behind cover.

FA623.3. Shoulder the semiautomatic rifle/carbine.

FA623.4. Obtain the cheek weld with the semiautomatic rifle/carbine.

FA623.6. Obtain sight alignment with the semiautomatic rifle/carbine.

FA623.7. Obtain sight picture with the semiautomatic rifle/carbine.

FA623.8. Control the trigger until the semiautomatic rifle/carbine discharges.

FA623.9. Release pressure on the trigger until the trigger resets.

FA623.10. Follow through after the cartridge is fired.

Accurately shooting a rifle/carbine requires learning the fundamentals of marksmanship. These fundamentals include grip, stance, sight alignment, sight picture, trigger control, follow-through, breath control, and concentration.

Shooting Stances for Semiautomatic Rifle/Carbine

Semiautomatic rifles/carbines are fired from several positions: standing, kneeling, low kneeling, low ready, prone and barricade.

Standing Position

To shoot a semiautomatic rifle/carbine from the standing position,

1. Stand with your feet approximately shoulder-width apart.

2. Keep your weight on the balls of your feet.

3. Bend your knees slightly so you can move in any direction.

4. Move your weapon-side foot back slightly, or stand with your head and shoulders square to the target, body weight forward.

5. With your shooting hand, grip the pistol grip with your trigger finger alongside the receiver. *(FA623.2.)*

6. Place the rifle/carbine butt high against your shoulders so that its sights are at eye level.

7. Place your support hand under the front of the stock/fore-end in a position that best helps you support and steady the rifle/carbine.

8. Lean slightly forward from the waist.

9. Place the butt of the stock between the shoulder and the collar bone so that your cheek naturally touches the top of the stock.

Kneeling Position

To shoot a semiautomatic rifle/carbine from the kneeling position, point the firearm in a safe direction and follow these steps:

1. Kneel on your strong knee.

    a. Keep the rifle's muzzle pointed toward the target.

    b. Keep your finger off the trigger.

2. Extend your support leg toward the target with your foot flat on the ground.

3. Hold the rifle as you do in the standing position.

To assume the low kneeling position,

1. From the kneeling position, lower your weight onto your weapon-side leg.

2. Turn down your ankle.

3. Sit on the inside of your ankle. (Do not sit back too far; doing so causes poor balance.)

4. Hold the semiautomatic rifle/carbine as you do in the standing position.

For all these positions, you should perform the following:

1. Extend your support leg toward the target with your foot flat on the ground.

2. For maximum support, point your toes toward the target.

3. To prevent side movement, turn your support toes slightly inward by pivoting on your heel. When in position, you may push your support foot forward or pull it back slightly to lower or raise the muzzle.

4. Position the lower part of your support leg to provide maximum support for controlling the semiautomatic rifle/carbine. From a front view, the lower support leg appears nearly vertical. In this position, your support leg supports your body weight.

5. Place the back of the triceps of your support arm against the forward part of your knee.

6. Do not rest your elbow on your knee.

Low Ready Position

Use the low ready position only in the standing or kneeling positions. It is a position of readiness to begin firing the semiautomatic rifle/carbine or take appropriate action.

1. Hold the semiautomatic rifle/carbine's butt in your shoulder pocket.

2. Point the barrel at an angle of approximately 45 degrees with the ground. This helps you use your peripheral vision and quickly react to a threat.

You may also begin from the port arms position, normally used when moving from one safe position to another: Hold your weapon across your chest. Keep the muzzle pointed up in a safe direction.

Prone Position

To shoot a semiautomatic rifle/carbine from the prone position,

1. Stand facing the target, and place your support hand on the stock/pistol grip in front of the trigger guard.

2. Grasp the grip portion of the stock/pistol with your shooting hand.

3. Spread your feet, shifting your weight slightly to the rear.

4. Kneel on both knees.

5. Lean forward and use your support hand to ease your body to the ground.

6. Place your support elbow on the ground.

7. Gripping the stock/pistol grip with your shooting hand, place the semiautomatic rifle/carbine's butt into your shooting shoulder pocket.

8. Grasp the small of the stock/pistol grip with your shooting hand.

9. Lower your weapon-side elbow to the ground so that your shoulders are approximately level.

10. Place your cheek on the stock in a position where you can obtain proper sight alignment.

11. Do not rest the magazine on your arm or let it touch the ground.

12. Position your body behind the rifle to absorb recoil.

The prone position is steadier than standing and kneeling positions, easier to assume, and presents a lower profile. You can easily adapt it to the use of cover and support. *(FA623.1.A.)*

Barricade Position

To assume the barricade position, you should stand in the open, next to the barricade, with your rifle/carbine in a ready position. Upon target stimulus/command, you should step back behind the barricade and assume a standing or kneeling position. Finally, remove the safety and fire the prescribed number of rounds.

Do not let your weapon touch the barricade's surface. The barricade is cover, not a resting place.

Stand or kneel a safe distance away from the barricade, and use the roll-out technique to gain maximum protection from behind cover. Positioning your weapon-side leg to the rear makes you a smaller, harder-to-hit target for the aggressor. *(FA608.5.C.)*

Shouldering the Semiautomatic Rifle/Carbine

To shoulder the semiautomatic rifle/carbine, you must place the rifle butt firmly into your shoulder pocket. Properly placing the butt reduces the effect of recoil, helps steady the rifle, and prevents the rifle butt from slipping into the shoulder.

To properly shoulder the rifle, do the following:

1. Hold the stock just behind the trigger guard with your shooting hand by placing your thumb on top of the stock and wrapping your middle, ring, and pinky fingers on the bottom of the stock just behind the trigger guard.

2. Place your trigger finger on the outside of the stock just above the trigger guard.

3. With your support hand, grasp the forward portion of the stock from underneath with your thumb on one side and remaining fingers on the other side.

4. Raise the rifle and place the butt of the stock into your shooting shoulder pocket. Your support elbow will be bent and your shooting-side elbow will be raised to create a pocket. To seat the rifle in your shoulder, pull back with your shooting hand. *(FA623.3.)*

Cheek Weld

The cheek weld provides firm contact between your cheek and the stock. To form a cheek weld, place your cheek firmly on the stock. The firm contact between your cheek and rifle enables your head and weapon to recoil as one unit. This aids in rapid recovery between rounds. *(FA623.4.)*

Sight Alignment and Sight Picture

Sight alignment is the relationship of the front and rear sights on a weapon. Sight picture is the relationship between the eye, front sight, rear sight, and the target.

For proper sight alignment and sight picture, you may try the following options:

1. Look through the rear sight aperture (hole or peep).

2. Align the top of the front sight in the center of the rear sight aperture.

3. Use your dominant eye to focus on the front sight. This may be altered if you are cross-eyed dominant.

4. Align the sights on the center mass of the target (the target will be blurry). *(FA623.6., FA623.7.)*

Breath Control

Breath control is important in the aiming process. If you breathe while trying to aim, the rise and fall of your chest moves the handgun vertically.

To hold your breath properly, inhale, exhale normally, and stop at the moment when you pause between breaths. The extended pause between breaths (respiratory pause) is the best time to fire the shot(s).

Trigger Control and Follow-through

Trigger control was previously defined on page 148. Place your trigger finger on the trigger. After you place your trigger finger on the trigger, keep it there until you fire *(FA623.8.)*. After the round discharges, allow the trigger to reset forward quickly. Your trigger finger should not lose contact with trigger. *(FA623.9.)*

Follow-through involves maintaining sight alignment before, during, and after firing a round. You must maintain proper grip, shooting stance, and finger placement on the trigger. You must also acquire a sight picture each time you fire the rifle/carbine. *(FA623.10.)*

Concentration

Concentration on the fundamentals is key to accurate and consistent shooting. For improved proficiency you should apply all the fundamentals simultaneously.

UNIT 5 | DRAWING AND HOLSTERING A HANDGUN

LESSON 1 | Drawing and Holstering a Handgun

OBJECTIVES

FA602.2. Disengage the holster retention device(s) for a holstered handgun.

FA602.4. Draw the handgun upward from a holster with the retention devices unfastened.

FA602.3. Acquire a proper grip on a holstered handgun.

FA601.5. Secure the handgun in the holster using retention device(s).

FA601.4.B.1. Use the thumb of the shooting hand on the rear of the slide to prevent cocking the semiautomatic pistol.

Section Vocabulary

handgun

Drawing a Handgun

Handgun refers to either the revolver or the semiautomatic pistol. The procedures are the same for both weapons. To draw a handgun properly, start in the shooting stance, hands near waist level, away from your weapon. On command, disengage the safety and holster retention devices and establish a proper grip. *(FA602.2.)*

To attain the proper grip, you should perform the following steps:

1. Keep your hand high on the backstrap.
2. Wrap your fingers around the grip.
3. Draw the handgun in an upward motion, keeping your trigger finger outside the trigger guard and off the trigger. *(FA602.4.)*
4. Lift the handgun upward so its muzzle clears the top of your holster. (Remember to keep your trigger finger outside the trigger guard.)
5. Thrust the muzzle straight toward the target as the support hand joins the shooting hand and firearm to form the proper two-handed shooting grip. If no threat is present, keep the muzzle pointed in a safe direction. *(FA602.3.)*

Holstering a Handgun

To holster a handgun, you should do the following:

1. Maintain a proper grip and keep your finger off the trigger and outside the trigger guard.
2. In the reverse order from drawing, smoothly return the handgun to your holster until you seat it properly.
3. Align the retention device components, and secure them together until locked. *(FA601.5.)*

Note: It is recommended for the semiautomatic pistol to use the thumb of your shooting hand on the rear of the slide to prevent the slide from moving to the rear while holstering. *(FA601.4.B.1.)*

UNIT 6 I LOADING AND UNLOADING

LESSON 1 I **Revolver**

Loading a Revolver

Select and adjust a gun belt to fit your waist. The belt should include a holster, belt keepers, speed loaders and speed loader case. Carry your speed loader case between your belt buckle and holster on your weapon side. For training and qualification, carry your extra ammunition in your shooting-side pants pocket.

Perform the following steps to fill a speed loader:

1. Inspect ammunition for proper caliber and defects.

2. Hold the speed loader in the fingers of your support hand so the charge holes face upward.

3. Unlock the speed loader.

4. With your shooting hand, place cartridges rim down in the charge holes.

5. Lock the cartridges in the speed loader.

6. Properly store the speed loader in the speed loader pouch. *(FA603.1.)*

To load a revolver, follow these steps:

1. Keep your finger outside the trigger guard.

2. Always keep the muzzle pointed in a safe direction. *(FA603.3.)*

3. Open the cylinder.

4. Locate and operate the cylinder release latch. *(FA603.4.)*

5. Place the revolver frame in your support hand, and then push/press the cylinder out of the frame with the ring and middle fingers of your support hand. *(FA603.5.)*

6. Cradle the revolver in your support hand just above your waistline, close to your body.

Hand Loading

1. With your two center fingers holding the cylinder open and your pinky and index fingers controlling the frame, position the revolver so its muzzle points at the ground.

2. Hold one cartridge between the thumb and index finger of your shooting hand.

3. Push the cartridge into a chamber of the cylinder.

4. With your thumb and fingers on the cylinder and barrel pointed towards the ground, rotate the cylinder and continue inserting cartridges until the cylinder chambers are full.

OBJECTIVES

FA603.1. Insert ammunition into a speed loader for a revolver.

FA603.3. Point the muzzle of the revolver in a safe direction.

FA603.4. Disengage the revolver's cylinder release latch.

FA603.5. Push/press the revolver's cylinder out of frame alignment.

FA603.7. Insert ammunition into the revolver's cylinder by hand.

FA603.6. Insert the ammunition into the revolver's cylinder using a speed loader.

FA604.4. Extract the spent revolver cartridge casings.

FA604.5. Inspect the cylinder chambers to ensure that all spent cartridge casings have been extracted.

5. When you have loaded all chambers, push the cylinder closed with your support hand thumb.

6. As you remove your two center fingers, rotate the cylinder until it locks in place. *(FA603.7.)*

Partial Hand Loading

When loading with less than six rounds, place each round together, leaving no space in between rounds. For revolvers where the cylinder rotates counter clockwise, the first round should be placed to the right of the top strap so the cylinder can rotate; place a live round in front of the barrel in line with the firing pin. For revolvers where the cylinder rotates clockwise, the first round should be placed to the left of the top strap so the cylinder can rotate; place a live round in front of the barrel in line with the firing pin. As you close the cylinder, it should be positioned so that the rounds fire in succession. *(FA603.7.)*

Partial load

Figure 3-15

Cylinder placement with partial load

Figure 3-16

Speed Loading

1. Grasp the loader's turn or push knob with the first three fingers of your shooting hand.

2. Align the cartridges protruding from the speed loader with the chambers in the cylinder.

3. Insert the cartridges as a unit into the chambers.

4. Turn or push the release knob so all the cartridges fall into the cylinder.

5. Allow the speed loader to drop to the ground.

6. Push the cylinder closed with your support hand thumb.

7. Use your support hand thumb and forefinger to rotate the cylinder until it locks into place. *(FA603.6.)*

Unloading

1. Hold the revolver in your shooting hand, and point it in a safe direction.

2. Locate and operate the cylinder release latch.

3. Open the cylinder by pushing it from the frame.

4. With your support hand under the trigger guard, use the two center fingers of your support hand to push open the cylinder and your index and little fingers to control the frame. (Place your index finger over the top strap and your pinky finger over the hammer.)

5. To unload the empty casings, cradle the revolver in your support hand. Then, hold the revolver vertically with its muzzle pointed up and push down on or strike the ejector rod using your thumb or the open palm of your shooting hand to eject the casings. Let the casings fall directly to the ground. Do not catch them. After unloading the revolver, visually inspect the cylinder chambers to ensure they are all empty. *(FA604.4., FA604.5.)*

UNIT 6 | LOADING AND UNLOADING
LESSON 2 | Semiautomatic Pistol

Select and adjust a gun belt to fit your waist. The belt should include a holster, belt keepers, and a magazine pouch. Carry the magazine pouch on the support side in a vertical position. When placing magazines in the pouch, face the front of the magazine toward the center of your body.

To load a magazine, perform the following steps:

1. Inspect ammunition for proper caliber and defects.

2. Hold the magazine with the follower facing up.

3. Pick up the ammunition and place the cartridge on the follower so its rim faces the back of the magazine, and sits in front of the magazine lips.

4. With your thumb, push the cartridge down to depress the follower into the magazine. Continue pressing down until the cartridge is under the magazine lips.

5. Continue filling until the magazine is full. Place only the correct number of rounds in the magazine. Do not add extra rounds.

6. Tap the back of the magazine on your palm to assure that the cartridges are seated.

7. Properly store the magazine in its pouch. *(FA613.5.A.)*

OBJECTIVES

FA613.5.A. Load the magazine for the semiautomatic pistol.

FA613.2. Point the muzzle of the semiautomatic pistol in a safe direction.

FA613.5. Insert a loaded magazine into the magazine well of the semiautomatic pistol.

FA613.6. Chamber a cartridge with the semiautomatic pistol.

FA614.4. Remove the magazine from the semiautomatic pistol.

FA614.5. Eject the cartridge from the chamber of the semiautomatic pistol.

To load a semiautomatic pistol, use your shooting hand to draw the pistol from your holster. While doing so, always keep the barrel pointed in a safe direction. *(FA613.2.)*

1. Open the magazine pouch with your support hand, and remove a magazine.

2. While pulling up on the magazine, place your index finger along the front of the magazine.

3. Holding the weapon in your shooting hand, bring it close to your body and angle the magazine well slightly inward.

4. Use your index finger to guide the magazine into the magazine well.

5. Push the magazine into the magazine well with enough force to lock the magazine into place. *(FA613.5.)*

6. Chamber a round by pulling the slide all the way to the rear and releasing, letting the slide travel forward on its own (slingshot; do not ride the slide forward). *(FA613.6.)*

7. De-cock/disengage if applicable.

The process of de-cocking varies, depending on the semiautomatic pistol's type: For Smith and Wesson, Beretta, and Ruger pistols, push the de-cock/safety lever down and then up with the thumb of your support hand. For a pistol with spring-loaded de-cock/safety lever, push the lever down with your shooting hand thumb and release. For Sig Sauer and HK pistols, push the de-cock lever down with your shooting hand and release.

To unload an equipped semiautomatic pistol, you should first engage the safety and then remove the magazine, holding the pistol in your shooting hand with the trigger finger outside the trigger guard. Press the magazine release button with your shooting hand thumb. Let the magazine fall to the ground. Do not attempt to catch it. *(FA614.4.)*

To eject the round from the chamber, use your support hand thumb and index finger to grab the slide and pull it to the rear several times. As you pull the slide back for the last time, push the slide stop up with your shooting hand thumb until the slide locks to the rear in the open position. Keep the muzzle pointed in a safe direction at all times. Make sure that your hand or fingers do not cover the pistol's ejection port. With the slide locked back, tilt the weapon and physically and visually inspect to make sure the chamber and magazine well are empty. *(FA614.5.)*

Empty Gun Reload

When the slide locks back due to an empty gun, you must reload. Remove your finger from the trigger. Press the magazine release, which allows the empty magazine to fall to the ground; do this while bringing the gun close to your body, angling the magazine well slightly inward. At the same time, retrieve a loaded magazine with your support hand and insert it into the magazine well. Chamber a live round and reassess the threat.

UNIT 6 | LOADING AND UNLOADING
LESSON 3 | Shotgun

Perform these steps to load a shotgun:

1. Grip the shotgun by the stock with your shooting hand. *(FA630.1.)*

2. Ensure the safety is engaged. *(FA630.3.)*

3. While gripping the shotgun, keep your trigger finger alongside the frame and keep the barrel pointed in a safe direction. *(FA630.2.)*

4. With your support hand, grasp the fore-end/slide and move it forward forcefully until the action locks into place. *(FA630.4.)*

You are now ready to load the ammunition.

1. Point the muzzle in a safe direction.

2. Choose the proper ammunition for your shotgun by finding the gauge on the headstamp.

3. Hold the shell in your support hand, and insert it into the magazine tube through the bottom of the receiver, crimped end first and brass to the rear.

4. Use your thumb to push the shell until it locks or clicks into the magazine tube.

5. Repeat Steps 1 through 3 until your magazine tube is full. *(FA630.5.)*

To chamber a round,

1. Hold the shotgun stock in your shooting hand, with its barrel pointed in a safe direction.

2. Depress the fore-end/slide release with your shooting hand index finger.

3. With your support hand, grip the fore-end/slide from underneath and pull it all the way to the rear. This moves a shell from the magazine tube onto the carrier.

4. Push the fore-end/slide forward forcefully until it locks in place. This closes the action and chambers a shell.

Make sure that none of your fingers are between the rear of the fore-end and the receiver. This can cause injury. *(FA630.6.)*

To unload your shotgun,

1. Engage the safety.

2. Hold your shotgun by the grip with your shooting hand, and point the muzzle in a safe direction. *(FA631.1.)*

3. With a round in the chamber, depress the action/slide release with your trigger finger. *(FA631.3.)*

OBJECTIVES

FA630.1. Hold the shotgun by the stock when loading.

FA630.3. Engage/move the safety.

FA630.2. When loading the shotgun, point the barrel in a safe direction.

FA630.4. Move the fore-end/slide forward, away from the receiver.

FA630.5. Insert shotgun shells into the magazine tube.

FA630.6. Chamber a shell when shells are inserted into the magazine tube of the shotgun.

FA631.1. Hold the loaded shotgun by the grip.

FA631.3. Engage the action/slide release of the loaded shotgun.

FA631.4. Remove any chambered shell through the ejection port of the shotgun.

FA631.5. Remove the shell(s) from the magazine tube of the shotgun.

FA631.6. Inspect the chamber and magazine tube of the unloaded shotgun to ensure that no shell remains.

4. Grip the fore-end/slide with your support hand.

5. Slowly pull the fore-end/slide to the rear until you expose the shell.

6. With your support hand, reach over the top and remove the chambered shell. *(FA631.4.)*

7. With the fore-end/slide two-thirds to the rear, push the shell carrier up into the receiver.

8. Place your support hand on the rear of the fore-end/slide, covering the loading port as you pull the slide to the rear and catch the shell from the magazine loading port.

To remove the remaining shells from the magazine tube, you should place your support hand thumb and index finger inside the receiver through the loading port and press the shell latch/stop against the receiver. This releases a round from the magazine tube *(FA631.5.)*. When you clear all rounds from the magazine tube, visually and physically inspect the chamber and magazine tube to make sure that there are no shells in the chamber. *(FA631.6.)*

Tactical Loading

A *tactical load* is a technique used to reload in a tactical situation. (Tactical loading is the preferred method.)

1. Point your shotgun's barrel in a safe direction or at your target.

2. While gripping your shotgun, keep your trigger finger alongside the frame. Pull the fore-end/slide to the rear to open the ejection port.

3. Wrap your support hand under your weapon, holding one round just below the ejection port opening, brass end toward the rear.

4. Roll the live round into the weapon though the open ejection port.

5. Close the action by pushing the fore-end/slide forward with your support hand, chambering the round.

6. With your support hand load the other rounds into your weapon through the loading port into the magazine tube.

UNIT 6 | LOADING AND UNLOADING
LESSON 4 | Semiautomatic Rifle/Carbine

To load a semiautomatic rifle/carbine, follow the following steps:

1. Load the magazine.

2. As you prepare the rifle/carbine, keep it pointed in a safe direction. Tap the back of the magazine to ensure that you seat the rounds properly.

3. Hold the rifle/carbine by its pistol grip with your shooting hand. Make sure to keep your trigger finger alongside the frame.

4. Engage the safety.

5. With the magazine properly aligned with the magazine well, push the magazine into the magazine well until the magazine locks into place.

6. To make sure the magazine is locked in place, try to pull it out. *(FA621.4.)*

7. Keeping the weapon pointed in a safe direction, pull the charging handle fully to the rear and release it. This allows the bolt to go forward, feeding a round into the chamber. *(FA621.5.)*

To unload the semiautomatic rifle/carbine, keeping the firearm pointed in a safe direction, you should perform the following steps:

1. Engage the safety.

2. Grip the rifle/carbine firmly and steadily so you do not lose control or drop the weapon as you unload.

3. Remove the magazine by depressing the magazine release button. Let the magazine drop to the ground. *(FA622.4.)*

4. To extract the cartridge from the chamber, you should grip the charging handle and pull the charging handle fully to the rear and release. These actions should eject any round in the chamber. Do not attempt to catch the ejected cartridge. *(FA622.5.)*

5. If the specific weapon you are using does not automatically lock the bolt back, you should pull the charging handle to hold the bolt to the rear. While holding the bolt to the rear, you should depress the bolt catch lever. Then, depress the bolt catch lever to release the charging handle. (Reset the charging handle back into the upper receiver.) This locks the action in the open position. *(FA622.6.)*

6. With the bolt locked back and the chamber open and fully visible, physically and visually inspect the chamber and magazine well to make sure that no rounds remain in the chamber. *(FA622.7.)*

OBJECTIVES

FA621.4. Insert a loaded magazine into the magazine well of the semiautomatic rifle/carbine.

FA621.5. Chamber a cartridge in the semiautomatic rifle/carbine.

FA622.4. Remove the magazine from the semiautomatic rifle/carbine.

FA622.5. Extract the cartridge from the chamber from a semiautomatic rifle/carbine with the magazine removed.

FA622.6. Lock the action in the "open" position on an unloaded semiautomatic rifle/carbine.

FA622.7. Inspect the unloaded semiautomatic rifle/carbine for any cartridges with the action locked in the "open" position.

UNIT 7 | USE OF COVER

LESSON 1 | Use of Cover

OBJECTIVES

FA608.2.A. Define *cover*.

FA608.2.B. Define *concealment*.

FA608.2.A.2. Identify tactical considerations in the use of cover and concealment.

FA608.2. Identify factors to consider before moving.

FA608.4. Use cover properly when given a threat.

FA608.5.A. Identify appropriate shooting stances from behind cover.

Using cover and concealment can be critical to an officer winning a confrontation. *Cover* is any object or obstacle that creates a bullet-resistant barrier between you and a threat. It includes, but is not limited to, such things as a solid concrete wall, a vehicle's engine block, or a concrete telephone pole. *(FA608.2.A.)*

Concealment is any object or group of objects that creates a visual barrier between you and a threat but may not stop a projectile. Examples include bushes, trees, and cars. The purpose of concealment is to hide your exact location *(FA608.2.B.)*. Cover can be concealment, but concealment is not necessarily cover.

Cover should be chosen for its bullet-stopping capabilities, not its size. Walls and doors made of materials that bullets can penetrate may serve as concealment. Do not consider them cover, however. The objective of cover is to save your life by stopping or deflecting bullets and to provide a safer environment while you evaluate a situation.

Tactical considerations in using cover include using cover whenever possible, and reloading behind cover whenever possible while observing the threat.

Consider these factors to determine appropriate cover:

- size—Ideally, the object should be large enough to fully conceal your body (for example, a vehicle or concrete wall). However, any cover is better than no cover.

- density—The cover should be capable of stopping a projectile.

- location—Choose cover that is tactically sound and positions you to engage a threat.

- versatility—Choose cover that gives you the most options, such as cover that positions you to use your shooting hand rather than your support hand or cover that enables you to change heights or shooting stances. *(FA608.2.A.2.)*

There are several factors to consider before moving to cover. For instance, never change your cover just for the sake of change. Select your next position before you move. Move closer only to gain a tactical advantage. Move using concealment—cars, trees, bushes—if available. You may need to run, crawl, or "duck walk" to reach cover. Move if you need to reach a safer location. Reload your firearm behind cover when possible. *(FA608.2.)*

When moving to cover, scan the area first. Your weapon should be in a ready position. You should be ready to engage the threat at any time, even while moving. Keep your finger off the trigger, outside the trigger guard. Be aware of foot placement. Move quickly and decisively; use concealment if available. Always be aware of alternative options. Don't lock yourself into a bad position. To properly use cover, keep your body and your firearm behind cover. Do not expose your body unnecessarily. Do not let the muzzle of your firearm extend beyond the cover object.

Exploit distance and angles. Do not "crowd" your cover. You do not have to be right behind your cover to use it effectively. Remember to judge your position of cover from your adversary's angle or viewpoint and keep your firearm and body off the cover. Leaning on your cover decreases your mobility, and it increases your chance of being hit by direct fire or a ricochet or splattered by debris when projectiles impact your cover. Remember that ricochet or debris may disable your firearm. Alter your shooting position from behind cover whenever possible. Muzzle flash may reveal your location, especially at night. *(FA608.4.)*

Stances from Behind Cover: Handgun
Barricade Standing (Roll-Out Method)

Follow this procedure for firing your handgun from the standing barricade position:

1. Start away from cover in your basic stance.

2. Draw your firearm from your holster, keeping your finger off the trigger; move to cover and identify your target.

3. Stay completely behind the barricade using it for cover.

4. Use your basic shooting position.

5. Roll out to your shooting-hand side. Expose only a small portion of your shoulder and head. Keep your firearm away from and behind the barricade. Do not let your firearm or hands rest on or touch the barricade.

Kneeling Barricade (Roll-Out Method)

Use this procedure for firing your handgun from the kneeling barricade position.

1. Start away from cover in your basic stance.

2. Draw your firearm from your holster, keeping your finger off the trigger; move to cover and identify your target.

3. Stay completely behind it and use it for cover.

4. Use a kneeling position behind cover.

5. Roll to your shooting-hand side. Remember to expose only a small portion of your shoulder and head and keep your firearm away from and behind the barricade. Also, do not let your firearm or hands rest on or touch the barricade.

Positions from Behind Cover: Shotgun and Rifle/Carbine
Barricade Standing (Roll-Out Method)

Use this procedure to fire a shotgun or rifle/carbine from the standing barricade position:

1. Start away from cover in your basic stance.

2. Keeping your finger off the trigger, move to cover and identify your target.

3. Stay completely behind the barricade using it for cover.

4. Roll out to your shooting-hand side. Remember to expose only a small portion of your shoulder and head and keep your firearm away from and behind the barricade. Also, do not let your firearm or hands rest on or touch the barricade.

Kneeling Barricade (Roll-Out Method)

Use this procedure for firing your shotgun or rifle/carbine from the kneeling barricade position.

1. Start away from cover in your basic stance.

2. Keeping your finger off the trigger, move to cover, take a kneeling position and identify your target.

3. Stay completely behind the barricade, using it for cover.

4. Roll to your shooting hand side. Remember to expose only a small portion of your shoulder and head and keep your firearm away from and behind the barricade. Also, do not let your firearm or hands rest on or touch the barricade. *(FA608.5.A.)*

UNIT 8 I WEAPONS MALFUNCTIONS

LESSON 1 I Revolver Malfunctions

OBJECTIVES

FA610.2. Keep the barrel of a weapon with a malfunction pointed in a safe direction.

FA610.1. Remove finger from trigger of a weapon with a malfunction.

FA610.3. Identify revolver malfunctions.

FA610.3.A.4. Identify a squib load in a revolver.

FA610.4.D.3. Switch to a secondary weapon when a squib load occurs in a loaded revolver.

FA610.4. Correct the revolver malfunction using the proper technique.

This section identifies types of malfunctions that may occur as you fire your weapon and instructs you on how to correct them. Knowing how to correct problems with your firearm is imperative: It may save your life. Malfunctions caused by ammunition can usually be prevented if the ammunition is inspected for defects before using it.

A *malfunction* is a condition that prevents a weapon from operating normally. Before trying to correct a malfunction on the weapons covered in this chapter, remember to perform the following steps:

1. Keep the barrel pointed in a safe direction. *(FA610.2.)*

2. Remove your finger from the trigger. *(FA610.1.)*

3. Identify the kind of malfunction and the proper technique for correcting it.

Revolver Malfunctions

Revolver malfunctions include failure to fire, misfire, a squib load, a casing caught under the extractor, or a frozen or improperly closed cylinder. *(FA610.3.)*

A *squib load* occurs when there is no powder or a partial burn of powder and the primer ignites. The result is incomplete propulsion of the bullet, which may lodge the projectile in the barrel. THIS IS A MAJOR SAFETY HAZARD. *(FA610.3.A.4.)*

A distinct sound is associated with a squib load. It is not as loud or forceful as the sound of a regular round firing. You hear a **pop** instead of a **bang** and feel much less recoil.

If this happens during training, do the following:

1. Stop firing.

2. Keep your weapon pointed downrange.

3. Raise your support hand.

4. Wait for an instructor to take the weapon.

Instructors are responsible for clearing this malfunction. During a deadly force encounter, go to a secondary weapon (if available). Retreat and move to cover. This description of a squib load and the procedure for handling it is the same for the semiautomatic pistol and rifle/carbine covered in this section. *(FA10.4.D.3.)*

Clearing Revolver Malfunctions

Suppose you pull the trigger and the hammer falls, but the round fails to detonate. You are experiencing a failure to fire. The following conditions cause a failure to fire:

The revolver is not loaded. To fix this, load the revolver.

A bad primer causes a misfire; that is, the primer fails to fire after the hammer nose or firing pin strikes it. The result is a dead round.

Dirt and debris may cause a malfunction. To fix this, you must unload and clean the weapon.

The rebound spring has been altered to make the trigger easier to pull, resulting in a light hammer fall. Only a certified armorer can fix this problem.

The strain screw has been backed out, cut, loosened, or altered to make the trigger easier to pull. The result is a light hammer fall. Only a certified armorer can fix this problem.

No student should alter a weapon. All weapons should meet factory standards.

The firing pin or hammer nose breaks; a certified armorer must fix it.

If the firing pin breaks during training, keep the weapon pointed in a safe direction, and raise your support hand to summon the range instructor. If this happens during a deadly force encounter, go to your secondary weapon (if available). Retreat and move to cover.

If a misfire occurs in training, keep the weapon pointed in a safe direction, pause momentarily, and then pull the trigger again. When you empty the cylinder, you will see an indentation on the primer of the round that caused the misfire. The projectile is still attached to the casing.

If a misfire occurs during a deadly force encounter, immediately pull the trigger again. If the weapon still fails to fire, use your secondary weapon (if available), and then retreat and move to cover.

Section Vocabulary

frozen cylinder

malfunction

squib load

Unloading the revolver sideways or failing to fully depress the extractor rod when unloading it may cause a casing to be caught under the extractor. You can prevent this malfunction by making sure to point the muzzle straight up when unloading the revolver. If it does occur, press and hold the extractor rod completely to the rear, with the cylinder open. Then, dislodge the casing from the cylinder using your finger.

A *frozen cylinder* is one that does not rotate. Causes can include dirt or debris under the extractor that locks the cylinder so it cannot rotate. To solve this problem, clean under the extractor. Bad ammunition (high primer) can also cause a frozen cylinder. The primer on the cartridge protrudes above the headstamp. This situation can be dangerous: opening the cylinder roughly can ignite the primer. To prevent this problem, check your ammunition before loading.

If the cylinder freezes or a loose extractor rod has backed out in the frame during training, you should keep your weapon pointed in a safe direction and raise your support hand to summon an instructor. The instructor will take the revolver and clear the ammunition.

Checking your revolver and ammunition before loading, as well as keeping your weapon clean, can prevent most malfunctions. *(FA610.4.)*

UNIT 8 | WEAPONS MALFUNCTIONS
LESSON 2 | Semiautomatic Pistol Malfunctions

Semiautomatic pistol malfunctions include a squib load, a failure to fire, a failure to feed, a failure to eject, a double feed, or a failure to extract. The leading cause of malfunctions in semiautomatic weapons is the failure to properly seat the magazine. *(FA620.3.A.)*

You can clear most malfunctions from the pistol (excluding a squib round) using two clearance methods. If available, move to cover to clear a malfunction in an actual armed confrontation.

Phase 1 Clearance: *Immediate Action Drill*

Use Phase 1 Clearance to fix failure to feed, failure to fire, stovepipe, and failure to extract malfunctions. The easiest way to remember this method is to learn the phrase Tap, Rack, Ready, Fire (if necessary).

When a malfunction occurs, you should perform the following steps:

1. Use your support hand to tap (**Tap**) the bottom of the magazine into the magazine well. If the magazine is not fully seated, tapping will seat it.

2. Reach up to the slide with your support hand, pull the slide to the rear, and then release it.

   This is the same action you use when loading your weapon (**Rack**). It extracts and ejects a bad round (if necessary) and chambers a new round.

3. **Ready**—In an actual armed confrontation, you must assess the situation. You either re-engage the subject if he or she remains a threat, or issue commands if the subject surrendered during the clearance drill.

4. Fire if necessary.

Phase 2 Clearance: *Immediate Action Drill*

If Phase 1 Clearance does not clear the malfunction or the malfunction is a double feed, use Phase 2 Clearance. A Phase 2 Clearance is more detailed and time consuming.

1. Lock the slide to the rear to release pressure on the recoil guide/spring and magazine.

2. Depress the magazine release; forcibly strip the magazine from the magazine well with the support hand.

3. Rotate the pistol towards the ejection port side and with your support hand, work the slide back and forth until you clear the barrel and chamber of any rounds or obstructions.

4. Place a new magazine in the magazine well, and use a sharp upward motion to seat the magazine.

OBJECTIVES

FA620.3.A. Identify the types of semiautomatic pistol malfunctions that may occur.

FA620.3.A.7. Identify a squib load in a semiautomatic pistol.

FA620.4. Correct the semiautomatic pistol malfunction using the proper technique(s).

5. Reach up to the slide with your support hand, pull the slide to the rear, and then release it (sling shot). This chambers a round.

6. Ready—Assess the situation. Re-engage the subject if he or she is still a threat, or issue verbal commands.

7. Fire if necessary.

Squib load (See the information on squib load in the Revolver section.) *(FA620.3.A.7.)*

A *failure to fire* occurs when the trigger is pulled, but the round fails to detonate. The following conditions cause a failure to fire:

The safety is engaged. Disengage the safety.

Failure to chamber a round. Correct this malfunction with the Phase 1 Clearance method—Tap, Rack, and Ready.

The magazine is not seated in the magazine well. Correct this malfunction by tapping the magazine into the magazine well.

The primer fails to fire after the firing pin or striker hits it. The result is a misfire and a dead round. Correct this malfunction with the Phase 1 Clearance method—Tap, Rack, and Ready.

In a *failure to feed*, the cartridge fails to feed into the chamber. This occurs when the magazine is not fully seated. Use the Phase 1 Clearance method—Tap, Rack, and Ready—to correct this malfunction, or insert a new magazine.

Failure to eject, often called a *stovepipe*, occurs when a fired cartridge case does not completely eject. The most common causes are a weak powder charge (bad ammunition), a dry weapon (not enough lubrication), and, if while firing, the shooter does not provide enough resistance for the slide to operate (limp wrist). Use the Phase 1 Clearance method—Tap, Rack, and Ready—to correct this malfunction. (Figure 3-17)

A *double feed* is a failure to extract the round in the chamber and a new round being fed from the magazine well. Causes include damaged or improperly dimensioned magazine lips or a faulty cartridge interrupter (in weapons with tubular magazines).

To clear a double feed, you must use the Phase 2 Clearance method:

Stovepipe   *Figure 3-17*

1. Lock the slide to the rear.

2. Depress the magazine release and forcefully strip the magazine from the magazine well.

3. Rotate the pistol towards the ejection port side and with your support hand, work the slide back and forth until you clear the barrel and chamber of any rounds or obstructions.

4. Reinsert a magazine and make sure it is fully seated.

5. Pull back on the slide, and release it to chamber a round (sling shot).

6. Assess the situation.

7. Fire if necessary.

Failure to extract occurs when the pistol fails to extract a spent casing from its chamber. The causes of this malfunction include a weak powder charge, dirt behind the extractor, a dirty chamber, a broken extractor, a damaged or worn rim on the case, or an over-expanded or cracked case.

To clear this malfunction, use the Phase 1 Clearance method. If you do not succeed, try the Phase 2 Clearance method. If the extractor is worn or broken, a certified armorer must repair the weapon. If the weapon is dirty, it must be cleaned.

During qualification, you must clear weapon malfunctions and continue firing. If you cannot return your weapon to firing condition after performing an immediate action drill, summon an instructor. *(FA620.4.)*

Section Vocabulary
double feed (handgun)
failure to eject (stovepipe)
failure to extract
failure to feed
failure to fire

UNIT 8 | WEAPONS MALFUNCTIONS
LESSON 3 | Shotgun Malfunctions

Shotgun malfunctions include the following: the shell fails to load from the magazine tube, the fore-end/slide fails to close fully, failure to feed, double feed, stacked feed, failure to fire, failure to extract, failure to open, failure to eject, failure to close, and stovepipes. *(FA637.3.)*

Clearing Shotgun Malfunctions

Shells fail to load into the magazine tube when a bent carrier prevents the shell from aligning with the magazine tube opening, the wrong ammunition is used, or the shell stop is defective.

To correct this malfunction, raise your support hand, keep your weapon pointed downrange, and summon the instructor to assist you.

It is possible for the fore-end/slide to fail to close fully. This results from a bent action bar, a jammed or bent shell stop, a foreign object or broken part in the action, or the shooter's failure to push the fore-end/slide completely forward. If one of the first three reasons caused the malfunction, raise your support hand, keep your weapon pointed

OBJECTIVES

FA637.3. Identify the shotgun malfunction.

FA637.4. Correct the shotgun malfunction using the proper technique(s).

downrange, and wait for an instructor to assist you. If you did not push the fore-end/slide completely forward, forcefully push the fore-end/slide forward, then lock it into place.

If the slide is cycled but the round does not feed, there is a failure to feed. The following conditions may cause a failure to feed:

The shell stop is holding back the shell.

The magazine follower is sticking in the magazine tube.

An improperly operating carrier prevents alignment of the shell.

Ammunition is inverted.

The fore-end or slide is not cycled completely.

The weapon is not loaded.

If one of the first four reasons caused the malfunction, raise your support hand, keep your weapon pointed downrange, and summon an instructor to assist you. If either of the last two reasons caused the malfunction, completely cycle the slide, then load the weapon.

A ***double feed*** occurs when the shell stop fails to retain a shell in the magazine tube after one has been moved onto the carrier. The action will not close. To correct this malfunction, you should press down on the nose of the shell on the carrier to expose the base of the shell still partially in the magazine tube. With your finger, push that shell back into the magazine tube until it locks in place. You must do this through the ejection port.

A ***stacked feed*** occurs when a round is in the chamber and the action is closed. The shell latch fails to keep a round in the magazine tube. Instead, it moves the round onto the carrier. The weapon still operates but you cannot load rounds until you remove the one in the chamber. You can correct this in two ways:

1. Fire the chambered round and cycle the slide.

2. If you cannot fire the round, engage the safety and remove your finger from the trigger guard. Depress the slide release and apply sufficient force to pull the fore-end/slide to the rear.

3. Depress the slide release and apply sufficient force to pull the fore-end/slide to the rear.

If the trigger is pulled, but the round fails to fire, this is a failure to fire. The following conditions cause a failure to fire: the safety is on, the chamber is empty, the round is bad, or the firing pin is broken. If a broken firing pin is the problem, a certified armorer must repair it.

To correct this malfunction,

1. If the safety is on, disengage it.

2. If the weapon is empty, load it.

3. If the weapon misfires, immediately cycle the weapon and fire, if appropriate, or assume the ready position on the target.

4. If taking these steps fails to correct the problem, raise your support hand, keep your weapon pointed downrange, and summon an instructor to assist you.

The shotgun fails to extract a spent casing from its chamber while it tries to feed a new round into the chamber at the same time. Called failure to extract, this malfunction's causes include a broken extractor or a worn extractor hook. To correct this malfunction, raise your support hand, keep your weapon pointed downrange, and summon an instructor to assist you. A certified armorer must repair a broken extractor or worn extractor hook.

A failure to open occurs when the shotgun's fore-end/slide will not cycle, and the shotgun will not open. Causes include not firing a round to release the fore-end/slide, failing to depress the fore-end/slide release, or an improperly maintained weapon.

If this malfunction results from improper maintenance, engage the safety and place your finger outside the trigger guard, then raise your support hand, keep your weapon pointed in a safe direction, and summon an instructor to assist you. If the malfunction occurs for the other reasons listed earlier, you can usually correct it by properly cycling the fore-end/slide.

A failure to eject occurs when an ejector is missing or broken, the shell is swollen and will not extract, or an ejector is bent or improperly positioned. To correct this malfunction, engage the safety by placing the finger outside the trigger guard, then raise your support hand, keep your weapon pointed in a safe direction, and summon an instructor to assist you.

When the bolt and ejection port trap a partially ejected shell, a stovepipe occurs. A shooter's failure to cycle the action properly causes this problem. To correct it, pull the slide all the way to the rear, and free the shell by using your hand. Then, cycle the slide forward to load the chamber.

If the officer's shotgun malfunctions in the field, he or she should immediately switch to his or her handgun. *(FA637.4.)*

Section Vocabulary
double feed (shotgun)
stacked feed

UNIT 8 | WEAPONS MALFUNCTIONS
LESSON 4 | Semiautomatic Rifle/Carbine Malfunctions

OBJECTIVES

FA628.4. Identify the semiautomatic rifle/carbine malfunctions.

FA628.4.A.7. Identify a squib load in a semiautomatic rifle/carbine.

FA628.5.H.3. Transition to a secondary means of defense when a squib load occurs.

FA628.5. Correct the malfunction of the semiautomatic rifle/carbine using the proper technique(s).

Semiautomatic rifle/carbine malfunctions include a squib load, failure to fire, failure to feed, failure to extract (double feed), or failure to eject (stovepipe). *(FA628.4.)*

Most malfunctions from a rifle/carbine (excluding a squib round) can be cleared using two clearance methods, or techniques:

Phase 1 Clearance: *Immediate Action Drill*

Use Phase 1 Clearance to fix failure to feed, failure to fire, stovepipe, and failure to extract malfunctions. The easiest way to remember this method is to learn the phrase Tap, Rack, Ready, Fire if necessary. In an actual armed confrontation, officers should transition to a secondary weapon and clear the malfunction when safe to do so.

When a malfunction occurs perform the following steps:

1. Use your support hand to tap (Tap) the bottom of the magazine into the magazine well. If the magazine is not fully seated, tapping will seat it.

2. Remain in your stance with your weapon still pointed at the target.

3. Reach up to the charging handle with your support hand, pull it to the rear, and release (sling shot).

   This is the same action you use when loading the weapon (Rack). It extracts and ejects a bad round (if necessary), and/or chambers a new round.

4. Ready—In an actual armed confrontation, you must assess the situation. You should either re-engage the subject if he or she remains a threat, or issue commands if the subject surrenders during the clearance drill.

5. Fire if necessary.

Phase 2 Clearance: *Immediate Action Drill*

If Phase 1 Clearance does not clear the malfunction or the malfunction is a double feed, use Phase 2 Clearance.

1. Lock the bolt to the rear to release pressure on the magazine.

2. Depress the magazine release; forcibly strip the magazine from the magazine well.

3. Remain in your stance with your weapon still pointed at the target.

4. With your support hand, work the charging handle back and forth until you clear the barrel and chamber of rounds or obstructions.

5. Place a new magazine in the magazine well, and use a sharp upward motion to seat the magazine.

6. Reach up to the charging handle with your support hand, pull it to the rear, and release (sling shot). This chambers a round.

7. Ready—Assess the situation. Re-engage the subject if he or she remains a threat, or issue verbal commands.

8. Fire if necessary.

Squib load (See the information on squib load in the Revolver section.) *(FA628.4.A.7.)*

In a training situation, an instructor will take the firearm. Instructors are responsible for clearing this malfunction.

During a deadly force encounter, transition to a secondary weapon or retreat. Immediately move to cover, if available. If an officer's rifle malfunctions, he or she should immediately switch to a handgun, if available. *(FA628.5.H.3.)*

If the trigger is pulled but the round fails to fire, this is a failure to fire. The following conditions cause a failure to fire:

The safety is engaged and you cannot pull the trigger. Disengage the safety.

Failure to chamber a round. Correct this malfunction with the Phase 1 Clearance method—Tap, Rack, Ready.

The primer fails to ignite after the firing pin strikes it. The result is a misfire and a dead round. Correct this malfunction with the Phase 1 Clearance method—Tap, Rack, Ready.

You insert the magazine, release the bolt forward, and disengage the safety. Then you pull or squeeze the trigger, and nothing happens. You are experiencing a failure to feed. This occurs when the magazine is not fully seated in the magazine well, the magazine is empty, the magazine spring is broken, or the magazine is not loaded properly.

Take these steps immediately:

1. Tap the bottom of the magazine upward to ensure proper seating.

2. Pull the charging handle completely to the rear, and release it. This chambers a round.

3. If the magazine well is empty, insert a new magazine.

4. Ready—Assess the situation. Re-engage the subject if he or she remains a threat, or issue commands if the subject surrendered.

5. Fire if necessary.

A failure to extract round (double feed) occurs when a spent casing remains in the chamber, blocking a new round from feeding into the chamber.

To clear a double feed,

1. Lock the bolt to the rear.

2. Remove the magazine.

3. Work the charging handle back and forth until you empty the chamber.

4. Reinsert the magazine.

5. Pull the charging handle completely to the rear, and release it to chamber a round.

6. Ready—Assess the situation.

7. Fire if necessary.

A stovepipe occurs when an empty casing fails to completely eject. Causes include a weak powder charge or a dry weapon (not enough lubrication).

Use the Phase 1 Clearance method to clear the caught casing:

1. Tap the bottom of the magazine upward to ensure proper seating.

2. Pull the charging handle completely to the rear while turning the ejection port towards the ground, and release the charging handle/lever. This ejects the caught round and chambers a new round.

3. Ready—Assess the situation.

4. Fire if necessary. *(FA628.5.)*

UNIT 9 | WEAPONS CLEANING
LESSON 1 | Revolver Cleaning

OBJECTIVES

FA609.1.A. Identify the proper supplies/tools to use when cleaning the revolver.

FA609.4. Clean the revolver, removing all lead, powder, debris, and dirt.

FA609.5. Lightly lubricate the revolver.

FA609.6. Reassemble the cleaned revolver dependent upon the make and model of the weapon.

FA609.7. Function check the cleaned revolver.

FA609.8. Return the revolver to safe storage and/or securely re-holster the weapon.

Cleaning your weapon is important. A clean weapon functions properly when it is needed. Field stripping and cleaning are routine maintenance for all weapons. Before cleaning your weapon, gather the supplies and tools you need, select a well-ventilated location for cleaning, and fieldstrip the weapon.

While field stripping and cleaning your revolver, remember to take these important steps:

1. Safety check the weapon.

2. Remove live ammunition from the cleaning area.

3. Release the cylinder catch and open the cylinder.

4. Visually and physically inspect the barrel and chambers for obstructions and ammunition.

Cleaning tools—Cleaning tools are caliber specific. Use the tools designated for the specific caliber of your weapon. A larger caliber cleaning brush or patch tip does not fit in a small weapon and may cause damage. A small tool may not completely clean your firearm. It is recommended that you observe the manufacturer's guidelines.

Solvent and lubricant—Several types and brands of cleaners and solvents are available. Use solvent and lubricant specifically designed for firearms maintenance.

Patches and swabs—Consider the weapon bore when choosing patches. Different materials have different absorption qualities.

The weapon cleaning kit could include the following items; bore brush, solvent, patches (cotton patches absorb more), nylon cleaning brush, Bore Snake®, cleaning pad, gun oil/lubricant (non-penetrating), rags, pipe cleaners, and Q-tips®. *(FA609.1.A.)*

> **FA609.9.** Appropriately dispose of all debris and contaminated/used cleaning supplies.
>
> **FA609.10.** Wash hands after cleaning a revolver.

Cleaning and Lubricating the Revolver

1. Remove all lead, powder, debris, and dirt. These substances can cause a malfunction if they build up. Be sure to remove as much of these materials as possible.

   a. Use a brushing technique to remove loose objects, loosen other substances, and help solvents and cleaners work better.

   Brush all surfaces of your firearm.

   The bore brush should clear the bore after each stroke.

   Push the brush all the way in, then bring it all the way out.

   Make sure to use a soft, non-marring brush on the firearm's outer finished surface. Do not use a brass brush on the firearm's exterior: it can damage the surface.

   Do not use a brass brush on the firearm's exterior: it can damage the surface.

   b. Brush with solvent—Solvents are designed to dissolve and loosen lead, powder, debris, and dirt. You can also use them to clean substances that brushing does not, such as lead, powder, or debris.

2. Pay special attention to the following areas on the revolver:

   cylinder—When the firearm discharges, it may blow powder and lead back over the cylinder's outer surface. These substances may be heavily concentrated on the cylinder's face.

   cylinder chambers—The chambers may contain unburned powder and lead.

   a. Insert the cleaning brush in each chamber.

   b. Slide it back and forth several times.

   bore—As the projectile travels down the bore, it leaves behind small amounts of material. If the projectile is lead, it leaves lead behind. If its jacket is brass, the projectile may leave some brass behind.

   a. Insert the cleaning brush in the barrel.

   b. Slide the cleaning brush back and forth several times.

   c. Push the brush all the way through, then pull it all the way out.

   area below the top strap—Lead and powder residue are deposited in this area when gases from fired rounds escape around the forcing cone.

   firing pin hole—Observe the firing pin hole to ensure that it is free of all debris.

ejector rod—Clean the area around and under the ejector rod.

extractor—Clean the area around and under the extractor. If the extractor does not work, you cannot empty or load the weapon.

3. After brushing these parts, wipe them with a clean patch and a small amount of cleaning solvent.

4. With a clean, dry patch, wipe all parts again to remove the solvent and debris.

You may need to repeat this action until the revolver is clean. *(FA609.4.)*

Lubricating your weapon is very important. Check your weapon at regular intervals to ensure it is properly lubricated. Also, check the manufacturer's recommended lubrication points and amounts. A little lubricant goes a long way. Excess lubrication can harm ammunition. Wipe it off using a clean, dry cloth. *(FA609.5.)*

When you finish cleaning and lubricating your revolver, you should follow these steps:

1. Reassemble the revolver. *(FA609.6.)*

2. Perform a function check of the revolver for proper operation. *(FA609.7.)*

3. Return the revolver to safe storage, or holster and secure it. *(FA609.8.)*

4. Properly dispose of all cleaning supplies. *(FA609.9.)*

5. Wash your hands with soap and water. *(FA609.10.)*

UNIT 9 | WEAPONS CLEANING

LESSON 2 | Semiautomatic Pistol Cleaning

While field stripping and cleaning your semiautomatic pistol, remember these important steps:

1. Safety check the weapon.

2. Remove live ammunition from the cleaning area.

3. Remove the magazine by pressing the magazine release and letting the magazine slide out of the magazine well or by stripping the magazine with your support hand. Place the magazine away from the weapon.

4. To lock the slide to the rear, pull on it and engage the slide stop or catch.

5. Visually and physically inspect the chamber, magazine well, and barrel. Look for ammunition casings and obstructions.

6. Remove the ammunition from the magazine(s).

7. Place the ammunition in a secure area away from the weapon. *(FA619.3.)*

It is recommended that you observe manufacturer's guidelines for cleaning your semiautomatic pistol. Make sure the tools you use do not invalidate the manufacturer's warranty or conflict with the manufacturer's recommendations.

The weapon cleaning kit could include a bore brush, solvent, patches (cotton patches absorb more), nylon cleaning brush, Bore Snake®, cleaning pad, gun oil/lubricant (nonpenetrating), rags, pipe cleaners, and Q-Tips®.

Cleaning Tools—Cleaning tools are caliber specific. Use the tools designated for the specific caliber of your weapon. A larger caliber cleaning brush or patch tip does not fit in a small weapon and may cause damage. A small tool may not completely clean a large firearm.

Solvent and Lubricant—Several types and brands of cleaners and solvents are available. Use solvent and lubricant specifically designed for firearms maintenance.

Patches and Swabs—Consider the weapon bore when choosing patches. Different materials have different absorption qualities. *(FA619.1.A.)*

Cleaning and Lubricating the Semiautomatic Pistol

1. Remove all lead, powder, debris, and dirt. These substances can cause a malfunction if they build up. Use the following processes:

   a. Brush properly—Use a back and forth brushing motion to remove loose objects, loosen other substances, and help solvents and cleaners work better.

OBJECTIVES
FA619.3. Field strip the semiautomatic pistol based on make and model of weapon.
FA619.1.A. Identify the proper supplies/tools to use when cleaning the semiautomatic pistol.
FA619.4. Clean the semiautomatic pistol, removing all lead, powder, debris, and dirt.
FA619.5. Lubricate the semiautomatic pistol using lubricant and cloth/patches.
FA619.6. Reassemble the cleaned semiautomatic pistol.
FA619.7. Function check the clean, reassembled semiautomatic pistol.
FA619.8. Return the cleaned semiautomatic pistol to safe storage and/or securely re-holster the weapon.
FA619.9. Appropriately dispose of all debris and contaminated/used cleaning supplies.
FA619.10. Wash hands after cleaning a semiautomatic pistol.

Brush all surfaces of your firearm.

The bore brush should clear the bore completely after each stroke.

It is important to use a soft, non-marring brush on the firearm's outer finished surface. Do not use a brass brush on the firearm's exterior: it can damage the surface.

b. Brush with solvent—Solvents are designed to dissolve and loosen lead, powder, debris, and dirt. You can also use them to clean substances that brushing does not, such as lead, powder, or debris.

c. Wipe all parts repeatedly to remove all of the solvent and debris until your semiautomatic pistol is clean. Use new clean, dry patches when necessary. *(FA619.4.)*

2. Pay special attention to the following areas of the semiautomatic pistol:

magazines—Clean magazines thoroughly and wipe dry. If magazines donot function properly, the firearm can malfunction.

bore—As the projectile travels down the bore, it leaves behind small amounts of the material it is made of. To thoroughly clean the bore, you should insert the cleaning brush into the bore's breech end, push the cleaning brush through until it clears the muzzle, and then pull it all the way out. Repeat this process until the bore of the barrel is clean.

recoil spring and guide—Clean thoroughly; dirt and debris hinder the weapon's blowback and cycle function.

slide—Clean the entire slide, outside and inside. Pay special attention to the slide rails. You can use Q-Tips.

extractor—Clean the extractor thoroughly. It must be able to catch the rim of a fired cartridge as the weapon cycles. If not, the next round cannot feed properly and a malfunction results.

firing pin hole—Observe the firing pin hole to ensure that it is free of all debris.

Lubricating your weapon is very important. Check your weapon at regular intervals to ensure it is properly lubricated. Also, check the manufacturer's recommended lubrication points and amounts.

1. Lubricate the frame or slide rails to reduce drag or friction between surfaces when the weapon cycles.

2. Lubricate any other points recommended by the manufacturer.

3. Remove excess lubrication. A little lubrication goes a long way. Excess lubrication can harm ammunition. Wipe it off using a clean, dry cloth. Heavy lubrication or solvents may destroy the primer and powder of loaded cartridges. Wipe the inside of the magazine dry; leave no lubricant. *(FA619.5.)*

When you finish cleaning and lubricating your pistol:

1. Reassemble the semiautomatic pistol and its magazines. *(FA619.6.)*

2. Perform a function check of the pistol for proper operation. *(FA619.7.)*

3. Return the pistol to safe storage, or holster and secure it. *(FA619.8.)*

4. Properly dispose of all cleaning supplies. *(FA619.9.)*

5. Wash your hands with soap and water. *(FA619.10.)*

UNIT 9 | WEAPONS CLEANING
LESSON 3 | Shotgun Cleaning

While field stripping and cleaning your shotgun, remember to take these important steps:

1. Safety check the weapon.

2. Remove live ammunition from the cleaning area.

3. Point the weapon in a safe direction, remembering the safety rules.

4. Verify that the safety is in the on position and the magazine tube or chamber contains no ammunition.

5. Ensure that the slide is at the rear and the ejection port is open. *(FA636.3.)*

It is recommended that you observe manufacturer's guidelines for cleaning your shotgun. Make sure the tools you use do not invalidate the manufacturer's warranty or conflict with the manufacturer's recommendations.

The shotgun cleaning kit could include a bore brush, patches, lubricant, Bore Snake®, cleaning rod, gun solvent, and a cloth.

Cleaning Tools—Cleaning tools are gauge specific. Use the tools designated for the specific gauge of your weapon. A larger gauge cleaning brush or patch tip does not fit into a smaller one and may cause damage. A smaller tool may not completely clean a larger firearm.

Solvent and Lubricant—Several types and brands of cleaners and solvents are available. Use solvent and lubricant specifically designed for firearms maintenance.

Patches and Swabs—Consider the weapon bore when choosing patches. Different materials have different absorption qualities. Follow the manufacturer's recommendations. *(FA636.1.A.)*

Cleaning and Lubricating the Shotgun

To remove all lead, powder, debris, and dirt from the shotgun,

1. Take the barrel off the weapon, if possible.

2. With a bore brush and cleaning rod, clean and brush the bore and chamber of the barrel. Repeatedly push the bore brush completely through the barrel until it appears at the opposite end.

3. Use a non-metallic brush with solvent to clean areas contaminated with powder residue.

OBJECTIVES

FA636.3. Field strip the shotgun based on make and model.

FA636.1.A. Identify the proper supplies/tools to use when cleaning the shotgun.

FA636.4. Clean the shotgun, removing all lead, powder, debris, and dirt.

FA636.5. Lubricate the shotgun.

FA636.6. Properly reassemble the shotgun.

FA636.7. Function check the cleaned, reassembled shotgun.

FA636.8. Return the cleaned shotgun to safe storage and/or securely re-case the weapon.

FA636.9. Appropriately dispose of all debris and contaminated/used cleaning supplies.

FA636.10. Wash hands after cleaning a shotgun.

4. Use a patch, cleaning rod, and solvent to clean the bore, replacing the patch as needed.

5. Run a clean patch through the barrel to remove excess solvent and dirt. Repeatedly push the patch through the barrel until it appears at the opposite end.

6. Clean every part of the shotgun, and wipe the parts dry with a clean patch. *(FA636.4.)*

7. Lightly lubricate all parts including the bore of the barrel. Too much lubricant may damage a shotgun. Lubricant acts as a magnet, attracting dirt, dust, packing debris, and unburned powder. *(FA636.5.)*

When you finish cleaning and lubricating your shotgun:

1. Reassemble the shotgun. *(FA636.6.)*

2. Perform a function check of the shotgun. *(FA636.7.)*

3. Return the shotgun to safe storage, or securely re-case it. *(FA636.8.)*

4. Properly dispose of all cleaning supplies. *(FA636.9.)*

5. Wash your hands with soap and water. *(FA636.10.)*

UNIT 9 | WEAPONS CLEANING

LESSON 4 | Semiautomatic Rifle/Carbine Cleaning

While field stripping and cleaning your rifle/carbine, remember these important points:

1. Safety check the weapon.

2. Remove live ammunition from the cleaning area.

3. Remove the magazine and secure it away from the weapon.

4. Verify that the chamber or magazine contains no ammunition.

5. Ensure the bolt is locked to the rear and the ejection port is open. *(FA627.3.)*

It is recommended that you observe manufacturer's guidelines for cleaning your semiautomatic rifle/carbine. Make sure the tools you use do not invalidate the manufacturer's warranty or conflict with the manufacturer's recommendations.

Equipment—A rifle/carbine cleaning kit could include swabs, a cleaning rod, lubricant(s), Bore Snake®, bore brush, cleaning solvent (non-penetrating), and cloth/patches.

Cleaning Tools—Cleaning tools are caliber specific. Use the tools designated for the specific caliber of your weapon. A larger caliber cleaning brush or patch tip does not fit into—and may damage—a smaller weapon. A small tool may not completely clean a large firearm.

Solvent and Lubricant—Several types and brands of cleaners and solvents are available. Use solvent and lubricant specifically designed for firearms maintenance.

Patches and Swabs—Consider the weapon bore when choosing patches. Different materials have different absorption qualities. *(FA627.1.A.)*

Cleaning and Lubricating the Rifle/Carbine

To remove all lead, powder, debris, and dirt from the rifle/carbine,

1. With a bore brush and cleaning rod, clean and brush the bore and chamber of the barrel from the chamber end. Repeatedly push the bore brush completely through the barrel until it appears at the opposite end.

2. Use a non-metallic brush with solvent to clean areas contaminated with powder residue.

3. Use a patch, cleaning rod, and cleaning solvent to clean the bore, replacing the patch as needed.

4. Run a clean patch through the barrel from the chamber end to remove solvent and dirt. Repeatedly push the patch through the barrel until it appears at the opposite end.

OBJECTIVES

FA627.3. Field strip the semiautomatic rifle/carbine based on make and model of weapon.

FA627.1.A. Identify the proper supplies/tools to use when cleaning the semiautomatic rifle/carbine.

FA627.4. Clean the semiautomatic rifle/carbine, removing all lead, powder, debris, and dirt.

FA627.5. Lubricate the semiautomatic rifle/carbine using lubricant and cloth/patches.

FA627.6. Reassemble the cleaned semiautomatic rifle/carbine dependent upon the make and model of weapon.

FA627.7. Function check the clean, reassembled semiautomatic rifle/carbine.

FA627.8. Return the cleaned semiautomatic rifle/carbine to safe storage and/or securely re-case the weapon.

FA627.9. Appropriately dispose of all debris and contaminated/used cleaning supplies.

FA627.10. Wash hands after cleaning a semiautomatic rifle/carbine.

5. Clean every part of the rifle/carbine and wipe the exterior parts dry with a clean patch. *(FA627.4.)*

6. Lightly lubricate all parts and the bore. *(FA627.5.)*

Cleaning the Magazine

1. Field strip the magazine and clean all parts with a patch and solvent.

2. Wipe parts with a clean patch upon completion.

3. Wipe the exterior parts of the magazine with a lightly lubricated cloth or patch.

4. Clean the inside of the magazine with a dry cloth or patch.

5. Make sure the inside of the magazine is entirely dry.

When you finish cleaning and lubricating your semiautomatic rifle/carbine:

1. Reassemble the firearm. *(FA627.6.)*

2. Function check the firearm to ensure that all parts operate. Ensure that the bolt moves freely and spring tension is good, the safety works in both the on and off positions, the magazine feeds into the magazine well and releases freely, and that all metal parts are clean and lightly coated with lubricant or oil, except for the inside of the magazine(s). *(FA627.7.)*

3. Return the rifle/carbine to safe storage, or securely re-case it. *(FA627.8.)*

4. Properly dispose of all cleaning supplies. *(FA627.9.)*

5. Wash your hands with soap and water. *(FA627.10.)*

UNIT 10 | SURVIVAL SHOOTING

LESSON 1 | Handgun

Drawing: Support Hand Only

To draw your handgun using your support hand, do the following:

1. Reach across the front or back of your body, and use the fingers of your support hand to find the retention device(s) for your holster.

2. With the fingers of your support hand, disengage the retention device(s).

3. Grip the handgun.

4. Safely draw the handgun from its holster.

5. Safely bring the handgun across your body, watching the muzzle and ensuring your finger is outside the trigger guard, and point it at the target. *(FA602.2.B.)*

Reload Handgun with One Hand Only

Although reloading your handgun with two hands is preferable, some circumstances dictate that you reload with only one hand.

Unload/Reload a Revolver Using the Right Hand

To unload a revolver using only your right hand, do the following:

1. Establish a firm grip on your revolver with your right hand, while keeping the muzzle pointed in a safe direction and keeping your finger off the trigger.

2. Maintaining control of your revolver, open the cylinder. Use the technique appropriate for the model of your revolver.

3. Push the cylinder open with your index finger.

4. Place your thumb through the opening in the frame, under the top strap and over the cylinder.

5. Point the muzzle straight up.

6. Depress the extractor rod with your index finger, and extract empty cartridges from the cylinder. *(FA604.6.)*

To reload a revolver using only your right hand, do the following:

1. Place the grip of the weapon against your stomach.

2. Grab the top strap with the fingers of your right hand.

3. Place the barrel behind the gun belt inside the front of your pants with its cylinder facing out.

4. With your right hand, remove a speed loader from the pouch and insert the cartridges into the cylinder.

OBJECTIVES

FA602.2.B. Disengage the holster retention device(s) with the support hand.

FA604.6. Unload the handgun using one hand.

FA603.9. Load a handgun using one hand.

5. Hold the front of the cylinder with your little and ring fingers.

6. Apply pressure on the cylinder to hold it in place.

7. With your thumb and forefinger, turn the knob on the speed loader to release the cartridges.

8. Grip the revolver with the "shooting grip," removing it from your waistband.

9. Close the cylinder using your right thumb. *(FA603.9.)*

Unload/Reload the Revolver Using the Left Hand

To unload a revolver using only your left hand, do the following:

1. Establish a firm grip on the revolver with your left hand, keep the muzzle pointed in a safe direction, and keep your finger off the trigger.

2. Maintaining control of your revolver, open the cylinder. Use the technique appropriate for the model of your revolver.

3. Open the cylinder by tapping the side of the cylinder against your holster.

4. Place your thumb on the top strap and your little finger over the hammer.

5. Move your thumb inside the frame, and put your index finger on the extractor rod.

6. Point the muzzle straight up.

7. Depress the extractor rod with your thumb or index finger, and remove empty shell casings from the cylinder. *(FA604.6.)*

To reload a revolver using only your left hand, do the following:

1. Place the barrel behind the gun belt inside the front of your pants with its cylinder facing out.

2. With your support hand remove the speed loader from the pouch and insert the cartridges into the cylinder.

3. Use your index, center, and ring fingers to control the cylinder, before releasing the cartridges.

4. With the thumb and index finger, turn the knob on the speed loader to release the cartridges.

5. Establish a firm shooting grip on your revolver, and remove it from your waistband.

6. Close the cylinder with your trigger finger. *(FA603.9.)*

UNIT 10 | SURVIVAL SHOOTING

LESSON 2 | Discretionary Shooting

Officers must be able to identify deadly threats to themselves or others and then respond using only the amount of force necessary. If a threat demands deadly force, an officer must be able to identify that threat, innocent bystanders, field of fire, and what lies beyond the field of fire; determine if cover is available; decide that deadly force is the only course of action; and respond as quickly as possible. An officer must use all of his or her faculties to make the right decision.

Threat Assessment

Upon arriving at the scene, scan the area for possible problems, including additional threats. The ability to assess a situation or subject depends largely on your observation skills, including the ability to recognize hazardous areas and potential weapons and identify areas that provide cover and/or concealment.

Your senses of sight, sound, smell, and touch increase your awareness of your surroundings. As you become more familiar with the normal conditions of those surroundings, you will also be more aware of and able to identify people, occurrences, and conditions that are out of place. *(FA608.1.)*

Movement

After you identify the threat, you may need to move to cover. To move effectively during an armed confrontation, you must be aware of many factors and be able to use different types of movement. Appropriate cover is any object big enough to hide your body, and strong enough to stop bullets.

As you move from cover to cover, you must move quickly, safely, and without hesitation. You must be aware of your surroundings and of the condition of your weapon (loaded, rounds available, etc.). You must also know what suffices for cover, decide where to move, know if the location you choose allows you to see the area where the threat originates, and know when to move.

Basic movement techniques and tactics follow, but they are not the only methods officers use. Always be open to new ideas and tactics that may give you options to help you survive an armed confrontation. *(FA608.3.B.)*

Lateral Slide-Step Movement (Crab Walk)

1. Stand square to the target with your legs apart and your body balanced.

2. Shift your weight to the balls of your feet to allow movement. Be careful not to cross your feet.

3. Keep your back straight and your knees slightly bent.

OBJECTIVES

FA608.1. Scan surroundings for possible threats.

FA608.3.B. Identify various methods of moving to cover and/or concealment.

4. Hold your firearm in a tactical ready stance.

5. Upon the direction to move, lead with the foot in that direction. For example, if you are going right, move your right foot first.

6. Keep your feet low to the ground, feeling for objects that may cause you to trip or block your movement. Stepping low also helps with balance.

7. Look toward the area of threat.

Discretionary Shooting Skills

Threat Recognition—The ability to distinguish a deadly threat from a nondeadly threat. You must take some type of appropriate action to neutralize a deadly threat, for example, firing a round at the target.

Reaction Time—This is the time you take to distinguish a deadly threat from a non-deadly threat and then take appropriate action.

Verbal Commands—Use these to identify yourself and direct the subject. Give loud, clear, and concise commands, saying, for example, "Police! Don't move!"

Reloading—Take proper cover and reload.

Use of Cover—Move to cover.

Weapon Status—Follow all safety rules when handling the weapon. Show awareness of the weapon's status, and respond to weapon malfunctions.

Engagement of Nondeadly Threat—Identify the nondeadly threat and respond with proper verbal commands.

Neutralized Target—Neutralize all deadly threats.

CHAPTER 4

CMS Criminal Justice Defensive Tactics

The public often focuses its attention on the daily work of criminal justice officers and their methods for controlling subject resistance when there is a question of the officer's use of force. Whether meeting resistance on the street or in a correctional facility, officers must be prepared to respond appropriately to control a situation where officer and public safety are in danger. The defensive tactics curriculum offers criminal justice basic recruits effective, tactically sound, and legally defensible training in defensive tactics and control techniques. This course teaches recruits to select and properly execute techniques that are reasonable and necessary given the circumstances and factors of a situation.

UNIT 1 | INTRODUCTION
LESSON 1 | Overview of Defensive Tactics Program

OBJECTIVES

DT501.5. Define *defensive tactics*.

Section Vocabulary

defensive tactics

Defensive tactics is a system of controlled defensive and offensive body movements used by criminal justice officers to respond to a subject's aggression or resistance. These techniques are based on a combination of martial arts, wrestling, and boxing *(DT501.5.)*. The physical skills in defensive tactics require practice and repetition to master. Fitness, strength, agility, balance, and flexibility are vital to the development of these skills.

The role of defensive tactics in law enforcement and corrections is to assist the officer in restraining or arresting a subject. Depending on the situation, officers will use various levels of force in the application of defensive tactics techniques.

The CMS Criminal Justice Defensive Tactics course provides basic recruits with training in the physical skills necessary for the use of force in controlling subjects and for self-defense. Although there is some classroom instruction, most of this course is physical training.

UNIT 1 | INTRODUCTION
LESSON 2 | Preparation for Defensive Tactics Training

OBJECTIVES

DT501.4. Apply strategies for optimal physical performance during a defensive tactics training program.

Because defensive tactics training is a physical endeavor, students should prepare for the activities required in this course by considering some changes in their daily habits. Students should eat a nutritious diet, get adequate rest, and stay sufficiently hydrated to maximize the benefit of this training *(DT501.4.)*. Making these changes will enhance physical performance and minimize the risk of injury.

Defensive tactics skills require physical fitness, strength, agility, balance, and flexibility. Because flexibility reduces the risk of injuries, stretching exercises should be conducted every day.

Stretching Exercises

Begin and end each session with stretching exercises. A warm-up session elevates the heart rate and increases blood circulation to the muscles, which saturates the muscles with oxygen. This helps the body prepare itself for the physical activity. A cool-down after physical activity redistributes the blood flow, causing the metabolic rate to decrease. This process helps the muscles relax and prevents the tightening of muscles, which is vital for the body to recover.

Stretching usually begins with a warm-up such as running in place, jumping jacks, push-ups, or any calisthenics exercises that last for 5–7 minutes to warm up the muscles, and increase heart rate, respiration, and perspiration. Stretching generally begins at the top of the body and moves to the bottom or vice versa. You should stretch until you feel mild to moderate tension. The following examples of stretching exercises are suitable for preparation for defensive tactics training.

Neck Stretch

While standing, lean your left ear to your left shoulder for a count of 10 seconds. Repeat on the opposite side. Stretch chin to chest and head to rear. Perform 2–3 sets in each direction.

Straight Arm Behind Back Stretch

While standing, place both arms behind your hips. With interlocking hands, slowly raise your arms behind your back for a count of 10–20 seconds. Keep your head upright and neck relaxed.

Behind Neck Tricep Stretch

While standing, raise your right arm above your head and bend the right arm. The elbow will be above your head. Using the opposite hand, grasp your elbow and slowly pull towards the midline of the back, moving your hand in between your shoulder blades. Hold the stretch for 10–20 seconds and repeat on the left side.

Arm Cross in Front of Chest

While standing, bring your straight right arm across your chest with the palm up. Grasp your upper arm above the elbow with your left hand and slowly pull in towards and across your chest. Hold for 10–20 seconds and repeat with the left arm.

Both Arms Up Above Head Stretch

While standing, bring both straight arms above the head with hands interlocking, palms facing up, and reach upward slowly while reaching slightly backward. Hold for 10–20 seconds.

Both Arms in Front of Chest Stretch

While standing with your feet shoulder-width apart, bring your arms from an overhead position slowly towards the front of your body, while rounding the back and stretching the shoulder blades apart. Hold for 10–20 seconds.

Forward Lunge Stretch

While standing, take a long step forward until your right knee is directly over your right foot. Keeping your back leg straight, your forward foot on the floor, and your hands on the front thigh, lower your hips slowly forward and down. The heel of your back foot may or may not be on the floor, depending on your flexibility. Hold the stretch for 10–20 seconds and repeat on the opposite side.

Butterfly Stretch

While seated, bend your legs toward each other with the soles of your shoes touching. Your legs should be relaxed and knees should be flat on the floor. (If you lack flexibility your knees may not rest on the floor.) Lean forward from the waist with a straight back. Bring your head as close to your feet as possible. Hold for 10–20 seconds.

Spinal Twist

Sitting with your legs extended straight, bend your right leg and bring your right foot to the outside of your left leg next to the knee. Place your right hand behind your hips for support. Push your right knee to the left with your left elbow while turning your upper body to the right and rotating your shoulders as far as possible. Hold for 10–20 seconds and repeat on the opposite side.

Supine Knee Flex Stretch

Lie on your back with your legs straight. Bring your right knee towards your chest, placing both hands below the knee while continually pulling the knee towards your chest. Hold the stretch for 10–20 seconds and repeat on the opposite side.

Seated Bent Knee Stretch

While seated with both legs bent, bring your right ankle to your left knee. Support your upper body by placing your palms on the floor with fingers pointing away from your body. Bring both legs towards your chest. Hold the stretch for 10–20 seconds and repeat on the opposite side.

Modified Hurdler's Stretch

While seated, put your right leg straight in front of your body. Bend your left leg and bring the sole of your left shoe facing the inside of your straight leg. Lean forward from the waist and grasp your toes while moving your chest as close to your straightened leg as possible. Hold the stretch for 10–20 seconds and repeat on the opposite side.

Straddle Stretch

Sit with your legs straight out in front, spread your legs as far as possible, and face your right leg grasping the toes of the right foot while leaning from the waist. Keep your buttocks on the floor and your back straight. Your chest should be directly over your right knee. Facing forward and keeping your back straight, lean your upper body forward towards the ground with your hands grasped as close to the toes as possible. Hold the stretch for 10–20 seconds and repeat on the opposite side.

Cardiovascular Conditioning

Cardiovascular training is any exercise that elevates the heart rate to a range between 60 to 85 percent of the maximum rate. When the heart rate is in that range, a person is training in a cardiovascular or aerobic state. Cardiovascular training has numerous health benefits. In addition to burning calories and eliminating body fat, it strengthens the heart and lungs. Since heart disease is the leading cause of premature death for both men and women, cardiovascular fitness is extremely important. Examples of cardiovascular exercises include walking, jogging, running, jumping rope, bicycling, swimming, and step aerobics.

Rest

Proper rest and sleep are necessary for reaching maximum performance and maintaining focus while engaged in physical training.

Nutrition

A nutritious diet and an adequate intake of water are necessary for optimal performance in defensive tactics training.

Section Vocabulary

cardiovascular training

Nutrient	Function	Sources
Protein	Provides energy; builds and repairs body cells; is part of various enzymes, hormones, antibodies	Meat, poultry, fish, eggs, legumes (such as lentils), milk and milk products, vegetables, grains
Carbohydrate	Provides energy needed by the brain, nervous system, red blood cells, and other cells	Breads, cereal grains, pasta, rice, fruit, vegetables, milk, sugar
Fat	Provides energy and essential fatty acids; carries other fat-soluble nutrients (vitamins); is part of cell membranes, membranes around nerves, hormones, bile (for fat digestion)	Meat, poultry, fish, milk and milk products, nuts and seeds, oils, butter, margarine, salad dressing

Essential nutrients in food *Figure 4-1*

UNIT 2 | USE OF FORCE

LESSON 1 | Force Guidelines

OBJECTIVES

DT501.2.A. Identify elements of the Florida Statutes as related to the use of force by criminal justice officers.

DT501.2.E. Explain the provisions of Chapters 944 and 945, F.S., related to the use of force by state correctional and correctional probation officers.

DT501.1.D. Explain the concept of objective reasonableness.

DT501.2.B. Explain that subject resistance and officer response may change rapidly.

DT501.2. Apply the legal authority for an officer's response to a subject's resistance.

DT501.2.C. Explain escalation, de-escalation, and disengagement.

DT501.1.B. Explain how the injury potential to an officer may affect his or her response.

DT501.2.B.1. Define *passive resistance.*

DT501.2.B.2. Define *active resistance.*

DT501.2.B.3. Define *aggressive resistance.*

DT501.2.B.4. Define *deadly force resistance.*

DT501.2.B.5. Define *physical control.*

DT501.2.B.6. Define *nonlethal weapon.*

DT501.2.A.1. Define *deadly force.*

Chapter 776, F.S. governs all use of force by criminal justice officers. Even though the statute refers to "law enforcement" officers, the legal guidelines regarding use of force apply equally to corrections and correctional probation officers. The statute identifies two general areas in which an officer's use of force is justified: to apprehend a subject and make an arrest, or to defend self or others.

Section 776.05, F.S. addresses the issue of an officer using force to make an arrest:

A law enforcement officer, or any person whom the officer has summoned or directed to assist him or her, need not retreat or desist from efforts to make a lawful arrest because of resistance—or threatened resistance to the arrest. The officer is justified in the use of any force:

(1) Which he or she reasonably believes to be necessary to defend himself or herself or another from bodily harm while making the arrest;

(2) When necessarily committed in retaking felons who have escaped; or

(3) When necessarily committed in arresting felons fleeing from justice. However, this subsection shall not constitute a defense in any civil action for damages brought for the wrongful use of deadly force unless the use of deadly force was necessary to prevent the arrest from being defeated by such flight and, when feasible, some warning had been given, and:

(a) The officer reasonably believes that the fleeing felon poses a threat of death or serious physical harm to the officer or others; or

(b) The officer reasonably believes that the fleeing felon has committed a crime involving the infliction or threatened infliction of serious physical harm to another person. *(DT501.2.A.)*

While Chapter 776, F.S., applies in general to all criminal justice officers, Chapter 944, F.S., specifically addresses the use of force by state correctional and correctional probabtion officers. Chapter 945, F.S., establishes that the Department of Corrections has jurisdiction over the supervisory and protective care, custody, and control of inmates and offenders.

Section 944.35, F.S. provides:

(1)(a) An employee of the department is authorized to apply physical force upon an inmate only when and to the extent that it reasonably appears necessary:

1. To defend himself or herself or another against such other imminent use of unlawful force;

2. To prevent a person from escaping from a state correctional institution when the officer reasonably believes that person is lawfully detained in such institution;

3. To prevent damage to property;

4. To quell a disturbance;

5. To overcome physical resistance to a lawful command; or

6. To administer medical treatment only by or under the supervision of a physician or his or her designee and only:

   a. When treatment is necessary to protect the health of other persons, as in the case of contagious or venereal diseases; or

   b. When treatment is offered in satisfaction of a duty to protect the inmate against self-inflicted injury or death. *(DT501.2.E.)*

DT501.2.A.2. Identify the essential criteria to determine the justification of the use of deadly force.

DT501.2.D. Identify the subject's ability, opportunity, and intent as it relates to the officer's response to resistance.

DT501.1.E. Explain the concept of totality of circumstances.

DT501.1.A. Identify various situational factors that may influence the use of force.

Objective Reasonableness

The courts have used the term ***objective reasonableness*** to describe the process for evaluating the appropriateness of an officer's response to a subject's resistance *(DT501.1.D.)*. Appropriate force is the amount of force reasonably necessary to make an arrest. The U.S. Supreme Court said in *Graham v. Connor*, 490 U.S. 386 (1989), that the reasonableness of a particular use of force must be judged from the perspective of how a reasonable officer on the scene would respond, rather than from the 20/20 perspective of hindsight. To determine if an officer's actions were objectively reasonable, the courts look at the facts and circumstances the officer knew when the incident occurred. Courts recognize that criminal justice officers must make split-second judgments about the amount of force needed in a particular situation under circumstances that are tense, uncertain, and rapidly evolving. *(DT501.2.B.)*

The officer's reasons for using force must be consistent with constitutional and statutory law, as well as agency policy and training guidelines. The Supreme Court has made clear that use of force is a seizure under the Fourth Amendment. Correctional officers must also consider that use of force may violate the Eighth Amendment's prohibition against cruel and unusual punishment.

An officer's agency may establish the specific techniques, tactics, and applications that an officer may use in an encounter with a resistant subject.

Authority to Use Force

Much litigation against criminal justice officers is not about the amount of force used, but whether the use of force was permitted at all. Though the law grants criminal justice officers the right to use force, this right is conditioned on their official authority.

Correctional officers have full-time authority over inmates due to the inmates' adjudication and suspension of civil rights. A law enforcement officer's authority to use force is established by the officer's reasonable belief that a crime has been, is being, or is about to be committed. Absent this belief, known as reasonable suspicion, a law enforcement officer has no authority over a subject, and thus no permission to use any amount of force at all. *(DT501.2.)*

Escalation, De-Escalation, and Disengagement

Force decisions may escalate and de-escalate rapidly in relation to the perceived threat. An officer's goal is to achieve subject compliance. *Compliance* is the verbal and/or physical yielding to an officer's authority without apparent threat of resistance or violence.

Escalation, de-escalation, and disengagement are important concepts in making legally and tactically sound, reasonable responses to resistance. *Escalation* is increasing the use of force or resistance. *De-escalation* is decreasing the use of force or resistance. *Disengagement* is discontinuing a command or physical use of force, for example, by breaking away from a subject *(DT501.2.C.)*. Officers are legally permitted to escalate their use of force as the subject escalates his or her level of resistance. The officer's choices are determined by the subject's actions and the risk of physical harm posed to the officer or others *(DT501.1.B.)*. Once the officer achieves control or compliance, he or she must de-escalate the use of force. Under certain circumstances, disengagement may be the best tactical option, for example, when the officer is waiting for backup, when the officer is injured or outnumbered, or when the suspect has superior firepower.

Force Guidelines

The *Force Guidelines* provide a framework for making decisions involving the reasonable use of force by criminal justice officers. The structure of the Force Guidelines is based on constitutional considerations and case law and describes appropriate decision making in a fluid and dynamic situation. The Guidelines consider the relationship between subject resistance and various situational factors in determining the officer's response options.

Subject Resistance Levels

Passive resistance is a subject's verbal and/or physical refusal to comply with an officer's lawful direction causing the officer to use physical techniques to establish control. *(DT501.2.B.1.)*

Some examples of passive resistance include the following:

- The subject refuses to move at the officer's direction.
- The subject peacefully protests at a political event in a public location.
- The subject refuses to take his hands out of his pockets or from behind his back.

Active resistance is a subject's use of physically evasive movements directed toward the officer such as bracing, tensing, pushing, or pulling to prevent the officer from establishing control over the subject. *(DT501.2.B.2.)*

Some examples of active resistance include the following:

- The subject physically anchors himself to a person or object to prevent himself from being removed.
- The subject braces or pulls away from the officer when the officer grips the subject's arm.
- The subject attempts to run when the officer touches or attempts to grab the subject's arm or shoulder.

Aggressive resistance is a subject's attacking movements toward an officer that may cause injury but are not likely to cause death or great bodily harm to the officer or others. *(DT501.2.B.3.)*

Some examples of aggressive resistance include the following:

- The subject balls up his fist and approaches the officer.
- The subject pushes the officer back as the officer tries to take the subject into custody.
- The subject grabs any part of the officer's body.

Deadly force resistance is a subject's hostile, attacking movements with or without a weapon that create a reasonable perception by the officer that the subject intends to cause and has the capability of causing death or great bodily harm to the officer or others. *(DT501.2.B.4.)*

Some examples of deadly force resistance include the following:

- A subject refuses to drop a knife when ordered to by the officer and moves toward the officer.
- A subject shoots or points a gun at an officer or other person.
- A subject tries to use a vehicle to run down an officer.

Officer Response Options

Officers should try to resolve a situation with the least amount of force necessary. Command presence and verbal communication often will defuse many volatile situations. Sometimes, however, these are not enough or officers may not have an opportunity to use them. An officer may have to use physical force to gain control of the situation. Physical force includes physical control, the use of nonlethal weapons, and deadly force. Officers need not apply force in gradually increasing steps in order to justify physical control or even deadly force. Instead, officers need to respond with all the force reasonably necessary for the circumstances in each specific situation.

Physical control is achieving compliance or custody through the use of empty-hand or leverage-enhanced techniques, such as pain compliance, transporters, restraint devices, takedowns, and striking techniques. *(DT501.2.B.5.)*

A ***nonlethal weapon*** is a weapon that is not fundamentally designed to cause death or great bodily harm *(DT501.2.B.6.)*. Some examples of nonlethal weapons include electronic control devices (ECD), dart-firing stun guns such as a TASER®, expandable batons, flashlights, and chemical agent sprays.

Deadly force is force that is likely to cause death or great bodily harm *(DT501.2.A.1.)*. Some examples of deadly force include use of a firearm, eye gouges, empty-hand strikes to the throat, and impact-weapon strikes to the side of the neck.

Section 776.06, F.S. states:

(1) The term "deadly force" means force that is likely to cause death or great bodily harm, and includes, but is not limited to:

   a. The firing of a firearm in the direction of the person to be arrested, even though no intent exists to kill or inflict great bodily harm; and

   b. The firing of a firearm at a vehicle in which the person to be arrested is riding.

Section 776.07, F.S., states:

> (2) A correctional officer or other law enforcement officer is justified in the use of force, including deadly force, which he or she reasonably believes to be necessary to prevent the escape from a penal institution of a person whom the officer reasonably believes to be lawfully detained in such institution under sentence for an offense or awaiting trial or commitment for an offense.

Use of deadly force may be an officer's first and only appropriate response to a perceived threat. Deadly force does not necessarily mean that someone died from the force used. It can cause great bodily harm or no harm at all. For example, returning fire is deadly force even if the officer misses the target.

The officer must base his or her decision to use deadly force as a defensive tactic on a clear, reasonable belief that he or she, a fellow officer, or another person, faces imminent danger of death or great bodily harm. *(DT501.2.A.2.)*

Factors for Deciding the Use of Deadly Force

Officers use three criteria for making deadly force decisions: ability, opportunity, and intent. *(DT501.2.D.)*

Ability refers to the subject having the means to carry out his or her intent to cause death or great bodily harm. An officer must determine whether the subject has the necessary means to cause death or great bodily harm to the officer or others. A weapon is not required; a subject must only have the apparent ability to carry out his or her intention. If the subject seems physically able to cause death or great bodily harm, then he has the ability. For example, a 6'4", 250-lb. muscular man threatening to do bodily harm to an officer does not necessarily need a weapon. By virtue of his size and physical condition, he has the apparent ability.

Opportunity means the subject is capable of carrying out an intention to cause death or great bodily harm to the officer or others. The subject's weapon often determines opportunity. For example, a suspect armed with a knife may not be an immediate threat to an officer standing far away. However, the same person standing closer or carrying a firearm certainly has the opportunity to carry out his intent to cause death or great bodily harm.

Intent is a reasonably perceived, imminent threat to an officer or another person based on the subject's actions, behaviors, words, or other indicators. It is a perception derived from the totality of the circumstances.

Officers should use the amount of force necessary and reasonable for the situation. If ability, opportunity, and intent are present and the officer cannot control the threat using lesser means, then deadly force is justified. When resistance de-escalates, so must the officer's response.

Totality of Circumstances

Totality of circumstances is a term the court uses to refer to all facts and circumstances known to the officer at the time, or reasonably perceived by the officer as the basis for, a use of force decision. The courts will look at the totality of circumstances in determining whether the decision was objectively reasonable and, therefore, legally justified. The totality of circumstances includes consideration of the subject's form of resistance, all reasonably perceived situational factors that may have an effect on the situation, and the response options available to the officer. *(DT501.1.E.)*

Some situational factors may include the following:

- severity of the crime

- subject is an immediate threat

- subject's mental or psychiatric history, if known to the officer

- subject's violent history, if known to the officer

- subject's combative skills

- subject's access to weapons

- innocent bystanders who could be harmed

- number of subjects versus number of officers

- duration of confrontation

- subject's size, age, weight, and physical condition

- officer's size, age, weight, physical condition, and defensive tactics expertise

- environmental factors, such as physical terrain, weather conditions, etc. (DT501.1.A.)

The Force Guidelines (see Figure 4-2 on the following page) recognizes that officers make use of force decisions based on the totality of circumstances at the time of the incident. Circumstances are fluid and dynamic. Formulating a valid response requires continual assessment as the situation changes.

Use of Force Reporting

Most agencies require an additional report anytime an officer uses force to control a subject. Officers need to clearly articulate the specific basis for their decisions regarding the use of force. For example, if deadly force was used, the officer should state exactly what the subject did that created the perception of the subject's ability, opportunity, and intent to cause death or great bodily harm. Simply stating "The suspect threatened me" is not sufficient.

Officers should remember that whatever is written on a use of force incident report will be seen by not only supervisors but also by a prosecutor, defense attorney, judge, and potentially many others. Officers should be careful to include every factor used in their use of force decision since factors added later will be viewed with suspicion.

Section Vocabulary
ability
active resistance
aggressive resistance
compliance
de-escalation
deadly force
deadly force resistance
disengagement
escalation
Force Guidelines
intent
nonlethal weapon
objective reasonableness
opportunity
passive resistance
physical control
totality of circumstances

Subject Resistance	Situational Factors
Is the subject verbally or physically resisting my lawful authority?	What subject factors influence this situation? Weapon? Physical size? Demeanor? Others?
Is the subject making attacking movements that are not likely to cause death or great bodily harm?	What officer factors influence this situation? Training? Experience? Physical size? Others?
Is the subject making attacking movements that are likely to cause death or great bodily harm?	What environmental factors influence this situation? Weather? Location? Presence of others?
Justification	**Officer's Response**
Were my actions reasonable based on the subject's resistance and the totality of the circumstances?	Can I physically control the subject?
Am I able to articulate the reasons for my actions?	Could I use a nonlethal weapon not meant to cause death or great bodily harm?
Was I in compliance with constitutional and state laws, agency policy, and training?	Is deadly force the appropriate option to prevent death or great bodily harm to myself or others?

Force guidelines–The decision making process

Figure 4-2

UNIT 2 | USE OF FORCE
LESSON 2 | Survival Stress Reaction

Survival Stress

Survival stress, sometimes called fear-induced stress, is stress caused by hormonal changes brought on by a perception of danger. The hormones cause an elevated heart rate that affects an officer's cognitive decision making skills *(IN015.1.H.)*. There are four instinctual reactions to fear-induced stress: fight, flight, posture, and submit.

During an encounter, survival stress occurs in both subject and officer. Some subjects may fight or flee, but some decide to do what an officer tells them (submit). Some react verbally and physically as if they may resist (*posturing*) until the moment of truth. Then, they submit, fight, or flee.

A subject may demonstrate posturing when an officer gives him a command. The subject expands his chest and begins to speak loudly, shouting, "You're not taking me!" He strikes his chest with his open hands while stepping back and forth, side to side as he yells the same words over and over. When the officer displays a higher level of force or backup officers arrive, the subject may back down and follow the officer's verbal directions with no force used. If the subject does not submit to the officer's authority, this posturing may be a precursor to a fight or an indication that the subject is preparing to run.

When an officer is in a physically or emotionally threatening situation, the officer's body adapts to help him or her react more effectively to the threat by releasing adrenaline and other hormones. By knowing this, the officer is better prepared to respond and to recognize his or her body's changes in response to trauma and other incidents of injury.

An officer should be aware of certain changes that occur to the body during and after survival stress including physiological changes, motor performance changes, visual performance changes, cognitive changes, and critical incident amnesia.

Physiological Changes *(IN015.1.H.1.)*

The heart rate and respiration increase.

Vascular flow moves away from the extremities. The body pulls the blood away from the arms and legs into the torso. This keeps the blood near vital organs in case of emergency and also protects the arms and legs (our weapons) from losing too much blood in case of injury.

Hearing is diminished—this is known as *auditory exclusion*.

Motor Performance Changes *(IN015.1.H.2.)*

There is a loss of fine motor skills at a heart rate of approximately 115 beats per minute. *Fine motor skills* refer to the muscle control required to make small, precise movements, such as unlocking handcuffs with a key.

Gross motor skills are enhanced as the heart rate reaches 150 beats per minute. ***Gross motor skills*** are the movements of the large or major muscles of the body, such as running, punching, or kicking.

There is a loss of complex motor skills at a heart rate of approximately 145 beats per minute. ***Complex motor skills*** combine fine and gross motor skills using hand and eye coordination timed to a single event, such as when driving a vehicle.

Catastrophic motor skill breakdown may occur when the heart rate exceeds 175 beats per minute.

There may be an increase in strength and speed for a short period of time.

The heart rate may spike during a violent encounter to well over 200 beats per minute.

Visual Performance Changes *(IN015.1.H.3.)*

Binocular vision is dominant. Both eyes remain open and it is very difficult to close just one eye.

There is a loss of peripheral vision and depth perception; this is known as tunnel vision.

There is a loss of near vision. This is one reason that most officers involved in shootings never see the sights of their firearms. Physiologically, it is nearly impossible to focus.

Cognitive Functions *(IN015.1.H.4.)*

The ***cognitive brain***, the part that logically thinks and plans, begins to shut down at 145 beats per minute.

Decision making is inhibited. The more choices you have, the slower you are to make a decision.

Reaction time increases. This may be because of too much stimuli to process quickly or because of denial that a violent encounter is actually happening.

In general, high levels of adrenaline caused by fear-induced stress are likely to result in extreme strength, an increase in speed, a decrease in fine motor skills, and an increased ability to ignore pain. In other words, strength goes way up and dexterity goes way down.

Threat Awareness

The Threat Awareness Spectrum (see Figure 4-3) illustrates how survival stress may affect an officer's reaction to a perceived threat. The desired state of awareness and readiness of an officer while on duty is Condition Yellow *(IN014.2.A.1.)*. This allows an officer to be ready to move to Condition Orange and Condition Red as appropriate for the situation. Officers should avoid Condition White and Condition Black.

Critical Incident Amnesia

Officers who encounter an extremely stressful situation such as an officer-involved shooting may show signs of post-traumatic stress disorder. They may also exhibit long-term memory loss, a temporary condition known as ***critical incident amnesia*** *(IN015.1.I.1.)*. Particular memory-related phenomena in traumatic situations may include the following:

During the actual incident, there is usually a sensory overload combined with a fixation on some particular aspect of the critical incident, often to the exclusion of all else.

Immediately after the incident, post-incident amnesia will often result in a failure to remember the majority of the information observed in the incident.

Condition White	Condition Yellow	Condition Orange	Condition Red	Condition Black
Unaware that a threat exists	General awareness of possible threats	Recognition that a threat exists	Specific threat identified and appropriate actions taken	Threat mismanaged due to panicked stress response
Attention is unfocused or preoccupied, and the officer is oblivious to potential danger in his or her environment.	Attention is focused, and the officer scans the environment for potential threats.	Awareness of a specific threat encourages preplanning and more intense focus. Physical indicators of stress may become evident.	The threat is assessed and managed through intensified cognitive and physical reactions. Survival stress functions become optimum.	Survival stress functions break down. Submission or freezing may occur.
Example: A person drives to work and does not remember the drive (automatic pilot).	*Example:* While on the job, an officer is in a state of relaxed awareness and notices what is going on around him or her.	*Examples:* A patrol officer observes a vehicle backed into a parking space at a convenience store with the engine running, considers the possibility of a robbery in progress, and begins tactical planning. A correctional officer observes an inmate with possible contraband and begins formulating a plan of action.	*Examples:* The patrol officer initiates the plan to engage the suspects as they exit the store. The correctional officer initiates the plan to engage the inmate.	*Examples:* The patrol officer panics and may not respond effectively. The correctional officer panics and may not respond effectively.

Threat awareness spectrum

Figure 4-3

After a healthy night's sleep, there is usually a memory recovery which will result in remembering the majority of what occurred. This memory is probably the most pure.

Within 72 hours, the final and most complete form of memory recovery will occur, but it will be at least partially reconstructed and therefore somewhat contaminated after the inevitable process of integrating available information from other sources, such as the news media.

Controlling the Effects of Survival Stress

Survival stress is a natural reaction to danger, but officers can prepare and increase their chances of controlling the effects of the stress *(IN015.3.A.)*. Officers can do the following:

Section Vocabulary

auditory exclusion

binocular vision

cognitive brain

complex motor skills

critical incident amnesia

fine motor skills

gross motor skills

posturing

survival stress/fear-induced stress

• pre-plan—The time to figure out what to do is before the confrontation begins. Emotions such as fear, anger, panic, anxiety, or any combination will be present during high stress events. If officers call upon their physical and mental training, they greatly improve their chances of surviving the violence.

• stay physically fit

• use deep breathing techniques

• rely on gross motor movements over fine and complex motor skills

• be prepared for resistance with every subject encounter

• maintain proficiency in physical skills—The skills officers develop will diminish without constant practice and use.

UNIT 3 | DEFENSIVE TACTICS TECHNIQUES
LESSON 1 | Fundamental Principles of Defensive Tactics

Fundamental Principles of Defensive Tactics

To properly and effectively perform defensive tactics techniques, you must be able to apply certain fundamental principles. *(DT501.3.U.)*

Balance—Maintaining a balanced posture is essential in performing any technique. To achieve balance, your head and hips must be aligned and your weight distributed evenly between your feet. If any one of these points is misaligned, you are not in balance. *Balance displacement* is a controlling technique used to break the subject's balance through the use of leverage principles. *(DT501.3.U.1.)*

Leverage—Leverage is using a great force against a weaker resistance. It is used in conjunction with joint manipulation and/or pain and mechanical compliance in order to gain control. *(DT501.3.U.2.)*

Pain compliance—Pain compliance is a subject's response to a combination of pain and verbal commands to stop resisting. *(DT501.3.U.3.)*

Mechanical compliance—An officer may gain control over a subject by applying pressure or leverage on a joint by locking it up so that no movement of the joint is possible, causing the subject to comply with verbal direction. *(DT501.3.U.4.)*

Joint manipulation—An officer may gain control over a subject by bending or twisting a joint in a direction that will cause pain or discomfort to the joint. *(DT501.3.U.5.)*

Motor dysfunction—An officer may gain control over a subject by using an incapacitation technique that causes temporary impairment of muscular control. *(DT501.3.U.6.)*

Fluid shock principle—For maximum effectiveness, most strikes are delivered utilizing penetration so that the striking object stays on or indented in the target for an instant allowing for energy transfer. When a major muscle mass is struck this way, it displaces the water content in the muscle and penetrates the nerves within, creating a shock wave. The effect on the subject will be greatly multiplied. This is known as the fluid shock principle. When delivering a strike, an officer strikes a muscle so that the striking object penetrates the muscle and nerves of the target area. This is a full transfer of kinetic energy that increases the power of the strike. *(DT501.3.U.7.)*

OBJECTIVES

DT501.3.U. Describe the fundamental principles of applying defensive tactics.

DT501.3.U.1. Explain the use of balance in applying defensive tactics.

DT501.3.U.2. Explain how leverage is used in the application of defensive tactics.

DT501.3.U.3. Explain the use of pain compliance in applying defensive tactics.

DT501.3.U.4. Describe the use of mechanical compliance in applying defensive tactics.

DT501.3.U.5. Describe the use of joint manipulation to control a resistant subject.

DT501.3.U.6. Describe how to use motor dysfunction to control a resistant subject.

DT501.3.U.7. Identify the fluid shock principle.

Section Vocabulary

balance

balance displacement

fluid shock principle

joint manipulation

leverage

mechanical compliance

motor dysfunction

pain compliance

UNIT 3 | DEFENSIVE TACTICS TECHNIQUES

LESSON 2 | Threat Assessment: Threat Assessment and Response

OBJECTIVES

DT501.3.A.1. Identify the necessity of conducting a threat assessment.

DT501.1.C. Identify verbal and nonverbal cues in assessing threats.

DT501.3.A. Demonstrate officer presence.

DT501.3.A.4. Demonstrate the interview stance.

DT501.3.A.5. Demonstrate the offensive ready stance.

DT501.3.A.3.b. Identify relative positioning.

DT501.3.A.3. Demonstrate the slide step approach.

DT501.3.A.2. Demonstrate how to maintain a minimum reactionary gap.

DT501.3.A.3.a. Identify the danger zone.

DT501.3.B.1. Demonstrate hand clearing techniques.

DT501.3.A.1.a. Define *reaction time principle*.

DT501.3.I.1. Demonstrate evasion techniques.

DT501.3.I.2. Demonstrate redirection techniques.

Though it may be difficult to determine factors that constitute a specific threat, there are certain facts, circumstances, and conditions that, when taken together, may be perceived by an officer as threatening.

An officer's assessment of a perceived threat is critical for safety and influences his or her actions when dealing with a situation. The more information an officer has, the better prepared he or she will be to assess the situation. All factors, whether obvious or not, should be considered when assessing threats. *(DT501.3.A.1.)*

Officers must recognize that threats may be fluid and constantly changing. Officers should continuously analyze situations for their threat potential.

Subject Behavior

There are certain verbal and nonverbal cues that indicate the possibility of subject aggression or posturing. *(DT501.1.C.)*

Verbal cues may include abnormal stuttering, serious and specific swearing, and specific verbal threats.

Nonverbal cues may include the following:

- increased breathing and pulse rates
- cessation of all movement
- clenched fists and quivering hands
- refusal to show palms of hands
- reddened or flushed face
- expanding veins showing prominently on face and forearms
- shifting of shoulders or change of stance
- target glance
- ignoring the officer
- rapid, angry movements

Excited Delirium

Officers should be aware of unusual symptoms exhibited by a subject upon initial contact or that may develop or intensify during the course of the confrontation. These symptoms may be indicators of serious issues, such as physical illness, mental illness, drug reaction or overdose, or post-traumatic stress disorder.

The unusual symptoms or behavior is usually attributed to a condition known as excited delirium. "***Excited delirium*** is a state of extreme mental and physiological excitement characterized by exceptional agitation and hyperactivity, overheating, excessive tearing of the eyes, hostility, superhuman strength, aggression, acute paranoia, and endurance without apparent fatigue" (Lewinski, 2006).

A subject in a state of excited delirium could die suddenly and without explanation, a death sometimes referred to as Sudden Death Syndrome. Unfortunately, the death may be wrongly attributed to the actions of an officer or his or her use of certain levels of force.

When confronting a subject with unusual symptoms, an officer should immediately seek medical attention. Be careful of the position in which the subject is restrained. Take care to maintain an open airway, and ensure continuous breathing and proper circulation until medical help arrives.

Environmental Factors

Some potential environmental factors that should also be considered in threat assessment may include weather, traffic conditions, terrain, presence of animals, presence of bystanders, and potential weapons.

Presence

Officer presence is your ability to convey to subjects and onlookers that you are able and ready to take control. Subjects' and onlookers' reaction toward you depends on their perceptions of how you present yourself.

You should be aware of and interpret nonverbal communication. Some movements and gestures are clues to escalating aggression, for example, clenched fists, shifting feet, or hidden hands. Subjects also observe your actions to determine your attitudes and intentions. Officer presence is your first response to any situation. By simply arriving on the scene, an officer affects a subject or situation. *(DT501.3.A.)*

Command presence is the way you carry yourself. Your presence can determine whether a subject's resistance escalates or de-escalates. A good command presence projects an image of confidence in your skills and abilities to perform the task at hand. Important aspects of command presence include personal appearance (uniform and personal grooming), erect posture, and alertness and attention to surroundings.

Stances
Interview Stance *(DT501.3.A.4.)*

Stand with head, hips, and feet aligned.

Place your feet shoulder-width apart with the knees slightly bent.

Angle your body to the subject with the strong side away.

Place your hands above waist level. (See Figure 4-4)

Offensive Ready Stance *(DT501.3.A.5.)*

Stand with your head, hips, and feet aligned.

Plant your feet slightly wider than shoulder-width apart with the knees in a deep crouch.

Interview stance

Figure 4-4

Offensive ready stance *Figure 4-5*

Reactionary gap   *Figure 4-6*

Your body is angled to the subject with the strong side away.

Place your hands at your face level and towards your center. (See Figure 4-5)

Relative Positioning

When preparing to approach a subject, an officer must place him- or herself in the safest possible position. *Relative positioning* describes an officer's position in relation to the subject. *(DT501.3.A.3.b.)* (See Figures 4-8 & 4-9)

Body movement refers to how you approach a subject or enter a scene. The manner and direction from which you approach a subject and the distance you maintain from the subject throughout the interaction are based on your assessment of the threat and potential harm present.

The *slide step* is used when preparing to engage or disengage from a subject in close proximity. Use this method to maintain balance and an appropriate stance:

Maintain a balanced stance with head, hips, and feet aligned.

Step with your lead foot.

Slide your trailing foot forward.

Keep your feet shoulder-width apart. *(DT501.3.A.3.)*

The distance you must keep between you and the subject in order to react effectively against a sudden threat is the *reactionary gap* (See Figure 4-6). This distance is generally 6–9 feet if you have visual control of the subject's hands, or 25 feet when you cannot see the subject's hands. *(DT501.3.A.2.)*

The area within the reactionary gap is the *danger zone*. Anytime an officer is in the danger zone, the potential for physical harm increases. *(DT501.3.A.3.a.)*

1

2

Hand-clearing technique

Figure 4-7

Visual control of the hands is the ability to see both the subject's hands and to know that those hands hold no weapons.

When approaching a subject, you may use the following hand-clearing technique:

Maintain an appropriate reactionary gap.

Visually scan the area for potential threats.

Assume an appropriate stance.

Identify yourself as an officer, if appropriate.

Use clear, concise verbal commands.

Tell the subject to expose both palms. *(DT501.3.B.1.)* (See Figure 4-7)

Reaction time principle is the amount of time it takes for the brain to process a physical threat and the body to respond *(DT501.3.A.1.a.)*. This process involves perceiving and analyzing the threat, formulating a strategy, and initiating motor action(s). In other words, the officer sees the threat, figures out what to do, and then takes action.

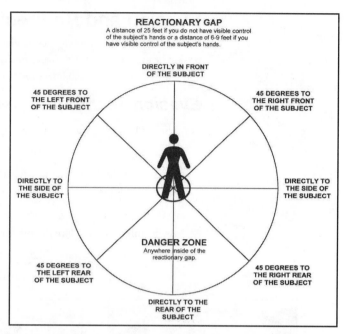

Relative positioning diagram

Figure 4-8

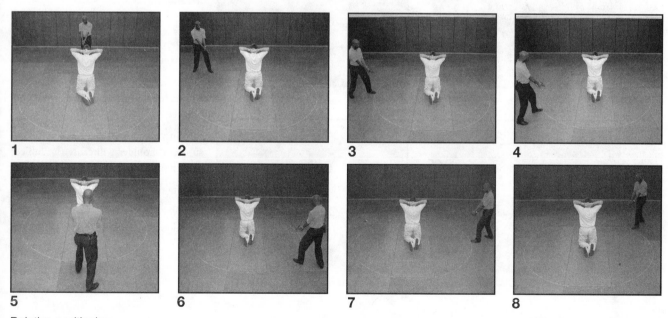

Relative positioning

Figure 4-9

Evasion and Redirection

Evasive and redirection movements are used to avoid or redirect an attack. ***Evasion*** is simply shifting your body or side stepping to avoid the attack. ***Redirection*** is using the hands to move the subject away. Using evasive and redirecting tactics may allow time to disengage, escape, or use other force options.

Evasion Technique *(DT501.3.I.1.)*

Use loud, clear verbal commands throughout the application of the technique.

Assume the offensive ready stance.

Sidestep the direct line of attack to either the strong or supporting side. Direct line of attack simply means the direction that the subject comes from. Sidestepping to either side gets you out of the subject's way.

Face the subject.

As the subject passes, face the subject and maintain an offensive ready stance.

The offensive ready stance positions the officer to respond if the subject attacks again.

Follow up with an appropriate technique(s). (See Figure 4-10)

1

2

3

4

Evasion technique

Redirection Technique *(DT501.3.I.2.)*

Use loud, clear verbal commands throughout the application of the technique.

Assume the offensive ready stance.

Sidestep the direct line of attack to either the strong or supporting side.

As the subject passes, redirect the subject by pushing the subject away and off balance.

Striking the upper back or side of the subject's shoulder will cause the subject to spin off balance.

Maintain an offensive ready stance.

Follow up with an appropriate technique(s). (See Figure 4-11)

Figure 4-10

Redirection technique

Figure 4-11

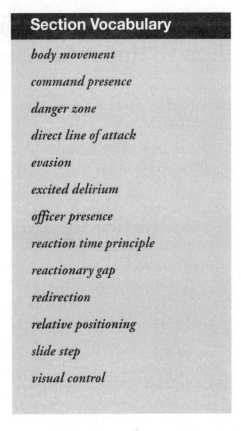

UNIT 3 | DEFENSIVE TACTICS TECHNIQUES

LESSON 3 | Threat Assessment: Communication and Commands

OBJECTIVES

DT501.3.B. Demonstrate applicable verbal direction.

Section Vocabulary

communication

dialogue

touch

verbal direction

Communication transcends all levels of a use of force exchange. Unlike a category of force, communication is a part of all officer-subject interactions. Officers are encouraged to use communication before, during, and after a confrontation. Communication is necessary to continually gauge compliance. In a use of force situation, resistance begins when a subject fails to submit to an officer's authority. When an officer gives a verbal command, an evaluation will determine if escalation may become necessary.

Communication is the exchanging of information through verbal and nonverbal methods which provides valuable insight into the likelihood of cooperation and compliance of a subject.

Dialogue is a controlled, non-emotional communication between an officer and a subject aimed at problem solving and communication. Used as a strategy, dialogue is intentionally designed to gain rapport and exchange information.

Verbal direction is the use of proper, clear, and concise commands to let a subject know what you need or expect him or her to do. The ability to give verbal direction is usually the first step in controlling the subject's actions. Establish yourself as a criminal justice officer. Give clear and concise commands. Make sure that your commands are loud enough for the subject to hear. *(DT501.3.B.)*

Touch is a nonthreatening, noncustodial physical contact and can be used to support or emphasize a verbal command. It can be effective to enhance your communication; however, you must evaluate carefully so as not to escalate a subject's resistance.

UNIT 3 | DEFENSIVE TACTICS TECHNIQUES
LESSON 4 | Control Tactics: Pressure Points

Pressure points are techniques used to control resistant behavior by utilizing pain compliance. Pressure or leverage is applied using a fingertip or thumb tip to a target nerve, joint, or sensitive area causing pain and compliance to verbal direction. These techniques do not work on every person or in all situations but are generally effective.

The two main components of pressure point techniques are as follows:

- *touch pressure*—touching the location of a nerve or sensitive area and applying continual, uninterrupted pressure with the tip of the finger(s) or thumb until the subject complies.

- *stabilization*—immobilizing the subject's head so the subject cannot move or escape. Be careful not to apply too much pressure or torque on the neck or spine when stabilizing the head.

As soon as the subject complies by obeying your commands, release pressure to stop the pain. On all pressure point techniques, applying pressure longer than 3–5 seconds without a response may result in an adrenaline surge. This may cause the subject to exhibit symptoms similar to survival responses, inability to feel pain, extraordinary strength, or auditory exclusion. *(DT501.3.H.)*

Exercise caution when applying a pressure point technique. The subject's hands are free and you must move inside the danger zone. Also be aware of the possibility of being bitten by the subject.

Pressure point techniques covered in this lesson include the following:

- under the jaw
- hollow behind the ear
- hollow behind the collarbone
- under the nose
- hollow of the neck

Under the Jaw

This technique works well to bring a seated, kneeling, or prone subject to a standing position.

> Approach the subject safely.
>
> Use loud, repetitive verbal commands to let the subject know what you want him to do.
>
> Stabilize the subject's head. Locate the pressure point under the jawbone.
>
> Apply pressure until compliance.

OBJECTIVES

DT501.3.H. Demonstrate pressure point techniques.

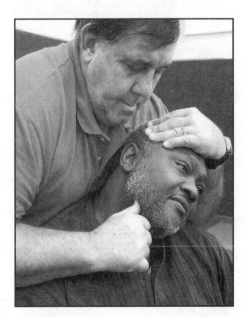

Pressure points–
Under the jaw

Figure 4-12

Decrease the pressure when the subject complies. Do not release control, just the pressure. If the subject begins to resist again, reapply the pressure.

Follow up with an appropriate technique(s). (See Figure 4-12)

Hollow Behind the Ear

Applying pressure to the sensitive area in the hollow behind the ear is a good technique to use on a seated or prone subject or a subject who is holding onto a fixed object.

Approach the subject safely.

Use loud, repetitive verbal commands to let the subject know what you want him to do.

Stabilize the subject's head and locate the pressure point in the vicinity of the hollow behind the ear.

Apply pressure inward and toward the nose until compliance.

Decrease the pressure when the subject complies. Do not release control, just the pressure. If the subject begins to resist again, reapply the pressure.

Follow up with an appropriate technique(s). (See Figure 4-13)

Hollow Behind the Collarbone

Use this technique when you want a standing subject to sit, lie down, or move to another location. You can employ this technique from either the front or the side of the subject.

Approach the subject safely.

Use loud, repetitive verbal commands to let the subject know what you want him to do.

Stabilize the subject.

Locate the pressure point behind the collarbone.

Apply pressure toward the feet until compliance.

Decrease the pressure when the subject complies. Do not release control, just the pressure. If the subject begins to resist again, reapply the pressure.

Follow up with an appropriate technique(s). (See Figure 4-14)

Under the Nose

Approach the subject safely.

Use loud, repetitive verbal commands to let the subject know what you want him to do.

Stabilize the subject.

Locate the pressure point under the base of the nose.

Apply pressure upward toward the center of the brain until compliance.

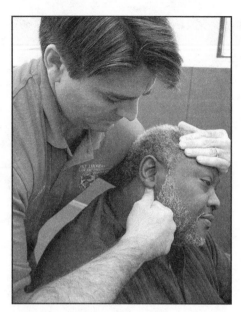

Pressure points—
Hollow behind the ear

Figure 4-13

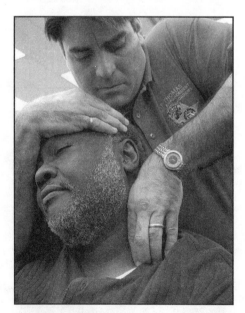

Pressure points—
Hollow behind the collarbone

Figure 4-14

Decrease the pressure when the subject complies. Do not release control, just the pressure. If the subject begins to resist again, reapply the pressure.

Follow up with an appropriate technique(s). (See Figure 4-15)

Hollow of the Neck

This technique performed at the jugular notch is usually used for thwarting an attack by balance displacement.

Approach the subject safely.

Use loud, repetitive verbal commands to let the subject know what you want him to do.

Stabilize the subject.

Locate the pressure point in the hollow of the front of the neck, just above the sternum.

Apply pressure inward until compliance.

For pain compliance, apply pressure inward and downward toward the stomach. For gag reflex, apply pressure inward and upward toward the back of the neck.

Decrease the pressure when the subject complies. Do not release control, just the pressure. If the subject begins to resist again, reapply the pressure.

Follow up with an appropriate technique(s). (See Figure 4-16)

Section Vocabulary
pressure points
stabilization
touch pressure

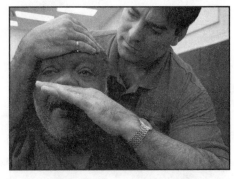

Pressure points–   Figure 4-15
Under the nose

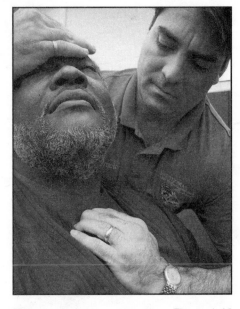

Pressure points–   Figure 4-16
Hollow of the neck

UNIT 3 | DEFENSIVE TACTICS TECHNIQUES

LESSON 5 | Control Tactics: Escorts and Transporters

OBJECTIVES

DT501.3.F. Demonstrate escort and transporter techniques.

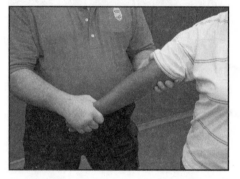

Escort position   Figure 4-17

Officers may encounter subjects who refuse to obey their commands but demonstrate no physical resistance. Pain compliance, mechanical compliance, and/or joint manipulation techniques can be used to move the unwilling subject from one location to another. These techniques are called escorts and transporters. These escort and transporter techniques are the basis for some takedowns.

Escorts

The *escort* position is a technique used to move a subject from one point to another without using pain compliance. It provides minimal control of the subject through leverage. If a subject resists, you may transition to a transporter technique.

Transporters

Transporters, sometimes called *come-along holds*, are techniques used to move a subject from one point to another with pain compliance and/or mechanical compliance.

When using an escort or transporter technique, you enter the danger zone and should always be aware of your weapon's proximity to the subject.

The following are escort and transporter techniques included in this lesson:

- escort position
- bent wrist
- finger lock
- hammer lock
- shoulder lock *(DT501.3.F.)*

Escort Position

An escort may be your first physical contact with a subject. You apply pressure or leverage on a joint to lock it and the subject complies.

Use loud, clear verbal commands throughout the application of the technique.

Maintain an appropriate stance.

Make contact with the subject's arm by controlling the upper arm just above the elbow and wrist simultaneously.

Turn the subject's palm so that it is facing you.

Move the subject, or follow up with an appropriate technique(s). (See Figure 4-17)

Bent Wrist Transporter

The bent wrist transporter transitions from the escort position when the subject tries to resist by pulling his arm away. Effective joint manipulation causes pain compliance, making the subject move in the direction you are leading.

1

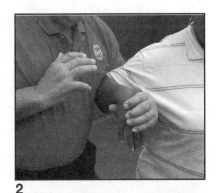

2

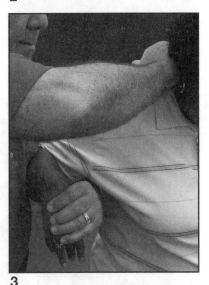

3

Bent wrist transporter   *Figure 4-18*

- Use loud, clear verbal commands throughout the application of the technique.

- Maintain an appropriate stance.

- Make contact with the subject's arm by controlling the upper arm just above the elbow and wrist simultaneously.

- Pull the subject's elbow/arm sharply towards the rear, bending the arm at the elbow.

- Secure the subject's elbow firmly against your torso.

- Simultaneously bend the subject's wrist by placing both hands on the subject's hand.

- Apply pressure to the back of the subject's hand toward the subject's elbow.

- Control or move the subject, or follow up with an appropriate technique(s). (See Figure 4-18)

Finger Lock Transporter

The finger lock transporter is usually effective because you hyperextend the subject's fingers, bending them in a direction they are not meant to go. The subject's pain usually leads to compliance.

- Use loud, clear verbal commands throughout the application of the technique.

- Maintain an appropriate stance.

- Make contact with the subject's arm by controlling the upper arm just above the elbow and wrist simultaneously.

- Pull the subject's elbow/arm sharply towards the rear.

- Grabbing the subject's index and middle fingers, rotate the palm upward with the fingers pointed down.

- Secure the subject's elbow firmly against your torso.

- Maintain rearward pressure on the fingers.

- Control or move the subject, or follow up with an appropriate technique(s). (See Figure 4-19)

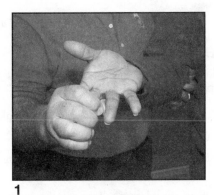

1

Finger lock transporter

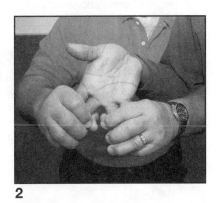

2

Figure 4-19

Hammer Lock Transporter

The hammer lock is a useful technique applied when a subject tries to pull away from the escort position or a bent wrist or finger lock transporter. This technique uses pain compliance and mechanical compliance with the subject's arm behind his back.

Use loud, clear verbal commands throughout the application of the technique.

Maintain an appropriate stance.

Make contact with the subject's arm by controlling the upper arm just above the elbow and wrist simultaneously.

Mirror the controlled hand and rotate the subject's controlled hand while sweeping the subject's hand behind his back.

Maintain control by bending the wrist.

Control or move the subject, or follow up with an appropriate technique(s). (See Figure 4-20)

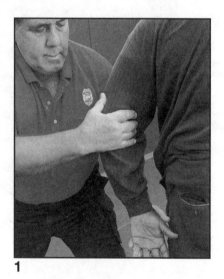
1

2

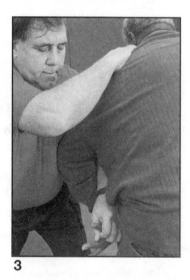
3

Hammer lock transporter

Figure 4-20

Shoulder Lock Transporter

The shoulder lock transporter is a good controlling technique because of the position in which you put the subject's arm. This transporter incorporates pain compliance, joint manipulation, and balance displacement.

Use loud, clear verbal commands throughout the application of the technique.

Maintain an appropriate stance.

Make contact with the subject's arm by controlling the upper arm just above the elbow and wrist simultaneously.

Raise the elbow upward, then roll the shoulder forward.

Push the controlled arm behind the subject's back over your forearm placing your hand on the subject's tricep.

Reach across the subject's back grabbing the opposite shoulder to bring him to an upright position.

Maintain control, or follow up with an appropriate technique(s). (See Figure 4-21)

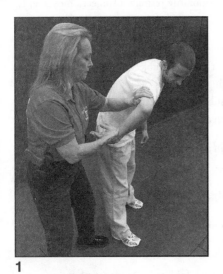

1

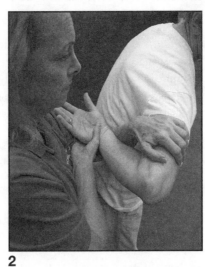

2

Shoulder lock transporter

Figure 4-21

UNIT 3 | DEFENSIVE TACTICS TECHNIQUES
LESSON 6 | Control Tactics: Restraint Devices

OBJECTIVES

DT501.3.D. Demonstrate using restraint devices.

Handcuffs

Restraint devices are tools designed to temporarily restrain a subject's movements, such as handcuffs.

Handcuffs are temporary restraining devices used frequently to control a subject. Because handcuffing does not render a subject harmless, subjects should be continuously monitored to ensure officer safety. Applying handcuffs places the officer inside the reactionary gap or the danger zone. The subject may attempt to resist after the first handcuff is applied. Prepare to respond with an appropriate control technique.

The handcuffing procedure must be done in a controlled manner, thereby minimizing potential harm to both officer and subject.

Using the nomenclature illustration, identify the parts of handcuffs.

Handcuffs or any other restraining device must be kept in working order.

To properly holster or load the handcuffs, do the following:

- Preset the single strands through the pawl, folding key ways together.
- The single strands should point forward, with chain links or hinge downward.

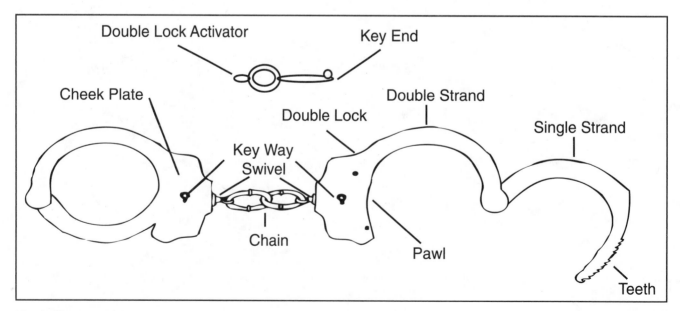

Handcuffs nomenclature

Figure 4-22

Handcuffing Technique

Handcuffing techniques may vary depending on the compliance level of the subject, but the basic steps for applying handcuffs are as follows:

Use loud, clear verbal commands throughout the application of the technique.

Visually inspect and direct the subject into a preparatory position for handcuffing.

Approach the subject.

> • *Note:* If a weapon has been drawn, safely manage the weapon before approaching the subject.

Draw the handcuffs from the holder.

Place one handcuff on one wrist.

Place the other handcuff on the other wrist.

Check for tightness.

Double lock the handcuffs.

Search the subject. *(DT501.3.D.)*

This technique can be used from a variety of positions including standing from a rear or front approach (see Figure 4-23a), kneeling (see Figure 4-23b), or prone (see Figure 4-23c).

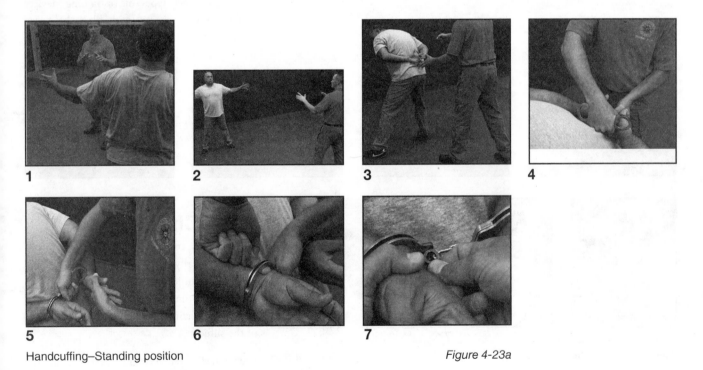

Handcuffing–Standing position

Figure 4-23a

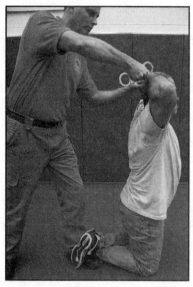

Handcuffing–
Kneeling position

Figure 4-23b

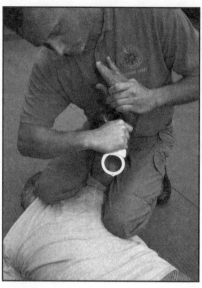

Handcuffing–
Prone position

Figure 4-23c

With noncompliant subjects, use controlling techniques to apply the handcuffs.

Removing Handcuffs

To remove handcuffs, follow these steps:

Use loud, clear verbal commands throughout the application of the technique.

Visually inspect and direct the subject into a preparatory position for removing handcuffs.

Approach the subject.

Draw the handcuff key.

Remove the handcuff from one wrist and close cuff.

Control the subject's uncuffed hand.

Remove the other handcuff and close it.

Move away from the subject. (See Figure 4-23d)

There are other types of restraining devices including waist chains (with black box), leg restraints (leg irons), and flexible leg restraints that may be used in different circumstances.

1   2   3   4

5   6   7

Removing handcuffs

Figure 4-23d

Waist Chains

Waist chains are another type of restraining device, typically used by correctional officers to secure a subject, particularly when moving an inmate from one location to another. To apply waist chains, you will need verbal control of the subject.

Use loud, clear verbal commands throughout the application of the technique.

Position the subject by having him face you with his hands in front and palms facing each other. The subject's hands should be approximately 6 inches away from his body.

Facing the subject, you will place the handcuffs on his wrists, check for tightness, and then double lock the cuffs.

Attach the black box to the handcuffs from the bottom up. Insert the elongated end of the chain to the backside of the black box.

Direct the subject to turn around, wrapping the chain around his waist through the belt loops.

Have the subject pull his hands toward his body to take the slack out of the chain. Use a padlock to go through both lengths of the chain and secure on the subject's side. (See Figure 4-24a)

Leg Restraints

Leg restraints, also called leg irons, are generally used along with waist chains to limit the movement of a subject. To apply leg restraints:

Use loud, clear verbal commands throughout the application of the technique.

Hold the leg restraints with the double bar facing the subject's legs. This will ensure that the key holes are facing down.

Have the subject lean against a wall or kneel on a chair to maintain a balanced stance. Apply the leg restraints to each ankle, check for tightness, and then double lock them. (See Figure 4-24b)

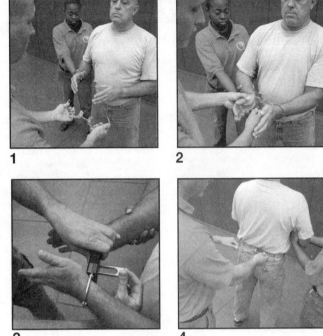

1   **2**

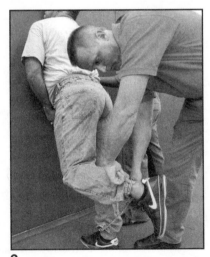

3   **4**

5
Waist chains   *Figure 4-24a*

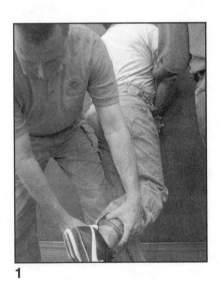

1

Leg restraints   *Figure 4-24b*

Section Vocabulary

handcuffs

restraint devices

Flexible Leg Restraints

Flexible leg restraints are a useful tool for restraining a subject who is kicking, trying to run away, or posing a safety threat. Applying flexible leg restraints is best performed by more than one officer.

Use loud, clear verbal commands throughout the application of the technique.

Control the subject by handcuffing him and placing him in the prone position. Your partner will control the subject's upper body, either with a three-point pin or a wrist compression.

Move close to the subject and kneel or squat near the subject's legs. Control the subject's legs by grabbing and wrapping your hands around them, working your way to the subject's feet.

While holding the subject's feet together, slide the restraints over the lower half of the subject's legs. Keep the restraints above the subject's ankles.

Tighten the restraint device by pulling the excess portion. The restraint should be tight enough to restrict leg movement while allowing normal blood flow.

To further restrict the subject's movement, clip the excess to the handcuff chain by bending the subject's legs at the knees to a 90-degree angle behind the subject. Place the subject in a sitting position or lying on his side to keep pressure off the diaphragm.

UNIT 3 | DEFENSIVE TACTICS TECHNIQUES
LESSON 7 | Control Tactics: Frisks and Searches

A *search* is a government intrusion into a place in which a person has a reasonable expectation of privacy.

Because inmates and probationers have a significantly reduced expectation of privacy, searches by corrections and probation officers are much less limited by Fourth Amendment concerns.

Three search techniques are typically used in the defensive tactics context: pat down, custodial, and inmate. *(DT501.3.E.)*

OBJECTIVES

DT501.3.E. Demonstrate conducting physical frisks and searches.

Pat Down Technique

A *pat down* is a physical frisk of a subject conducted in a predetermined pattern to locate weapons. Before a law enforcement officer may conduct a pat down, he or she must have reasonable suspicion that the subject is armed. (See F.S. §901.151, Florida Stop and Frisk Law.) *Reasonable suspicion* is facts or circumstances which reasonably indicate that the person has committed, is committing, or is about to commit a violation of the law.

"The purpose of a pat down is not to discover evidence of a crime but to allow the officer to pursue his or her investigation without fear of violence." See *Adams v. Williams*, 407 U.S. 143 (1972).

Under the *plain feel doctrine*, the officer may seize any object "whose contour or mass" he or she identifies as apparent contraband. See *Minnesota v. Dickerson*, 508 U.S. 366 (1993). An officer may only pat down the outside of the clothing for weapons.

When conducting a pat down, you should do the following:

Use loud, clear verbal commands throughout the application of the technique.

Be aware of verbal and nonverbal cues that indicate the probability of aggressive behavior. Remember that you are in the danger zone.

Visually scan the subject while assuming the interview stance.

Have the subject lift his arms to tighten clothing so you can visually search potential concealment areas, such as the waistline.

Have the subject move his hands away from his body.

Have the subject place his hands in a way so they can be controlled.

Physically control the subject's hands.

Keep the subject off balance.

Conduct the pat down in a predetermined pattern.

Follow up with appropriate action.

If you find a weapon, take possession of it and place it beyond the subject's reach in a safe location. If handcuffing is not tactically sound, you may use an alternate weapon, incapacitate the subject, or draw your firearm. (See Figure 4-25)

1

Pat down technique

2

Figure 4-25

Custodial Search Technique

A *custodial search technique* is used when a subject is taken into custody in an unsecured environment. Unlike the pat down, this is a complete search of the subject.

A custodial search of a subject should be done in a systematic and predetermined pattern using the *quadrant search approach*, which is dividing the body into four sections horizontally and vertically. During this close contact inside the danger zone, an officer is most vulnerable to a subject's physical assault. The officer should handcuff first and then search.

The primary purpose of a custodial search is to detect potential weapons and/or contraband. By searching the subject's body, an officer should be able to detect items hidden in the subject's clothing or on his body. The officer may search inside the waistband and pockets; however, he or she must be careful to avoid being injured by sharp objects, for example, needles and razor blades.

An officer should follow agency policy regarding searching a subject of the opposite sex. He or she may modify the hand position to avoid the appearance of inappropriate contact. If possible, there should be a witness to the search.

When searching a handcuffed subject, the officer should:

Use loud, clear verbal commands throughout the application of the technique.

Keep the subject off balance.

Physically control the subject's hands.

Conduct the search in a predetermined pattern. The groin is one of the most commonly overlooked areas. Remain professional and focus on conducting a proper, thorough search.

Follow up with appropriate action. (See Figure 4-26)

Custodial search technique   *Figure 4-26*

Inmate Search Techniques

Searches of inmates are primarily designed to uncover contraband, prevent escapes, maintain sanitary standards, and eliminate safety hazards. There are three types of inmate searches: clothed, strip/unclothed, and body cavity.

Clothed Search

Clothed searches of inmates can be conducted at random by officers during the course of their daily routine. A search of a clothed male inmate may be conducted by a female officer. A clothed search of a female inmate by a male officer will be conducted only during an emergency situation as determined by the shift supervisor. The only exception to this provision is an instance when time and circumstances do not permit the presence of a female officer or consultation with the shift supervisor. If there is an imminent threat of physical violence, a search may be needed to secure the inmate to prevent injury to staff or other inmates.

Like the custodial search of a subject, the clothed search utilizes the quadrant search approach. In an institutional setting, however, handcuffing is not required because there is little risk of escape. Officers should be aware, though, of their vulnerability to a physical assault.

To conduct a clothed search, do the following:

Inmate search technique– *Figure 4-27*
Clothed search

> Use loud, clear verbal commands throughout the application of the technique.
>
> Have the inmate remove the contents of his or her pockets and take off his or her shoes and hat.
>
> Inspect the shoes, hat, and personal effects before proceeding.
>
> Keep the inmate off balance.
>
> Maintain visual contact with the inmate's hands.
>
> Conduct the search in a predetermined pattern.
>
> Follow up with appropriate action. (See Figure 4-27)

Strip/Unclothed Search

A strip/unclothed search is done visually. The officer does not touch the inmate during the search.

Strip/unclothed searches of inmates may be conducted only by correctional officers who are of the same sex as the inmate, except in emergency circumstances. Inmates will generally be unclothed and searched upon their arrival at the correctional institution after returning from court, other institutions, any place where they may have come in contact with the public, or after an escape or attempted escape. There may be other occasions for a strip/unclothed search based upon agency policy, or if there is reason to believe an inmate possesses contraband.

Before the strip/unclothed search can be conducted, the inmate must be moved out of view of the inmate population. Only the inmate and staff involved will be present during the search.

To conduct a strip/unclothed search, do the following:

Use loud, clear verbal commands throughout the application of the technique.

Have the inmate remove all clothing.

Search the inmate's hair, ears, and mouth (dentures must be removed).

Visually check the entire body including armpits, hands, pubic region, between the toes, soles of the feet, inner portions of the legs, and rectum. Any bandages or casts should be thoroughly examined by medical staff.

Search every article of clothing and personal property, including collars, cuffs, lapels, seams, and linings. Examine shoes for split soles, false linings, and removable insoles or heels.

Follow up per agency policy based on the results of the search.

Body Cavity Search

Body cavity searches of inmates may be conducted only by appropriate health services staff members in accordance with agency policy.

UNIT 3 | DEFENSIVE TACTICS TECHNIQUES

LESSON 8 | Sudden Attacks: Blocks

OBJECTIVES

DT501.3.I.3. Demonstrate blocking techniques.

Blocks are reactionary techniques using the arms, legs, or body to deflect or redirect an impending strike from a subject to areas of the body.

Blocks to defend three areas of the body are covered in this section: the upper area, the mid area, and the low area. *(DT501.3.I.3.)*

Upper Area Block

In the upper area, the arm should be used in a motion to deflect a strike to the neckline up to the top of the head. The officer has the option of transitioning to another technique. (See Figure 4-28)

Mid Area Block

In the mid area, the arm should be used in a motion to deflect a strike to the center chest/stomach area and the face. The officer has the option of transitioning to another technique. (See Figure 4-29)

Upper area block

Figure 4-28

Low Area Block

In the low area, the arm and/or leg should be used in a motion to deflect a strike to the area below the beltline. The officer has the option of transitioning to another technique.

After every block, an officer should be prepared to counter with an appropriate technique designed to end the attack. (See Figure 4-30)

1

2

Mid area block

Figure 4-29

Low area block   *Figure 4-30*

OBJECTIVES

DT501.3.I.6. Identify target areas for empty-hand strikes.

DT501.3.I.4. Demonstrate striking techniques.

DT501.3.I.5. Demonstrate kicking techniques.

DT501.3.J. Demonstrate distraction techniques.

An *empty-hand striking technique* is any impact technique using hands, arms, elbows, feet, legs, knees, or head to strike a subject in an offensive or defensive situation. The entire body can be used as a weapon. This could include punching, hitting, kicking, or slapping.

In striking techniques, there are specific target areas *(DT501.3.I.6.)*. Some target areas involve nerve motor points in muscles. When struck, the impact may cause disruption of nerve tissue leading to incapacitation and/or motor dysfunction. Strikes to the skeletal structure are also effective.

Target Areas—Empty Hand Strikes

DF means deadly force and NDF refers to nondeadly force.

Front of Shoulder (NDF)—Strike this target area with an empty hand. The expected effect is to disable or cause temporary motor dysfunction.

Top of Forearm (NDF)—Strike the top of the forearm with an empty hand. The expected effect is to disable or cause temporary motor dysfunction.

Inside of Forearm (NDF)—Strike the inside of the forearm with an empty hand. The expected effect is to disable or cause temporary motor dysfunction.

Outside of Thigh (NDF)—Strike the outside of the thigh with an empty hand, leg, or knee. The expected effect is to disable or cause temporary motor dysfunction.

Inside of Thigh (NDF)—Strike the inside of the thigh with an empty hand, leg, or knee. The expected effect is to disable or cause temporary motor dysfunction.

Center of Abdomen (NDF)—The center of the abdomen can be struck with an empty hand. The expected effect when striking this area will be to disable or cause temporary respiratory or motor dysfunction.

Top of Calf (NDF)—Strike the top of the calf with an empty hand, foot, knee, or leg. The expected effect is to disable or cause temporary motor dysfunction.

Chest (NDF)—The chest area can be struck with an empty hand. The expected effect when striking this area with an empty hand will be to incapacitate the subject.

Side of Neck (NDF)—Strike the side of the neck with an empty hand to cause incapacitation and/or temporary motor dysfunction.

Head (NDF)—The expected effect is to distract or incapacitate. Strikes to certain areas of the head have the potential for injury depending on the amount of force used.

Throat (DF)—Striking the throat with an empty hand is considered deadly force.

Eyes (NDF)—Striking the eyes with an empty hand is an act of nondeadly force, but gouging the eyes is an act of deadly force.

Groin (NDF)—The expected effect of striking this area with an empty hand, knee, or leg is to incapacitate. Striking a subject in the groin may be an effective escape from a close-quarter body hold. (See Figure 4-31)

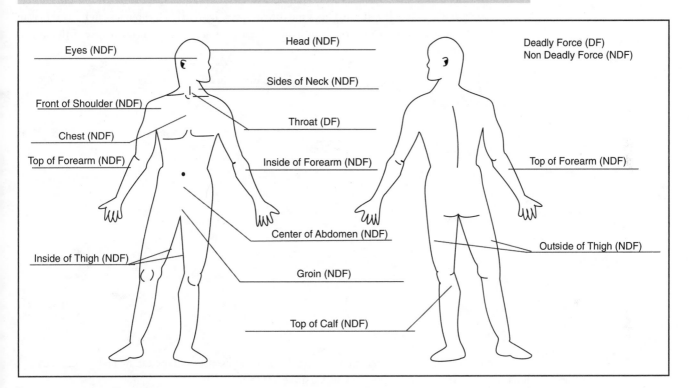

Target areas–Empty hand strikes

Figure 4-31

There are two methods of delivering strikes: penetration and snap-back.

There are two different types of strikes: swinging or thrusting. A swinging strike generates less power on impact due to the greater amount of surface area of the target. A thrusting strike magnifies the delivered power due to the smaller surface area making contact with the target area.

When delivering a strike, an officer strikes a muscle using the fluid shock principle. The penetration of the muscle and nerves in the target area results in a full transfer of kinetic energy that increases the power of the strike. All targets are struck with the intention of preventing or stopping aggressive action.

Two variables account for the amount of power generated in a strike. These are the amount of mass delivered with the striking weapon (i.e., fist, foot, baton) and the velocity (speed) at which it is delivered. To generate maximum power effectively, an officer needs a wide stable stance. He or she must twist the upper torso and hips into the strike allowing the maximum amount of mass to complement the striking weapon. The faster the strike, the more power will be generated.

A strike using a ***snap-back*** delivery method is retracted very quickly, thus enabling multiple strikes, creating distance, setting up the next techniques, and causing distraction to the subject. A snap-back may be delivered with any body part used for striking, kicking, punching, etc. A boxer's jab is one example of a snap-back.

Some strikes may be used as distraction techniques. ***Distraction*** is a technique that interrupts the subject's concentration so that energy is redirected from the current focus. Distraction techniques can be used to gain space when you are held in a close-quarter body hold and can assist in applying other defensive tactics such as takedowns and transporters.

There are several types of striking and kicking techniques covered in this section: *(DT501.3.1.4., DT501.3.1.5.)*

- palm heel strike
- punches
- hammer fist strike
- elbow strike
- forearm strike
- knee strike
- backfist strike
- front kick
- back kick
- side kick
- angle kick

Other strikes may be more appropriate in certain situations as distractions for escaping body holds, such as a head butt, foot stomp, shin scrape, or knuckle strike. *(DT501.3.J)*

1

Palm heel strike

2

Figure 4-32

Palm Heel Strike

You can use the palm heel strike to defuse a situation and gain control of a subject. This strike may be delivered to the center of the subject's chest primarily as a distraction technique or to the forehead as an incapacitating technique.

Use loud, clear verbal commands throughout the application of the technique.

Thrust the hand forward striking the target area with the palm heel of the hand.

Rotate your shoulders and hips to deliver the strike.

Follow up with an appropriate technique(s). (See Figure 4-32)

Knuckle Strike

The knuckle strike has multiple uses such as an escape, to open a subject's hand, for pain compliance, or as a distraction.

Use loud, clear verbal commands throughout the application of the technique.

Assume an appropriate position.

Identify the target area.

Make a half fist.

Use the foreknuckle to strike the specific target area.

Follow up with an appropriate technique(s). (See Figure 4-33)

Knuckle strike   Figure 4-33

Punches

The purpose of a punch is to gain control of a situation by stunning the subject before using other techniques, such as a takedown followed by handcuffing.

Use loud, clear verbal commands throughout the application of the technique.

Assume an appropriate position.

Identify the target area.

Make a fist. To make a proper fist, roll the fingers, tuck, and lock into the palm of the hand with thumb pressure.

Use the knuckles to strike the specific target area.

Follow up with an appropriate technique(s). (See Figure 4-34)

Punches can be executed from multiple angles and delivered to different areas of the body. Examples include jabs, crosses, hooks, upper cuts, overhands, or a variety of combinations.

Punches   Figure 4-34

Hammer Fist Strike

The hammer fist strike is one of the most powerful strikes you can use. A properly delivered strike combined with fluid shock usually causes the subject to release his grip in a situation where the subject suddenly grabs your wrist, equipment, or part of your clothing. Using a hammer fist temporarily incapacitates the subject and allows you to escalate, de-escalate, or disengage.

Use loud, clear verbal commands throughout the application of the technique.

Assume an appropriate position.

Identify the target area.

Make a fist.

Use the bottom of the fist to strike the specific target area.

Follow up with an appropriate technique(s). (See Figure 4-35)

1   **2**

Hammer fist strike   Figure 4-35

1   2

Backfist strike   *Figure 4-36*

Backfist Strike

A properly delivered backfist strike can often give you a tactical advantage and may incapacitate or break the concentration of the attacker.

Use loud, clear verbal commands throughout the application of the technique.

Assume an appropriate position.

Identify the target area.

Make a fist.

Use the back of the fist to strike the specific target area.

Follow up with an appropriate technique(s). (See Figure 4-36)

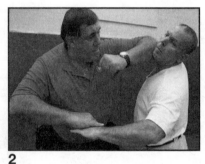

1   2

Elbow strike   *Figure 4-37*

Elbow Strike

The elbow strike may be used as an initial or follow-up strike to incapacitate the subject and create distance when in close range to the subject. This strike is not executed with the tip of the elbow but with the area of the arm approximately one inch below or above the elbow.

Use loud, clear verbal commands throughout the application of the technique.

Make a proper fist.

Flex your elbow.

Rotate your body and strike the subject.

Follow up with an appropriate technique(s). (See Figure 4-37)

Forearm Strike

A forearm strike is used to stop or impede an attack or to distract or incapacitate a subject. You may use this strike when a subject suddenly moves toward you and reaches to grab you.

Use loud, clear verbal commands throughout the application of the technique.

Extend the arm and bend the elbow slightly.

Rotate your body and strike the subject.

Follow up with an appropriate technique(s). (See Figure 4-38)

Knee Strike

You can use the knee strike when you are in close proximity to a resistant or combative subject. Use it to gain control or distance.

Use loud, clear verbal commands throughout the application of the technique.

Drive your knee forward into the target area.

Follow up with an appropriate technique(s). (See Figure 4-39)

Forearm strike   *Figure 4-38*

Knee strike   *Figure 4-39*

Front Kick

When an aggressive subject advances toward you, the front kick can be used to stop the subject's forward momentum.

Use loud, clear verbal commands throughout the application of the technique.

Transfer your balance to the support leg.

Lifting the knee, snap the foot forward.

Strike the target with either the ball or bridge of the foot.

Follow up with an appropriate technique(s). (See Figure 4-40)

Back Kick

Use loud, clear verbal commands throughout the application of the technique.

Transfer your balance to the support leg.

Lifting the knee, thrust the foot rearward.

Strike the target with the heel of the foot.

Follow up with an appropriate technique(s). (See Figure 4-41)

1
Front kick

2

Figure 4-40

1
Back kick

2

Figure 4-41

Side Kick

Use loud, clear verbal commands throughout the application of the technique.

Transfer your balance to the support leg.

Lifting the knee, thrust the foot to the side.

Strike the target with the blade or heel of the foot.

1 Side kick

2

Figure 4-42

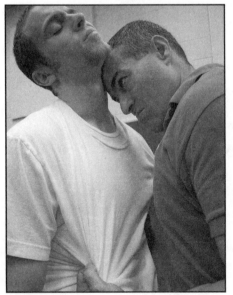

1 Angle kick

2

Figure 4-43

Head butt   Figure 4-44

Follow up with an appropriate technique(s). (See Figure 4-42)

Angle Kick

The angle kick can have an incapacitating effect on a subject who begins to attack you. For maximum effectiveness, use fluid shock. This kick can be delivered without getting close to the subject.

Use loud, clear verbal commands throughout the application of the technique.

Transfer your balance to the support leg.

Lift the knee of the kicking leg and rotate the hip.

Either snap or thrust the leg toward the target area.

Strike the target with the shin, ball, or top of the foot.

Follow up with an appropriate technique(s). (See Figure 4-43)

Head Butt

A **head butt** is a distraction technique that inflicts pain and temporarily diverts a subject's attention, redirecting the physical power of the subject's attack. It can also facilitate your escape from a body hold and can incapacitate the subject.

Use loud, clear verbal commands throughout the application of the technique.

Assume an appropriate position.

Identify the target area.

The best target area for a head butt is the soft tissue of the subject's face or head.

Using the frontal lobe (the top of the forehead) or the occipital area (back of the head), thrust the head into the specific target area.

Follow up with an appropriate technique(s). (See Figure 4-44)

Foot Stomp

A *foot stomp* is a distraction technique that inflicts pain and temporarily diverts a subject's attention, redirecting the physical power of the subject's attack. It can be used to facilitate your escape or to apply controlling techniques. The foot stomp is very effective when a subject attacks from the front or from the rear in close quarters.

Use loud, clear verbal commands throughout the application of the technique.

Assume an appropriate position.

Transfer your weight.

Lift the other leg, bending at the knee.

Using the heel of the foot, deliver a downward thrust to the subject's foot.

Follow up with an appropriate technique(s). (See Figure 4-45)

1 **2**

Foot stomp

Figure 4-45

Shin Scrape

A ***shin scrape*** is a distraction technique that inflicts pain and temporarily diverts an attacking subject's attention. With this technique, you must raise your foot and apply downward pressure on the subject's shin. It does not require much effort or strength but, properly performed, the shin scrape is very effective in allowing you to escape from a body hold.

Use loud, clear verbal commands throughout the application of the technique.

Assume an appropriate position.

Transfer your weight.

Lift the other leg, bending at the knee.

Turning the foot either to the inside or to the outside, deliver a downward scraping thrust along the subject's shin.

Follow up with an appropriate technique(s). (See Figure 4-46)

1 **2**

Shin scrape

Figure 4-46

UNIT 3 | DEFENSIVE TACTICS TECHNIQUES
LESSON 10 | Sudden Attacks: Takedowns

OBJECTIVES

DT501.3.G. Demonstrate takedown techniques.

Takedowns are techniques used to bring a resisting subject from a standing position to the ground making it easier to control him. Usually, a three-point pin is used to control the subject for handcuffing. After a takedown, you may escalate, de-escalate, or disengage depending on your assessment of the situation.

Most takedowns use mechanical compliance and/or balance displacement to place the subject safely on the ground.

There are several types of takedown techniques covered in this section:

- straight arm takedown
- hammerlock takedown
- shoulder lock takedown
- outside wrist takedown
- inside wrist takedown *(DT501.3.G.)*

Straight Arm Takedown

This technique is very versatile and allows you to move into a control position for a resistant subject. The key to this technique is to maintain control of the subject's straight arm.

Use loud, clear verbal commands throughout the application of the technique.

Assume an appropriate position, usually an escort position.

Slightly pull the subject off balance straightening his arm, pulling his wrist downward with his palm toward you to your outside hip.

Move your outside leg rearward, rotating your hips.

Apply downward pressure to the elbow while maintaining control of the wrist.

Drop to your inside knee and place the subject in a prone position.

Follow up with an appropriate technique(s). (See Figure 4-47)

1

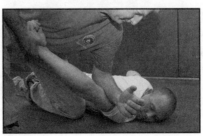

2

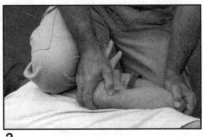

3

Straight arm takedown

Figure 4-47

Hammer Lock Takedown

From a hammer lock transporter:

Use loud, clear verbal commands throughout the application of the technique.

Sweep the outside leg rearward, rotating the hips.

Drop to your inside knee and place the subject in a prone position.

Follow up with an appropriate technique(s). (See Figure 4-48)

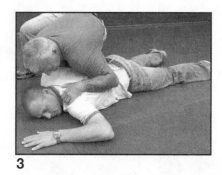

1   2   3

Hammer lock takedown

Figure 4-48

Shoulder Lock Takedown

From a shoulder lock transporter:

Use loud, clear verbal commands throughout the application of the technique.

Sweep the outside leg rearward, rotating the hips.

Drop to your inside knee and place the subject in a prone position.

Follow up with an appropriate technique(s). (See Figure 4-49)

1   2   3   4

Shoulder lock takedown

Figure 4-49

Outside Wrist Takedown

The outside wrist takedown can be an effective option if an aggressive subject touches you in a threatening manner.

Use loud, clear verbal commands throughout the application of the technique.

The subject reaches out toward your upper body.

Grab the subject's hand with your thumb placed in the back of the subject's hand, wrapping your fingers around the base of his thumb.

Rotate the subject's hand toward the outside of your body, reinforcing the grip with your other hand.

Rotate your hips and step forward.

Apply downward pressure on the subject's hand, bringing him onto his back.

Follow up with an appropriate technique(s). (See Figure 4-50)

Inside Wrist Takedown

The inside wrist takedown can be an effective option if an aggressive subject touches you in a threatening manner.

Use loud, clear verbal commands throughout the application of the technique.

The subject reaches out toward your upper body.

Grab the subject's hand with your thumb placed in the back of the subject's hand, wrapping your fingers around the blade edge of his hand.

Rotate the subject's hand, anchoring it in the center of your chest and reinforcing the grip with your other hand.

Quickly step rearward, forcing the subject's thumb down and his fingers toward his face.

Maintain pressure until the subject is controlled.

Follow up with an appropriate technique(s). (See Figure 4-51)

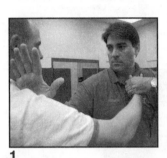
1

2

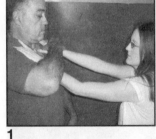
3

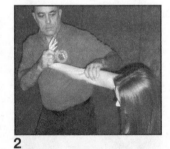
4

Outside wrist takedown

Figure 4-50

1

2

3

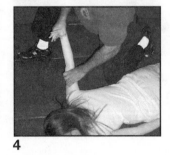
4

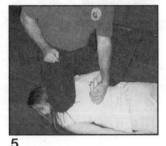
5

Inside wrist takedown

Figure 4-51

UNIT 3 I DEFENSIVE TACTICS TECHNIQUES
LESSON 11 I Sudden Attacks: Upright Grappling Body Holds

One of the most common attacks an officer may face is an upright grappling position. *Grappling* is the use of body mechanics to leverage or control a subject. When engaged in a grappling hold, an officer should consider methods of stabilizing, controlling, and securing a resistant subject.

There are several types of upright grappling body holds covered in this section:

- escape from front chokehold
- escape from rear chokehold
- escape from front body hold over/under arms
- escape from rear body hold over/under arms
- escape from headlock
- escape from front football tackle

Transition to Ground Control:

- hip roll
- leg sweep *(DT501.3.K.)*

OBJECTIVES

DT501.3.K. Demonstrate upright grappling body hold techniques.

Escape from a Front Chokehold

The purpose of the escape from a front chokehold is to break away from a subject who grabs you around the throat from the front. This technique involves maintaining balance, disengaging, and following up with other techniques. You may also need to apply a distraction technique before the escape from a front chokehold. Subject factors and officer factors dictate what distraction to use and when.

The front choke is life threatening. Execute this technique immediately.

Use loud, clear verbal commands throughout the application of the technique.

Step straight back with the strong side leg and raise your lead side arm as you swing the lead side arm up and over the subject's arm to break the hold (windmill).

Follow up with an appropriate technique(s). (See Figure 4-52)

Pressure to the jugular notch and bob-and-weave can also be effective escapes from a front chokehold.

1

2

3

Escape from front chokehold

Figure 4-52

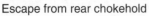

1   **2**   **3**

Escape from rear chokehold   *Figure 4-53*

Escape from a Rear Chokehold

The rear chokehold is usually the result of a surprise attack or a struggle with a combative subject. Being in a rear chokehold for an extended period can cause serious injury. Escape is crucial.

Use loud, clear verbal commands throughout the application of the technique.

Tuck your chin and lower your center of gravity.

Hold the subject's arm to your chest.

Maintain control of the subject's arm.

Drop to your attacked side knee, pull down, and twist toward your other side.

Roll the subject to the ground.

Follow up with an appropriate technique(s). Protect the airway. (See Figure 4-53)

Escape from Front Body Hold Over/Under Arms

A front body hold is usually the result of a surprise attack. A subject applying this type of hold on you can cause serious injury. Use your hands, feet, and legs to perform a distraction technique and escape.

Use loud, clear verbal commands throughout the application of the technique.

Lower your center of gravity.

Perform one or more striking techniques or pressure points to the appropriate target areas.

Follow up with an appropriate technique(s).

1   **2**

Escape from front body hold over/under arms   *Figure 4-54*

For escaping over the arms, create distance between you and the subject by putting the palms on the subject's hips (hip check). (See Figure 4-54)

Escape from Rear Body Hold Over/Under Arms

A rear body hold is usually the result of a surprise attack. A subject who grabs you in a rear body hold can exert force strong enough to the ribcage that breathing becomes difficult or serious injury may occur. Immediate escape is imperative.

Use loud, clear verbal commands throughout the application of the technique.

Lower your center of gravity.

Perform one or more striking techniques and/or finger peel to break the subject's grip.

Follow up with an appropriate technique(s). (See Figure 4-55)

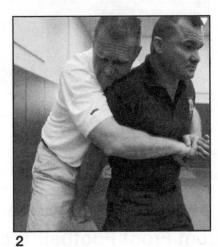

1   **2**   **3**

Escape from rear body hold over/under arms   *Figure 4-55*

Escape from Headlock

The headlock is usually the result of a surprise attack or a struggle with a combative subject. Being in a headlock for an extended period can cause serious injury. Escape is crucial. To escape from a headlock, you must react quickly and apply leverage.

When a subject applies a headlock, turn your face into the subject's torso to establish an airway and protect vital areas of your face.

Strikes and distraction techniques are effective for escaping from a headlock. A wide stance is necessary to establish good balance.

> Use loud, clear verbal commands throughout the application of the technique.
>
> Establish an airway, and a wide stance.
>
> Perform one or more striking techniques or pressure points to the appropriate target areas.
>
> Force the subject's head back, while giving verbal commands.
>
> Follow up with an appropriate technique(s). (See Figure 4-56)

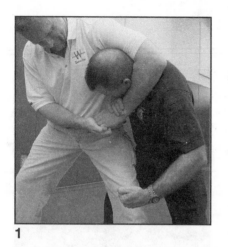

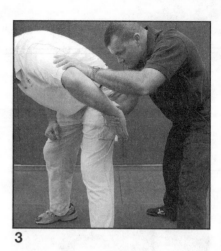

1   **2**   **3**

Escape from headlock

Figure 4-56

Escape from Front Football Tackle

The football tackle is usually the result of a surprise attack or a struggle with a combative subject. Avoid being taken to the ground, and instead drive the subject to the ground.

Use loud, clear verbal commands throughout the application of the technique.

Take an extended step backward and lower your center of gravity.

Raise your arms in an offensive ready position.

Stop the subject's forward motion with double forearm strikes to both clavicle areas.

Bend your elbow and place it on the subject's back alongside the spine at the shoulder blade.

Apply downward pressure with the elbow and force the subject to the ground.

Follow up with an appropriate technique(s).

To escape from a Rear Football Tackle, execute a front fall and use appropriate ground-fighting technique(s). (See Figure 4-57)

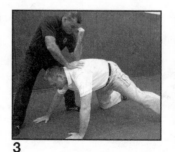

1   **2**   **3**   **4**

Escape from front football tackle

Figure 4-57

Hip Roll

A hip roll is an effective defense against a subject who closes the gap and tries to control your upper body.

From an upright grappling position:

> Use loud, clear verbal commands throughout the application of the technique.
>
> Place your hip into the subject's lower abdomen.
>
> Lower your center of gravity.
>
> Pull subject over the hip and direct him to the ground. (See Figure 4-58)

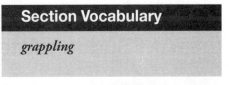

Section Vocabulary

grappling

1　2　3　4

Hip roll

Figure 4-58

Leg Sweep

The leg sweep uses leg-to-leg contact to upset the subject's balance from an upright grappling position.

> Use loud, clear verbal commands throughout the application of the technique.
>
> Assume an appropriate position.
>
> Use your leg in a sweeping motion to direct the subject to the ground.
>
> Follow up with an appropriate technique(s). (See Figure 4-59)

1　2　3　4

Leg sweep

Figure 4-59

UNIT 3 | DEFENSIVE TACTICS TECHNIQUES
LESSON 12 | Sudden Attacks: Vascular Neck Restraints

OBJECTIVES

DT501.3.R. Demonstrate a simulation of a vascular neck restraint technique.

Note: This lesson is optional for Law Enforcement, Corrections, and Correctional Probation.

The ***vascular neck restraint*** is a physical restraint compressing certain veins and arteries in the neck to cause a subject to lose consciousness for a brief period of time. *(DT501.3.R.)*

Historically, the vascular neck restraint has been favored for its high probability of effectiveness in controlling a resistant subject. Unexplained in-custody deaths in previous years which are now attributed to Sudden Death Syndrome caused many criminal justice agencies to restrict the use of this technique. New research establishes the physiology of this technique as safe and without contraindications in the general population.

"While no technique is completely risk free, there is no valid medical reason to routinely expect grievous bodily harm or death following the correct application of the vascular neck restraint by professional criminal justice officers with standardized training and technique." (National Study on Neck Restraints in Policing, June 2007, Canadian Police Research Centre).

The vascular neck restraint is not recommended on elderly persons, pregnant women, children, or persons with apparent disabilities due to their unique physiology.

Standard Vascular Neck Restraint

Apply a standard vascular neck restraint by following these steps:

Use loud, clear verbal commands throughout the application of the technique.

Wrap your arm around the subject's neck so you can apply equal pressure to each side of the neck using your forearm and bicep by positioning your elbow in front of the subject's throat.

Rotate the restraining forearm with palm down and grip that hand with your free hand. Your arm is aligned just below the subject's jaw line. The windpipe should be protected by the space created by the bend of the elbow.

Apply pressure by using your bicep as a brace and closing your forearm towards your bicep.

Stabilize the subject's head between your body and arm.

Compress the neck until you get compliance or unconsciousness.

Follow up with appropriate technique(s). (See Figures 4-60, 61, 62)

Because this is a vascular restraint, releasing the hold will quickly replenish the blood flow and immediately revive the subject. Subject should regain consciousness within approximately 30 seconds. If not, render medical aid.

Vascular Neck Restraint: Basic Position

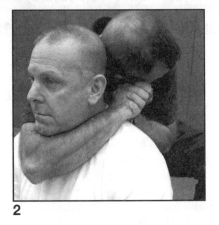

Section Vocabulary

vascular neck restraint

Vascular neck restraint–Basic position

Figure 4-60

Vascular Neck Restraint: From Front

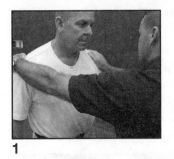

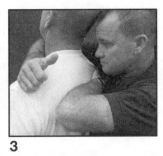
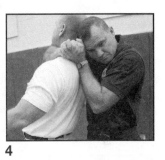

Vascular neck restraint–From front

Figure 4-61

Vascular Neck Restraint: From Rear

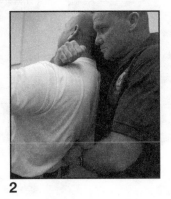
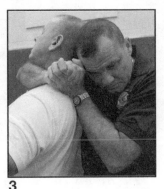

Vascular neck restraint–From rear

Figure 4-62

UNIT 3 | DEFENSIVE TACTICS TECHNIQUES
LESSON 13 | Ground Maneuvers: Falling Techniques

OBJECTIVES

DT501.3.C. Demonstrate falling techniques.

Falling techniques are useful if a subject attacks, pushes, or hits you with enough force to send you to the ground, or if you trip over an unexpected obstacle.

Falling properly reduces the potential for injury and minimizes the stunning effect associated with falling, so you can assume an effective defensive position. Returning to a defensive stance puts you in a position to defend against further attack or control the subject.

This lesson covers four types of falls: front fall, rear fall, shoulder roll, and side fall. *(DT501.3.C.)*

Front Fall

Use loud, clear verbal commands while completing the fall.

Extend your bent arms slightly in front of your chest as in a natural bracing position.

Fall forward to a prone position contacting the ground with the palms, forearms, and feet, keeping your mouth closed but exhaling upon impact. If falling with an unholstered weapon, make contact with the ground with just one palm.

Follow up with an appropriate technique(s). (See Figure 4-63)

1

Front fall

2

3

Figure 4-63

Rear Fall

Use loud, clear verbal commands while completing the fall.

Tuck your chin into your chest.

Bend your knees into a squatting position and roll backward.

As your back makes contact with the ground, swing both of your arms out and strike the ground with the palms of both hands while exhaling.

Follow up with an appropriate technique(s). (See Figure 4-64)

1 **2** **3**

Rear fall

Figure 4-64

Shoulder Roll

Use loud, clear verbal commands while completing the fall.

Tuck your chin into your chest and roll forward onto the ground making contact with the outside edge of the bladed hand with your palms facing out and elbows flexed.

Continue rolling from shoulder diagonally across to lower back.

Follow up with an appropriate technique(s). (See Figure 4-65)

1 **2** **3** **4**

Shoulder roll

Figure 4-65

Side Fall

Use loud, clear verbal commands while completing the fall.

Tuck your chin on your chest.

Bend your knees into a squatting position and roll to the rear quarter and to one side.

Relax the body as you fall.

Don't land flat. Dissipate the shock by rolling after hitting the ground.

As your body makes contact with the ground, you may swing the same side arm and strike the ground with the palm to minimize impact.

Exhale to relax your body and prevent you from having the wind knocked out of you.

Follow up with an appropriate technique(s). (See Figure 4-66)

1   2   3   4

Side fall

Figure 4-66

UNIT 3 | DEFENSIVE TACTICS TECHNIQUES
LESSON 14 | Ground Maneuvers: Ground Escapes

Ground fights present unique challenges to criminal justice officers because of the officers' equipment and the likelihood of a sudden deadly force assault. Other factors including general fitness level, physical size, maneuverability, loss of visibility, multiple subjects, environmental conditions, and the inability to disengage immediately all complicate the ground fight.

Some positive features of ground fights include the following:

- The subject is close to you, allowing you to keep and maintain physical control.
- The subject does not have the support of a strong stance to generate power for striking.
- The subject is usually working against time and fearful that you may receive back-up or other assistance.

Some negative features of ground fights include the following:

- The subject has immediate access to all of your equipment.
- The ground is often a rough surface which can quickly scratch and tear the skin.
- Equipment can become painful as you roll on the ground.
- Ground fighting is an anaerobic physical activity which will quickly tire you.
- The subject has easy access to your vital areas.

Ground escape techniques covered in this section include:

- foundation
- escape to the standing position
- hip escapes
- ground defense position
- defend and escape from the supine position
- defend and escape from side control
- defend and escape from a full mount
- defend and escape from a rear mount
- defend and escape from a head-to-head prone attack *(DT501.3.L.1.)*

OBJECTIVES

DT501.3.L.1. Demonstrate ground escape techniques.

1

Foundation

2

Figure 4-67

Foundation

From lying on the back:

Use loud, clear verbal commands throughout the application of the technique.

Using an extended arm, prop the upper body off the ground (posting).

Posting is supporting the balance of the body using a limb.

Bend the knees with feet on the ground.

Keep your free hand up in a defensive position to protect vital areas.

Follow up with an appropriate technique(s). (See Figure 4-67)

Escape to the Standing Position

Your ability to get up safely from a ground encounter is critical. The objective of this technique is to prepare you to get back up on your feet while protecting your face, head, body, and weapon from an aggressive subject.

This technique is used to gain time and distance between you and the aggressive subject. If distance is not gained, the subject may have the ability to get on top of you or strike you while you are attempting to get up and get away.

From the foundation position:

Use loud, clear verbal commands throughout the application of the technique.

Push up on the reactionary foot and strong arm simultaneously. This will lift the hips off the ground. The base arm and leg will support the body weight.

Use your free hand to protect the vital areas.

Once distance is established, get up by moving your leg under your body and move to a standing position.

Maintain an appropriate stance, and follow up with an appropriate technique(s). (See Figure 4-68)

1　　**2**　　**3**　　**4**

Escape to standing position

Figure 4-68

Hip Escapes

The purpose of hip escapes is to move from side to side while avoiding or defending an attack. The movement in a hip escape is also known as ***shrimping***.

Use loud, clear verbal commands throughout the application of the technique.

From the foundation, tuck the chin to the chest to protect your neck and back of your head.

Push off with one foot, force your hips up, and push out towards the opposite side. Your hands will simulate a pushing motion, as if pushing the subject away.

Follow up with an appropriate technique(s). (See Figure 4-69)

 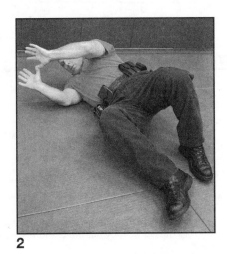 

1　　**2**　　**3**

Hip escapes

Figure 4-69

Ground Defense Position

If you are knocked to the ground and unable to recover immediately to the standing position, you must go to a ground defense position. While in the ground defense position, you may have the ability to access a weapon or escape to a standing position.

Use loud, clear verbal commands throughout the application of the technique.

From the foundation position, tuck your chin to your chest, with your arms and hands up protecting vital areas. Your legs will be up, knees bent toward the chest, and feet slightly canted.

Defend by kicking the subject in the knees, shins, or other available targets.

Lift your hips off the ground and use your feet to rotate in a circular motion. Propel forward, backward, and in circular motions by using hips and feet. Follow the subject's movement while still on your back.

Follow up with an appropriate technique(s). (See Figure 4-70)

1   2   3   4

Ground defense position

Figure 4-70

Defend and Escape from the Supine Position

This position builds on the ground defense position. You will defend while on your back with legs up and feet kicking the subject. Defending and escaping from the open guard position will be used when the subject attempts to force himself between or over the top of your legs.

From the ground defense position:

Use loud, clear verbal commands throughout the application of the technique.

Stop the subject's forward movement by shoving your legs out toward the subject and getting your feet against his hips.

Keep your feet on the subject's hips as he moves around and leans into you.

If the subject leans against you in an attempt to strike, transfer one foot to the subject's chest while the other foot remains on his hip.

Once your feet are in place, shove the subject back and away. Create distance and quickly escape to the standing position.

Follow up with an appropriate technique(s). (See Figure 4-71)

 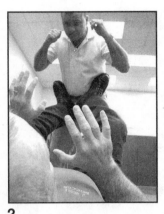  

1   **2**   **3**   **4**

Defense and escape from the supine position

Figure 4-71

Defend and Escape from Side Control

When a person is controlling you from the side pressing down against you with his chest or using his arms to control your head and hips, he may prevent you from moving or escaping. It is also easy for the subject to deliver strikes and disarm you.

This can be one of the worst positions to be caught in. You must be able to escape, escalate, or get to your weapon.

From the ground defense position:

> Use loud, clear verbal commands throughout the application of the technique.
>
> As the subject attacks from the right side, bring your left arm across and underneath the subject's neck. Push up, lifting the subject's head to gain distance.
>
> Place your right hand on the subject's left hip blocking any hip movement.
>
> Escape by moving your hips to the left to create more distance. At the same time, place your right hand on the subject's hip to control and push away.
>
> Follow up with an appropriate technique(s). (See Figure 4-72)

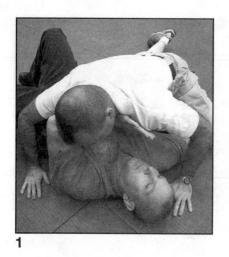

Defense and escape from side control

Figure 4-72

Defend and Escape from a Full Mount

When you are in a ground fight, the subject may sit on top of your chest, stomach, or waist and use his body weight to hold you down. In this position, you are subject to a variety of attacks such as strikes from different angles and being choked. The objective of this technique is to teach you to defend and escape.

From the ***supine position*** (lying on the back face up):

Use loud, clear verbal commands throughout the application of the technique.

The subject mounts you from the waist to the chest.

Control the subject's wrists to prevent strikes or choke attempts.

Block the subject's leg by placing your foot to the outside of the subject's leg.

Control the subject's wrist on the same side. Pull the subject's arm in and hold it tight to your body.

Push up with your foot and drive your hips up to a bridge. Thrust the subject forward while you roll the subject onto his back. You will end up on top and between the subject's legs.

Follow up with an appropriate technique(s). (See Figure 4-73)

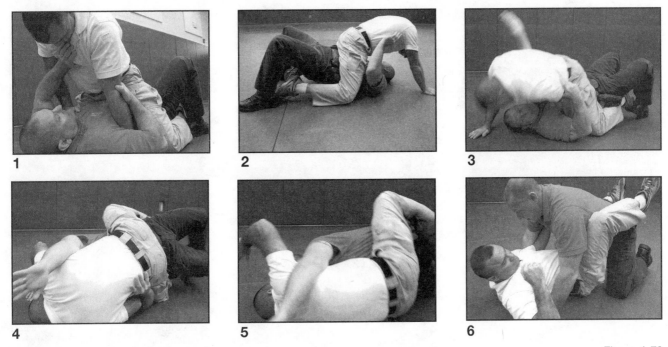

Defend and escape from a full mount

Figure 4-73

Defend and Escape from a Rear Mount

When you are in a ground fight, the subject may sit on top of your back and use his body weight to hold you down. In this position, you are subject to a variety of attacks and strikes to the back of the head and neck. If you have a weapon, it may be vulnerable.

From the **_prone position_** (lying on the stomach face down):

Use loud, clear verbal commands throughout the application of the technique.

The subject mounts your lower back and places his legs to the outside of your legs to control you. The subject holds you down with his body weight.

Keep your hands around your head for protection from punches to the back of the head and the side of your face.

Cover and trap either of the subject's legs.

Roll towards and onto the trapped leg.

Follow up with an appropriate technique(s). (See Figure 4-74)

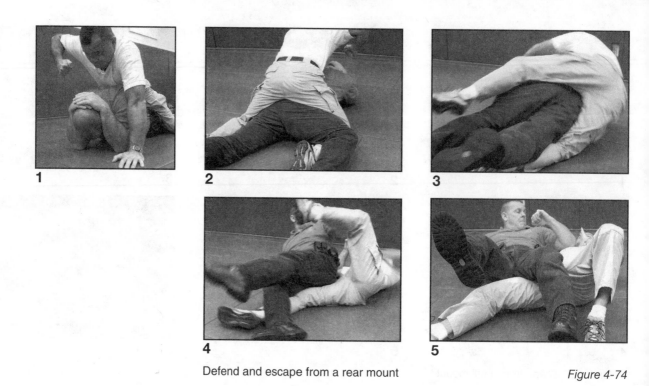

Defend and escape from a rear mount

Figure 4-74

Defend and Escape from a Head-to-Head Prone Attack

When you are in a ground fight, the subject may grab your head and/or shoulder and use his body weight to hold you down. In this position, you are subject to being choked. If you have a weapon, it may be vulnerable.

From the prone position:

> Use loud, clear verbal commands throughout the application of the technique.
>
> If you are being choked, grab the choking arm, pull down, and attempt to establish an airway.
>
> Attempt to turn your head and pull your jaw down into empty space.
>
> Attempt to roll onto your weapon side.
>
> If you are no longer being choked and your weapon is not in danger, this may be your stalling position.
>
> If you are still being choked, attempt to brace the elbow of one arm and compress the subject's wrist on the same side to force a release.
>
> If the hold cannot be broken, use other force options.
>
> When the subject releases you, disengage, and follow up with an appropriate technique(s). (See Figure 4-75)

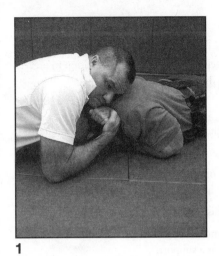

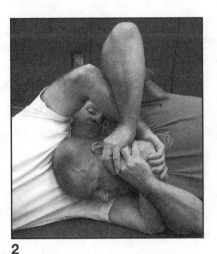

1　　　　　　　　　　　　**2**

Defend and escape from a head-to-head prone attack　　　*Figure 4-75*

Section Vocabulary

posting

prone position

shrimping

supine position

UNIT 3 | DEFENSIVE TACTICS TECHNIQUES
LESSON 15 | Ground Maneuvers: Ground Control

A ground fight is very exhausting and requires tremendous bursts of energy for short periods of time. **Stalling** is a tactical method of safely controlling a suspect until you physically recover or reassess the situation, or backup arrives. The stalling techniques presented here are based on leverage, not strength.

Stalling techniques for ground control covered in this lesson include:

- scarf hold
- arm bar
- disengaging from the scarf hold
- seated stall
- follow-up from the seated stall
- straddle stall *(DT501.3.L.2.)*

OBJECTIVES

DT501.3.L.2. Demonstrate ground control techniques.

Scarf hold   *Figure 4-76*

Scarf Hold

The most basic of the stalling positions is the scarf hold. This hold uses leverage tactics to hold the subject down while keeping you in a strategic position to prevent him from attacking critical areas such as the head, throat, or weapon.

Follow these steps for the scarf hold:

Use loud, clear verbal commands throughout the application of the technique.

The subject is on his back.

Sit between the arm of the subject and one side of his body. If you are wearing a weapon, place your weapon side against the ribcage of the subject, if possible.

Face the subject's head and lean against his ribcage.

Place the arm closest to his head around the backside of his neck and place it underneath his head using your forearm as a support.

Press your weight onto the subject's chest. Slide your opposite arm under his shoulder closest to you and clasp your hands together.

Lower your head and turn your face away from the subject.

Keep your feet 90° perpendicular to the subject.

From this position, you may continue to hold the subject, escalate, or disengage.(See Figure 4-76)

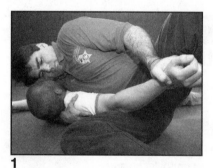
1

2

Arm bar   *Figure 4-77*

Arm Bar

The arm bar is a variation of the scarf hold which utilizes a joint lock to control a subject on the ground.

From the scarf hold grip:

Use loud, clear verbal commands throughout the application of the technique.

Release your clasped hands while maintaining control of the subject's shoulder with your arm around his neck.

Grab the subject's closest arm with your free hand palm down.

Slide your bottom leg upward so that your thigh is close to the subject's shoulder.

Place the tricep of the subject's arm in an extended position across your thigh.

Use your chest to compress the subject's chest as you push down on the subject's wrist. You may use your leg to trap the extended arm. This gives more control and strength and frees your hand.

From this position, you may continue to hold the subject, escalate, or disengage. (See Figure 4-77)

Disengaging from the Scarf Hold

To disengage from a scarf hold and/or arm bar, follow these steps:

Shoulder Lock

From the arm bar position, pass the subject's arm toward his head.

Release your grip and place your free hand on the tricep of the subject.

Push the subject's arm towards his head and place your head on the outside of his tricep to pin his arm against his face.

Clasp your hands and push against the subject's arm with your head. (See Figure 4-78)

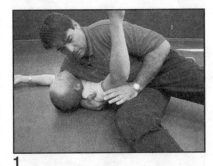

1   Shoulder lock

2

Figure 4-78

Disengaging

Move to your knees.

Release your grip and place your hand on the subject's shoulder.

Push his shoulder and pull your other arm towards you as you stand up.

Exit towards the subject's head.

Follow up with an appropriate technique(s). (See Figure 4-79)

1   Disengaging

2

Figure 4-79

Seated Stall

This technique is useful when a subject grabs you from behind and attempts to control your upper body.

Follow these steps for a seated stall:

Use loud, clear verbal commands throughout the application of the technique.

From a seated position where the subject is behind you, attempt to capture one or both of the subject's arms by using your arms and trapping them between your body and upper arm.

Control the subject's arms above the elbow to eliminate the subject's movement.

Turn your head downward to protect your throat.

Perform a joint lock by capturing the arm and controlling the elbow joint. Compress it against your forearm using an arm wrap.

From this position, you may continue to hold the subject, escalate, or disengage.(See Figure 4-80)

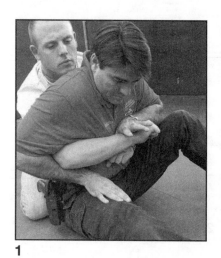

1

Seated stall

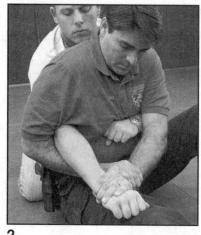

2

Figure 4-80

Follow-up from the Seated Stall

The ability to disengage is important if approached by multiple subjects while in the seated stall.

From the seated stall position:

Use loud, clear verbal commands throughout the application of the technique.

Place an arm bar on the subject while in the seated stall position.

Using your legs, swivel in the direction of the controlled arm.

Lay back as you lift the subject's arm.

As the subject falls forward onto his chest, bridge your mid-section using the outside leg and rotate toward the subject's back.

Place his arm in the small of his back as you maintain your grip.

Complete the movement by rotating onto your knees.

Handcuff or disengage. (See Figure 4-81)

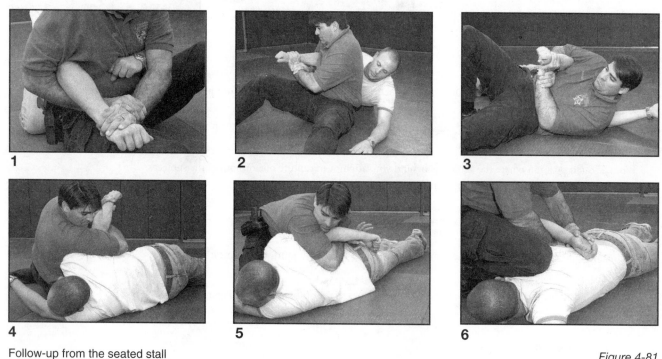

1   **2**   **3**

4   **5**   **6**

Follow-up from the seated stall

Figure 4-81

Straddle Stall

Possibly the worst tactical position that you can find yourself in is when a subject has you on your back and is sitting on your chest. The straddle stall gives an officer an opportunity to survive a barrage of punches to the face. You will remain on the bottom, but the attacker will not be able to strike you in the face or throat. Your firearm will be out of reach covered by the subject's legs.

Follow these steps for a straddle stall:

Use loud, clear verbal commands throughout the application of the technique.

The subject sits on your chest as you lie on your back.

With the subject positioned on your chest, sit up and grab the subject around the waist with both arms.

Depending on how the subject positions himself, it may be necessary to precede the following steps with a maneuver. Place your elbows on the thighs of the subject pushing down and scoot forward.

Pull the subject down on top of you.

Place your forehead into the chest or stomach of the subject. Move your head left or right to breathe and avoid attack.

From this position, you may continue to hold the subject, escalate, or disengage. (See Figure 4-82)

Section Vocabulary

stalling

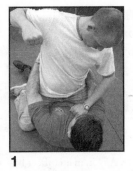

1

2

3

Straddle stall

Figure 4-82

UNIT 3 | DEFENSIVE TACTICS TECHNIQUES
LESSON 16 | Intermediate Weapons: Impact Weapons

OBJECTIVES

DT501.3.N.1. Identify target areas for impact weapon strikes.

DT501.3.N. Demonstrate impact weapon techniques.

Note: The lesson on Impact Weapons is optional for Law Enforcement, Corrections, and Correctional Probation.

Intermediate weapons are tools used when empty-handed control is ineffective, but the subject's level of resistance does not merit deadly force. Though intermediate weapons may cause death or great bodily harm, they are not fundamentally designed to do so.

A strike with an impact weapon affects a subject psychologically when he sees an officer use the weapon in a controlled, competent manner. It gives the impression of a well-trained officer and emphasizes his or her authority and command presence.

The most common types of intermediate weapons include the following:

- impact weapons such as batons or weapons of opportunity
- specialty impact weapons such as bean bags or baton rounds
- electronic control devices, such as a dart-firing stun gun like TASER®
- chemical agents

An ***impact weapon*** is any object used for striking. Impact weapons may disable or cause temporary motor dysfunction. ***Temporary motor dysfunction*** is a type of incapacitation that causes temporary impairment of muscle control, such as a charley horse.

The most common impact weapon is the baton. Even though new intermediate weapons have been developed, such as OC spray and dart-firing stun guns, the baton remains a standard tool for some criminal justice agencies.

The baton is not the only impact weapon available to an officer. Any item an officer has at hand may be used as a potential impact weapon when needed, such as a broomstick, flashlight, clipboard, or radio. These unconventional impact weapons are also known as ***weapons of opportunity***.

An ***interview stance with an impact weapon*** is a low profile stance with the weapon held partially hidden behind the leg.

An ***offensive ready stance with an impact weapon*** is a high profile stance with the weapon held at a shoulder position to enable a rapid strike.

There are specific target areas for striking with an impact weapon. *(DT501.3.N.1.)*

Target Areas—Impact Weapons Strikes

DF means deadly force and NDF refers to nondeadly force.

Front of Shoulder (NDF)—Jab this target area with an impact weapon. The expected effect is to disable or cause temporary motor dysfunction.

Top of Forearm (NDF)—Strike the top of the forearm with an impact weapon. The expected effect is to disable or cause temporary motor dysfunction.

Inside of Forearm (NDF)—Strike the inside of the forearm with an impact weapon. The expected effect is to disable or cause temporary motor dysfunction.

Outside of Thigh (NDF)—Strike the outside of the thigh with an impact weapon. The expected effect is to disable or cause temporary motor dysfunction.

Inside of Thigh (NDF)—Strike the inside of the thigh with an impact weapon. The expected effect is to disable or cause temporary motor dysfunction.

Center of Abdomen (NDF)—Jab the center of the abdomen with an impact weapon. The expected effect will be to disable or cause temporary respiratory or motor dysfunction.

Top of Calf (NDF)—Strike the top of the calf with an impact weapon. The expected effect is to disable or cause temporary motor dysfunction.

Side of Neck (DF)—Striking the side of the neck with an impact weapon is deadly force.

Head (DF)—Striking the head with an impact weapon is deadly force.

Throat (DF)—Striking the throat with an impact weapon is deadly force.

Groin (DF)—Striking the groin with an impact weapon is deadly force. (See Figure 4-83 on next page)

The most common techniques using an impact weapon are impact weapon thrusts, impact weapon swings, and impact weapon blocks. *(DT501.3.N.)*

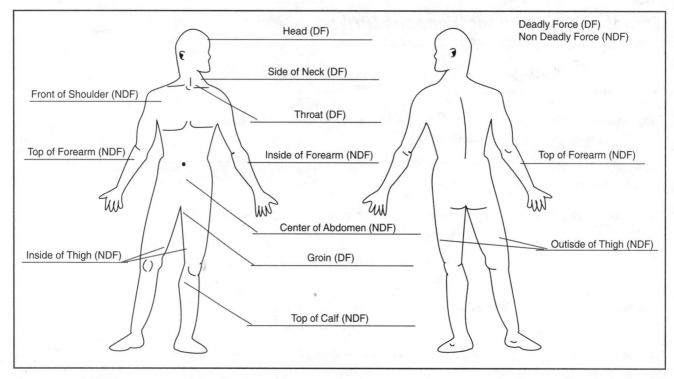

Head (DF)

Side of Neck (DF)

Front of Shoulder (NDF)

Throat (DF)

Top of Forearm (NDF)

Inside of Forearm (NDF)

Deadly Force (DF)
Non Deadly Force (NDF)

Top of Forearm (NDF)

Center of Abdomen (NDF)

Inside of Thigh (NDF)

Groin (DF)

Outisde of Thigh (NDF)

Top of Calf (NDF)

Target areas: impact weapon strikes

Figure 4-83

1

2

Impact weapon thrusts

Figure 4-84

Impact Weapon Thrusts

This technique can be executed in all directions with the tip, back, or shaft of the impact weapon. Generally, the weapon is thrust in a straight line into a target.

Use loud, clear verbal commands throughout the application of the technique.

Assume an appropriate position.

Hold the impact weapon with one or both hands.

Thrust the impact weapon into an appropriate target area.

Follow up with an appropriate technique(s). (See Figure 4-84)

Impact Weapon Swings

This technique can be executed with the shaft or edge of the impact weapon. Generally, the weapon is swung in a circular motion to the target.

This technique is also appropriate for use with weapons of opportunity, such as a flashlight, radio, or cell phone.

Use loud, clear verbal commands throughout the application of the technique.

Assume an appropriate position.

Hold the impact weapon with one or both hands.

Swing the impact weapon to an appropriate target area.

Follow up with an appropriate technique(s). (See Figure 4-85)

1   **2**   **3**

Impact weapon swings   *Figure 4-85*

Impact Weapon Blocks

Blocks are reactionary techniques. A block places the impact weapon between the officer and the subject. Scan blocks pull across the body. Power blocks push against the attacking arm.

Use loud, clear verbal commands throughout the application of the technique.

Assume appropriate hand position.

Hold the impact weapon with one or both hands.

Sweep or push the impact weapon across the front of the body, defending against attack.

Follow up with an appropriate technique(s). (See Figure 4-86)

Impact weapon blocks   *Figure 4-86*

Section Vocabulary

electronic control device (ECD) or electronic immobilization device

impact weapon

intermediate weapon

interview stance with an impact weapon

offensive ready stance with an impact weapon

temporary motor dysfunction

weapon of opportunity

Electronic Control Devices

Electronic control devices (ECD) (also called *electronic immobilization devices*) are weapons that utilize a battery-powered current of electricity. The current is high voltage and low amperage and is considered safe when used on people. These devices control a subject through an artificial contraction of the muscles which may cause extreme muscular tension and complete structural dysfunction.

Types of electronic control devices include dart-firing stun gun (TASER®), handheld stun gun, electronic shield, electronic belt, electronic sleeve, etc.

UNIT 3 | DEFENSIVE TACTICS TECHNIQUES
LESSON 17 | Nonlethal Intermediate Weapons: Chemical Agents

OBJECTIVES

DT501.3.Q.1. Identify the types of chemical agents used by criminal justice officers.

DT501.3.Q.1.a. Identify the active ingredient in oleo capsicum.

DT501.3.Q.2.a. Identify the use of the Scoville Heat Unit (SHU) in measuring the burning effect of chemical agents.

DT501.3.Q.2. Identify the physical effects of a chemical agent on a subject.

DT501.3.Q.2.b. Describe the correct responses to a subject's prolonged or severe reactions to chemical agent contamination.

DT.501.3.Q.4.a. Identify decontamination procedures for contamination from a chemical agent.

Types of Chemical Agents

Criminal justice officers primarily use two types of chemical agents to control resistant subjects: *oleo-resin capsicum (OC)* and/or *orthochlorobenzal-malononitrile (CS)*. *(DT501.3.Q.1.)*

Both are generally deployed in the form of handheld canisters and chemical projectiles. Special operations units may use other deployment systems such as pepper foggers or gas guns.

Although OC has become the preferred chemical agent of criminal justice agencies worldwide, CS may also be used in some applications.

CS is an irritant agent that causes burning and tearing eyes, nasal discharge, and skin and upper respiratory irritation. The chemical, when it makes contact with skin, gives the sensation of pain by activating and irritating the neural transmitters of the body. Though there is no actual burning caused by the chemical, there is the sensation of an intense burn once contaminated.

OC, commonly called *pepper spray*, is an inflammatory agent that causes tearing and involuntary closing of the eyes, nasal discharge, sneezing, disorientation, and a sensation of respiratory distress. The skin will turn red due to the inflammation and show mild signs of puffiness. These effects will wear off generally in 20–40 minutes, though some cases have been reported to last longer.

Contents of OC Spray

Oleo-resin capsicum is a natural derivative of the cayenne pepper, although there are some synthetic forms. The active ingredient in OC is known as capsaicin which produces the heat felt when it makes contact with human tissue. *(DT501.3.Q.1.a.)*

The heat value of capsicum is measured in ***Scoville Heat Units*** (SHU) *(DT501.3.Q.2.a.)*. The SHU scale was originally designed for determining the heat properties (burning sensation) of peppers for the restaurant industry. Bell peppers are at the low end of the scale and cayenne pepper is higher on the scale. This is a fitting measurement for a chemical agent like OC which is in essence nothing more than a vegetable product voluntarily ingested by countless persons in the form of food and medicine. Though it is true that OC is hot, SHUs are not to be equated with thermal degrees, and as such, do not present the burning dangers associated with fire.

Within the formula, capsicum is mixed with a propellant consisting of carbon dioxide, nitrogen, or isobutane, whose function is to expel the active ingredient from the canister. In addition, the formula will include water, vegetable oil, or alcohol based solutions, which hold the capsicum suspended so that the material does not sink to the bottom. This solution allows the capsicum material to remain suspended so that it is discharged evenly with every spray. This precludes the need for shaking the canister before deployment.

Alcohol-based sprays can create a potential fire hazard if sprayed directly into a flame or used in conjunction with electronic control devices. However, alcohol-based sprays adhere better to skin, making them more effective.

Effects of OC

OC has been proven to be highly effective on a majority of the population. There may be circumstances in which OC will not deliver the expected results. Any of the following factors could influence the results of the OC: a poorly placed discharge where the OC does not make contact with the subject's face, the subject's mindset or past experience with the chemical agent, or the subject's drug use, psychosis, or a high pain tolerance.

This chemical agent has the most desired effects when sprayed directly at the subject's head. Caution should be used when discharging any chemical directly into the eyes due to the compressed nature of the chemical that discharges at a potentially dangerous velocity. The effects of a direct discharge into the eyes has been known to cause slight tears in the eye membranes which could lead to complications.

When OC enters the eyes, it causes them to involuntarily close. The subject will feel an intense burning sensation and the capillaries of the eyes will dilate, causing the eyes to appear bloodshot. If the chemicals are inhaled, they will often cause coughing and gasping. If the gag reflex is activated, the chemicals may cause gagging and even vomiting. These are common reactions due to the irritation of the skin and slight swelling of the lining of the throat. The nasal cavity will also swell causing significant discharge of mucus, and sneezing *(DT501.3.Q.2.)*. Officers should always use caution when approaching subjects who have been contaminated to prevent cross-contamination.

OC is particularly effective on moist areas of the body including lips, tongue, and sweaty areas. A subject's reaction to being sprayed can include a loss of balance, loss of coordination, anger, anxiety, fear, and/or panic.

There have been cases documented where subjects have died inexplicably after being taken into police custody. Some subjects had been contaminated with OC which raised concerns that OC caused their deaths. While some unexplained deaths have been attributed to contamination by chemical agents, studies have shown that OC may be a contributing factor of the excited state of the subject, but there is no known evidence that OC caused their deaths. Recall from an earlier lesson the unusual behaviors that indicate a subject may be in a crisis state and in need of immediate medical attention when encountered.

Officers are required to adhere to certain standards of care for each person contaminated by OC. Visual contact should be maintained with each contaminated person until the person has recovered. If unusual behavior is observed, immediately seek medical attention. If symptoms are acute, stabilize the subject, maintain an open airway, and assure continuous breathing and proper circulation *(DT501.3.Q.2.b.)*. The manufacturer's Material Safety Data Sheet (MSDS) for the chemical agent used should be easily accessible.

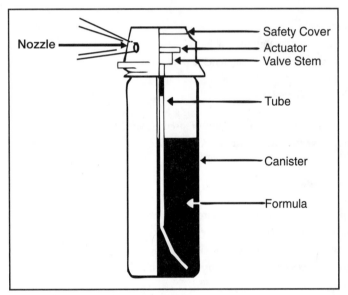

Chemical agent
canister nomenclature

Figure 4-87

The OC Canister

Follow the manufacturer's recommendations to maintain the canister in working order.

Though chemical canisters may dent or bend, there is generally no need to be concerned with the canisters leaking. Major manufacturers of these chemical contaminants have intentionally designed the canisters to be soft, pliable, and resistant to cracking and splitting. (See Figure 4-87)

Documentation

The use of a chemical agent is considered a use of force and should be documented according to agency policy. Document the contamination and the decontamination procedures taken.

Decontamination Procedures

Decontamination procedures are an essential component of the proper use of chemical agents. The chemical agent's effects will wear off in time; however, decontamination may decrease the period of discomfort. Whenever a subject is contaminated, the officer should follow the decontamination procedures as prescribed by agency policy. This standard of care should take place as soon as the subject is under control. *(DT.501.3.Q.4.a.)*

When an officer must use a chemical agent on a suspect or encounters a person who has been accidentally contaminated, he or she should not leave that person unattended while the effects of the contaminant are evident.

Psychological Decontamination

Contamination by a chemical agent may also have psychological effects on the contaminated person. The officer should tell the person who is contaminated to remain calm and reassure the person that the contaminant causes no lasting effects and that the effects should dissipate within 20–40 minutes. This repeated reassurance will help prevent anxiety and panic, behaviors that can endanger the officer and others.

Physical Decontamination

While psychologically decontaminating the subject, an officer may also guide the person through the process of physical decontamination.

Strobing—After contamination, the person should never wipe or rub his eyes with his fingers. Doing so may rub small particles into the eye which can ultimately damage the cornea. Instead, the person should begin by strobing his eyes. *Strobing* is forcefully blinking the eyes using all the muscles in the face, including those in the forehead. This forceful blinking helps clear the vision and activates the tear ducts. Tears help clear the eyes and wash away particles of contaminant.

Breathing—The person should also concentrate on breathing to draw his attention from the burning sensation the contaminant causes. Focusing on the discomfort may cause the person to shut down and panic. A rhythmic inhale through the mouth and then a forceful exhale through the nose will cause the mucous glands to begin working and the nose to run. This will clear the nasal passages and sinuses of mucus containing contaminant particles.

Removing Contaminants—After strobing the eyes and breathing rhythmically, the person may remove contaminants from his skin which will reduce the chemical agent's effects.

Air—The chemical agent's effects will wear off in time by mere exposure to air, i.e., standing in a breeze or in front of a fan.

Water—The person should use large amounts of running water to irrigate his eyes and facial skin.

Decontaminant solutions—There is no absolute antidote for chemical agents, but decontaminant solutions, such as baby shampoo, may decrease contamination effects. Many manufacturers produce solutions that are easy to carry in patrol vehicles and require little or no cleanup. The eyes should be rinsed with water and dabbed with an uncontaminated towel to lift the contaminant from skin. Scrubbing or using oil-based soaps to decontaminate can cause the contaminant to adhere to the skin and prolong decontamination time.

Medical personnel should treat prolonged or severe reactions.

Section Vocabulary

oleo-resin capsicum (OC)

orthochlorobenzal-malononitrile (CS)

pepper spray

Scoville Heat Units

strobing

UNIT 3 | DEFENSIVE TACTICS TECHNIQUES
LESSON 18 | Weapon Defense and Control: Weapon Retention

OBJECTIVES

DT501.3.P. Demonstrate weapon retention techniques.

Approximately 7.6 percent of officers murdered in the line of duty are killed with their own weapon. During a confrontation with a subject, an officer must control his or her weapons to keep the suspect from taking them.

An officer must remember that he or she brings weapons to every encounter. Therefore, maintaining an appropriate reactionary gap is one of the most effective methods in preventing the disarming of an officer. This becomes more difficult in close-quarter combat situations. Officers must protect their weapons along with their vital areas while engaged in a fight.

The following techniques are covered in this lesson:

- retention of intermediate weapon in carrier/holster
- drawn baton retention
- holstered handgun retention
- drawn handgun retention *(DT501.3.P.)*

Retention of Intermediate Weapon in Carrier/Holster

This technique is applicable to all intermediate weapons worn on the belt, such as a baton, chemical agent canister, or dart-firing stun gun.

The best defense against a subject grabbing your intermediate weapon is to maintain the reactionary gap. This technique works from a front and rear grab.

Use loud, clear verbal commands throughout the application of this technique.

Cover the subject's hand with your hand and maintain downward pressure.

Adjust your stance to maintain balance.

Deliver strikes to appropriate target areas.

Follow up with an appropriate technique(s). (See Figure 4-88)

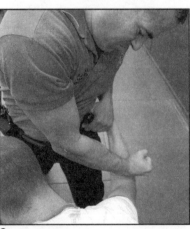

1   2

Retention of intermediate weapon in carrier

Figure 4-88

Drawn Baton Retention

This technique works on one- and two-handed grabs.

When the drawn baton is grasped:

> Adjust stance to maintain balance.
>
> Rotate the long end of the baton upward and from the outside to inside, releasing the subject's grip.
>
> Pull the baton back and away.
>
> Follow up with an appropriate technique(s). (See Figure 4-89)

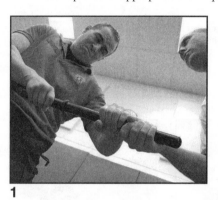  

1   **2**   **3**

Drawn baton retention   *Figure 4-89*

Holstered Handgun Retention

This technique should not be used unless the holster is firmly affixed to the belt.

When a subject grabs your holstered handgun:

> Use loud, clear verbal commands throughout the application of this technique.
>
> Grab the bottom of your holster and lift outward. This cants the weapon into your body and prevents removal of the weapon.
>
> Adjust your stance to maintain balance.
>
> Deliver strikes to appropriate target areas as you twist your body and increase pressure on the subject's grip.
>
> Follow up with an appropriate technique(s). (See Figure 4-90)

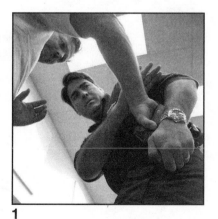 

1   **2**

Holstered handgun retention   *Figure 4-90*

Drawn Handgun Retention

The cradle handgun retention technique is used when the subject grabs a drawn handgun's barrel. The person holding a handgun's barrel has greater leverage than the person holding its grip. The cradle changes the leverage to the officer's advantage.

When a subject grabs your handgun:

Use loud, clear verbal commands throughout the application of this technique.

Widen your stance and lower your center of gravity.

Step forward and bring the handgun closer to your chest.

Wrap your nonweapon arm under the handgun and subject's hand and clamp them tightly to your chest.

Lever the gun barrel upward to release it from the subject's grasp.

Step back and create distance from the subject.

Follow up with an appropriate technique(s). (See Figure 4-91)

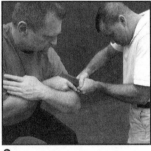
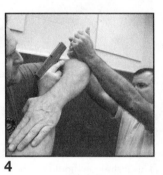

1   **2**   **3**   **4**

Drawn handgun retention

Figure 4-91

UNIT 3 | DEFENSIVE TACTICS TECHNIQUES
LESSON 19 | Weapon Defense and Control: Handgun Disarming

Disarming techniques are a last resort when an officer believes that the subject is going to shoot him or her.

Many factors affect an officer's decision to employ disarming techniques:

- the proximity of the officer to the subject
- the officer's belief that the subject is going to shoot him or her
- the presence of other potential victims in the immediate area
- the consideration of other reasonable options
- the mindset and commitment to disarm the subject regardless of personal injury or initial failure

This technique relies on several principles to be effective:

- **Surprise**—Do not telegraph to the subject that you plan to counterattack.

Telegraphing is small eye, hand, or foot movements in the direction that you plan to move.

- **Action is faster than reaction**—When you enter the danger zone to deal with a subject, you are the initiator. The subject must react to your threat.

- **Verbal distraction**—Reaction time increases when a subject processes two or more pieces of information at the same time. For example, ask the subject a question immediately prior to taking action.

- **Physical proximity**—To initiate this technique, the subject's handgun must be within arm's reach.

You can execute the technique equally well from either side. Although this lesson pertains to the handgun, you can apply the same concepts to a long gun. Your primary objective is to get the muzzle pointed in a different direction than toward you. *(DT501.3.S.)*

After you are in position and make the decision to initiate the technique, speed, intensity, and follow-through are paramount.

Handgun Cycles of Operation

If you grab a revolver with the hammer cocked, you may stop it from firing by grabbing the hammer and preventing the firing pin from striking.

If you grab the revolver's cylinder, you can prevent it from cycling to the next round.

If you grab over the top of a semiautomatic pistol, you may stop the slide from cycling. However, one shot may fire and the barrel will become very hot. You may also experience temporary flash blindness.

OBJECTIVES

DT501.3.S. Demonstrate handgun disarming techniques.

Front Disarming Technique

Use this technique when confronted by a subject pointing a gun at you. This technique must be applied with speed and an element of surprise.

Position yourself within arm's reach of the subject's handgun.

Use dialogue to distract the subject.

Place your hands at about shoulder height, palms facing the subject.

Pivot and thrust with one hand to grab the subject's handgun and push it farther away from you.

Bring up the opposite hand and grab the barrel from underneath.

Drive the weapon toward the subject's center line straight up to a vertical position.

Drive the barrel toward the subject's head as you rip the weapon straight back and create distance.

Draw your own weapon and issue verbal commands.

Follow up with an appropriate technique(s). (See Figure 4-92)

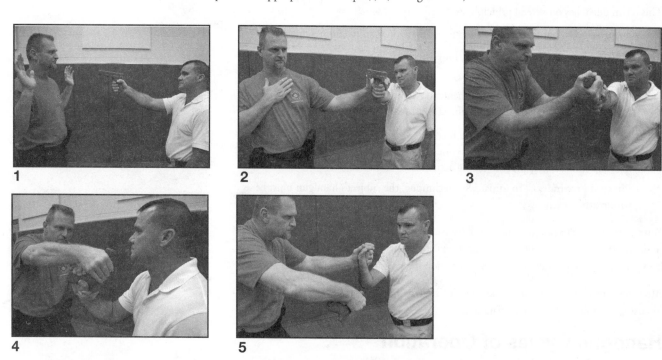

Front disarming technique

Figure 4-92

Rear Disarming Technique

Use this technique if a subject has a gun pointed at your back. This technique must be applied with speed and an element of surprise.

Establish a dialogue with the subject.

Move back toward the subject as you talk.

Raise your hands to shoulder height, palms facing forward.

Step back and quickly turn around.

As you turn, simultaneously use your closest arm to strike the subject's arm that holds the firearm in order to deflect the weapon.

Grab the gun's barrel with both hands.

Drive the weapon towards the subject's center line straight up to a vertical position.

Drive the barrel toward the subject's head as you rip the weapon straight back and create distance.

Draw your own weapon and issue verbal commands.

Follow up with an appropriate technique(s). (See Figure 4-93)

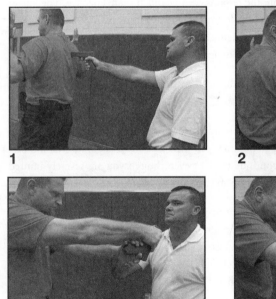

1

2

3

4

5

Rear disarming technique

Figure 4-93

LESSON 20 | **Weapon Defense and Control: Defense Against Edged Weapons**

OBJECTIVES

DT501.3.O. Demonstrate defense against edged weapons techniques.

An officer may be involved in an encounter where the subject is armed with a weapon. Knife fighting is a sophisticated technique and this portion of the curriculum provides only a basic knowledge of an edged weapon attack.

Defense against an edged weapon, bottle, club, or other blunt instrument may require a deadly force response, but only as a last resort. Officers should deploy empty-hand techniques against edged weapon attacks when no other options are available.

An edged weapon attack that involves distance or an impending threat gives you time to plan and react to the attack. One that happens suddenly and up close gives you limited options and more than likely will dictate a defense with empty hands. There is usually no time to disengage or select a weapon for defense. Empty-hand skills may be necessary when attacked at close range only if no other options are available.

If you identify a threat early on, the response can be much more effective. The longer it takes you to identify the attack, the less time you have to react. Awareness will help you recognize cues and early warning signs. Redirecting techniques are used to avoid or redirect an attack to give you time to disengage and escape.

The safe distance for an officer to be able to react to an edged weapon attack without injury is approximately 25 feet.

Before an incident occurs, you should make mental preparation that you will be cut. Develop a survival mindset to continue to fight even though you are severely injured until you are able to stop the aggression. Never give up!

Obstacles that may be used as a barrier between you and the subject, such as furniture, a vehicle, or clothing, are useful tools in defense against an edged weapon attack. Obstacles can slow down an attack and allow you to defend or to disengage from a situation, giving you time to utilize force options, control, or escape.

Knife Patterns

The following attack patterns are likely to be used from a knife-wielding subject:

- straight thrust (See Figure 4-94)

1

2

Knife patterns–Straight thrust

Figure 4-94

• overhead attack with one or two hands (See Figure 4-95)

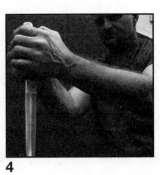

1   2   3   4

Knife patterns–Overhead attack, one or two hands

Figure 4-95

• slash forehand and backhand (See Figure 4-96)

1   2   3   4

Knife patterns–Slash forehand and backhand

Figure 4-96

• reverse grip (See Figure 4-97)

Knife patterns–
Reverse grip

Figure 4-97

• cross X pattern with up and down movements (See Figure 4-98)

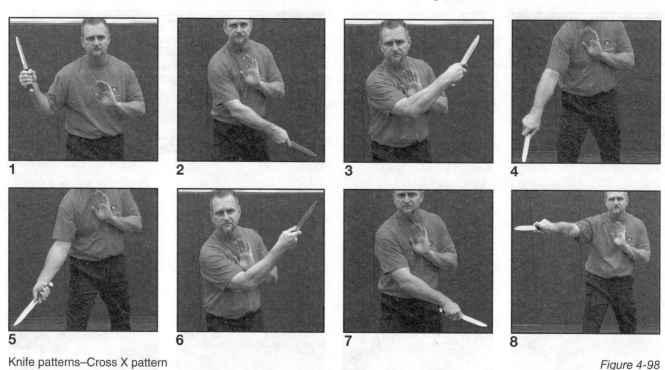

Knife patterns–Cross X pattern

Figure 4-98

Defensive Movements

The following movements may be used to defend against a spontaneous, close-quarter, edged weapon attack:

- **Evade**—Move or pivot away from the attacker.

- **Secure**—Capture the weapon arm and secure it.

- **Redirect**—Redirect the weapon arm.

- **Control**—Use a takedown to put the subject in a prone position (lying on the stomach face down,) disarm, and use a restraint device. (See Figure 4-99)

Use loud verbal commands before, during, and after the attack.

1

2

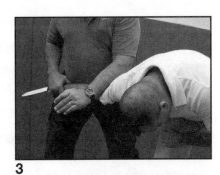

3

Redirection and Evasion Techniques

Redirection and evasive movements are used to avoid or redirect an edged weapon attack. Evasion is simply shifting your body or side stepping to avoid the attack. Redirection is using your hands to move the subject away. Using evasive and redirecting tactics may allow time to disengage, escape, or use other force options.

When redirecting, move in an angle or circle away from the attacker. Most people can run faster going forward than backward so the attacker has the advantage. By circling or angling away from the attack, the attacker has to adjust his direction of travel.

4

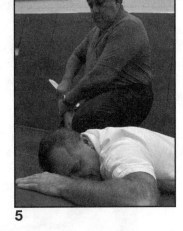

5

Defensive movements

Figure 4-99

Redirection Techniques

To perform redirection techniques, follow these steps:

Use loud, clear verbal commands throughout the application of the technique.

As the subject attacks, pivot backward to evade his forward movement.

Simultaneously bring both hands up in front of your face to protect vital areas.

Push or slap at the subject's upper arm or shoulder to create distance.

Move away from the subject at an angle or circle.

Follow up with an appropriate technique(s).

Techniques for defense against edged weapons covered in this lesson include:

• defense against an overhead stab with an edged weapon

• defense against a straight/underhand thrust with an edged weapon

• defense against a forehand slash with an edged weapon

• defense against a backhand slash with an edged weapon *(DT501.3.O.)*

Defense Against an Overhead Stab with an Edged Weapon (1)

As in all the edged weapon defenses, speed, surprise, and clearing your body from the path of the weapon are key elements to success.

Use loud, clear verbal commands throughout the confrontation.

As the subject strikes down with the weapon, step to the outside of the attacking arm.

Simultaneously overlap your hands forming a V to grab and control the subject's wrist.

Step back and pivot to the rear while forcing the subject's attacking arm downward.

Rotate the subject's arm elbow up.

Control the subject's arm with downward pressure on the elbow.

Keep the subject's arm straight with his wrist above his shoulder.

Take the subject down as in a straight arm takedown or outside wrist takedown.

Apply pressure to the back of the subject's wrist to facilitate the weapon's release.

Secure the edged weapon.

Follow up with an appropriate technique(s). (See Figure 4-100)

 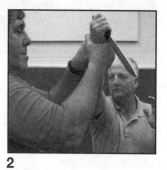  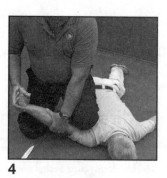

1   **2**   **3**   **4**

Defense against overhead stab with edged weapon (1)

Figure 4-100

Defense Against an Overhead Stab with an Edged Weapon (2)

Use loud, verbal commands throughout the confrontation.

Palm strike the subject's upper chest near his shoulder with both hands to stop the movement of the weapon arm.

Using your arm closest to the subject's weapon arm, capture and secure his arm by encircling it. At the same time, strike the throat or face with your other hand or elbow.

Utilize multiple strikes until the subject is disarmed and under control or until you can safely disengage.

Use a takedown to put the subject in a prone handcuffing position. (See Figure 4-101)

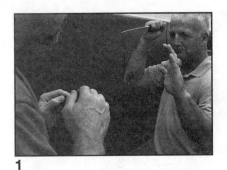
1

2

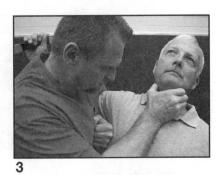
3

Defense Against a Straight/Underhand Thrust with an Edged Weapon

Use loud, clear verbal commands throughout the confrontation.

As the subject strikes with the weapon, step to the outside of the attacking arm.

With both hands, simultaneously grab and control the subject's wrist as you move your hips back. At the same time, push the weapon away from your body and strike the subject in the face with a head butt.

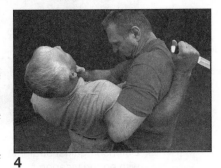
4

Defense against overhead stab with edged weapon (2)

5

Figure 4-101

Pivot to the outside while trapping the subject's arm between your arm and body with the subject's elbow up.

Control the subject's arm with downward pressure on the elbow.

Keep the subject's arm straight with his wrist above his shoulder.

Take the subject down by forcing his chest to the ground.

Apply pressure to the back of the subject's wrist to facilitate the weapon's release.

Secure the edged weapon.

Follow up with an appropriate technique(s). (See Figure 4-102)

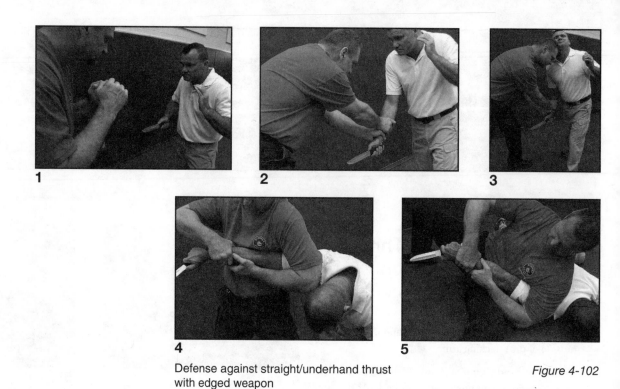

Defense against straight/underhand thrust with edged weapon

Figure 4-102

Defense Against a Forehand Slash with an Edged Weapon (1)

Use loud, verbal commands throughout the confrontation.

As the subject strikes with the weapon, step to the inside of the attacking arm.

Simultaneously overlap your hands forming a V to grab and control the subject's wrist.

Step back and pivot to the rear while forcing the subject's attacking arm downward.

Rotate the subject's arm elbow up.

Control the subject's arm with downward pressure on the elbow.

Keep the subject's arm straight with his wrist above his shoulder.

Take the subject down by forcing his chest to the ground.

Apply pressure to the back of the subject's wrist to facilitate the weapon's release.

Secure the edged weapon.

Follow up with an appropriate technique(s). (See Figure 4-103)

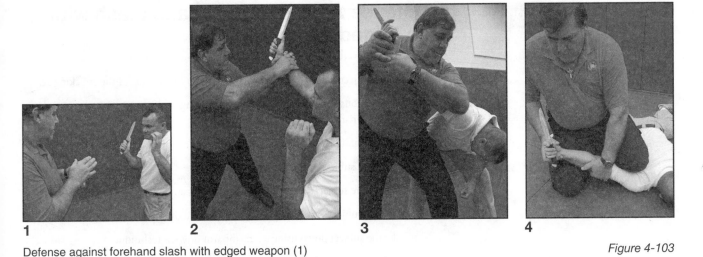

Defense against forehand slash with edged weapon (1)

Figure 4-103

Defense Against a Forehand Slash with an Edged Weapon (2)

Use loud, verbal commands throughout the confrontation.

Palm strike the subject's upper chest near his shoulder with both hands to stop the movement of the weapon arm.

Using your arm closest to the subject's weapon arm, capture and secure his arm by encircling it. At the same time, strike the throat or face with your other hand or elbow.

Utilize multiple strikes until the subject is disarmed and under control or until you can safely disengage.

Use a takedown to put the subject in a prone handcuffing position. (See Figure 4-104)

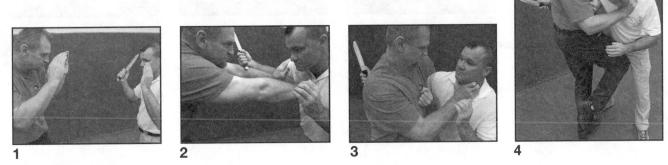

Defense against forehand slash with edged weapon (2)

Figure 4-104

Section Vocabulary

prone position

Defense Against a Backhand Slash with an Edged Weapon

Use loud, verbal commands throughout the confrontation.

As the subject strikes with the weapon, step to the outside of the attacking arm.

Simultaneously overlap your hands forming a V to grab and control the subject's wrist.

Step back and pivot to the rear while forcing the subject's attacking arm downward.

Rotate the subject's arm elbow up.

Control the subject's arm with downward pressure on the elbow.

Keep the subject's arm straight with his wrist above his shoulder.

Take the subject down using a straight arm or wrist technique.

Apply pressure to the back of the subject's wrist to facilitate the weapon's release.

Secure the edged weapon.

Follow up with an appropriate technique(s). (See Figure 4-105)

  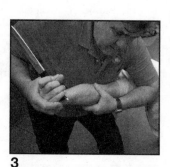 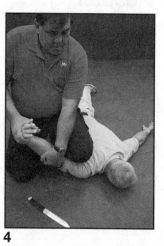

1 **2** **3** **4**

Defense against backhand slash with edged weapon

Figure 4-105

UNIT 3 | DEFENSIVE TACTICS TECHNIQUES
LESSON 21 | Deadly Force Techniques

Deadly force is usually associated with the use of a firearm. However, certain empty-hand techniques and unconventional weapons can be used effectively in a deadly force encounter. Empty-hand techniques become deadly force when they have the capability of causing great bodily harm or even death. A good example is a ground fight that turns into a deadly threat when a subject attempts to choke or bite you, gouge your eyes, or grab your gun. If you cannot access a weapon, then an empty-hand technique may help stop or disable your attacker, giving you the chance to recover to a different position.

Some empty-hand techniques can become deadly force if applied to a specific target area of the body that is likely to result in great bodily harm or death. Some examples of deadly force techniques include the thumb strike, elbow strike, and eye gouge. *(DT501.3.T.)*

Deadly Force Thumb Strike

Form a fist with your strong hand.

Extend your thumb past the middle knuckle of your index finger.

Squeeze your hand tightly so that the pad of the thumb pushes firmly against the index finger.

Allow it to curl upward to form a slight bend that will lock the middle knuckle of the thumb.

Using good control, deliver a strike to various areas of the subject. Some examples of striking areas include the throat and eyes. (See Figure 4-106)

The throat and eyes are two examples of effective target areas for a deadly force thumb strike.

Deadly Force Elbow Strike

The deadly force elbow strike uses the tip of the elbow to target a specific area where great bodily harm may result. To be a deadly force strike, certain target areas must be stabilized.

Some target areas for a deadly force elbow strike include the following:

- temple
- side of jaw
- bridge of nose
- back of the head
- throat (See Figure 4-107)

OBJECTIVES

DT501.3.T. Demonstrate the simulation of deadly force techniques.

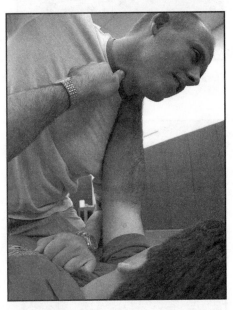

Deadly force thumb strike   *Figure 4-106*

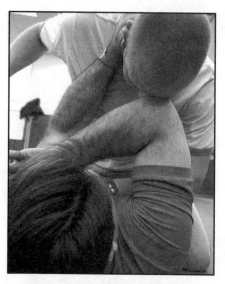

Deadly force elbow strike   *Figure 4-107*

Deadly Force Eye Gouge

Your fingers or spear hand can be used to strike or rake the attacker's eyes. (See Figure 4-108)

Use of Alternative Weapons

Any item an officer has at hand may be used as a potential weapon in a time of need. In fact, any extension of the body may be a weapon, such as a flashlight, a ballpoint pen, keys, or a pocket knife held in the hand. It is the use of the item that qualifies the item as a weapon. For instance, a firearm is just a firearm until it is used for a defensive purpose; however, an ashtray or coffee mug which is not perceived as a weapon becomes a weapon if used to strike someone.

A deadly weapon is any item used to cause death or great bodily harm. For example, a ballpoint pen directed to the eye becomes a deadly weapon. An officer in a deadly force situation should not hesitate to use unconventional weapons if available and necessary.

Deadly force eye gouge   *Figure 4-108*

CHAPTER 5

Dart-Firing Stun Gun

Stun guns are one type of ***electronic control device***, a device that uses a high voltage, low-power electrical charge to induce involuntary muscle contractions to temporarily incapacitate a noncompliant subject. Technology has progressed from the basic hand-held stun gun to a weapon that propels darts up to 35 feet. This weapon is called the ***dart-firing stun gun (DFSG)***, and propels electrified darts/probes/electrodes/barbs (these terms will be used interchangeably throughout this chapter). The use and effects of dart-firing stun guns have been a topic of discussion in the media, among law enforcement officers and administrators, and within the scientific and medical professions. This chapter will introduce an officer to the basics of the stun gun, particularly the dart-firing stun gun, and provide knowledge of its practical use.

UNIT 1 I USE OF THE DART-FIRING STUN GUN

LESSON 1 I Use of the Dart-Firing Stun Gun

OBJECTIVES

DFSG521. Summarize basic training or equivalency requirements for dart-firing stun gun use.

DFSG522. Summarize required annual training for dart-firing stun gun use.

DFSG519. Describe statutorily authorized use of a dart-firing stun gun.

DFSG523. Explain lawful possession and use of a dart-firing stun gun by a civilian.

DFSG525. Provide a brief history of stun guns.

DFSG524. Describe the basic nomenclature and mechanics of a stun gun.

DFSG526. Describe the basic nomenclature and mechanics of a dart-firing stun gun.

DFSG540. Explain use as a drive stun device.

DFSG527. Describe the proper maintenance, care, and storage of the dart-firing stun gun.

DFSG528. Explain that a dart-firing stun gun is intended to prevent injury to the subject involved and other persons present.

DFSG535. Describe the possible effects that a dart-firing stun gun has on the human body.

DFSG549. Explain medical considerations involving dart-firing stun gun use.

In 2006, the Florida legislature created F.S. §943.1717 as a response to inconsistent stun gun use statewide. This legislation governs the training and use of dart-firing stun guns by law enforcement in Florida. Florida statute requires that any law enforcement officer authorized by his or her employing agency to operate a dart-firing stun gun must attend either the Commission-approved dart-firing stun gun course during basic recruit training or an equivalent training course provided by the officer's employing agency. *(DFSG521.)*

Not every criminal justice agency authorizes its officers to carry dart-firing stun guns. However, if an officer is employed by an agency that does, he or she may be required to go through supplemental agency training before being allowed to operate the weapon. If the officer's agency allows the use of the dart-firing stun gun and has authorized the officer to carry it, he or she is required by the CJSTC to attend annual re-training of at least one hour on its use. *(DFSG522.)*

Legal Aspects of Dart-Firing Stun Gun Use

As defined in F.S. §943.1717 and §790.01(4)(b), a dart-firing stun gun is categorized as a **nonlethal** (force level that is not intended to cause death or great bodily harm) weapon. It is used to control a person during an arrest or to control a person in custody when resistance escalates from passive physical resistance to active physical resistance and the person has the apparent ability to physically threaten the officer or others, or the person is preparing or attempting to flee or escape. These statutory guidelines provide the minimum criteria for use of a dart-firing stun gun. The appropriate and necessary use of a dart-firing stun gun will be determined on the basis of the officer's training and experience and assessment of all pertinent circumstances. *(DFSG519.)*

Authorized Civilian Use

Stun guns and dart-firing stun guns are available for purchase and legal use by civilians in Florida. According to F.S. §790.01(4) (b), "it is not a violation of this section for a person to carry, for purposes of lawful self-defense in a concealed manner," a dart-firing stun gun. Further, F.S. §790.053(2) (b) states that a person may openly carry a dart-firing stun gun for purposes of lawful self-defense. *(DFSG523.)*

History of Stun Guns

The stun gun was invented in the 1960s by John Cover. He intended to create an electric, nonlethal weapon to control violent criminal behavior. This new weapon was called a TASER®, an acronym for Thomas A. Swift's Electrical Rifle. Its name references an early 1900s children's novel by Victor Appleton. Electronic control devices (the words "devices" and "tools" will be used synonymously throughout this chapter) are all generally built using the same principle, which is delivering relatively low power (amperage and wattage) coupled with high voltage to a subject. Compliance is gained either through pain or involuntary muscle contractions causing incapacitation enabling the officer to restrain the subject.

Early in its development, the stun gun itself had to make physical contact with a subject because the electrodes were fixed to the device. This type of stun gun has been manufactured in various sizes and shapes but is usually small and easy to hold. Currently, the two most common types of stun guns are the basic stun gun and the dart-firing stun gun. Additionally, there are several different types of electronic control tools including shields, batons, and restraint devices. The shield is generally used for riot control and in correctional settings. The restraint devices are not seen as much as other delivery systems. The first dart-firing stun gun was developed in 1974 and is the most widely used tool to date for law enforcement officers in Florida. *(DFSG525.)*

TASER® International

One example of a dart-firing stun gun is the TASER® International TASER® device, which is a stun gun with the ability to reach its subject from up to 35 feet. The TASER® device is shaped like a handgun and uses compressed gas to propel two small darts which are connected by wire to the TASER® device.

The TASER® device is primarily used by law enforcement, the military, and security guards. However, civilians are increasingly using TASER® devices as self-defense weapons.

How Stun Guns Work

If a person is struck by lightning or sticks a finger in an electrical outlet, the current can maim or even kill, but in smaller doses, electricity is harmless. An **amp (ampere)** is the measure of electrical current or power. High voltage won't injure a subject if the current (or amps) is low. For example, a harmless carpet static discharge is equal to 30,000 volts. Low voltage can injure if the current is high enough. Stun guns operate at low average currents.

Electricity follows the path of least resistance. In order for a stun gun to operate, electricity must be able to flow between the probes. The path of least resistance on a dart-firing stun gun is between the probes. The wider the probes spread on the target, the greater the effectiveness of the weapon. Electricity will not pass to others in contact with the subject unless contact is made directly between or on the probes. An officer should remember that electricity can arc through clothing and even some bullet-resistant materials. If the officer were to expose a subject who was submerged or standing in water to a dart-firing stun gun, it would not cause electrocution or increase the power applied to the subject (See Figure 5-1).

The basic idea of a stun gun is to disrupt the body's communication system by generating a high-voltage, low-amperage electrical charge. In simple terms, the charge has a lot of pressure behind it but not much intensity. When a stun gun is pressed

DFSG550. Explain how to handle an impaired, ill, injured or pregnant subject.

DFSG551. Explain the after-care considerations of dart-firing stun gun use.

DFSG520. Explain legal justification of use of a dart-firing stun gun.

DFSG530. Describe how to properly use verbal skills to de-escalate a situation and avoid the use of the dart-firing stun gun when practical.

DFSG529. Explain why not every subject displaying an active physical resistance will necessitate the use of a dart-firing stun gun.

DFSG534. Explain why use of a dart-firing stun gun in a punitive manner is prohibited.

DFSG537. Identify that a dart-firing stun gun is not a substitute for a firearm.

DFSG532. Describe primary and alternative sites on the body to target with a dart-firing stun gun.

DFSG531. Describe areas to avoid targeting with a dart-firing stun gun.

DFSG533. Describe environmental conditions to consider prior to using a dart-firing stun gun.

DFSG501. Explain how to properly utilize backup officer(s) to gain compliance and handcuff a subject during use of a dart-firing stun gun.

DFSG502. Explain the use of multiple exposures to gain compliance.

DFSG503. Summarize the need to stay current on dart-firing stun gun policy issues and trends.

DFSG504. Demonstrate how to properly document use of force reports involving dart-firing stun gun use.

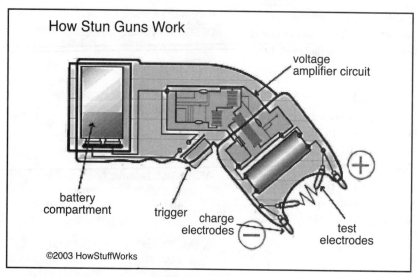

Stun gun

Figure 5-1

against a subject and the trigger is held, the charge passes into the subject's body. Since it has a fairly high voltage, the charge will pass through heavy clothing and skin, but the charge is not intense enough to damage the subject's body unless it is applied for extended periods. It does affect the subject's nervous system. First, the charge combines with the electrical signals from the subject's brain, making it very difficult to decipher any messages. The subject has a hard time telling his or her muscles to move and may become confused, unbalanced, and incapacitated. Also, the current may be generated with a pulse frequency that mimics the body's own electrical signals. In this case, the current will tell the subject's muscles to do a great deal of work in a short amount of time. Depending on shot placement, the subject's torso and limbs will either contract or extend. *(DFSG524.)*

Standard Stun Gun

Conventional stun guns have a simple design. They are about the size of a flashlight and work on nine-volt batteries. The circuitry includes multiple transformers and components that boost the voltage in the circuit, typically between 20,000 and 150,000 volts, and reduce the amperage. The electrodes are simply two plates of conducting metal positioned in the circuit with a gap between them. Since the electrodes are positioned along the circuit, they have a high voltage difference between them. If this gap is filled with a conductor (the subject's body), the electrical pulses will try to move from one electrode to the other, dumping electricity into the subject's nervous system (See Figure 5-2).

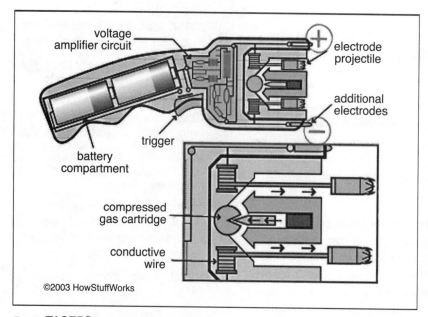

Basic TASER®

Figure 5-2

Dart-Firing Stun Guns

TASER® stun guns work the same basic way as ordinary stun guns, except the two charge electrodes aren't permanently joined to the housing. Instead, they are positioned at the ends of long conductive wires attached to the gun's electrical circuit. Pulling the trigger breaks open a compressed gas cartridge inside the gun, launching them through the air; the attached conductive wires trail behind. This is the same basic firing mechanism of a BB gun (See Figure 5-3).

15, 21, LS, & XP25 Compressed Air Cartridges

The electrodes are fitted with small barbs so that they will grab onto a subject's clothing. When the electrodes are attached, the current travels down the wires into the subject. The main advantage of this design is that it stuns subjects from a greater distance (typically 15 to 25 feet for patrol and 35 feet for SWAT/Special Operations). The disadvantage is that if an officer misses or only one probe hits, he or she must reload to attempt a second shot. A **cycle** is the predetermined amount of time (usually five seconds) that a stun device will discharge automatically when activated.

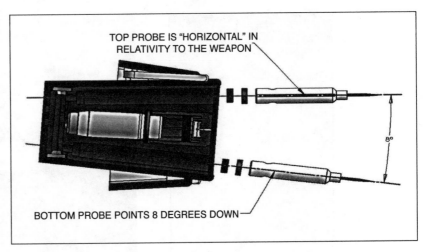

TOP PROBE IS "HORIZONTAL" IN RELATIVITY TO THE WEAPON

8°

BOTTOM PROBE POINTS 8 DEGREES DOWN

Top probe

Figure 5-3

Some TASER® stun guns have a built-in shooter-identification system. When fired, the gun also releases dozens of confetti-sized identification tags that tell investigators which gun was fired and at what location. Some also have a computer system that records the time and date of shots. *(DFSG526.)*

Use as a Drive Stun Device

Drive stun, or touch stun, occurs when the front of the dart-firing stun gun is directly touched to the body of the resisting subject, and the electrical charge is passed to the subject's body. In this mode, the dart-firing stun gun works as a conventional stun gun and is a pain-compliance tool only. The drive stun can be used when the suspect is too close to the dart-firing stun gun operator or when a probe application would be hard to make (e.g., a suspect and an officer are fighting, and the dart-firing stun gun operator cannot get a clear shot on the suspect). The drive stun does not incapacitate a subject but may assist an officer in taking a subject into custody.

To use as a drive stun (without firing probes), the officer should remove the live cartridge and apply the weapon directly to a subject. Ideal target areas of the body are large muscle mass areas or areas with high nerve concentration such as the side of the neck, inside of the thigh, or abdomen and leg areas (excluding the chest area if possible). (See Figure 5-5 on page 304.) If the first choice of target area is not effective, an officer may consider a different area of application, use of an additional cycle of application, or alternative force option. The drive stun generally does not cause incapacitation. Because of this, officers frequently find themselves in prolonged struggles with violent suspects whom they end up drive stunning several times in several different locations on the body. This often results in multiple discharges, causing scratches on the suspect's body and numerous **signature marks**, which are marks left on a subject's body after a drive stun application (See Figure 5-4 on the next page).

An effective alternative technique is for an officer to use a drive stun with a live cartridge. For example, the officer fires a dart-firing stun gun, and the probes are discharged into the resisting subject. A drive stun is then applied away from the probes to achieve neuromuscular incapacitation. In addition, if only one probe strikes a subject, the drive stun will act as a second probe by completing the cycle. This tactic also works even if both

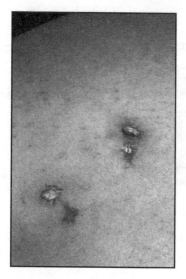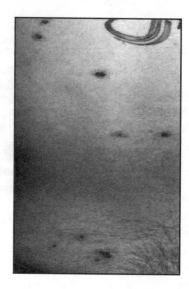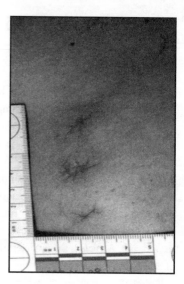

Drive stun signature marks

Figure 5-4

probes strike the subject. If the probe spread is very minimal due to a close shot or a drive stun with a live cartridge, a drive stun away from the probes will increase the spread and cause incapacitation. Probe hits are almost always more desirable than drive stuns. They are more effective (neuromuscular vs. pain compliance), can be applied from a safe distance, usually require fewer cycles, and cause fewer injuries. *(DFSG540.)*

Maintenance, Care, and Storage

While most electronic control devices have specific maintenance requirements, there are some considerations that apply to all. An officer should keep the device clean and dry as much as possible. If it gets wet, the officer should make sure it is turned off and put in a clean, dry place until it dries completely. An officer should never test the device while it is still wet. Storage will be based on the manufacturers' recommendation and agency policy. Prolonged storage in extreme temperatures should be avoided. *(DFSG527.)*

Effects on the Human Body

Although use of a dart-firing stun gun is intended to prevent injury to the subject and other people present, the device itself has a very powerful physical effect *(DFSG528.)*. The human body uses electricity to move its muscles. A dart-firing stun gun essentially overwhelms that electrical system, causing temporary paralysis/incapacitation. A 7 to 15-watt system works as a pain compliance tool and does not interfere with a person's nervous system. A 26-watt system overrides the body's sensory and motor nervous system but has not been shown to interfere with respiration or heartbeat.

When dart-firing stun gun probes hit a subject, the weapon transmits electric impulses that interfere with the electric impulses used by the human nerve system to communicate with the skeletal muscles, causing physical incapacitation, or ***electro-muscular disruption (EMD)***. Therefore, the subject immediately loses control of his or her body and falls to the ground, incapable of any coordinated action. Possible effects of use could include the subject immediately falling to the ground, yelling or screaming, having involuntary muscle contractions, freezing in place with legs locked, feeling dazed for several seconds or minutes, experiencing vertigo or a temporary tingling sensation, experiencing critical stress amnesia, not remembering any pain, and/or exhibiting minor signature marks from contact.

The subject may not show any physical effects from the contact but may have sustained injuries from a fall as a result of contact with the dart-firing stun gun. These injuries are usually minor in nature. However, there are circumstances where more severe injuries could occur. At this time, there is no evidence that age is a contributing factor in injuries. Also, there is no evidence that electrical energy alone causes significant injury to an unborn fetus or an expectant mother. Manufacturers and independent studies assert that the use of these devices has no residual medical impact on subjects. There is no basis to establish that stun guns pose unacceptable health risks when used appropriately on healthy subjects. The fall that results from use of a dart-firing stun gun, if it occurred from elevated heights or other hazardous areas, could cause more significant injuries. *(DFSG535.)*

Medical Considerations

Sudden In-custody Death Syndrome (SDS) is a broad classification for unexplained in-custody deaths, usually occurring 20 minutes to 2 hours after the suspect has been taken into custody. In nearly all cases of unexplained deaths involving in-custody subjects, the victim has exhibited bizarre behavior due to delusional, agitated, or stimulant drug-induced mental states.

SDS is an emerging medical diagnosis for the following well-documented medical maladies: excited delirium and *drug-induced psychosis*, which is a form of psychosis resulting from drug use. It can cause hallucinations and/or delusions or positional asphyxia, which is death as a result of body position that interferes with the ability to breathe.

Researchers have noted this phenomenon for more than a century. Though there are few diagnostic methods to accurately predict an onset of SDS, there are some consistent indicators which alert a trained professional that a subdued person is more susceptible to the onset of SDS. The most common factors that are relevant to criminal justice officers are the visible signs of distress or indicators that a subject may be suffering from excited delirium. Some indicators of this condition include unusual or psychotic behavior, disorientation, intense sweating, hot, feverish skin, delirious and/or delusional behavior, extreme paranoia, continuously racing pulse, and/or a history of drug abuse or use.

The quickest and safest way for an officer to handle a subject in this condition is to notify EMS as soon as possible, use a dart-firing stun gun to incapacitate if necessary, and restrain the subject at the earliest possible point using the least restrictive means possible. *(DFSG549.)*

Impaired, Ill, or Pregnant Subjects

In as safe and practical a manner as possible, an officer should attempt to discern if a subject is impaired. Although most subjects who are emotionally or mentally disturbed or under the influence of drugs or alcohol usually comply, some do not. Agency policy should be followed in these situations. An officer must be aware that the typical physiological responses to the dart-firing stun gun are not always present in impaired subjects. As in any high risk situation, the officer should be prepared to adapt to the situation and take other tactical action. In general, the best approach to handling subjects suffering from any form of psychosis is to restrain them as quickly as possible to protect them and others from potential injury. Also, an officer should follow agency policy when encountering an obviously pregnant or ill subject. *(DFSG550.)*

After Care

All persons who have been subjected to dart-firing stun gun use should be monitored regularly while in custody, even if they are receiving medical care. In accordance with training and agency policy, an officer should consider removing the probes if all signs of resistance are gone. Probes that have been removed from the skin should be treated as biohazard sharps. If excessive bleeding is observed, medical attention should be sought immediately. Additionally, an officer should clean and bandage any wounds per agency policy. An officer should look for and treat any possible secondary injuries and seek medical attention if the condition requires it. Trained medical professionals should remove all deeply embedded probes or probes that penetrate sensitive tissue areas (i.e., neck, face, groin, female breast, etc.). *(DFSG551.)*

Use of Force Considerations

Claims that officers used excessive force in the course of an arrest, investigatory stop, or other seizure are analyzed under the Fourth Amendment's objective reasonableness standard *(Graham v. Conner,* 490 U.S. 386 1989). Use of force incidents are judged on whether a reasonable person would believe the officers' actions were justifiable based on the totality of circumstances known to officers at the time the force was used. The officer must consider, without regard to underlying intent or motivation, his or her authority to use force and the totality of the circumstances, much of which officers may have no control over. In these instances the officer must be able to articulate justification verbally for why he or she chose to utilize the DFSG. Florida Statute also requires officers to consider using a DFSG only when a subject is actively, physically resisting.*(DFSG520.)*

The court has established law on the use of a TASER® in the case of *Draper vs. Reynolds,* 369 F3d 1270 (11th Cir. 2004). Video of the traffic stop led the court to conclude that if the officer had attempted handcuffing without the use of the TASER®, it would have escalated into a serious physical struggle. The one-time shock of a suspect with a TASER® did not constitute excessive force and was reasonably proportionate when the subject repeatedly refused verbal commands and became hostile, belligerent, and uncooperative during the stop.

Many law enforcement officials claim that in some situations, stun guns can be an effective alternative to more harmful methods such as traditional firearms and batons. "Numerous recent independent studies—including an extensive, multi-million dollar three-year study conducted by the United Kingdom's Association of Chief Police Officers (ACPO) in consultation with the British Police Scientific Development Branch (PSDB), the British Defense Science and Technology Laboratory (DSTL) and the British Defense Scientific Advisory Council Sub-committee on the Medical Implications of Less-lethal Weapons (DOMILL), as well as a U.S. Department of Defense (DOD) study involving approximately 20 medical and research doctors from academic, government and private institutions—have reaffirmed the life-saving value of TASER® technology. According to TASER® International, these studies have determined TASER® technology, although not risk-free, is among the safest use-of-force options available." (http://taser.com/research/Pages/FAQGeneral.aspx, 2011, FAQs).

Assessing the Situation

An officer should first attempt to gain control of a situation by using verbal commands. Many physical encounters can be avoided by this process, often referred to as verbal de-escalation. By disengaging or de-escalating, an officer gives the subject another opportunity to comply with lawful commands and avoid the use of the dart-firing stun gun. If all efforts to verbally de-escalate the situation are exhausted or are not feasible, the use of a dart-firing stun gun may be warranted. *(DFSG530.)*

Not every situation where a subject displays an active physical resistance calls for the application of a dart-firing stun gun. During these encounters, an officer must continually assess whether to engage or disengage and decide on the appropriate force option. Many times, the most prudent approach may be for the officer to fend off the initial assault then disengage and reassess. From this point, the officer can either escalate to a higher force option or de-escalate to a lower force option as the situation dictates *(DFSG529.)*. Whenever possible, this should be done from a position of cover. If an officer decides to use a dart-firing stun gun, he or she will be expected to articulate that, based on training, experience, and assessment of the circumstances, use of the device was the best force option for the situation.

Lawful Authority

The dart-firing stun gun is not to be used to coerce a subject to give statements or perform an illegal act. Use of a DFSG in a punitive manner without lawful authority may be violating a citizen's civil rights and be subject to the following decision:

U.S. Code Title 42 Chapter 21 Subchapter 1 Section 1983: Civil action for deprivation of rights states that:

> "Every person who, under color of any statute, ordinance, regulation, custom, or usage, of any State or Territory or the District of Columbia, subjects, or causes to be subjected, any citizen of the United States or other person within the jurisdiction thereof to the deprivation of any rights, privileges, or immunities secured by the Constitution and laws, shall be liable to the party injured in an action at law, suit in equity, or other proper proceeding for redress, except that in any action brought against a judicial officer for an act or omission taken in such officer's judicial capacity, injunctive relief shall not be granted unless a declaratory decree was violated or declaratory relief was unavailable." *(DFSG534.)*

Tactical Considerations

The use of a dart-firing stun gun is not a substitute for the use of a firearm. However, this does not exclude its use in place of a firearm when an officer is afforded the time, reasonable cover, and a backup officer *(DFSG537.)*. Once the decision to use a dart-firing stun gun has been made, an officer must consider a number of tactical factors including the following:

- What is the most effective area of the body to target?
- What is the physical environment around the subject?
- Are there officer safety concerns or danger to the subject or nearby public?
- Is there cover or concealment available for an officer?
- Is there a time constraint?
- Is backup present or en route?
- At what point in the encounter might an additional dart-firing stun gun application be required?

Targeting

The primary target of a subject's body should be low center mass or large muscle groups such as the back, buttocks, and legs. The chest area should be avoided when possible. (See Figure 5-5 on the next page.) Alternative target sites might be the back near the shoulders or the back of the legs where, if clothed, the

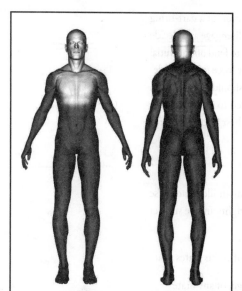

Preferred target areas are illustrated in dark shading and light areas should be avoided when possible.

Preferred target areas   Figure 5-5

clothing fits tighter and the probes will conduct electricity to the subject more effectively *(DFSG532.).* The physical positioning of a subject, the clothing he or she is wearing, and how he or she is wearing it could also play a big role in the effectiveness of a dart-firing stun gun application. The dart-firing stun gun may not be as effective when the subject has on loose-fitting or very thick clothing. The intentional targeting of a subject's head, neck, face, chest, or groin should be avoided when possible because of a higher likelihood of potential for injury to the subject. *(DFSG531.).*

Safety Considerations

Officers must observe the subject and be aware at all times of the methods subjects may use to defeat a dart-firing stun gun including where a subject's hands are. He or she must also be prepared to intervene when necessary with an additional application/cycle or other methods of control.

There are a number of safety factors to consider prior to the use of a dart-firing stun gun. For instance, if a subject is encountered in an elevated position, such as on a ledge or stairwell, the officer should consider that if he or she fires a dart-firing stun gun, the subject may become incapacitated and injure him- or herself upon falling. If a subject is operating a vehicle or machinery and is incapacitated by a dart-firing stun gun, there is a possibility that the subject could turn the vehicle into an uncontrolled, deadly object. If a subject is in or could fall into water when hit with a dart-firing stun gun, the subject could drown. If a flammable chemical spray has been deployed on a subject, the dart-firing stun gun could ignite the subject. An officer should follow his or her agency's policies and procedures regarding the use of OC sprays and dart-firing stun guns. If a subject is in an environment containing hazardous materials or potentially flammable, volatile, or explosive materials that could be ignited as a result of firing the dart-firing stun gun, the subject could ignite when hit with a dart-firing stun gun. *(DFSG533.).*

Utilizing Backup

An officer should try to have at least one backup officer present to handcuff the subject after the officer with the dart-firing stun gun has gained compliance. The primary officer will be operating the dart-firing stun gun and the backup officer(s) will take physical control of the subject. By taking advantage of the time the subject is incapacitated, the backup officer moves in and secures him or her, while the primary officer maintains control through the use of a dart-firing stun gun.

While the cycle (five seconds) is active, the officer may not be able to manipulate the subject's arms or legs to handcuff them. At this point, the subject is usually no longer trying to resist and wants to comply but has little or no muscular control and may appear to be resisting. It is for the officer's (and the subject's) safety that the officer be aware of the subject's potential uncontrollable overreaction in these situations. *(DFSG501).*

Multiple Exposures

Experts in the field agree that there is no definitive number of exposures to the electricity that a dart-firing stun gun produces. The reasonableness standard will help in the decision-making process. For example, an officer who is left alone several minutes away from the nearest backup and is facing a large subject who is threatening to do serious bodily harm to the officer may decide to use a dart-firing stun gun. At the end of the cycle, the subject still refuses to comply. An officer may continue demanding compliance and deliver another cycle. Several cycles may be necessary until another officer arrives on scene to assist or until the subject stops physically resisting. *(DFSG502.)*

Current Dart-Firing Stun Gun Policy Issues and Trends

An officer should stay up to date on case law, department policies, and current trends regarding dart-firing stun guns. The manufacturer may provide updates. Also, subjects expecting encounters with law enforcement may be putting objects or shields under their clothing to render the dart-firing stun gun ineffective. They may also "stop, drop, and roll" to pull out darts. If a subject begins to roll, an officer should close the distance, move with the subject, and keep sufficient slack in the wire to maintain electrical contact. Additionally, subjects may wait for the cycle to stop then pull out the darts and may even begin to run away. An officer must be prepared to close in and utilize a drive stun or transition to another force option to stop the suspect from leaving. *(DFSG503.)*

Documenting Dart-Firing Stun Gun Use

Prompt and accurate reporting of the decision to use a dart-firing stun gun is required. An officer's employing agency will have specific policy and training on when and how to document this use. *(DFSG504.)*

Section Vocabulary

amp (ampere)

cycle (cycling)

dart-firing stun gun (DFSG)

drug-induced psychosis

electro-muscular disruption (EMD)

electronic control device

nonlethal

signature marks

sudden in-custody death syndrome (SDS)

CHAPTER 6

Criminal Justice Officer Physical Fitness Training

The following is an outline of the Physical Fitness training for the Florida Criminal Justice Standards and Training Commission (CJSTC) Basic Recruit Training Programs. This information is intended to demonstrate what will be expected of Basic Recruit Training students and provide instruction on how to prepare for each component of the evaluations. An evaluation will be conducted in the first two weeks of training and again in the last two weeks of training. Each component score will be recorded separately on the designated CJSTC form.

Basic Recruit Training Programs

Criminal Justice Officer Physical Fitness Training Programs: Table of Course Numbers and Hours

Course/Program	Course Number	Physical Fitness Course Hours	Estimated Fitness Training Hours Per Week
Criminal Justice Officer Physical Fitness Training: Florida CMS Law Enforcement Basic Recruit Training Program	CJK_0096	*60 Hours	3
Criminal Justice Officer Physical Fitness Training: Traditional Correctional Officer Basic Recruit Training Program	CJK_0280	*40 Hours	3
Criminal Justice Officer Physical Fitness Training: Florida Correctional Probation Basic Recruit Training Program	CJK_0281	*34 Hours	3

*Note: The physical fitness training hours are based on the total instructional hours of the each of the basic recruit training programs.

Frequently Asked Questions
What are the physical training requirements for Basic Recruit Training Programs?

Answer: There are five physical fitness components that will be measured at the beginning and end of Basic Recruit Training Programs.

1. **Vertical Jump.** This measures leg power and consists of measuring how high a person jumps.

2. **One Minute Sit-ups.** This measures abdominal or trunk muscular endurance. While lying on his or her back, the student will be given one minute to do as many bent leg sit ups as possible.

3. **300 Meter Run.** This measures anaerobic power or the ability to make an intense burst of effort for a short time period or distance. This component consists of sprinting 300 meters.

4. **Maximum Push-ups.** This measures the muscular endurance of the upper body. This component consists of doing as many push-ups as possible until muscular fatigue develops.

5. **1.5 Mile Run.** This measures aerobic power or cardiovascular endurance (stamina over time). To complete this component, the student must run or walk as fast as possible for a distance of 1.5 miles.

Why was this physical fitness test selected?

Answer: In 2006, the curriculum developmental staff re-examined the need for physical fitness training programs within the Basic Recruit Training Programs. Public safety studies have shown there are several physical tasks that are job related. These tasks are necessary to perform essential functions of the job. There is ample data to document that physical fitness components are the underlying and predictive factors for performing tasks such as:

- sustained pursuit/aerobic power
- sprints/anaerobic power
- dodging/aerobic/anaerobic power and flexibility
- lifting and carrying/muscular strength and endurance/anaerobic power
- dragging, pulling and pushing/muscular strength and endurance/anaerobic power
- jumping and vaulting/anaerobic power/leg power and strength
- crawling/muscular endurance/flexibility/body fat composition
- use of force/muscular strength and endurance/anaerobic power
- use of force/muscular strength and endurance/aerobic power

Studies conducted by the Cooper Institute for Aerobics Research (CIAR) have determined the areas and levels of physical fitness which are necessary for performing the essential functions of a law enforcement officer.

Are there any minimum physical fitness standards for entry into the Basic Recruit Training Programs?

Answer: There are no entry standards. However, a trainee should enter the Basic Recruit Training Programs at a fitness level which will provide him or her with the potential for successful completion all of the physical fitness goals by the last two weeks of training.

How can trainees prepare themselves to take the physical fitness test?

Answer: The CJSTC Training Academies will make available an informational handout to all recruits which will outline proven workout routines that trainees can follow to prepare themselves for the test.

What will happen to a trainee who is injured and cannot participate in all aspects of the test?

Answer: Applicants must come prepared to participate in all components of the assessment during the first week of training. Trainees who are injured during basic training and are unable to complete testing at exit must successfully complete the training and testing at a later date when approved by their physician. A graduation certificate cannot be earned until this is accomplished.

My agency has a different set of standards that applicants must meet. Do my agency standards have to conform to the Academy standards?

Answer: Agencies are encouraged to develop their own physical fitness programs and standards that exceed the CJSTC goals. However, agency recruits will still have to complete the physical fitness training and the exit evaluation for the Basic Recruit Training Program to be successfully completed.

Vertical Jump

Purpose

This is a measure of jumping or explosive power.

Equipment

1. Vertical measuring apparatus fixed to a smooth wall

2. Some way to mark extension when jumping (e.g., chalk dust, Velcro)

Procedure

1. Participant stands with one side toward the wall, feet together, and reaches up as high as possible to mark his or her standard reach.

2. Participant jumps as high as possible and marks the highest point of the jump. Participant must jump from both feet in a stationary stance. Arms may be pumped and thrust upward.

3. Score is the total inches, to the nearest 1/2 inch, above the standard reach mark.

4. Record the best of three trial scores.

1   **2**   **3**

Vertical jump

Figure 6-1

How to Prepare for Vertical Jump

Training must be specific to the target activity, and therefore each component has a different training routine.

Vertical Jump

A good way to prepare for this component is to do plyometrics training. The basic plyometrics exercise routine consists of three exercises: double leg vertical jump, single leg vertical jump, and the double leg hop. Perform each exercise with 1 set of 10 repetitions, 3 days a week. Do the repetitions without stopping, and rest three minutes between each set of the exercise.

Double Leg Vertical Jump

Intensity Level: High

Starting Position: Stand with the feet shoulder-width apart.

Direction of Jump: Vertical

Arm Action: Double arm action

Starting Action: Perform a rapid counter movement, and jump as high as possible.

Ascent: Thrust arms upward vigorously, and reach as high as possible.

Descent: When the feet hit the ground, jump again immediately without a stutter step.

Double Leg Hop

Intensity Level: Medium

Starting Position: Stand with the feet shoulder-width apart.

Direction of Jump: Horizontal, with a vertical component

Arm Action: Double arm action

Starting Action: Jump from both legs, and strive for maximal distance.

Ascent: Think about "hanging" in the air.

Descent: Land in the starting position and immediately repeat the movement.

Single Leg Vertical Jump

Intensity Level: High

Starting Position: Stand with one foot on the ground.

Direction of Jump: Vertical

Arm Action: Double arm action

Starting Action: Perform a rapid counter movement, and jump as high as possible.

Ascent: The arms should be thrust upward vigorously and reach as high as possible.

Descent: When the foot hits the ground, immediately jump without a stutter step.

(Emphasis should be placed on maximum height and quick, explosive takeoffs. Repeat this exercise with the opposite leg after a brief rest of 15–30 seconds.)

One Minute Sit-ups

Purpose

This measures abdominal muscular endurance.

Procedure

One minute sit-ups Figure 6-2

1. The participant starts by lying on his or her back, knees bent, heels flat on the floor, with the fingers laced and held behind the head. Avoid pulling on the head with the hands. The buttocks must remain on the floor with no thrusting of the hips.

2. A partner holds the feet down firmly.

3. The participant then performs as many correct sit ups as possible in one minute.

4. In the up position, the subject should touch elbows to knees and then return until the shoulder blades touch the floor.

5. A participant's score equals the total number of correct sit ups. Any resting must be done in the up position.

6. Breathing should be as normal as possible, and the participant should not hold his or her breath.

How to Prepare for Sit-ups

1. Estimate the number of correct sit ups you can do in one minute. Multiply that number by .75 (75%). Round the result to the lowest number. This will be the number of repetitions (sit ups) you will do per set.

2. Warm up with some light activity of your choice such as a stationary bike, walking or jogging on the treadmill, light calisthenics, etc.

3. Perform the number of sit ups (correct form) determined in the calculation done in #1 above.

4. Rest no longer than 60 seconds, and do another set of repetitions.

5. Repeat #3 and #4 until you have done 3 to 5 sets of repetitions. Even though the last sets may be difficult, maintain proper form. If you have to hesitate longer on the floor on the last sets to get in the full number, then do so, but rest no longer than necessary. It is important that you perform all the repetitions.

6. Do this routine every other day. Increase the number of reps per set by 1 or 2 each week.

Note: If you are unable to do at least 5 reps per set, you will need to modify your routines in order to complete sufficient repetitions to address muscular endurance. You should follow a crunch or curl routine for your abdominals, and also get assistance in designing leg exercises (multi-hip machine or leg lifts) to address the hip flexors. Also, you could use an abdominal machine in a fitness facility using a light enough resistance to get in 15 reps per set for 3 sets.

300 Meter Run

300 meter run — *Figure 6-3*

Purpose

This is a measure of anaerobic power.

Equipment

1. Stopwatch

2. 400 meter running track or any measured 300 meter flat surface with sufficient distance to slow to a stop

Procedure

1. Warm up and stretching should precede testing.

2. The participant should run 300 meters at his or her maximal level of effort. Record the amount of time used to complete the required distance.

3. The participant should walk for 3–5 minutes immediately following the test to cool down. This is an important safety practice.

4. *Note:* Students may walk, if necessary. However, the time will be recorded as the amount of time used to walk.

How to Prepare for the 300 Meter Run

To prepare for this component, it is a good idea to do interval training. The first step is to time yourself for an all-out effort at 110 yards. This is called your initial time, or IT. The second step is to divide your IT by .80 to get your training time.

Maximum Push-ups

Purpose

This measures the muscular endurance of the upper body (anterior deltoid, pectoralis major, triceps).

Maximum Standard Push-ups

Procedure

1. The participant's hands are placed shoulder-width apart, with fingers pointing forward. Some part of the hands must lie within a vertical line drawn from the outside edge of the shoulders to the floor.

2. Start from the up position: the arms are fully extended with elbows locked with both hands and both feet only touching the floor. The participant must keep the back straight at all times and lower the chest to approximately three inches from the floor. A small rubber ball or sponge (3 inches in dimension) can be placed on floor to check for distance. The participant then returns to the up position with the elbows fully locked. This is one repetition.

3. Resting is permitted only in the up position. The back must remain straight during resting.

4. When the participant elects to stop or cannot continue, the total number of correct push-ups is recorded as the score. There is no time limit for this exercise.

Maximum standard push-up

Figure 6-4

Modified (Knee) Push-up for Women

Note: Modified Push-ups—Women candidates may choose to use the standard or modified push-ups.

1. The participant's hands are placed shoulder-width apart, with fingers pointing forward. Knees are bent, ankles crossed. Only hands and knees should touch the floor.

2. Descend until elbows are bent approximately 90 degrees, then straighten arms and return to starting position.

3. The participant must keep the back straight at all times and lower the chest to approximately three inches from the floor. A small rubber ball or sponge (3 inches in dimension) can be placed on floor

to check for distance. The participant then returns to the up position with the elbows fully locked. This is one repetition.

4. Resting is permitted only in the up position. The back must remain straight during resting.

5. When the participant elects to stop or cannot continue, the total number of correct pushups is recorded as the score. There is not a time limit for this exercise.

Modified push-up

Figure 6-5

How to Prepare for Push-ups

1. Estimate the maximum number of correct push-ups you can do in one minute.

2. Multiply that number by .75 (75%). Round the result to the lowest number. This will be the number of repetitions (push-ups) you will do per set.

3. Warm up with some light activity of your choice, such as a stationary bike, walking or jogging on the treadmill, light calisthenics, etc.

4. Perform the number of push-ups (correct form) determined in the calculation done in #2 above.

5. Rest no longer than 60 seconds, and then do another set of repetitions.

6. Repeat #4 and #5 until you have done 3 to 5 sets of repetitions. Even though the last sets may be difficult, maintain proper form. If you have to hesitate longer on the floor on the last sets to complete the full number, then do so, but rest no longer than necessary. It is important that you complete all the repetitions.

7. Do this routine every other day. Increase the number of reps per set by 1 or 2 each week.

Note: Women may prepare for the push-ups using either the standard push-up or the modified knee push-up.

Note: If you are unable to do at least 5 reps per set, then you will have to adjust the above calculations on modified push-ups (from the knees) in order to keep the number of reps high enough to address muscular endurance. You should also get assistance in designing a strength routine using selectorized machines, including chest, arms and trunk exercises.

1.5 Mile Run

Purpose

The 1.5 mile run is a measure of aerobic power (cardiovascular endurance). The objective in the 1.5 mile run is to cover the distance as fast as possible.

Equipment

1. Stopwatch

2. Indoor or outdoor track or another suitable flat running area measured to 1.5 miles

Procedure

1. Participants should not eat a heavy meal or smoke for at least 2–3 hours prior to the test. Participants should warm up and stretch thoroughly prior to running.

2. The participant runs 1.5 miles as fast as possible.

3. Participants should not physically touch one another during the run, unless it is to render first aid.

4. Finish times should be recorded.

5. Upon completion of the run, participants should cool down by walking for about 5 minutes to prevent venous pooling (i.e., pooling of the blood in the lower extremities which reduces the return of blood to the heart and may cause cardiac arrhythmia).

Note: Student may walk if necessary; however, the time will be recorded as the amount of time walked.

How to Prepare for 1.5 Mile Run

To prepare for this test, you need to gradually increase your running endurance. Begin at the level you can accommodate, and use a walk and run workout format. Run a short distance, walk for a while, and then run again. Begin slowly and then proceed to the next level by improving your overall running or walking time.

Acknowledgement: Our thanks to the Indiana Law Enforcement Academy for allowing us to use their materials in the development of the physical fitness course materials.

GLOSSARY

A

abandonment: the relinquishing of a right or interest with the intention of never again claiming it (First Aid)

ABCs: airway, breathing, and circulation; assessment begins with ABCs (First Aid)

abdominal evisceration: an open wound where organs protrude from the abdominal cavity (First Aid)

ability: the capacity a subject has to carry out his or her intent (Defensive Tactics)

abrasion: an open wound caused by scraping, shearing away, or rubbing the outermost skin layer (First Aid)

ABS (anti-lock braking system): a computerized braking system that automatically slows and stops the vehicle when the driver applies a hard, steady pressure to the brake pedal (Vehicle Operations)

active resistance: a subject's use of physically evasive movements directed toward the officer; examples include bracing, tensing, pushing, or pulling to prevent the officer from establishing control over the subject (Defensive Tactics)

acuity: sharpness of vision (Vehicle Operations)

advanced directive: documents a patient's request to withhold specific medical care (First Aid)

AED: automated external defibrillator (First Aid)

aggressive resistance: a subject's attacking movements toward an officer that may cause injury but are not likely to cause death or great bodily harm to the officer or others (Defensive Tactics)

AIDS: Acquired Immune Deficiency Syndrome; caused by HIV (First Aid)

airborne disease: any infection spread from person to person through the air; caused by breathing in microscopic, disease-bearing organisms called pathogens (First Aid)

amniotic sac: the bag of fluid surrounding the fetus (First Aid)

amp (ampere): the measure of electrical current or power (DFSG)

amputation: the gross removal of an appendage, complete or incomplete (First Aid)

anaphylaxis: a severe allergic reaction in which air passages swell and restrict breathing; caused by insect bites or stings, pollen, medications, foods, chemicals, or other substances (First Aid)

apex: the center point of any curve (Vehicle Operations)

arterial bleeding: bright red blood spurting from a wound, indicating a severed or damaged artery (First Aid)

asthma: results from the narrowing of airway passages, causing breathing difficulties (First Aid)

auditory exclusion: a survival stress reaction in which hearing is diminished (Defensive Tactics)

AVPU: method for identifying four levels of patient responsiveness: alert, verbal, pain, and unresponsiveness (First Aid)

avulsion: an injury characterized by a flap of skin, torn or cut, that may not be completely loose from the body (First Aid)

B

balance: a position in which the head is over the hips, and the hips are over and between the feet; necessary for performing defensive tactics (Defensive Tactics)

balance displacement: a controlling technique used to break the subject's balance through the use of leverage principles (Defensive Tactics)

barricade position: a position behind cover (Firearms)

binocular vision: a survival stress reaction in which both eyes remain open, and it is very difficult to close just one eye (Defensive Tactics)

birth canal: the passage the fetus is pushed through during delivery (First Aid)

block: reactionary techniques using the arms, legs, or body to deflect or redirect a subject's impending strike to other certain areas of the body (Defensive Tactics)

body movement: refers to how an officer approaches a subject or enters a scene (Defensive Tactics)

breach of duty: the failure of an officer to act or failure to act appropriately (First Aid)

bruising: an obvious discoloration (black and blue) of the soft tissue at the injury site (First Aid)

BSI (body substance isolation): controlling infection by separating patients from each other; includes two basic behaviors: the use of medical PPE and personal behaviors that reduce risk (First Aid)

C

caliber: the measurement used to identify different cartridge (projectile) sizes (Firearms)

capillary bleeding: dark red blood oozing from a wound, indicating damaged capillaries (First Aid)

cardiac muscles: the muscles in the heart that constantly work to expand and contract it (First Aid)

cardiovascular training: any exercise that elevates the heart rate to a range between 60 and 85 percent of the maximum rate (Defensive Tactics)

Cartridge Parts and Types (Firearms)
Parts
   case: the metal, plastic, or paper container that holds all parts of a round of ammunition: primer, powder charge, and bullet

   rim: the edge on the base of a cartridge case that stops the progress of the case into the chamber

   crimp (shotgun only): the part of the case mouth that bends inward to grip the bullet; with shotgun shells, the term applies to the closure at the case mouth

   headstamp: markings found on the head of ammunition that indicate the caliber or gauge and identify the manufacturer

   shot (shotgun): spherical pellets of various sizes, usually made of lead

   primer: small metal cup containing the detonating mixture used to ignite the propellant or powder charge

   powder: propellant used in most firearms; produces a large volume of gas when ignited

   wad(s) (shotgun)—the only part not found in any other centerfire cartridge; this is used to seal/confine gases; can be made of plastic or compressed cardboard

   bullet: portion of the cartridge that becomes a projectile when in flight

   round: complete ammunition cartridge that contains all parts of ammunition; a military term meaning one single cartridge

Types
   birdshot: normally used for bird hunting or practice; this shell has a load of small diameter lead or steel shot pellets; used for training purposes

   double-aught buckshot: 2 3/4-inch shell with nine .33 caliber lead pellets or a 3-inch magnum shell with twelve .32 caliber pellets; penetrates solid wood doors, drywall, and wood walls at close range

   rifled slug: single, hollow lead bullet that weighs from 7/8 to 1 1/8 ounce; is .72 caliber and penetrates most materials but not solid steel

caster effect: the tendency for a vehicle travelling forward to straighten from a turn when the driver releases the steering wheel (Vehicle Operations)

CDC: Center for Disease Control & Prevention (First Aid)

central nervous system: located in the brain and spinal cord; components are the body's mainframe computer where all communication and control originate (First Aid)

centrifugal force: the reaction to centripetal force; force that pushes a vehicle toward the outside of a turn (Vehicle Operations)

centripetal force: the force that pulls a vehicle toward the inside of a turn (Vehicle Operations)

cervix: the neck of the uterus; contains a mucus plug (First Aid)

chemical burn: occurs when a burning chemical comes into contact with skin (First Aid)

circulatory system: pumps blood throughout the body; consists of the heart, blood vessels, and blood (First Aid)

closed chest injury: results from blunt trauma to the chest area; damages internal organs and/or causes internal bleeding (First Aid)

closed fracture: a fracture in which the skin at the injury site remains intact (First Aid)

CO (carbon monoxide): a potentially poisonous byproduct of combustion (First Aid)

cognitive brain: the part of the brain that logically thinks and plans (Defensive Tactics)

color vision: the ability to distinguish colors (Vehicle Operations)

command presence: the way an officer carries him- or herself (Defensive Tactics)

communication: the exchanging of information through verbal and nonverbal methods; provides valuable insight into the likelihood of cooperation and compliance of a subject (Defensive Tactics)

complex motor skills: a combination of fine and gross motor skills using hand/eye coordination timed to a single event (Defensive Tactics)

compliance: the verbal and/or physical yielding to an officer's authority without apparent threat of resistance or violence (Defensive Tactics)

concealment: an object or group of objects that creates a visual barrier between an officer and a threat but may not stop a projectile (Firearms)

constant radius: a turn that remains the same throughout, getting neither wider nor smaller (Vehicle Operations)

contusion: a closed injury that is discolored and painful at the injury site (First Aid)

counter steering: turning the vehicle's front tires in the desired direction to regain traction (Vehicle Operations)

cover: anything that creates a bullet-resistant barrier between an officer and a threat (Firearms)

CPR: cardiopulmonary resuscitation (First Aid)

critical incident amnesia: after a stressful situation, a temporary condition that causes difficulty in transferring information into long-term memory (Defensive Tactics)

CS (orthochlorobenzal-malononitrile): a type of chemical agent commonly used by law enforcement usually in the form of hand-held canisters and chemical projectiles (Defensive Tactics)

custodial search technique: a complete search of the subject used when a subject is taken into custody in an unsecured environment (Defensive Tactics)

cyanosis: changes in circulation causing the lips, palms, and nail beds to turn blue (First Aid)

cycle (cycling): the predetermined amount of time (usually five seconds) that a stun device will discharge automatically when activated (DFSG)

D

danger zone: the area within the reactionary gap (Defensive Tactics)

deadly force: force that is likely to cause death or great bodily harm (Defensive Tactics)

deadly force resistance: a subject's hostile, attacking movements, with or without a weapon, that create a reasonable perception by the officer that the subject intends to cause and has the capability of causing death or great bodily harm to the officer or others (Defensive Tactics)

decreasing radius: a turn that gets tighter during the turn much like a circle getting smaller (Vehicle Operations)

de-escalation: decreasing the use of force or resistance (Defensive Tactics)

defensive tactics: a system of controlled defensive and offensive body movements used by criminal justice officers to respond to a subject's aggression or resistance (Defensive Tactics)

depth perception: the ability to judge distance and space (Vehicle Operations)

DFSG (dart-firing stun gun): a hand-held stun gun which propels electrified darts/probes (DFSG)

diabetes: a disease in which the body does not produce or properly use insulin (First Aid)

dialogue: controlled, nonemotional communication between an officer and a subject, aimed at problem solving and communication (Defensive Tactics)

digestive system: ingests and digests food and nutrients; includes the stomach, pancreas, liver, gallbladder, and small and large intestines (First Aid)

dilation: the first stage of labor; begins with the initial contraction and continues until the fetus enters the birth canal (First Aid)

direct line of attack: the direction that a subject comes from (Defensive Tactics)

disengagement: the discontinuing of commands or the physical use of force; breaking away from a subject (Defensive Tactics)

dislocation: an injury occurring when the end of a bone comes out of its socket at the joint (First Aid)

distraction technique: a technique that interrupts the subject's concentration so that energy is redirected from the current focus (Defensive Tactics)

DNR/DNRO: Do Not Resuscitate or Do Not Resuscitate Order; documents the terminally or chronically ill patient's wish to refuse resuscitation (First Aid)

DOTS: deformities, open injuries, tenderness, and swelling; injuries and symptoms to look for during a physical assessment of a potentially injured person (First Aid)

double-action only: a firearm in which every round fires double action with the hammer at rest against the rear of the slide (Firearms)

double feed: a weapon malfunction which is caused by a failure to extract the round in the chamber and a new round being fed from the magazine well (Firearms)

double/single: a pistol in which the hammer must be manually cocked and the first round fires double action but the subsequent rounds fire single action (Firearms)

drug-induced psychosis: a form of psychosis which can result from drug use, typically causing hallucinations and/or delusions (DFSG)

duty life: the recommended time that ammunition can be expected to be reliable (Firearms)

duty to act: the duty to take some action to prevent harm to another and for the failure of which an officer may be liable depending on the relationship of the parties and the circumstances (First Aid)

E

electrical burn: occurs when manmade or natural (lightning) electricity comes into contact with the skin and body, causing the skin or internal organs to burn (First Aid)

electronic control device: a device that uses a high voltage, low-power electrical charge to induce involuntary muscle contractions to temporarily incapacitate a non-compliant subject (also known as electronic immobilization device) (Defensive Tactics, DFSG)

EMD (electro-muscular disruption): external electric impulses that interfere with the electric impulses used by the human nerve system to communicate with the skeletal muscles, causing physical incapacitation (DFSG)

emergency move: a relocation performed when a patient is in immediate danger or when the patient's location prevents providing care to him or her or another patient (First Aid)

empty-hand striking technique: any impact technique using hands, arms, elbows, feet, legs, knees, or head to strike a subject in an offensive or defensive situation (Defensive Tactics)

EMS system (emergency medical services system): network of trained professionals linked to provide advanced, out-of-hospital care for victims of a sudden traumatic injury or illness (First Aid)

EMT (emergency medical technician): emergency medical technicians who have advanced, specialized training that enables them to provide comprehensive care to patients (First Aid)

escalation: increasing the use of force or resistance (Defensive Tactics)

escort: a technique used to move a subject from one point to another without using pain compliance; provides minimal control of the subject through leverage (Defensive Tactics)

evasion: shifting one's body or side-stepping to avoid an attack (Defensive Tactics)

evasion technique: shifting one's body or side stepping to avoid an attack (Defensive Tactics)

evisceration: an open wound where the organs protrude (First Aid)

excited delirium: a state of extreme mental and physiological excitement due to extreme drug use; characterized by extreme agitation, hyperthermia, hostility, and exceptional strength and endurance without apparent fatigue; can lead to death (Defensive Tactics)

expressed consent: consent that is clearly and unmistakably stated (First Aid)

expulsion: the second stage of labor; the fetus moves through the birth canal and is delivered (First Aid)

eye-targeting: looking in the desired direction of travel to avoid an obstacle and steering in that direction (Vehicle Operations)

F

failure to eject (stovepipe): a weapon malfunction that occurs when a fired round does not completely eject (Firearms)

failure to extract (double feed): a weapon malfunction that occurs when a spent casing remains in the chamber while a new cartridge enters the chamber (Firearms)

failure to feed: a weapon malfunction that occurs when the cartridge fails to feed into the chamber (Firearms)

failure to fire: a weapon malfunction that occurs when the trigger is pulled, but the round fails to detonate (Firearms)

fear-induced stress: survival stress (Defensive Tactics)

femur: thighbone; the longest and strongest bone in the human body (First Aid)

fine motor skills: the muscle control required to make small, precise movements (Defensive Tactics)

flail chest: a closed chest injury that occurs when two or more adjacent ribs are fractured in two or more places and become free floating (First Aid)

fluid shock principle: the principle that describes the result of strikes that are delivered utilizing penetration of the muscle or nerves of the target area so that the striking object stays on or indented in the target for an instant, which allows for a full transfer of kinetic energy that displaces the water content in the muscle and creates a shock wave, greatly multiplying the effect of the strike by producing intense pain and immobilizing the subject (Defensive Tactics)

follow-through: the maintenance of sight alignment before, during, and after firing a round (Firearms)

foot stomp: a distraction technique applied with a downward thrust to the subject's foot to inflict pain, temporarily divert the subject's attention, and redirect the physical power of the subject's attack (Defensive Tactics)

Force Guidelines: a framework for making decisions involving the reasonable use of force by criminal justice officers (Defensive Tactics)

fracture: a bone break (First Aid)

frostbite: a localized injury from overexposure to cold (First Aid)

frozen cylinder: a cylinder that does not rotate (Firearms)

full thickness burn: a third-degree burn that damages all skin layers and affects muscles and nerves; causes skin to look waxy, white, or charred (First Aid)

G

gauge: a measurement of shotgun bores derived from the number of bore-sized balls of lead per pound (Firearms)

Good Samaritan Act: protects physicians who render emergency care from civil suits; Florida's Good Samaritan Act also protects first aid providers (First Aid)

grappling: the use of body mechanics to control a subject (Defensive Tactics)

gross motor skills: the movements of the large or major muscles of the body (Defensive Tactics)

H

handcuffs: temporary restraining devices used frequently to control a subject (Defensive Tactics)

handgun: a revolver or semiautomatic pistol (Firearms)

head butt: a distraction technique using the frontal lobe or back of the head to make contact with the subject's face, head, or other target area to inflict pain, temporarily divert a subject's attention, and redirect the physical power of the subject's attack (Defensive Tactics)

heart attack: caused by oxygen deprivation to part of the heart, typically from a blocked blood vessel (First Aid)

hematoma: a closed injury that evidences as a discolored lump (see swelling) (First Aid)

hepatitis A virus: a highly infectious disease spread by person-to-person contact, generally through fecal contamination or oral ingestion (First Aid)

hepatitis B virus: a highly infectious disease spread through sexual contact, sharing contaminated needles (through intravenous drug use), or through blood transfusions (First Aid)

hepatitis C virus: the most common chronic bloodborne infection; primarily transmitted through direct contact with human blood, from sharing needles or drug paraphernalia, or from an infected mother delivering her baby (First Aid)

HIPAA (Health Insurance Portability and Accountability Act of 1996): protects the rights of patients and restricts the release of patient information (First Aid)

HIV (Human Immunodeficiency Virus): bloodborne virus that attacks the immune system and causes AIDS; transmission occurs primarily during sexual contact with an infected individual, when intravenous drug users share contaminated needles, from infected mother to unborn child, and from contact with blood, certain body fluids, and tissue from an infected individual (First Aid)

hyperthermia: occurs when the body cannot recover from fluid loss (First Aid)

hypothermia: the excessive cooling of the body's core temperature (First Aid)

I

ICS: Incident Command System (First Aid)

impact weapon: any object used for striking (Defensive Tactics)

implied consent: consent inferred from conduct rather than from direct expression (First Aid)

incipient skid: a skid that occurs just before tires lose traction during braking; the tires lock and cause a skid (aka impending skid) (Vehicle Operations)

incipient spin: a skid that occurs just before the drive tires lose traction during acceleration (Vehicle Operations)

increasing radius: a turn that becomes wider during the turn much like a circle getting larger (Vehicle Operations)

informed consent: a person's agreement to allow something to happen, made with full knowledge of the risks involved and the alternatives (First Aid)

inhalation burn: occurs when a patient has a burn to any part of the airway (First Aid)

insulin: the hormone needed to convert sugar, starches, and other food into energy needed for daily life (First Aid)

intent: a reasonably perceived, imminent threat to an officer or another person (Defensive Tactics)

intermediate weapon: a tool used when empty-handed control is ineffective, but the subject's level of resistance does not merit deadly force; baton, OC spray, dart-firing stun gun (Defensive Tactics)

interview stance with an impact weapon: a low profile stance with the weapon held partially hidden behind the leg (Defensive Tactics)

involuntary muscles: smooth muscles that carry out many automatic body functions (First Aid)

J

joint manipulation: a method of gaining control over a subject by bending or twisting a joint in a direction that will cause pain or discomfort to the joint (Defensive Tactics)

L

labor: the final phase of pregnancy; begins the birthing process (First Aid)

laceration: an open wound in soft tissue (First Aid)

leverage: using a great force against a weaker resistance (Defensive Tactics)

LOC (level of consciousness): a patient's mental status due to illness or injury (First Aid)

M

malfunction: a condition that prevents a weapon from operating normally (Firearms)

MCI (multiple casualty incident): an incident that involves more than one victim (First Aid)

mechanical compliance: a method used to gain control over a subject by applying pressure or leverage on a joint by locking it up so that no movement of the joint is possible, causing the subject to comply with verbal direction (Defensive Tactics)

medic alert: a bracelet, necklace, or card that alerts medical personnel to a specific medical condition (First Aid)

motor dysfunction: a method of gaining control over a subject by using an incapacitation technique that causes temporary impairment of muscular control (Defensive Tactics)

MRSA (methicillin-resistant staphylococcus aureus): a type of bacteria that is highly contagious and resistant to certain antibiotics; causes a skin infection that is red, swollen, painful, or warm to the touch; may have purulent drainage or appear to be a spider bite, pimple, or boil (First Aid)

muscular system: gives the body shape, protects internal organs, and provides body movement (First Aid)

N

negligence: failure to use due or reasonable care in a situation, resulting in harm to another (Legal); failure to exercise the standard of care that a reasonably prudent person would have exercised in a similar situation; conduct that falls below the legal standard established to protect others against unreasonable risk of harm, except for conduct that is intentionally, wantonly, or willfully disregardful of other's rights (First Aid)

nervous system: controls voluntary and involuntary body activity, supports higher mental functions such as thought and emotion, allows the individual to be aware of and react to the environment, and keeps the rest of the body's systems working together (First Aid)

night vision: the ability to see clearly in darkness (Vehicle Operations)

nonlethal: force that is not intended to cause death or great bodily harm; nondeadly (DFSG)

nonlethal weapon: a weapon that is not fundamentally designed to cause death or great bodily harm (Defensive Tactics)

O

objective reasonableness: a term the courts have used to describe the process for evaluating the appropriateness of an officer's response to a subject's resistance (Defensive Tactics)

occlusive: airtight (First Aid)

offensive ready stance with an impact weapon: a high profile stance with the weapon held at a shoulder position to enable a rapid strike (Defensive Tactics)

officer presence: an officer's ability to convey to subjects and onlookers that he or she is ready and able to take control (Defensive Tactics)

OC (oleo-resin capsicum): a type of chemical agent commonly used by law enforcement, usually in the form of hand-held canisters and chemical projectiles (Defensive Tactics)

open chest injury: an injury that occurs when penetration opens the chest area (First Aid)

open fracture: a fracture where the skin at the injury site is broken, and the bone may protrude through the skin (First Aid)

opportunity: a subject's capacity for carrying out an intention to cause death or great bodily harm to others (Defensive Tactics)

over steer: the tendency of a vehicle to steer into a sharper turn than the driver intends (Vehicle Operations)

P

pain compliance: a subject's response to a combination of pain and verbal commands to stop resisting (Defensive Tactics)

partial thickness burn: second-degree burn that damages the first two skin layers, which blister and feel very painful (First Aid)

passive resistance: a subject's verbal and/or physical refusal to comply with an officer's lawful direction causing the officer to use physical techniques to establish control (Defensive Tactics)

pat down: a physical frisk of a subject conducted in a predetermined pattern to locate weapons (Defensive Tactics)

pepper spray: an inflammatory agent that causes tearing and involuntary closing of the eyes, nasal discharge, sneezing, disorientation, and perceived respiratory distress; also known as OC (Defensive Tactics)

peripheral nervous system: includes nerves that connect to the spinal cord and branch out to every other part of the body; serves as a two-way communication system (First Aid)

peripheral vision: ability to see above, below, and to the sides (Vehicle Operations)

physical control: achieving compliance or custody through the use of empty-hand or leverage-enhanced techniques, such as pain compliance, transporters, restraint devices, takedowns, and striking techniques (Defensive Tactics)

pitch: the transfer of a vehicle's weight from front to rear or rear to front; occurs during acceleration or braking (Vehicle Operations)

PIT (pursuit immobilization technique): pursuit termination technique in which an officer uses the patrol vehicle to make contact with the violator's vehicle (Vehicle Operations)

placenta: the disk-shaped inner lining of the uterus; provides nourishment and oxygen to a fetus (First Aid)

placental: the third stage of labor during which the placenta separates from the uterine wall and moves through the birth canal for delivery (First Aid)

plain feel doctrine: permits an officer to seize any object "whose contour or mass" he or she identifies as apparent contraband during a pat down (Defensive Tactics)

PMS: when examining extremities for potential injuries, indicates what to check for: pulse, and motor and sensory function (First Aid)

point shooting: a technique used when a shooter cannot use the sights on the weapon or he or she has no time to align the sight properly; the firearm is viewed as an extension of the arm and pointed at the target (Firearms)

positional asphyxia: death as a result of a body position that interferes with one's ability to breathe (First Aid)

posting: supporting the balance of the body using a limb (Defensive Tactics)

posturing: behavior in which a subject acts verbally and physically as if he or she may resist (Defensive Tactics)

PPE (personal protective equipment): items that protect individuals from harmful substances, infections, or other people; includes eye protection, gloves, shields, and biohazard bags (First Aid)

pressure points: techniques used to control resistant behavior by utilizing pain compliance (Defensive Tactics)

prone position: lying on the stomach face down (Defensive Tactics)

PSI (pounds per square inch): used to measure tire pressure (Vehicle Operations)

puncture wound: the result of driving a sharp or blunt, pointed object into soft tissue (First Aid)

pursuit: an active attempt by an officer in an authorized emergency vehicle to stop a vehicle that is being operated to elude apprehension or otherwise fails to stop after the driver realizes that the vehicle is being lawfully directed to stop (Vehicle Operations)

Q

quadrant search approach: dividing the body into four sections horizontally and vertically during a search (Defensive Tactics)

R

radius: the distance from the center to the outside of a circle (Vehicle Operations)

reaction time principle: the amount of time it takes for the brain to process a physical threat and for the body to respond (Defensive Tactics)

reactionary gap: the distance an officer must keep between him- or herself and the subject in order to react effectively against a sudden threat (Defensive Tactics)

reasonable suspicion: the facts or circumstances that reasonably indicate that a person has committed, is committing, or is about to commit a violation of the law (Defensive Tactics)

recovery position: a position where the patient is rolled over (preferably onto the left side) with knees slightly bent; helps maintain an open airway if the patient vomits and may prevent positional asphyxia (First Aid)

redirection: using one's hands to move the subject away (Defensive Tactics)

relative positioning: an officer's position in relation to the subject (Defensive Tactics)

respiratory system: delivers oxygen to and removes carbon dioxide from the blood (First Aid)

restraint devices: tools such as handcuffs designed to temporarily restrain a subject's movements (Defensive Tactics)

rifled slug: a single, hollow lead bullet (Firearms)

roadblock: use of vehicles, barricades, cones, or other objects to partially or completely block traffic flow (Vehicle Operations)

roll: the transfer of a vehicle's weight from side to side (Vehicle Operations)

rolling friction: traction created when a vehicle's tires constantly rotate against the road surface without losing contact (Vehicle Operations)

S

SAMPLE: signs and symptoms, allergies, medications, past history, last oral intake, events; method to help an officer acquire information useful in determining causes of injury or illness (First Aid)

SCU (Scoville heat unit): a measure of the heat properties (burning sensation) of capsicum in OC spray (Defensive Tactics)

SDS (Sudden In-custody Death Syndrome): a broad classification for unexplained in-custody deaths; usually occurs twenty minutes to two hours after the suspect has been taken into custody (DFSG)

search: a government intrusion into a place in which a person has a reasonable expectation of privacy (Defensive Tactics)

shelf life: the recommended time that ammunition can be expected to be reliable, from manufacture time to issue time (Firearms)

shin scrape: a distraction technique applied by raising the foot and applying downward pressure on the subject's shin to inflict pain and temporarily divert an attacking subject's attention (Defensive Tactics)

shock: failure of the heart and blood vessels (circulatory system) to maintain enough oxygen-rich blood flowing to the vital organs of the body (First Aid)

shooting hand: the dominant or strong hand that is used to fire a gun (Firearms)

shrimping: the movement in a hip escape; moving from side to side while avoiding or defending against an attack (Defensive Tactics)

sight alignment: the relationship of the front sight and rear sight with the shooter's eye (Firearms)

sight picture: the relationship between the eye, front sight, rear sight, and target (Firearms)

signature marks: the marks left on a subject's body after drive stun applications (DFSG)

single-action: a firearm in which the hammer must be cocked before the weapon can be fired (Firearms)

skeletal system: the supporting framework for the body, giving it shape and protecting vital organs; attains mobility from the attached muscles and manufactures red blood cells (First Aid)

skid: the loss of rolling friction that occurs when a vehicle's wheels lock and do not turn while the vehicle is still moving (Vehicle Operations)

skin: the protective covering for the inside of the body; provides a barrier against bacteria and other harmful substances and organisms; acts as a communication organ; helps regulate body temperature (First Aid)

slide: results when the loss of rolling friction causes loss of traction; the vehicle's wheels still rotate but they do not control the vehicle's movement (Vehicle Operations)

slide step: used when preparing to engage or disengage from a subject in close proximity (Defensive Tactics)

snap-back: a strike that is retracted very quickly, thus enabling multiple strikes, creating distance, setting up the next techniques, and causing distraction to the subject (Defensive Tactics)

squib load: a weapon malfunction that occurs when a lack of powder or a partial burn of powder causes the primer to ignite (Firearms)

stabilization: immobilizing the subject's head so the subject cannot move or escape (Defensive Tactics)

stacked feed: a weapon malfunction that occurs when a round is in the chamber and the action is closed (Firearms)

stalling: a tactical method of safely controlling a suspect until an officer can physically recover, reassess the situation, or backup arrives (Defensive Tactics)

stance: the posture a shooter assumes while firing a shot (Firearms)

START (Simple Triage And Rapid Treatment): a method of triage that assesses a large number of victims rapidly using personnel with limited medical training (First Aid)

STD (sexually transmitted disease): infection transmitted through sexual contact; among the most common infectious diseases (First Aid)

strobing: forcefully blinking the eyes using all the muscles in the face, including those in the forehead (Defensive Tactics)

stroke: damage to part of the brain due to the rupture or blockage of a blood vessel (First Aid)

sucking chest injury: type of open chest injury in which air and/or blood escapes into the area surrounding the lungs, creating a change in the pressure in the chest cavity (First Aid)

superficial burn: first-degree burn that damages the first layer of skin; becomes red and feels very painful (First Aid)

supine position: lying on the back face up (Defensive Tactics)

support hand: the hand that assists the shooting hand (Firearms)

survival stress: stress caused by hormonal changes brought on by a perception of danger (also known as fear-induced stress) (Defensive Tactics)

swelling: soft tissue that is raised when blood or other body fluids pool beneath the skin at the injury site (First Aid)

T

tactical load: technique used to reload in a tactical situation (Firearms)

takedowns: techniques used to bring a resisting subject from a standing position to the ground, making it easier to control him or her (Defensive Tactics)

TB (tuberculosis): a highly infectious airborne disease (First Aid)

telegraphing: small eye, hand, or foot movements in the direction that an officer plans to move (Defensive Tactics)

temporary motor dysfunction: a type of incapacitation that causes temporary impairment of muscle control (Defensive Tactics)

thermal burn: a burn that occurs when an external heat source comes into contact with the skin (First Aid)

threshold braking: pressing lightly on the brake pedal and then continuously applying increasing pressure to slow or stop the vehicle without losing traction (Vehicle Operations)

totality of circumstances: a term the court uses to refer to all facts and circumstances reasonably perceived by the officer as the basis for a use of force decision (Defensive Tactics)

touch: nonthreatening, noncustodial physical contact that can be used to support or emphasize a verbal command (Defensive Tactics)

touch pressure: touching the location of a nerve or sensitive area and applying continual, uninterrupted pressure with the tip of the finger(s) or thumb until the subject complies (Defensive Tactics)

tourniquet: a device, such as a bandage, that restricts blood flow to an extremity such as an arm or leg (First Aid)

transporters: techniques used to move a subject from one point to another with pain compliance and/or mechanical compliance (also known as come-along holds) (Defensive Tactics)

triage: a system of sorting and classifying of patients; determines order in which patients receive medical attention; assesses a large number of victims rapidly (First Aid)

trigger control: results when the trigger finger pulls the trigger straight back with increasing yet constant and steady pressure until the firearm discharges (Firearms)

tunnel vision: a loss of peripheral vision and depth perception that often occurs during survival stress situations (Defensive Tactics)

U

umbilical cord: connects the fetus and the mother; provides nourishment to the fetus (First Aid)

under steer: the tendency of a vehicle to turn less sharply than the driver intends (Vehicle Operations)

universal precautions: procedures designed to prevent transmission of HIV, hepatitis B virus, and other blood-borne pathogens (First Aid)

USDOT: United States Department of Transportation (First Aid)

uterus: the organ that holds the developing fetus (First Aid)

V

vascular neck restraint: a physical restraint compressing certain veins and arteries in the neck to cause a subject to lose consciousness for a brief period of time (Defensive Tactics)

venous bleeding: bleeding where dark red blood flows steadily from a wound, indicating a severed or damaged vein (First Aid)

verbal direction: the use of proper, clear, and concise commands to let a subject know what an officer needs or expects him or her to do (Defensive Tactics)

visual control: the ability to see both the subject's hands and to know that those hands hold no weapons (Defensive Tactics)

voluntary muscles: muscles used for deliberate acts, such as chewing, lifting, and running (First Aid)

W

weapon of opportunity: an item an officer has at hand that can be used as a potential impact weapon when needed, such as a broomstick, flashlight, clipboard, or radio (Defensive Tactics)

wheel tracking: the phenomenon of the rear wheels following an inside path in relation to the front wheels during a turn (Vehicle Operations)

Y

yaw: the transfer of a vehicle's weight causing an end-for-end motion resulting in the vehicle turning 180 degrees (Vehicle Operations)

COURT CASE INDEX

INDEX

REFERENCES

Chapter 1 CMS Law Enforcement Vehicle Operations

U.S. Department of Transportation, Federal Highway Administration, Office of Motor Carriers. (1997). *Commercial Vehicle Preventable Accident Manual: A Guide to Countermeasures* (3rd ed.). Niles, IL: U.S. Triodyne Incorporated.

Chapter 2 CMS First Aid for Criminal Justice Officers

Beckstrom, Gus. (Eds.). (2007). *Florida Crimes, Motor Vehicles, & Related Laws with Criminal Jury Instruction.* (2007–2008 ed.). Longwood, FL: LexisNexis Law Enforcement.

Centers for Disease Control and Prevention Healthcare-Associated Methicillin Resistant Staphylococcus Aureus (MRSA). (24 October 2007). Retrieved from: http://www.cdc.gov/mrsa/index.html

Garner, B. A. (Eds.). (1999). *Black's Law Dictionary.* (7th ed. abridged.). Eagan, MN: West Group.

Handel, Kathleen A. (1992). *American Red Cross First Aid: Responding to Emergencies.* Little, Brown and Company. New York, NY: The American Red Cross.

Limmer, D., Karren, K. J., & Hafen, B. Q. (2003). *First Responder: A Skills Approach.* (6th ed.).Upper Saddle River, NJ: Prentice Hall.

Merriam Webster. (2003) *Webster's Medical Speller.* (2nd ed.). Springfield, MA: Merriam-Webster, Incorporated.

Mish, F. C. (Ed.). (2002) *Merriam-Webster's collegiate dictionary.* (10th ed.). Springfield, MA: Merriam-Webster, Incorporated.

National Safety Council, American Academy of Orthopedic Surgeons. (2001.) *First Responder: Your First Response in Emergency Care.* (3rd ed.). Sudbury, MA: U.S. Jones and Bartlett Publishers.

U.S. Department of Transportation, National Highway Traffic Safety Administration & United States Department of Health and Human Services, Maternal and Child Health Bureau. (1990). *First Responder: National Standard Curriculum.* Washington, DC: U.S.

United States Naval Hospital Corpsman 3 & 2 Training Manual. (1989.) NAVEDTRA 10669-C. Philadelphia, PA.

Chapter 3 CMS Criminal Justice Firearms

National Rifle Association. *Law Enforcement Handgun / Shotgun Instructor Manual.* Fairfax, VA: National Rifle Association.

Chapter 4 CMS Criminal Justice Defensive Tactics

Lewinski, Bill. (2005). *Destroying Myths & Discovering Cold Facts about Controversial Force Issues: 10 Training Tips for Handling "Excited Delirium."* The Force Science Research Center. Retrieved from: http://www.forcescience.org

Hall, Christine, & Butler, Chris. (2007). Technical Report TR-03-02007: *National Study on Neck Restraints in Policing.* Canadian Police Research Centre. Retrieved from: http://www.cprc.org/

Chapter 5 Dart-Firing Stun Gun

All ©Karbon Arms copyrighted names and products registered (including Stinger's ICE Shield™ and Band-It™) Karbon Arms, Inc.

All Registered TASER® names and products and "Top Probe" diagram and 3 "signatures"—TASER International, Inc. Copyright 1998–2011

Harris, Tom. (2000). "Stun Gun Diagram" and "How Stun Guns Work" *How stun guns work.* Retrieved from: http://electronics.howstuffworks.com/stun-gun3.htm

NOTES

NOTES

NOTES

NOTES

NOTES

NOTES

NOTES

NOTES